The Philosophical Writings of Descartes

VOLUME I

These two volumes provide a completely new translation of the philosophical works of Descartes, based on the best available Latin and French texts. They are intended to replace the only reasonably comprehensive selection of his works in English, by Haldane and Ross, first published in 1911. All the works included in that edition are translated here, together with a number of additional texts crucial for an understanding of Cartesian philosophy, including important material from Descartes' scientific writings. The result should meet the widespread demand for an accurate and authoritative edition of Descartes' philosophical writings in clear and readable modern English.

Contents

The Philosophical Writings of
DESCARTES

translated by
JOHN COTTINGHAM
ROBERT STOOTHOFF
DUGALD MURDOCH

VOLUME I

CAMBRIDGE
UNIVERSITY PRESS

CAMBRIDGE UNIVERSITY PRESS
Cambridge, New York, Melbourne, Madrid, Cape Town,
Singapore, São Paulo, Delhi, Tokyo, Mexico City

Cambridge University Press
32 Avenue of the Americas, New York NY 10013-2473, USA

www.cambridge.org
Information on this title: www.cambridge.org/9780521288071

First published 1985
21st printing 2009

A catalogue record for this publication is available from the British Library.

ISBN 978-0-521-28807-1 Paperback

Contents

Early Writings

Rules for the Direction of the Mind

General Introduction

The aim of this two-volume edition is to provide a completely new translation of the philosophical writings of Descartes, based on the original Latin and French texts. Although many of Descartes' philosophical works are now available in English either individually or in various selections, the only tolerably comprehensive edition remains that of Haldane and Ross, which first appeared in 1911.[1] But although it has come to be regarded as the standard English edition, HR omits many works which are crucial for a full understanding of Descartes' philosophy. The present work, by contrast, aims to be as comprehensive as possible. Considerations of space have prevented us from being as inclusive as some, no doubt, would have wished; we have not, for example, included any of Descartes' letters, partly because an excellent selection is already available in English.[2] But as well as including all the works to be found in Haldane and Ross, *viz.* the *Discourse on the Method, Meditations, Objections and Replies, Rules for the Direction of the Mind, The Search for Truth, Comments on a Certain Broadsheet, The Passions of the Soul* and selections from the *Principles of Philosophy*, we have also provided extracts from Descartes' *Early Writings*, from *The World, Treatise on Man, Optics* and *Description of the Human Body*; our selection from the *Principles*, moreover, includes many articles not translated in Haldane and Ross. In general, we have construed the term 'philosophical' in a fairly generous way, so as to include, as well as Descartes' more celebrated metaphysical and epistemological works, a fair selection of his scientific writings (on physiology, psychology, physics and cosmology), which are likely to be of interest to students of philosophy and allied disciplines.

Descartes wrote with equal fluency in Latin and French, and published in both languages; within his lifetime some of his Latin works were

---

1 *The Philosophical Works of Descartes*, tr. Elisabeth S. Haldane and G. R. T. Ross (Cambridge: CUP, 1911, repr. 1931).
2 *Descartes, Philosophical Letters*, tr. A. Kenny (Oxford: OUP, 1970: repr. Oxford: Blackwell, 1980).

subsequently translated into French, and some of his French works into Latin. Our own translations of Descartes' works are made, in each case, from the original language in which they were composed (for further details see translators' prefaces to the individual works). Where subsequent translations approved by Descartes provide important additional material, this has also been translated, but in footnotes or within diamond brackets <...>, to distinguish it from the original material. We have thus firmly rejected the practice of Haldane and Ross, whose translation, e.g. in the case of the *Meditations* and *Principles*, is based on an uneasy amalgam of the original Latin and later French editions, with the result that the reader is frequently left in the dark as to whether a given rendering corresponds to Descartes' original words or to the formulation of one of his contemporary translators.

We have endeavoured to make our translations as accurate as possible, while at the same time attempting to produce readable modern English. Where Descartes employs technical terms which are now obsolete (e.g. 'objective reality') or uses expressions which are liable to cause difficulty to the modern student, we have supplied explanatory footnotes. But apart from this, we have tried to make the translations stand on their own feet. Often we have found that the choice of a particular English word or phrase hinges on a complex chain of philosophical argument which it it is impossible to summarize adequately in a brief footnote; to do justice to the issues involved would have required a formidable exegetical apparatus which would greatly have reduced the space available for presenting Descartes' own writings. We have also rejected the device, used sporadically by Haldane and Ross and others, of inserting unexplained original Latin or French phrases when the translation is difficult or problematical; such a proceeding merely tends to puzzle the reader having no French or Latin, and is of doubtful value to those who are able to consult the original texts for themselves. In cases where we have found it necessary to refer to Latin or French terms in our footnotes, we have always explained their meaning.

In dividing the material between the two volumes, we have decided to place the *Meditations* and the *Objections and Replies* together, since they are interconnected in the closest possible way, and were originally published by Descartes as a single book. These works comprise the bulk of Volume Two; also included is *The Search for Truth*, whose exact date is uncertain but which was probably composed in the same period as the *Meditations*, and deals with many of the same themes. Volume One contains all the remaining works, arranged in chronological order. Each work is preceded by an introductory note giving details of its composition and original publication. Comprehensive philosophical indexes are included at the end of each volume, and each volume also contains a brief chronological table of Descartes' life and works.

Our translations are based on the texts to be found in the standard twelve-volume edition of Descartes' works by Adam and Tannery (known as AT).[1] We have, however, consulted many other editions, and where these have been of particular value they are mentioned in the prefaces to individual works. Important departures from the text in AT are recorded in footnotes. Where the text is abridged, omitted material is indicated by dots, thus . . ., and further information is supplied in a footnote. For each work we have supplied, in the margins, running cross-references to the page number of the relevant volume of AT. It should be noted that, unless otherwise indicated, all comments in footnotes are those of the translators, not of Descartes.

The work of translation has been divided as follows: John Cottingham has translated the *Meditations, Objections and Replies, Early Writings, Principles of Philosophy* and *Description of the Human Body*; Robert Stoothoff has translated *The World, Treatise on Man, Discourse on the Method, Optics, The Passions of the Soul* and the first half of *The Search for Truth*; and Dugald Murdoch has translated the *Rules for the Direction of the Mind, Comments on a Certain Broadsheet* and the second half of *The Search for Truth*. All the members of the team have, however, scrutinized each other's work, and made numerous suggestions, many of which have found their way into the final versions.

We are happy to acknowledge our debt to the many previous translators, editors and writers – too numerous to list here – who have contributed to our understanding of Descartes' works. In a project of this size it is no empty formality to acknowledge our own responsibility for the shortcomings that undoubtedly remain; we can only enter as our plea the words with which Descartes himself concluded the *Meditations – naturae nostrae infirmitas est agnoscenda.*

John Cottingham
University of Reading, England

Robert Stoothoff
Dugald Murdoch
University of Canterbury, New Zealand.

---

1 *Oeuvres de Descartes*, edited by Ch. Adam and P. Tannery (revised edition, Paris: Vrin/C.N.R.S., 1964–76).

Chronological table of Descartes' life and works

1596	born at La Haye near Tours on 31 March
1606–14	attends Jesuit college of La Flèche at Anjou[1]
1616	takes *Baccalauréat* and *Licence* in law at University of Poitiers
1618	goes to Holland; joins army of Prince Maurice of Nassau; meets Isaac Beeckman; composes a short treatise on music, the *Compendium Musicae*
1619	travels in Germany; 10 November: has vision of new mathematical and scientific system
1622	returns to France; during next few years spends time in Paris, but also travels in Europe
1628	composes *Rules for the Direction of the Mind*; leaves for Holland, which is to be his home until 1649, though with frequent changes of address
1629	begins working on *The World*
1633	condemnation of Galileo; abandons plans to publish *The World*
1635	birth of Descartes' natural daughter Francine, baptized 7 August (died 1640)
1637	publishes *Discourse on the Method*, with *Optics*, *Meteorology* and *Geometry*
1641	*Meditations on First Philosophy* published, together with *Objections and Replies* (first six sets)
1642	second edition of *Meditations* published, with all seven sets of *Objections and Replies* and *Letter to Dinet*
1643	Cartesian philosophy condemned at the University of Utrecht; Descartes' long correspondence with Princess Elizabeth of Bohemia begins
1644	visits France; *Principles of Philosophy* published

---

1 Descartes is known to have stayed at La Flèche for eight or nine years, but the exact dates of his arrival and departure are uncertain. Baillet places Descartes' admission in 1604, the year of the College's foundation (A. Baillet, *La vie de M. Des-Cartes* (1691), vol. 1, p. 18).

Early Writings

Translator's preface

An inventory of Descartes' papers made at Stockholm after his death mentions a small notebook containing various early writings, apparently composed during Descartes' travels in Europe during the years 1619–22. The notebook is now lost, but a copy taken by Leibniz was later discovered and published under the title *Cogitationes Privatae* ('Private thoughts') in 1859. This Latin text, as published with minor corrections in Volume x of Adam and Tannery,[1] is the source of the extracts translated below.

According to Descartes' biographer Adrien Baillet (1649–1706), the original notebook (which he inspected) was divided into various sections under different headings. These included *Praeambula* ('Preliminaries') with the motto 'The fear of the Lord is the beginning of wisdom'; *Experimenta* ('Observations'); and *Olympica* ('Olympian matters'). The probable positionings of these headings are indicated below, though the correct grouping and ordering of the extracts is a matter of conjecture, since no divisions or headings were provided in Leibniz' copy. A detailed study of the Early Writings may be found in Henri Gouhier, *Les Premières Pensées de Descartes* (Paris: Vrin, 1958).

J.C.

1 See General Introduction, above p. x.

Preliminaries

213   Actors, taught not to let any embarrassment show on their faces, put on a mask. I will do the same. So far, I have been a spectator in this theatre which is the world, but I am now about to mount the stage, and I come forward masked.

214   In my youth, when I was shown an ingenious invention, I used to wonder whether I could work it out for myself before reading the inventor's account. This practice gradually led me to realize that I was making use of definite rules.

   Science is like a woman: if she stays faithful to her husband she is respected; if she becomes common property she grows to be despised.

   In the case of most books, once we have read a few lines and looked at a few of the diagrams, the entire message is perfectly obvious. The rest is added only to fill up the paper.

   The mathematical treasure trove of Polybius, citizen of the world.[1] This work lays down the true means of solving all the difficulties in the science of mathematics, and demonstrates that the human intellect can achieve nothing further on these questions. The work is aimed at certain people who promise to show us miraculous discoveries in all the sciences, its purpose being to chide them for their sluggishness and to expose the emptiness of their boasts. A further aim is to lighten the agonizing toil of those who struggle night and day with the Gordian knots of this science, and who squander their intellectual resources to no avail. The work is offered afresh to learned men throughout the world and especially to the distinguished brothers of the Rose Croix in Germany.[2]

---

1 Evidently a pseudonym which Descartes contemplated using.
2 'Afresh': what Descartes means here is not known. The reference to the Rosicrucians may well be ironical.

The sciences are at present masked, but if the masks were taken off, 215 they would be revealed in all their beauty. If we could see how the sciences are linked together, we would find them no harder to retain in our minds than the series of numbers.

For each of us there is a set limit to our intellectual powers which we cannot pass. Those who, through lack of intelligence, cannot make discoveries by employing first principles, will still be able to recognize the true worth of the sciences, and this will enable them to arrive at a correct judgement of the value of things.

Observations

I use the term 'vices' to refer to the diseases of the mind, which are not so easy to recognize as diseases of the body. This is because we have frequently experienced sound bodily health, but have never known true health of the mind.

I notice that if I am sad or in danger and preoccupied by some serious undertaking, I sleep deeply and eat voraciously. But if I am full of joy, I do not eat or sleep.

In a garden we can produce shadows to represent certain shapes, such as trees; or we can trim a hedge so that from a certain perspective it 216 represents a given shape. Again, in a room we can arrange for the rays of the sun to pass through various openings so as to represent different numbers or figures; or we can make it seem as if there are tongues of flame, or chariots of fire, or other shapes in the air. This is all done by mirrors which focus the sun's rays at various points. Again, we can arrange things so that when the sun is shining into a room, it always seems to come from the same direction, or seems to go from west to east. This is all done by parabolic reflectors: the sun's rays must fall on a concave mirror on the roof, and the mirror's focal point must be in line with a small hole, on the other side of which is another concave mirror with the same focal distance, which is also aligned on the hole. This causes the sun's rays to be cast in parallel lines inside the room.[1]

In the year 1620, I began to understand the fundamental principles of a wonderful discovery.

1 The original of this piece is in French and not, as is the case with all the other extracts, in Latin.

In November 1619, I had a dream involving the Seventh Ode of
Ausonius, which begins *Quod vitae sectabor iter* ['What road in life shall I
follow?'].[1]

217   It is just as valuable to be censured by friends as it is splendid to be
praised by enemies. We desire praise from those who do not know us, but
from friends we want the truth.

In the minds of all of us there are certain elements which once aroused,
however slightly, produce strong emotions. Thus, if a high-spirited child
is scolded, he will not weep but get angry, whereas another child will
weep. If we are told that some disaster has occurred we are sad; but if we
are afterwards told that some wicked man was responsible, we become
angry. In moving from one passion to another, we pass through
intermediate related passions. But often there will be a more violent
transition from one passion to its opposite, as when in the course of a
lively banquet we suddenly hear news of some misfortune.

Olympian matters[2]

Just as the imagination employs figures in order to conceive of bodies, so,
in order to frame ideas of spiritual things, the intellect makes use of
certain bodies which are perceived through the senses, such as wind and
light. By this means we may philosophize in a more exalted way, and
develop the knowledge to raise our minds to lofty heights.

It may seem surprising to find weighty judgements in the writings of
the poets rather than the philosophers. The reason is that the poets were
driven to write by enthusiasm and the force of imagination. We have
within us the sparks of knowledge, as in a flint: philosophers extract
them through reason, but poets force them out through the sharp blows
of the imagination, so that they shine more brightly.

1 The dream occurred in Descartes' famous 'stove-heated room' in southern Germany
(probably Ulm). According to Baillet, Descartes went to bed on 10 November 1619 'full
of enthusiasm, convinced he had discovered the foundations of a marvellous science'. He
then had three consecutive dreams. In the first he was assailed by phantoms and a
whirlwind, and felt a pain in his side which he feared had been produced by some evil
demon. In the second he heard a terrible noise like a thunderclap. In the third he opened a
volume of poetry and found the verse quoted here (by Decius Magnus Ausonius, a
Roman poet of the fourth century A.D., who lived in Bordeaux). On waking, Descartes
interpreted his dreams as evidence of his destiny to produce a new mathematical and
scientific system, and made a vow to the Virgin to visit her shrine at Loretto. Full details
of the episode are given in Adrien Baillet's *Life of Descartes* (*La Vie de M. Des-Cartes*,
1691), vol. I, pp. 80–6 (quoted in AT x 180ff).

2 According to Baillet, a description by Descartes of his discovery in 1619 of the
'foundations of a wonderful science' originally belonged in this section of the notebook.

The pronouncements of the learned can be reduced to a very small number of general rules.

Before the end of November I shall head for Loretto. I intend to go 218 there on foot from Venice, if this is feasible and is the custom. If not, I will make the pilgrimage with all the devotion that anyone could normally be expected to show.

At all events I will complete my treatise before Easter, and if I can find publishers, and I am satisfied with what I manage to produce, I shall publish it. This is the promise I have made today, 23 February 1620.

There is a single active power in things: love, charity, harmony.

The things which are perceivable by the senses are helpful in enabling us to conceive of Olympian matters. The wind signifies spirit; movement with the passage of time signifies life; light signifies knowledge; heat signifies love; and instantaneous activity signifies creation. Every corporeal form acts through harmony. There are more wet things than dry things, and more cold things than hot, because if this were not so, the active elements would have won the battle too quickly and the world would not have lasted long.

'God separated the light from the darkness.' This text in Genesis means that God separated the good angels from the bad angels. The text cannot be understood literally, since a privation cannot be separated from a positive state. God is pure intelligence.

The Lord has made three marvels: something out of nothing; free will; and God in Man.

Man has knowledge of natural things only through their resemblance to the things which come under the senses. Indeed, our estimate of how much truth a person has achieved in his philosophizing[1] will increase the 219 more he has been able to propose some similarity between what he is investigating and the things known by the senses.

The high degree of perfection displayed in some of their actions makes us suspect that animals do not have free will.[2]

---

1 Here, as often in Descartes, the terms 'philosophy', 'philosophize' etc. include what would nowadays be called scientific reasoning.
2 See below, *Discourse*, part 5, p. 139 and *Principles*, part 1, art. 37, p. 205.

Rules for the Direction of the Mind

Translator's preface

Descartes' *Rules for the Direction of the Mind* (*Regulae ad Directionem Ingenii*) was written in Latin, probably in 1628 or a few years earlier, but was not published during the author's lifetime. A Dutch translation of the work appeared in Holland in 1684, and the first Latin edition was published in Amsterdam by P. and J. Blaeu in 1701.[1]

In the inventory of Descartes' papers made at Stockholm shortly after his death in 1650 the work is listed as 'Nine notebooks bound together, containing part of a Treatise on clear and useful Rules for the Direction of the Mind in the Search for Truth'. The original manuscript, which is lost, passed to Claude Clerselier, one of Descartes' staunchest supporters, who showed the work to several scholars, including Antoine Arnauld. The manuscript was seen also by Adrien Baillet, Descartes' biographer, who gave a summary of its contents in his *La Vie de Monsieur Des-Cartes* (1691). Leibniz bought a copy of the original manuscript in Amsterdam in 1670, and this copy has survived among the Leibniz papers in the Royal Public Library at Hanover.

The *Rules* was originally intended to contain three parts, each comprising twelve rules. The second set of twelve rules is incomplete, ending at Rule Twenty-one, and only the headings of Rules Nineteen to Twenty-one are given. The final set of twelve Rules is entirely missing; it appears that Descartes left this project unfinished. The first twelve Rules are concerned with simple propositions and the two cognitive operations by means of which they are known, intuition and deduction. The second set deal with what Descartes calls 'perfectly understood problems', i.e. problems in which the object of inquiry is a unique function of the data and which can be expressed in the forms of equations. Problems of this sort are confined largely to the sphere of mathematics. The projected third set of Rules would have dealt with 'imperfectly understood problems', i.e. problems which, owing to the multiplicity of the data involved, resist expression in the form of an equation; problems of this sort are prominent in the empirical sciences. Descartes had intended to

---

1   R. *Des-Cartes Opuscula posthuma, physica et mathematica.*

show how imperfectly understood problems can be reduced to perfectly understood ones.

The present translation is based primarily on the text in Volume x of Adam and Tannery.[1] There are differences of detail between the Amsterdam edition of 1701 and the Hanover manuscript; they were probably based on different copies of the original manuscript. Where the two texts differ, the 1701 edition in most cases provides the better reading, and Adam and Tannery generally follow this text. In several instances, however, readings other than those adopted by Adam and Tannery have been preferred in the present translation; these are described in footnotes when the variants are not given in Adam and Tannery, or when neither of the alternative variants yields an obviously preferable reading. The critical edition of Giovanni Crapulli[1] has been a useful supplement to Adam and Tannery, and several of Crapulli's readings have been adopted.

In the footnotes the Amsterdam edition of 1701 is referred to as A, and the Hanover manuscript as H.

D.M.

1 See General Introduction, p. x above.
2 *René Descartes: Regulae ad directionem ingenii: texte critique établi par Giovanni Crapulli avec la version hollandaise du XVIIème siècle* (The Hague: Martinus Nijhoff, 1966).

Rule One

The aim of our studies should be to direct the mind with a view to forming true and sound judgements about whatever comes before it.

Whenever people notice some similarity between two things, they are in the habit of ascribing to the one what they find true of the other, even when the two are not in that respect similar. Thus they wrongly compare the sciences, which consist wholly in knowledge acquired by the mind, with the arts, which require some bodily aptitude and practice. They recognize that one man cannot master all the arts at once and that it is easier to excel as a craftsman if one practises only one skill; for one man 360 cannot turn his hand to both farming and harp-playing, or to several different tasks of this kind, as easily as he can to just one of them. This has made people come to think that the same must be true of the sciences as well. Distinguishing the sciences by the differences in their objects, they think that each science should be studied separately, without regard to any of the others. But here they are surely mistaken. For the sciences as a whole are nothing other than human wisdom, which always remains one and the same, however different the subjects to which it is applied, it being no more altered by them than sunlight is by the variety of the things it shines on. Hence there is no need to impose any restrictions on our mental powers; for the knowledge of one truth does not, like skill in one art, hinder us from discovering another; on the contrary it helps us. Indeed, it seems strange to me that so many people should investigate with such diligence the virtues of plants,[1] the motions of the stars, the transmutations of metals, and the objects of similar disciplines, while hardly anyone gives a thought to good sense – to universal wisdom. For every other science is to be valued not so much for its own sake as for its contribution to universal wisdom. Hence, we have reason to propose this as our very first rule, since what makes us stray from the correct way of seeking the truth is chiefly our ignoring the general end of universal

1 The translation here follows the texts of A and H: AT, following an emendation by Leibniz, read 'the customs of men, the virtues of plants . . .'

9

wisdom and directing our studies towards some particular ends. I do not mean vile and despicable ends such as empty glory or base gain: specious arguments and tricks suited to vulgar minds clearly provide a much more 361 direct route to these ends than a sound knowledge of the truth could provide. I have in mind, rather, respectable and commendable ends, for these are often more subtly misleading – ends such as the pursuit of sciences conducive to the comforts of life or to the pleasure to be gained from contemplating the truth, which is practically the only happiness in this life that is complete and untroubled by any pain. We can indeed look forward to these legitimate fruits of the sciences; but if we think of them during our studies, they frequently cause us to overlook many items which are required for a knowledge of other things, because at first glance they seem of little use or of little interest. It must be acknowledged that all the sciences are so closely interconnected that it is much easier to learn them all together than to separate one from the other. If, therefore, someone seriously wishes to investigate the truth of things, he ought not to select one science in particular, for they are all interconnected and interdependent. He should, rather, consider simply how to increase the natural light of his reason, not with a view to solving this or that scholastic problem, but in order that his intellect should show his will what decision it ought to make in each of life's contingencies. He will soon be surprised to find that he has made far greater progress than those who devote themselves to particular studies, and that he has achieved not only everything that the specialists aim at but also goals far beyond any they can hope to reach.

362   ## *Rule Two*

We should attend only to those objects of which our minds seem capable of having certain and indubitable cognition.

All knowledge[1] is certain and evident cognition. Someone who has doubts about many things is no wiser than one who has never given them a thought; indeed, he appears less wise if he has formed a false opinion about any of them. Hence it is better never to study at all than to occupy ourselves with objects which are so difficult that we are unable to distinguish what is true from what is false, and are forced to take the doubtful as certain; for in such matters the risk of diminishing our knowledge is greater than our hope of increasing it. So, in accordance with this Rule, we reject all such merely probable cognition and resolve to believe only what is perfectly known and incapable of being doubted. Men of learning are perhaps convinced that there is very little indubitable

1 Lat. *scientia*, Descartes' term for systematic knowledge based on indubitable foundations.

knowledge, since, owing to a common human failing, they have disdained to reflect upon such indubitable truths, taking them to be too easy and obvious to everyone. But there are, I insist, a lot more of these truths than such people think – truths which suffice for the sure demonstration of countless propositions which so far they have managed to treat as no more than probable. Because they have thought it unbecoming for a man 363 of learning to admit to being ignorant on any matter, they have got so used to elaborating their contrived doctrines that they have gradually come to believe them and to pass them off as true.

Nevertheless, if we adhere strictly to this Rule, there will be very few things which we can get down to studying. For there is hardly any question in the sciences about which clever men have not frequently disagreed. But whenever two persons make opposite judgements about the same thing, it is certain that at least one of them is mistaken, and neither, it seems, has knowledge. For if the reasoning of one of them were certain and evident, he would be able to lay it before the other in such a way as eventually to convince his intellect as well. Therefore, concerning all such matters of probable opinion we can, I think, acquire no perfect knowledge, for it would be presumptuous to hope that we could gain more knowledge than others have managed to achieve. Accordingly, if my reckoning is correct, out of all the sciences so far devised, we are restricted to just arithmetic and geometry if we stick to this Rule.

Yet I do not wish on that account to condemn that method of philosophizing which others have hitherto devised, nor those weapons of the schoolmen, probable syllogisms,[1] which are just made for controversies. For these exercise the minds of the young, stimulating them with a certain rivalry; and it is much better that their minds should be informed with opinions of that sort – even though they are evidently 364 uncertain, being controversial among the learned – than that they should be left entirely to their own devices. Perhaps without guidance they might head towards a precipice, but so long as they follow in their masters' footsteps (though straying at times from the truth), they will surely hold to a course that is more secure, at least in the sense that it has already been tested by wiser heads. For our part, we are very glad that we had a scholastic education of this sort. But we are now freed from the oath which bound us to our master's words and are old enough to be no longer subject to the rod. So if we seriously wish to propose rules for ourselves which will help us scale the heights of human knowledge, we must include, as one of our primary rules, that we should take care not

---

1 I.e. syllogisms whose premisses are believed, but not known, to be true.

to waste our time by neglecting easy tasks and occupying ourselves only with difficult matters. That is just what many people do: they ingeniously construct the most subtle conjectures and plausible arguments on difficult questions, but after all their efforts they come to realize, too late, that rather than acquiring any knowledge, they have merely increased the number of their doubts.

Of all the sciences so far discovered, arithmetic and geometry alone are, as we said above, free from any taint of falsity or uncertainty. If we are to give a careful estimate of the reason why this should be so, we should bear in mind that there are two ways of arriving at a knowledge of things – through experience and through deduction. Moreover, we must note that while our experiences of things are often deceptive, the deduction or pure inference of one thing from another can never be performed wrongly by an intellect which is in the least degree rational, though we may fail to make the inference if we do not see it. Furthermore, those chains with which dialecticians[1] suppose they regulate human reason seem to me to be of little use here, though I do not deny that they are very useful for other purposes. In fact none of the errors to which men – men, I say, not the brutes – are liable is ever due to faulty inference; they are due only to the fact that men take for granted certain poorly understood observations,[2] or lay down rash and groundless judgements.

These considerations make it obvious why arithmetic and geometry prove to be much more certain than other disciplines: they alone are concerned with an object so pure and simple that they make no assumptions that experience might render uncertain; they consist entirely in deducing conclusions by means of rational arguments. They are therefore the easiest and clearest of all the sciences and have just the sort of object we are looking for. Where these sciences are concerned it scarcely seems humanly possible to err, except through inadvertence. Yet we should not be surprised if many prefer of their own accord to apply their minds to other arts, or to philosophy. The reason for this is that everyone feels free to make more confident guesses about matters which are obscure than about matters which are clear. It is much easier to hazard some conjecture on this or that question than to arrive at the exact truth about one particular question, however straightforward it may be.

Now the conclusion we should draw from these considerations is not that arithmetic and geometry are the only sciences worth studying, but rather that in seeking the right path of truth we ought to concern

---

1 Descartes' term for scholastic logic see below, *Principles*, p. 186.
2 Lat. *experimenta*; see footnote on the equivalent French term *expériences*, p. 143 below.

ourselves only with objects which admit of as much certainty as the demonstrations of arithmetic and geometry.

Rule Three

Concerning objects proposed for study, we ought to investigate what we can clearly and evidently intuit[1] or deduce with certainty, and not what other people have thought or what we ourselves conjecture. For knowledge[2] can be attained in no other way.

We ought to read the writings of the ancients, for it is of great advantage to be able to make use of the labours of so many men. We should do so both in order to learn what truths have already been discovered and also to be informed about the points which remain to be worked out in the various disciplines. But at the same time there is a considerable danger that if we study these works too closely traces of their errors will infect us and cling to us against our will and despite our precautions. For, once writers have credulously and heedlessly taken up a position on some controversial question, they are generally inclined to employ the most subtle arguments in an attempt to get us to adopt their point of view. On the other hand, whenever they have the luck to discover something certain and evident, they always present it wrapped up in various 367 obscurities, either because they fear that the simplicity of their argument may depreciate the importance of their finding, or because they begrudge us the plain truth.

But even if all writers were sincere and open, and never tried to palm off doubtful matters as true, but instead put forward everything in good faith, we would always be uncertain which of them to believe, for hardly anything is said by one writer the contrary of which is not asserted by some other. It would be of no use to count heads, so as to follow the view which many authorities hold. For if the question at issue is a difficult one, it is more likely that few, rather than many, should have been able to discover the truth about it. But even if they all agreed among themselves, their teaching would still not be all we need. For example, even though we know other people's demonstrations by heart, we shall never become mathematicians if we lack the intellectual aptitude to solve any given problem. And even though we have read all the arguments of Plato and Aristotle, we shall never become philosophers if we are unable to make a sound judgement on matters which come up for discussion; in this case what we would seem to have learnt would not be science but history.

---

1 Lat. *intueri*, literally 'to look, gaze at'; used by Descartes as a technical term for immediate mental apprehension.
2 Lat. *scientia*; see footnote on p. 10 above.

Furthermore, we would be well-advised not to mix any conjectures into the judgements we make about the truth of things. It is most important to bear this point in mind. The main reason why we can find nothing in ordinary philosophy which is so evident and certain as to be

368 beyond dispute is that students of the subject first of all are not content to acknowledge what is clear and certain, but on the basis of merely probable conjectures venture also to make assertions on obscure matters about which nothing is known; they then gradually come to have complete faith in these assertions, indiscriminately mixing them up with others that are true and evident. The result is that the only conclusions they can draw are ones which apparently rest on some such obscure proposition, and which are accordingly uncertain.

But in case we in turn should slip into the same error, let us now review all the actions of the intellect by means of which we are able to arrive at a knowledge of things with no fear of being mistaken. We recognize only two: intuition and deduction.[1]

By 'intuition' I do not mean the fluctuating testimony of the senses or the deceptive judgement of the imagination as it botches things together, but the conception of a clear and attentive mind, which is so easy and distinct that there can be no room for doubt about what we are understanding. Alternatively, and this comes to the same thing, intuition is the indubitable conception of a clear and attentive mind which proceeds solely from the light of reason. Because it is simpler, it is more certain than deduction, though deduction, as we noted above, is not something a man can perform wrongly. Thus everyone can mentally intuit that he exists, that he is thinking, that a triangle is bounded by just three lines, and a sphere by a single surface, and the like. Perceptions such as these are more numerous than most people realize, disdaining as they do to turn their minds to such simple matters.

369 In case anyone should be troubled by my novel use of the term 'intuition' and of other terms to which I shall be forced to give a different meaning from their ordinary one, I wish to point out here that I am paying no attention to the way these terms have lately been used in the Schools. For it would be very difficult for me to employ the same terminology, when my own views are profoundly different. I shall take account only of the meanings in Latin of individual words and, when appropriate words are lacking, I shall use what seem the most suitable words, adapting them to my own meaning.

The self-evidence and certainty of intuition is required not only for apprehending single propositions, but also for any train of reasoning

---

1 *inductio* in A, almost certainly a misprint for *deductio*.

whatever. Take for example, the inference that 2 plus 2 equals 3 plus 1: not only must we intuitively perceive that 2 plus 2 make 4, and that 3 plus 1 make 4, but also that the original proposition follows necessarily from the other two.

There may be some doubt here about our reason for suggesting another mode of knowing in addition to intuition, *viz.* deduction, by which we mean the inference of something as following necessarily from some other propositions which are known with certainty. But this distinction had to be made, since very many facts which are not self-evident are known with certainty, provided they are inferred from true and known principles through a continuous and uninterrupted movement of thought in which each individual proposition is clearly intuited. This is similar to the way in which we know that the last link in a long chain is connected to the first: even if we cannot take in at one 370 glance all the intermediate links on which the connection depends, we can have knowledge of the connection provided we survey the links one after the other, and keep in mind that each link from first to last is attached to its neighbour. Hence we are distinguishing mental intuition from certain deduction on the grounds that we are aware of a movement or a sort of sequence in the latter but not in the former, and also because immediate self-evidence is not required for deduction, as it is for intuition; deduction in a sense gets its certainty from memory. It follows that those propositions which are immediately inferred from first principles can be said to be known in one respect through intuition, and in another respect through deduction. But the first principles themselves are known only through intuition, and the remote conclusions only through deduction.

These two ways are the most certain routes to knowledge that we have. So far as our powers of understanding are concerned, we should admit no more than these and should reject all others as suspect and liable to error. This does not preclude our believing that what has been revealed by God is more certain than any knowledge, since faith in these matters, as in anything obscure, is an act of the will rather than an act of the understanding. And if our faith has a basis in our intellect, revealed truths above all can and should be discovered by one or other of the two ways we have just described, as we may show at greater length below.

Rule Four 371

We need a method if we are to investigate the truth of things.

So blind is the curiosity with which mortals are possessed that they often direct their minds down untrodden paths, in the groundless hope that they will chance upon what they are seeking, rather like someone who is consumed with such a senseless desire to discover treasure that he continually roams the streets to see if he can find any that a passer-by might have dropped. This is how almost every chemist, most geometers, and many philosophers pursue their research. I am not denying that they sometimes are lucky enough in their wanderings to hit upon some truth, though on that account I rate them more fortunate than diligent. But it is far better never to contemplate investigating the truth about any matter than to do so without a method. For it is quite certain that such haphazard studies and obscure reflections blur the natural light and blind our intelligence. Those who are accustomed to walking in the dark weaken their eye-sight, the result being that they can no longer bear to be in broad daylight. Experience confirms this, for we very often find that people who have never devoted their time to learned studies make sounder and clearer judgements on matters which arise than those who have spent all their time in the Schools. By 'a method' I mean reliable

372 rules which are easy to apply, and such that if one follows them exactly, one will never take what is false to be true or fruitlessly expend one's mental efforts, but will gradually and constantly increase one's knowledge[1] till one arrives at a true understanding of everything within one's capacity.

There are two points here which we should keep in mind: we should never assume to be true anything which is false; and our goal should be to attain knowledge of all things. For, if we do not know something we are capable of knowing, this is simply because we have never discovered a way that might lead us to such knowledge, or because we have fallen into the opposite error.[2] But if our method properly explains how we should use our mental intuition to avoid falling into the opposite error and how we should go about finding the deductive inferences that will help us attain this all-embracing knowledge, then I do not see that anything more is needed to make it complete; for as I have already said, we can have no knowledge[1] without mental intuition or deduction. The method cannot go so far as to teach us how to perform the actual operations of intuition and deduction, since these are the simplest of all and quite basic. If our intellect were not already able to perform them, it would not comprehend any of the rules of the method, however easy they might be. As for other mental operations which dialectic[3] claims to direct with the help of those already mentioned, they are of no use here, or rather should be

373 reckoned a positive hindrance, for nothing can be added to the clear light of reason which does not in some way dim it.

1 Lat. *scientia*; see footnote on p. 10 above.
2 I.e. rejecting what is true through undue scepticism.
3 See footnote on p. 12 above.

So useful is this method that without it the pursuit of learning would, I think, be more harmful than profitable. Hence I can readily believe that the great minds of the past were to some extent aware of it, guided to it even by nature alone. For the human mind has within it a sort of spark of the divine, in which the first seeds of useful ways of thinking are sown, seeds which, however neglected and stifled by studies which impede them, often bear fruit of their own accord. This is our experience in the simplest of sciences, arithmetic and geometry: we are well aware that the geometers of antiquity employed a sort of analysis which they went on to apply to the solution of every problem, though they begrudged revealing it to posterity. At the present time a sort of arithmetic called 'algebra' is flourishing, and this is achieving for numbers what the ancients did for figures. These two disciplines are simply the spontaneous fruits which have sprung from the innate principles of this method. I am not surprised that, where the simplest objects of these disciplines are concerned, there has been a richer harvest of such fruits than in other disciplines in which greater obstacles tend to stifle progress. But no doubt these too could achieve a perfect maturity if only they were cultivated with extreme care.

That is in fact what I have principally aimed at achieving in this treatise. I would not value these Rules so highly if they were good only for solving those pointless problems with which arithmeticians and geometers are inclined to while away their time, for in that case all I could credit myself with achieving would be to dabble in trifles with greater subtlety than they. I shall have much to say below about figures 374 and numbers, for no other disciplines can yield illustrations as evident and certain as these. But if one attends closely to my meaning, one will readily see that ordinary mathematics is far from my mind here, that it is quite another discipline I am expounding, and that these illustrations are more its outer garments than its inner parts. This discipline should contain the primary rudiments of human reason and extend to the discovery of truths in any field whatever. Frankly speaking, I am convinced that it is a more powerful instrument of knowledge than any other with which human beings are endowed, as it is the source of all the rest. I have spoken of its 'outer garment', not because I wish to conceal this science and shroud it from the gaze of the public; I wish rather to clothe and adorn it so as to make it easier to present to the human mind.

When I first applied my mind to the mathematical disciplines, I at once read most of the customary lore which mathematical writers pass on to us. I paid special attention to arithmetic and geometry, for these were said to be the simplest and, as it were, to lead into the rest. But in neither 375 subject did I come across writers who fully satisfied me. I read much about numbers which I found to be true once I had gone over the calculations for myself. The writers displayed many geometrical truths before my very eyes, as it were, and derived them by means of logical arguments. But they did not seem to make it sufficiently clear to my mind why these things should be so and how they were discovered. So I was not surprised to find that even many clever and learned men, after dipping into these arts, either quickly lay them aside as childish and pointless or else take them to be so very difficult and complicated that they are put off at the outset from learning them. For there is really nothing more futile than so busying ourselves with bare numbers and imaginary figures that we seem to rest content in the knowledge of such trifles. And there is nothing more futile than devoting our energies to those superficial proofs which are discovered more through chance than method and which have more to do with our eyes and imagination than our intellect; for the outcome of this is that, in a way, we get out of the habit of using our reason. At the same time there is nothing more complicated than using such a method of proof to resolve new problems which are beset with numerical disorder. Later on I wondered why the founders of philosophy would admit no one to the pursuit of wisdom who was unversed in mathematics[1] – as if they thought that this discipline was the easiest and most indispensable of all for cultivating and preparing the mind to grasp other more important sciences. I came to suspect that they were familiar with a kind of mathematics quite different from the one which prevails today; not that I thought they had a perfect knowledge of it, for their wild exultations and thanksgivings for trivial discoveries clearly show how rudimentary their knowledge must have been. I am not shaken in this opinion by those machines[2] of theirs which are so much praised by historians. These mechanical devices may well have been quite simple, even though the ignorant and wonder-loving masses may have raised them to the level of marvels. But I am convinced that certain primary seeds of truth naturally implanted in human minds thrived vigorously in that unsophisticated and innocent age – seeds which have been stifled in us through our constantly reading and hearing all sorts of errors. So the same light of the mind which enabled them to see (albeit without knowing why) that virtue is preferable to pleasure, the good preferable to the useful, also enabled them to grasp true ideas in philosophy and mathematics, although they were not yet able fully to master such sciences. Indeed, one can even see some traces of this true mathematics, I think, in Pappus and Diophantus[3] who, though not of

376

---

1 A reference to Plato's Academy, over the entrance to which was inscribed the motto, 'No one ignorant of geometry may enter.'
2 Perhaps an allusion to mechanical devices such as the wooden dove (which could fly) constructed by Archytas of Tarentum, a friend of Plato.
3 Greek mathematicians working in Alexandria in the third century A.D.

that earliest antiquity, lived many centuries before our time. But I have come to think that these writers themselves, with a kind of pernicious cunning, later suppressed this mathematics as, notoriously, many inventors are known to have done where their own discoveries were concerned. They may have feared that their method, just because it was so easy and simple, would be depreciated if it were divulged; so to gain our admiration, they may have shown us, as the fruits of their method, some barren truths proved by clever arguments, instead of teaching us the method itself, which might have dispelled our admiration. In the present age some very gifted men have tried to revive this method, for the method seems to me to be none other than the art which goes by the outlandish name of 'algebra' – or at least it would be if algebra were divested of the multiplicity of numbers and incomprehensible figures which overwhelm it and instead possessed that abundance of clarity and simplicity which I believe the true mathematics ought to have. It was these thoughts which made me turn from the particular studies of arithmetic and geometry to a general investigation of mathematics. I began my investigation by inquiring what exactly is generally meant by the term 'mathematics'[1] and why it is that, in addition to arithmetic and geometry, sciences such as astronomy, music, optics, mechanics, among others, are called branches of mathematics. To answer this it is not enough just to look at the etymology of the word, for, since the word 'mathematics' has the same meaning as 'discipline',[2] these subjects have as much right to be called 'mathematics' as geometry has. Yet it is evident that almost anyone with the slightest education can easily tell the difference in any context between what relates to mathematics and what to the other disciplines. When I considered the matter more closely, I came to see that the exclusive concern of mathematics is with questions of order or measure and that it is irrelevant whether the measure in question involves numbers, shapes, stars, sounds, or any other object whatever. This made me realize that there must be a general science which explains all the points that can be raised concerning order and measure irrespective of the subject-matter, and that this science should be termed *mathesis universalis*[3] – a venerable term with a well-established meaning – for it covers everything that entitles these other sciences to be called branches of mathematics. How superior it is to these subordinate sciences both in utility and simplicity is clear from the fact that it covers all they deal with, and more besides; and any difficulties it involves apply to these as well, whereas their particular subject-matter involves difficulties which it lacks. Now everyone knows the name of this subject and without even

377

378

---

1 Descartes uses the term *mathesis*, from the Greek, μάθησις, literally 'learning'.
2 Lat. *disciplina*, from *discere*, 'to learn'.
3 I.e. 'universal mathematics'.

studying it understands what its subject-matter is. So why is it that most people painstakingly pursue the other disciplines which depend on it, and no one bothers to learn this one? No doubt I would find that very surprising if I did not know that everyone thinks the subject too easy, and if I had not long since observed that the human intellect always bypasses subjects which it thinks it can easily master and directly hurries on to new and grander things.

379   Aware how slender my powers are, I have resolved in my search for knowledge of things to adhere unswervingly to a definite order, always starting with the simplest and easiest things and never going beyond them till there seems to be nothing further which is worth achieving where they are concerned. Up to now, therefore, I have devoted all my energies to this universal mathematics, so that I think I shall be able in due course to tackle the somewhat more advanced sciences, without my efforts being premature. But before I embark on this task I shall try to bring together and arrange in an orderly manner whatever I thought noteworthy in my previous studies, so that when old age dims my memory I can readily recall it hereafter, if I need to, by consulting this book, and so that, having disburdened my memory, I can henceforth devote my mind more freely to what remains.

Rule Five

The whole method consists entirely in the ordering and arranging of the objects on which we must concentrate our mind's eye if we are to discover some truth. We shall be following this method exactly if we first reduce complicated and obscure propositions step by step to simpler ones, and then, starting with the intuition of the simplest ones of all, try to ascend through the same steps to a knowledge of all the rest.

This one Rule covers the most essential points in the whole of human endeavour. Anyone who sets out in quest of knowledge of things must

380   follow this Rule as closely as he would the thread of Theseus if he were to enter the Labyrinth. But many people either do not reflect upon what the Rule prescribes, or ignore it altogether, or presume that they have no need of it. They frequently examine difficult problems in a very disorderly manner, behaving in my view as if they were trying to get from the bottom to the top of a building at one bound, spurning or failing to notice the stairs designed for that purpose. Astrologers all do likewise: they do not know the nature of the heavens and do not even make any accurate observations of celestial motions, yet they expect to be able to delineate the effects of these motions. So too do most of those who study mechanics apart from physics and, without any proper plan, construct

new instruments for producing motion. This applies also to those philosophers who take no account of experience and think that truth will spring from their brains like Minerva from the head of Jupiter.

All those just mentioned are plainly violating this Rule. But the order that is required here is often so obscure and complicated that not everyone can make out what it is; hence it is virtually impossible to guard against going astray unless one carefully observes the message of the following Rule.

Rule Six

In order to distinguish the simplest things from those that are complicated and to set them out in an orderly manner, we should attend to what is most simple in each series of things in which we have directly deduced some truths from others, and should observe how all the rest are more, or less, or equally removed from the simplest.

Although the message of this Rule may not seem very novel, it contains nevertheless the main secret of my method; and there is no more useful Rule in this whole treatise. For it instructs us that all things can be arranged serially in various groups, not in so far as they can be referred to some ontological genus (such as the categories into which philosophers divide things[1]), but in so far as some things can be known on the basis of others. Thus when a difficulty arises, we can see at once whether it will be worth looking at any others first, and if so which ones and in what order.

In order to be able to do this correctly, we should note first that everything, with regard to its possible usefulness to our project, may be termed either 'absolute' or 'relative' – our project being, not to inspect the isolated natures of things, but to compare them with each other so that some may be known on the basis of others.

I call 'absolute' whatever has within it the pure and simple nature in question; that is, whatever is viewed as being independent, a cause, simple, universal, single, equal, similar, straight, and other qualities of that sort. I call this the simplest and the easiest thing when we can make use of it in solving problems.

The 'relative', on the other hand, is what shares the same nature, or at least something of the same nature, in virtue of which we can relate it to the absolute and deduce it from the absolute in a definite series of steps. The concept of the 'relative' involves other terms besides, which I call 'relations': these include whatever is said to be dependent, an effect, composite, particular, many, unequal, dissimilar, oblique, etc. The further

---

1 For example, the Aristotelian categories of substance, quality, quantity, relation, etc.

removed from the absolute such relative attributes are, the more mutually dependent relations of this sort they contain. This Rule points out that all these relations should be distinguished, and the interconnections between them, and their natural order, should be noted, so that given the last term we should be able to reach the one that is absolute in the highest degree, by passing through all the intermediate ones.

The secret of this technique consists entirely in our attentively noting in all things that which is absolute in the highest degree. For some things are more absolute than others from one point of view, yet more relative from a different point of view. For example, the universal is more absolute than the particular, in virtue of its having a simpler nature, but it can also be said to be more relative than the particular in that it depends upon particulars for its existence, etc. Again, certain things sometimes are really more absolute than others, yet not the most absolute of all. Thus a species is something absolute with respect to particulars, but with respect to the genus it is relative; and where measurable items are concerned, extension is something absolute, but among the varieties of extension 383 length is something absolute, etc. Furthermore, in order to make it clear that what we are contemplating here is the series of things to be discovered, and not the nature of each of them, we have deliberately listed 'cause' and 'equal' among the absolutes, although their nature really is relative. Philosophers, of course, recognize that cause and effect are correlatives; but in the present case, if we want to know what the effect is, we must know the cause first, and not *vice versa*. Again, equals are correlative with one another, but we can know what things are unequal only by comparison with equals, and not *vice versa*, etc.

Secondly, we should note that there are very few pure and simple natures which we can intuit straight off and *per se* (independently of any others) either in our sensory experience or by means of a light innate within us. We should, as I said, attend carefully to the simple natures which can be intuited in this way, for these are the ones which in each series we term simple in the highest degree. As for all the other natures, we can apprehend them only by deducing them from those which are simple in the highest degree, either immediately and directly, or by means of two or three or more separate inferences. In the latter case we should also note the number of these inferences so that we may know whether the separation between the conclusion and the primary and supremely simple proposition is by way of a greater or fewer number of steps. And the chain of inferences – which gives rise to those series of objects of investigation to which every problem must be reduced – is such throughout that the problem can be investigated by a reliable method. 384 But since it is not easy to review all the connections together, and moreover, since our task is not so much to retain them in our memory as to distinguish them with, as it were, the sharp edge of our mind, we must seek a means of developing our intelligence in such a way that we can discern these connections immediately whenever the need arises. In my experience there is no better way of doing this than by accustoming ourselves to reflecting with some discernment on the minute details of the things we have already perceived.

The third and last point is that we should not begin our studies by investigating difficult matters. Before tackling any specific problems we ought first to make a random selection of truths which happen to be at hand, and ought then to see whether we can deduce some other truths from them step by step, and from these still others, and so on in logical sequence. This done, we should reflect attentively on the truths we have discovered and carefully consider why it was we were able to discover some of these truths sooner and more easily than others, and what these truths are. This will enable us to judge, when tackling a specific problem, what points we may usefully concentrate on discovering first. For example, say the thought occurs to me that the number 6 is twice 3: I may then ask what twice 6 is, *viz.* 12; I may, if I like, go on to ask what twice 12 is, *viz.* 24, and what twice 24 is, *viz.* 48, etc. It would then be easy for me to deduce that there is the same ratio between 3 and 6 as between 6 and 12, and again the same ratio between 12 and 24, etc., and hence that the numbers 3, 6, 12, 24, 48, etc. are continued proportionals. All of this is so clear as to seem almost childish; nevertheless when I think carefully about it, I can see what sort of complications are involved in all the 385 questions one can ask about the proportions or relations between things, and in what order the questions should be investigated. This one point encompasses the essential core of the entire science of pure mathematics.

For I notice first that it was no more difficult to discover what twice 6 is than twice 3, and that whenever we find a ratio between any two magnitudes we can always find, just as easily, innumerable others which have the same ratio between them. The nature of the problem is no different when we are trying to find three, four, or more magnitudes of this sort, since each one has to be found separately and without regard to the others. I next observe that given the magnitudes 3 and 6, I easily found[1] a third magnitude which is in continued proportion, *viz.* 12, yet, when the extreme terms 3 and 12 were given, I could not find just as easily the mean proportional, 6. If we look into the reason for this, it is obvious that we have here a quite different type of problem from the preceding one. For, if we are to find the mean proportional, we must attend at the

---

1 Reading *invenerim*, A (following Crapulli) rather than *inveneris* ('you found'), H and AT.

same time to the two extreme terms and the ratio between them, in order to obtain a new ratio by dividing this one.[1] This is a very different task from that of finding a third magnitude, given two magnitudes in continued proportion.[2] I can go even further and ask whether, given the numbers 3 and 24, it would be just as easy to find one of the two mean
386 proportionals, *viz.* 6 and 12. Here we have another sort of problem again, an even more complicated one than either of the preceding ones. We have to attend not just to one thing or to two but to three different things at the same time, if we are to find a fourth.[3] We can go even further and see whether, given just 3 and 48, it would be still more difficult to find one of the three mean proportionals, *viz.* 6, 12 and 24. At first sight it does indeed seem to be more difficult. But then the thought immediately strikes us that this problem can be split up and made easier: first we look for the single mean proportional between 3 and 48, *viz.* 12; then we look for a further mean proportional between 3 and 12, *viz.* 6; then another between 12 and 48, *viz.* 24. In that way we reduce the problem to one of the second kind described above.

Moreover, from these examples I realize how in our pursuit of knowledge of a given thing we can follow different paths, one of which is much more difficult and obscure than the other. If, for example, we are asked to find the four proportionals, 3, 6, 12, 24, given any two consecutive members of the series, such as 3 and 6, or 6 and 12, or 12 and 24, it will be a very easy task to find the others. In this case we shall say that the proposition we are seeking is investigated in a direct way. But if two alternate numbers are given, such as 3 and 12, or 6 and 24, and we are to work out the others from these, in that case we shall say that the problem is investigated indirectly by the first method. Likewise, if we are to find the intermediate numbers, 6 and 12, given the two extremes, 3
387 and 24, then the problem will be investigated indirectly by the second method. I could thus go on even further and draw many other conclusions from this one example. But these points will suffice to enable the reader to see what I mean when I say that some proposition is deduced 'directly' or 'indirectly', and will suffice to make him bear in mind that on the basis of our knowledge of the most simple and primary things we can make many discoveries, even in other disciplines, through careful reflection and discriminating inquiry.

---

1 The problem: to find an x such that $3/x = x/12$.
2 The problem: to find an x such that $3/6 = 6/x$.
3 The problem: to find an x and y such that $3/x = x/y = y/24$.

Rule Seven

In order to make our knowledge[1] complete, every single thing relating to our undertaking must be surveyed in a continuous and wholly uninterrupted sweep of thought, and be included in a sufficient and well-ordered enumeration.

It is necessary to observe the points proposed in this Rule if we are to admit as certain those truths which, we said above, are not deduced immediately from first and self-evident principles. For this deduction sometimes requires such a long chain of inferences that when we arrive at such a truth it is not easy to recall the entire route which led us to it. That is why we say that a continuous movement of thought is needed to make good any weakness of memory. If, for example, by way of separate operations, I have come to know first what the relation between the magnitudes A and B is, and then between B and C, and between C and D, and finally between D and E, that does not entail my seeing what the relation is between A and E; and I cannot grasp what the relation is just from those I already know, unless I recall all of them. So I shall run through them several times in a continuous movement of the imagination, simultaneously intuiting one relation and passing on to the next, until I have learnt to pass from the first to the last so swiftly that memory is left with practically no role to play, and I seem to intuit the whole thing at once. In this way our memory is relieved, the sluggishness of our intelligence redressed, and its capacity in some way enlarged. 388

In addition, this movement must nowhere be interrupted. Frequently those who attempt to deduce something too swiftly and from remote initial premises do not go over the entire chain of intermediate conclusions very carefully, but pass over many of the steps without due consideration. But, whenever even the smallest link is overlooked the chain is immediately broken, and the certainty of the conclusion entirely collapses.

We maintain furthermore that enumeration is required for the completion of our knowledge.[1] The other Rules do indeed help us resolve most questions, but it is only with the aid of enumeration that we are able to make a true and certain judgement about whatever we apply our minds to. By means of enumeration nothing will wholly escape us and we shall be seen to have some knowledge on every question.

In this context enumeration,[2] or induction, consists in a thorough investigation of all the points relating to the problem at hand, an investigation which is so careful and accurate that we may conclude with

1 Lat. *scientia*; see footnote on p. 10 above.
2 Reading *hic*, A, H (following Crapulli), rather than *haec* ('This enumeration'), AT.

manifest certainty that we have not inadvertently overlooked anything.
389 So even though the object of our inquiry eludes us, provided we have
made an enumeration we shall be wiser at least to the extent that we shall
perceive with certainty that it could not possibly be discovered by any
method known to us. If we have managed to examine all the humanly
accessible paths towards the object of our inquiry (which we often do),
we shall be entitled confidently to assert that knowledge of it lies wholly
beyond the reach of the human mind.

We should note, moreover, that by 'sufficient enumeration' or 'induction' we just mean the kind of enumeration which renders the truth of
our conclusions more certain than any other kind of proof (simple
intuition excepted) allows. But when our knowledge of something is not
reducible to simple intuition and we have cast off our syllogistic fetters,
we are left with this one path, which we should stick to with complete
confidence. For if we have deduced one fact from another immediately,
then provided the inference is evident, it already comes under the heading
of true intuition. If on the other hand we infer a proposition from many
disconnected propositions, our intellectual capacity is often insufficient
to enable us to encompass all of them in a single intuition; in which case
we must be content with the level of certainty which the above operation
allows. In the same way, our eyes cannot distinguish at one glance all the
links in a very long chain; but, if we have seen the connections between
each link and its neighbour, this enables us to say that we have seen how
the last link is connected with the first.

I said that this operation should be 'sufficient', because it can often be
deficient and hence liable to error. For sometimes, even though we survey
390 many points in our enumeration which are quite evident, yet if we make
even the slightest omission, the chain is broken and the certainty of the
conclusion is entirely lost. Again, sometimes we do cover everything in
our enumeration, yet fail to distinguish one thing from another, so that
our knowledge of them all is simply confused.

The enumeration should sometimes be complete, and sometimes
distinct, though there are times when it need be neither. That is why I
said only that the enumeration must be sufficient. For if I wish to
determine by enumeration how many kinds of corporeal entity there are
or how many are in some way perceivable by the senses, I shall not
assert that there are just so many and no more, unless I have previously
made sure I have included them all in my enumeration and have
distinguished one from another. But if I wish to show in the same way
that the rational soul is not corporeal, there is no need for the
enumeration to be complete; it will be sufficient if I group all bodies
together into several classes so as to demonstrate that the rational soul

cannot be assigned to any of these. To give one last example, say I wish to show by enumeration that the area of a circle is greater than the area of any other geometrical figure whose perimeter is the same length as the circle's. I need not review every geometrical figure. If I can demonstrate that this fact holds for some particular figures, I shall be entitled to conclude by induction[1] that the same holds true in all the other cases as well.

I said also that the enumeration must be well-ordered, partly because there is no more effective remedy for the defects I have just listed than a well-ordered scrutiny of all the relevant items, and partly because, if every single thing relevant to the question in hand were to be separately 391 scrutinized, one lifetime would generally be insufficient for the task, for either there would be too many such things or the same things would keep cropping up. But if we arrange all of the relevant items in the best order, so that for the most part they fall under definite classes, it will be sufficient if we look closely at one class, or at a member of each particular class, or at some classes rather than others. If we do that, we shall at any rate never pointlessly go over the same ground twice, and thanks to our well-devised order, we shall often manage to review quickly and effortlessly a large number of items which at first sight seemed formidably large.

In such cases the order in which things are enumerated can usually be varied; it is a matter for individual choice. For that reason, if our choice is to be intelligently thought out we should bear in mind what was said in Rule Five. In the more frivolous of man's skills there are many things whose method of invention consists entirely in arranging things in this orderly way. Thus if you want to construct a perfect anagram by transposing the letters of a name, there is no need to pass from the very easy to the more difficult, nor to distinguish what is absolute from what is relative, for these operations have no place here. All you need do is to decide on an order for examining permutations of letters so that you never go over the same permutations twice. The number of these permutations should, for example, be arranged into definite classes, so that it becomes immediately obvious which ones present the greater prospect of finding what you are looking for. If this is done, the task will seldom be tedious; it will be mere child's play.

Now, these last three Rules should not be separated. We should 392 generally think of them together, since they all contribute equally to the perfection of the method. It was immaterial which of them we expounded first. We are giving only a brief account of them here, for our task in

---

1 'Induction' here seems to have its standard sense of 'inference from particular instances of something to all instances'.

the remainder of the treatise will be confined almost entirely to explicating in detail what we have so far covered in general terms.

Rule Eight

If in the series of things to be examined we come across something which our intellect is unable to intuit sufficiently well, we must stop at that point, and refrain from the superfluous task of examining the remaining items.

The three preceding Rules prescribe and explain the order to be followed; the present Rule shows when order is absolutely necessary, and when it is merely useful. It is necessary that we examine whatever constitutes an integral step in the series through which we must pass when we proceed from relative terms to something absolute or *vice versa*, before considering all that follows in the series. Of course if many things belong to a given step, as is often the case, it is always useful to survey all of them in due order. But we are not forced to follow the order strictly and rigidly; generally we may proceed further, even although we do not have clear knowledge of all the terms of the series, but only of a few or just one of them.

393

This Rule is a necessary consequence of the reasons I gave in support of Rule Two. But it should not be thought that this Rule contributes nothing new to the advancement of learning, even though it seems merely to deter us from discussing certain things and to bring no truth to light. Indeed, all it teaches beginners is that they should not waste their efforts, and it does so in practically the same manner as Rule Two. But it shows those who have perfectly mastered the preceding seven Rules how they can achieve for themselves, in any science whatever, results so satisfactory that there is nothing further they will desire to achieve. If anyone observes the above Rules exactly when trying to solve some problem or other, but is instructed by the present Rule to stop at a certain point, he will know for sure that no amount of application will enable him to find the knowledge[1] he is seeking; and that not because of any defect of his intelligence, but because of the obstacle which the nature of the problem itself or the human condition presents. His recognition of this point is just as much knowledge[1] as that which reveals the nature of the thing itself; and it would, I think, be quite irrational if he were to stretch his curiosity any further.

Let us illustrate these points with one or two examples. If, say, someone whose studies are confined to mathematics tries to find the line

394   called the 'anaclastic' in optics[2] – the line from which parallel rays are so

---

1 Lat. *scientia*; see footnote on p. 10 above.
2 Descartes solved this problem in Discourse 8 of his *Optics*.

refracted that they intersect at a single point – he will easily see, by following Rules Five and Six, that the determination of this line depends on the ratio of the angles of refraction to the angles of incidence. But he will not be able to find out what this ratio is, since it has to do with physics rather than with mathematics. So he will be compelled to stop short right at the outset. If he proposes to learn it from the philosophers or derive it from experience, he will achieve nothing, for that would be to violate Rule Three. Besides, the problem before him is composite and relative; and it is possible to have experiential knowledge which is certain only of things which are entirely simple and absolute, as I shall show in the appropriate place. Again, it is no use his assuming some particular ratio between the angles in question, one he conjectures to be most likely the real one; for in that case what he was seeking to determine would no longer be the anaclastic – it would merely be the line which was the logical consequence of his supposition.

Now take someone whose studies are not confined to mathematics and who, following Rule One, eagerly seeks the truth on any question that arises: if he is faced with the same problem, he will discover when he goes into it that the ratio between the angles of incidence and the angles of refraction depends upon the changes in these angles brought about by differences in the media. He will see that these changes depend on the manner in which a ray passes through the entire transparent body,[1] and that knowledge of this process presupposes also a knowledge of the nature of the action of light. Lastly, he will see that to understand the latter process he must know what a natural power in general is – this last being the most absolute term in this whole series. Once he has clearly ascertained this through mental intuition, he will, in accordance with Rule Five, retrace his course through the same steps. If, at the second step, he is unable to discern at once what the nature of light's action is, in accordance with Rule Seven he will make an enumeration of all the other natural powers, in the hope that a knowledge of some other natural power will help him understand this one, if only by way of analogy – but more of this later.[2] Having done that, he will investigate the way in which the ray passes through the whole transparent body. Thus he will follow up the remaining points in due order, until he arrives at the anaclastic itself. Even though the anaclastic has been the object of much fruitless research in the past, I can see nothing to prevent anyone who uses our method exactly from gaining a clear knowledge of it.

But let us take the finest example of all. If someone sets himself the

395

---

1 Lat. *totum diaphanum*, the very fluid 'subtle matter' which Descartes took to be the medium of the transmission of light. Cf. *Optics*, p. 154 below.
2 This topic is not discussed in the extant portions of the *Rules*. See however *Optics*, Discourses 1 and 2 (pp. 152–64 below).

problem of investigating every truth for the knowledge of which human reason is adequate – and this, I think, is something everyone who earnestly strives after good sense should do once in his life – he will indeed discover by means of the Rules we have proposed that nothing can be known prior to the intellect, since knowledge of everything else depends on the intellect, and not *vice versa*. Once he has surveyed everything that follows immediately upon knowledge of the pure intellect, among what remains he will enumerate whatever instruments of knowledge we possess in addition to the intellect; and there are only two

396 of these, namely imagination and sense-perception. He will therefore devote all his energies to distinguishing and examining these three modes of knowing. He will see that there can be no truth or falsity in the strict sense except in the intellect alone, although truth and falsity often originate from the other two modes of knowing; and he will pay careful heed to everything that might deceive him, in order to guard against it. He will make a precise enumeration of all the paths to truth which are open to men, so that he may follow one which is reliable. There are not so many of these that he cannot easily discover them all by means of a sufficient enumeration;[1] this will seem surprising and incredible to the inexperienced. And as soon as he has distinguished, with respect to each individual object, between those items of knowledge which merely fill and adorn the memory and those which really entitle one to be called more learned – an easy task to accomplish . . .[2] he will take the view that any lack of further knowledge on his part is not at all due to any lack of intelligence or method, and that whatever anyone else can know, he too is capable of knowing, if only he properly applies his mind to it. He may often be faced with many questions which this Rule prohibits him from taking up; yet, because he sees clearly that these questions are wholly beyond the reach of the human mind, he will not regard himself as being more ignorant on that account. On the contrary, his very knowing that the matter in question is beyond the bounds of human knowledge will, if he is reasonable, abundantly satisfy his curiosity.

Now, to prevent our being in a state of permanent uncertainty about the powers of the mind, and to prevent our mental labours being misguided and haphazard, we ought once in our life carefully to inquire

397 as to what sort of knowledge human reason is capable of attaining, before we set about acquiring knowledge of things in particular. In order to do this the better, we should, where the objects of inquiry are equally simple, always begin our investigation with those which are more useful.

---

1 The translation follows the punctuation of A and H here. AT punctuate so as to give the sense '. . . enumeration. What will seem surprising is that as soon as . . .'
2 A lacuna in the texts A, H.

Our method in fact resembles the procedures in the mechanical crafts, which have no need of methods other than their own, and which supply their own instructions for making their own tools. If, for example, someone wanted to practise one of these crafts – to become a blacksmith, say – but did not possess any of the tools, he would be forced at first to use a hard stone (or a rough lump of iron) as an anvil, to make a rock do as a hammer, to make a pair of tongs out of wood, and to put together other such tools as the need arose. Thus prepared, he would not immediately attempt to forge swords, helmets, or other iron implements for others to use; rather he would first of all make hammers, an anvil, tongs and other tools for his own use. What this example shows is that, since in these preliminary inquiries we have managed to discover only some rough precepts which appear to be innate in our minds rather than the product of any skill, we should not immediately try to use these precepts to settle philosophical disputes or to solve mathematical problems. Rather, we should use these precepts in the first instance to seek out with extreme care everything else which is more essential in the investigation of truth, especially since there is no reason why such things should be thought more difficult to discover than any of the solutions to the problems commonly set in geometry, in physics, or in other disciplines.

But the most useful inquiry we can make at this stage is to ask: What is human knowledge and what is its scope? We are at present treating this as one single question, which in our view is the first question of all that 398 should be examined by means of the Rules described above. This is a task which everyone with the slightest love of truth ought to undertake at least once in his life, since the true instruments of knowledge and the entire method are involved in the investigation of the problem. There is, I think, nothing more foolish than presuming, as many do, to argue about the secrets of nature, the influence of the heavens on these lower regions, the prediction of future events, and so on, without ever inquiring whether human reason is adequate for discovering matters such as these. It should not be regarded as an arduous or even difficult task to define the limits of the mental powers we are conscious of possessing, since we often have no hesitation in making judgements about things which are outside us and quite foreign to us. Nor is it an immeasurable task to seek to encompass in thought everything in the universe, with a view to learning in what way particular things may be susceptible of investigation by the human mind. For nothing can be so many-sided or diffuse that it cannot be encompassed within definite limits or arranged under a few headings by means of the method of enumeration we have been discussing. But in order to see how the above points apply to the problem before us, we shall first divide into two parts whatever is relevant to the question; for the question ought to relate either to us, who have the capacity for knowledge, or to the actual things it is possible to know. We shall discuss these two parts separately.

Within ourselves we are aware that, while it is the intellect alone that is capable of knowledge,[1] it can be helped or hindered by three other faculties, *viz.* imagination, sense-perception, and memory. We must therefore look at these faculties in turn, to see in what respect each of them could be a hindrance, so that we may be on our guard, and in what respect an asset, so that we may make full use of their resources. We shall discuss this part of the question by way of a sufficient enumeration, as the following Rule will make clear.

We should then turn to the things themselves; and we should deal with these only in so far as they are within the reach of the intellect. In that respect we divide them into absolutely simple natures and complex or composite natures. Simple natures must all be either spiritual or corporeal, or belong to each of these categories. As for composite natures, there are some which the intellect experiences as composite before it decides to determine anything about them: but there are others which are put together by the intellect itself. All these points will be explained at greater length in Rule Twelve, where it will be demonstrated that there can be no falsity save in composite natures which are put together by the intellect. In view of this, we divide natures of the latter sort into two further classes, *viz.* those that are deduced from natures which are the most simple and self-evident (which we shall deal with throughout the next book), and those that presuppose others which experience shows us to be composite in reality. We shall reserve the whole of the third book for an account of the latter.[2]

Throughout this treatise we shall try to pursue every humanly accessible path which leads to knowledge of the truth. We shall do this very carefully, and show the paths to be very easy, so that anyone who has mastered the whole method, however mediocre his intelligence, may see that there are no paths closed to him that are open to others, and that his lack of further knowledge is not due to any want of intelligence or method. As often as he applies his mind to acquire knowledge of something, either he will be entirely successful, or at least he will realize that success depends upon some observation which it is not within his power to make – so he will not blame his intelligence, even though he is forced to come to a halt; or, finally, he will be able to demonstrate that the thing he wants to know wholly exceeds the grasp of

1 See footnote on p. 10 above.   2 See Preface, p. 7 above.

the human mind – in which case he will not regard himself as more ignorant on that account, for this discovery amounts to knowledge[1] no less than any other.

Rule Nine

We must concentrate our mind's eye totally upon the most insignificant and easiest of matters, and dwell on them long enough to acquire the habit of intuiting the truth distinctly and clearly.

We have given an account of the two operations of our intellect, intuition and deduction, on which we must, as we said, exclusively rely in our acquisition of knowledge. In this and the following Rule we shall proceed to explain how we can make our employment of intuition and deduction more skilful and at the same time how to cultivate two special mental faculties, *viz.* perspicacity in the distinct intuition of particular things and discernment in the methodical deduction of one thing from another.

We can best learn how mental intuition is to be employed by comparing it with ordinary vision. If one tries to look at many objects at one glance, one sees none of them distinctly. Likewise, if one is inclined to attend to many things at the same time in a single act of thought, one does so with a confused mind. Yet craftsmen who engage in delicate operations, and are used to fixing their eyes on a single point, acquire through practice the ability to make perfect distinctions between things, however minute and delicate. The same is true of those who never let their thinking be distracted by many different objects at the same time, but always devote their whole attention to the simplest and easiest of matters: they become perspicacious. 401

It is, however, a common failing of mortals to regard what is more difficult as more attractive. Most people consider that they know nothing, even when they see a very clear and simple cause of something; yet at the same time they get carried away with certain sublime and far-fetched arguments of the philosophers, even though these are for the most part based on foundations which no one has ever thoroughly inspected. It is surely madness to think that there is more clarity in darkness than in light. But let us note, those who really do possess knowledge, can discern the truth with equal facility whether thay have derived it from a simple subject or from an obscure one. For once they have hit upon it, they grasp each truth by means of a single and distinct act which is similar in every case. The difference lies entirely in the route followed, which must surely be longer if it leads to a truth which is more remote from completely absolute first principles.

1 Lat. *scientia*; see footnote on p. 10 above.

Everyone ought therefore to acquire the habit of encompassing in his thought at one time facts which are very simple and very few in number –
402 so much so that he never thinks he knows something unless he intuits it just as distinctly as any of the things he knows most distinctly of all. Some people of course are born with a much greater aptitude for this sort of insight than others; but our minds can become much better equipped for it through method and practice. There is, I think, one point above all others which I must stress here, which is that everyone should be firmly convinced that the sciences, however abstruse, are to be deduced only from matters which are easy and highly accessible, and not from those which are grand and obscure.

If, for example, I wish to inquire whether a natural power can travel instantaneously to a distant place, passing through the whole intervening space, I shall not immediately turn my attention to the magnetic force, or the influence of the stars, or even the speed of light, to see whether actions such as these might occur instantaneously; for I would find it more difficult to settle that sort of question than the one at issue. I shall, rather, reflect upon the local motions of bodies, since there can be nothing in this whole area that is more readily perceivable by the senses. And I shall realize that, while a stone cannot pass instantaneously from one place to another, since it is a body, a power similar to the one which moves the stone must be transmitted instantaneously if it is to pass, in its bare state, from one object to another. For instance, if I move one end of a stick, however long it may be, I can easily conceive that the power which moves that part of the stick necessarily moves every other part of it instantaneously, because it is the bare power which is transmitted at that moment, and not the power as it exists in some body, such as a stone which carries it along.[1]

In the same way, if I want to know how one and the same simple cause
403 can give rise simultaneously to opposite effects, I shall not have recourse to the remedies of the physicians, which drive out some humours and keep others in; nor shall I prattle on about the moon's warming things by its light and cooling them by means of some occult quality. Rather, I shall observe a pair of scales, where a single weight raises one scale and lowers the other instantaneously, and similar examples.

Rule Ten

In order to acquire discernment we should exercise our intelligence by investigating what others have already discovered, and methodically

1 Cf. *Optics*, pp. 153–5 below.

survey even the most insignificant products of human skill, especially those which display or presuppose order.

The natural bent of my mind, I confess, is such that the greatest pleasure I have taken in my studies has always come not from accepting the arguments of others but from discovering arguments by my own efforts. It was just this that attracted me to the study of the sciences while I was still in my youth. Whenever the title of a book gave promise of a new discovery, before I read any further I would try and see whether perhaps I could achieve a similar result by means of a certain innate discernment. And I took great care not to deprive myself of this innocent pleasure through a hasty reading of the book. So frequently was I successful in this that eventually I came to realize that I was no longer making my way to the truth of things as others do by way of aimless and blind inquiries, with the aid of luck rather than skill; rather, after many trials I had hit upon some reliable rules of great assistance in finding the truth, and I then used these to devise many more. In this way I carefully elaborated my whole method, and became convinced that the method of study I had pursued from the outset was the most useful of all. 404

Still, since not all minds have such a natural disposition to puzzle things out by their own exertions, the message of this Rule is that we must not take up the more difficult and arduous issues immediately, but must first tackle the simplest and least exalted arts, and especially those in which order prevails – such as weaving and carpet-making, or the more feminine arts of embroidery, in which threads are interwoven in an infinitely varied pattern. Number-games and any games involving arithmetic, and the like, belong here. It is surprising how much all these activities exercise our minds, provided of course we discover them for ourselves and not from others. For, since nothing in these activities remains hidden and they are totally adapted to human cognitive capacities, they present us in the most distinct way with innumerable instances of order, each one different from the other, yet all regular. Human discernment consists almost entirely in the proper observance of such order.

It was for this reason that we insisted that our inquiries must proceed methodically. In these somewhat trivial subjects the method usually consists simply in constantly following an order, whether it is actually present in the matter in question or is ingeniously read into it. For example, say we want to read something written in an unfamiliar cypher which lacks any apparent order: what we shall do is to invent an order, so as to test every conjecture we can make about individual letters, words, or sentences, and to arrange the characters in such a way that by 405 an enumeration we may discover what can be deduced from them. Above all, we must guard against wasting our time by making random and unmethodical guesses about similarities. Even though problems such as these can often be solved without a method and can sometimes perhaps be solved more quickly through good luck than through method, nevertheless they might dim the light of the mind and make it become so habituated to childish and futile pursuits that thereafter it would always stick to the surface of things and would be unable to penetrate more deeply. But for all that we must not fall into the error of those who occupy their minds exclusively with serious and lofty issues, only to find that after much toil they gain, not the profound science they desired, but mere confusion. We must therefore practise these easier tasks first, and above all methodically, so that by following accessible and familiar paths we may grow accustomed, just as if we were playing a game, to penetrating always to the deeper truth of things. In this way we shall gradually find – much sooner than we might expect – that it is just as easy to deduce, on the basis of evident principles, many propositions which appear very difficult and complicated.

Some will perhaps be surprised that in this context, where we are searching for ways of making ourselves more skilful at deducing some truths on the basis of others, we make no mention of any of the precepts with which dialecticians[1] suppose they govern human reason. They prescribe certain forms of reasoning in which the conclusions follow with such irresistible necessity that if our reason relies on them, even though it 406 takes, as it were, a rest from considering a particular inference clearly and attentively, it can nevertheless draw a conclusion which is certain simply in virtue of the form. But, as we have noticed, truth often slips through these fetters, while those who employ them are left entrapped in them. Others are not so frequently entrapped and, as experience shows, the cleverest sophisms hardly ever deceive anyone who makes use of his untrammelled reason; rather, it is usually the sophists themselves who are led astray.

Our principal concern here is thus to guard against our reason's taking a holiday while we are investigating the truth about some issue; so we reject the forms of reasoning just described as being inimical to our project. Instead we search carefully for everything which may help our mind to stay alert, as we shall show below. But to make it even clearer that the aforementioned art of reasoning contributes nothing whatever to knowledge of the truth, we should realize that, on the basis of their method, dialecticians are unable to formulate a syllogism with a true

1 See footnote, p. 12 above.

conclusion unless they are already in possession of the substance of the conclusion, i.e. unless they have previous knowledge of the very truth deduced in the syllogism. It is obvious therefore that they themselves can learn nothing new from such forms of reasoning, and hence that ordinary dialectic is of no use whatever to those who wish to investigate the truth of things. Its sole advantage is that it sometimes enables us to explain to others arguments which are already known. It should therefore be transferred from philosophy to rhetoric.

Rule Eleven 407

If, after intuiting a number of simple propositions, we deduce something else from them, it is useful to run through them in a continuous and completely uninterrupted train of thought, to reflect on their relations to one another, and to form a distinct and, as far as possible, simultaneous conception of several of them. For in this way our knowledge becomes much more certain, and our mental capacity is enormously increased.

This is a good time to explain more clearly what was said about mental intuition in Rules Three and Seven. In one passage we contrasted it with deduction,[1] and in another only with enumeration,[2] which we defined as an inference drawn from many disconnected facts. But in the same passage we said that a simple deduction of one fact from another is performed by means of intuition.

It was necessary to proceed in that way, because two things are required for mental intuition: first, the proposition intuited must be clear and distinct; second, the whole proposition must be understood all at once, and not bit by bit. But when we think of the process of deduction as we did in Rule Three, it does not seem to take place all at once: inferring one thing from another involves a kind of movement of our mind. In that passage, then, we were justified in distinguishing intuition from deduction. But if we look on deduction as a completed process, as we did in 408 Rule Seven, then it no longer signifies a movement but rather the completion of a movement. That is why we are supposing that the deduction is made through intuition when it is simple and transparent, but not when it is complex and involved. When the latter is the case, we call it 'enumeration' or 'induction', since the intellect cannot simultaneously grasp it as a whole, and its certainty in a sense depends on memory, which must retain the judgements we have made on the individual parts of the enumeration if we are to derive a single conclusion from them taken as a whole.

---

1 See above, p. 15.   2 See above, p. 25.

All these distinctions had to be made in order to make clear the meaning of this Rule. Rule Nine dealt only with mental intuition; Rule Ten only with enumeration. The present Rule explains the way in which these two operations aid and complement each other; they do this so thoroughly that they seem to coalesce into a single operation, through a movement of thought, as it were, which involves carefully intuiting one thing and passing on at once to the others.

There is, we should point out, a twofold advantage in this fact: it facilitates a more certain knowledge of the conclusion in question, and it makes the mind better able to discover other truths. As we have said, conclusions which embrace more than we can grasp in a single intuition depend for their certainty on memory, and since memory is weak and unstable, it must be refreshed and strengthened through this continuous and repeated movement of thought. Say, for instance, in virtue of several operations, I have discovered the relation between the first and the second magnitude of a series, then the relation between the second and

409 the third and the third and fourth, and lastly the fourth and fifth: that does not necessarily enable me to see what the relation is between the first and the fifth, and I cannot deduce it from the relations I already know unless I remember all of them. That is why it is necessary that I run over them again and again in my mind until I can pass from the first to the last so quickly that memory is left with practically no role to play, and I seem to be intuiting the whole thing at once.

One cannot fail to see that in this way the sluggishness of the mind is redressed and its capacity even enlarged. But in addition we must note that the greatest advantage of this Rule lies in the fact that by reflecting on the mutual dependence of simple propositions we acquire the habit of distinguishing at a glance what is more, and what is less, relative, and by what steps the relative may be reduced to the absolute. For example, if I run through a number of magnitudes which are continued proportionals, I shall be struck by the following points. It is just as easy for me to recognize the relation between the first and the second magnitude, as between the second and the third, the third and fourth, etc., and the act of conceiving is exactly similar in each case. But it is more difficult for me to form a simultaneous conception of the relation of the second magnitude to the first and the third; and it is much more difficult still to conceive the way in which it depends on the first and fourth magnitudes, etc. These considerations enable me to understand why it is that, given only the first and second magnitudes, I can easily find the third and fourth, etc.: the reason is that the discovery is made by means of particular and distinct acts of conceiving. But if only the first and the

410 third are given, it will not be so easy for me to discern the intermediate

magnitude, for this can be done only by means of an act of conceiving which simultaneously involves two of the acts just mentioned. If only the first and the fourth magnitudes are given, it is even more difficult to intuit the two intermediate ones, for in this case three acts of conceiving are simultaneously involved. So, as a logical consequence, it might seem even more difficult to find the three intermediate magnitudes given the first and fifth. Yet this is not the case, owing to a further reason, which is that, although four acts of conceiving are joined together in the present example, they can nevertheless be separated, since four is divisible by another number. So I can obtain the third magnitude alone on the basis of the first and the fifth, then the second on the basis of the first and the third, etc. If one is used to reflecting on these and similar matters, whenever one investigates a new problem one will immediately recognize the source of the difficulty and the simplest method for dealing with it. And that is the greatest aid to knowledge of the truth.

Rule Twelve

Finally we must make use of all the aids which intellect, imagination, sense-perception, and memory afford in order, firstly, to intuit simple propositions distinctly; secondly, to combine[1] correctly the matters under investigation with what we already know, so that they too may be known; and thirdly, to find out what things should be compared with each other so that we make the most thorough use of all our human powers.

This Rule sums up everything that has been said above, and sets out a   411
general lesson the details of which remain to be explained as follows.

Where knowledge of things is concerned, only two factors need to be considered: ourselves, the knowing subjects, and the things which are the objects of knowledge. As for ourselves, there are only four faculties which we can use for this purpose, *viz.* intellect, imagination, sense-perception and memory. It is of course only the intellect that is capable of perceiving the truth, but it has to be assisted by imagination, sense-perception and memory if we are not to omit anything which lies within our power. As for the objects of knowledge, it is enough if we examine the following three questions: What presents itself to us spontaneously? How can one thing be known on the basis of something else? What conclusions can be drawn from each of these? This seems to me to be a complete enumeration and to omit nothing which is within the range of human endeavour.

Turning now to the first factor, I should like to explain at this point

---

1 Reading *componenda*, A; *comparanda*, H, 'to compare'.

what the human mind is, what the body is and how it is informed[1] by the mind, what faculties within the composite whole promote knowledge of things, and what each particular faculty does; but I lack the space, I think, to include all the points which have to be set out before the truth about these matters can be made clear to everyone. For my aim is always to write in such a way that I make no assertions on matters which are apt to give rise to controversy, without first setting out the reasons which led me to make them and which I think others may find convincing too.

412

But since I cannot do that here, it will be sufficient if I explain as briefly as possible what, for my purposes, is the most useful way of conceiving everything within us which contributes to our knowledge of things. Of course you are not obliged to believe that things are as I suggest. But what is to prevent you from following these suppositions if it is obvious that they detract not a jot from the truth of things, but simply make everything much clearer? This is just what you do in geometry when you make certain assumptions about quantity, which in no way weaken the force of the demonstrations, even though in physics you often take a different view of the nature of quantity.

Let us then conceive of the matter in the following way. First, in so far as our external senses are all parts of the body, sense-perception, strictly speaking, is merely passive, even though our application of the senses to objects involves action, *viz.* local motion; sense-perception occurs in the same way in which wax takes on an impression from a seal. It should not be thought that I have a mere analogy in mind here: we must think of the external shape of the sentient body as being really changed by the object in exactly the same way as the shape of the surface of the wax is altered by the seal. This is the case, we must admit, not only when we feel some body as having a shape, as being hard or rough to the touch etc., but also when we have a tactile perception of heat or cold and the like. The same is true of the other senses: thus, in the eye, the first opaque membrane receives the shape impressed upon it by multi-coloured light; and in the

413 ears, the nose and the tongue, the first membrane which is impervious to the passage of the object thus takes on a new shape from the sound, the smell and the flavour respectively.

This is a most helpful way of conceiving these matters, since nothing is more readily perceivable by the senses than shape, for it can be touched as well as seen. Moreover, the consequences of this supposition are no more false than those of any other. This is demonstrated by the fact that the concept of shape is so simple and common that it is involved in everything perceivable by the senses. Take colour, for example: whatever

1 A scholastic term conveying the Aristotelian notion that the soul is the 'form' of the body.

you may suppose colour to be, you will not deny that it is extended and consequently has shape. So what troublesome consequences could there be if – while avoiding the useless assumption and pointless invention of some new entity, and without denying what others have preferred to think on the subject – we simply make an abstraction, setting aside every feature of colour apart from its possessing the character of shape, and conceive of the difference between white, blue, red, etc. as being like the difference between the following figures or similar ones?

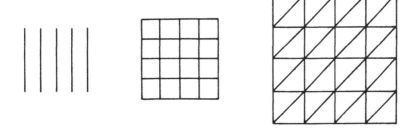

The same can be said about everything perceivable by the senses, since it is certain that the infinite multiplicity of figures is sufficient for the expression of all the differences in perceptible things.

Secondly, when an external sense organ is stimulated by an object, the figure which it receives is conveyed at one and the same moment to another part of the body known as the 'common' sense,[1] without any entity really passing from the one to the other. In exactly the same way I understand that while I am writing, at the very moment when individual letters are traced on the paper, not only does the point of the pen move, but the slightest motion of this part cannot but be transmitted simultaneously to the whole pen. All these various motions are traced out in the air by the tip of the quill, even though I do not conceive of anything real passing from one end to the other. Who then would think that the connection between the parts of the human body is less close than that between the parts of the pen? What simpler way of portraying the matter can be imagined?

Thirdly, the 'common' sense functions like a seal, fashioning in the phantasy[2] or imagination, as if in wax, the same figures or ideas which come, pure and without body, from the external senses. The phantasy is a

414

1 An Aristotelian expression signifying an internal sense which receives and co-ordinates impressions from the five external senses. See *De Anima*, III, 1, 425ª14.
2 Lat. *phantasia*, a term which for Descartes frequently means the same as *imaginatio*, though it is the term he prefers to use when speaking of the part of the brain in which the physical processes associated with imagining take place. When the latter use is clearly intended, the translation 'corporeal imagination' is adopted below.

genuine part of the body, and is large enough to allow different parts of it to take on many different figures and, generally, to retain them for some time; in which case it is to be identified with what we call 'memory'.

Fourthly, the motive power (i.e. the nerves themselves) has its origin in the brain, where the corporeal imagination is located; and the latter moves the nerves in different ways, just as the 'common' sense is moved by the external senses or the whole pen is moved by its lower end. This

415   example also shows how the corporeal imagination can be the cause of many different movements in the nerves, even though it does not have images of these movements imprinted on it, but has certain other images which enable these movements to follow on. Again, the pen as a whole does not move in exactly the same way as its lower end; on the contrary, the upper part of the pen seems to have a quite different and opposite movement. This enables us to understand how all the movements of other animals can come about, even though we refuse to allow that they have any awareness of things, but merely grant them a purely corporeal imagination. It also enables us to understand how there occur within us all those operations which we perform without any help from reason.

Fifthly, and lastly, the power through which we know things in the strict sense is purely spiritual, and is no less distinct from the whole body than blood is distinct from bone, or the hand from the eye. It is one single power, whether it receives figures from the 'common' sense at the same time as does the corporeal imagination, or applies itself to those which are preserved in the memory, or forms new ones which so preoccupy the imagination that it is often in no position to receive ideas from the 'common' sense at the same time, or to transmit them to the power responsible for motion in accordance with a purely corporeal mode of operation. In all these functions the cognitive power is sometimes passive, sometimes active; sometimes resembling the seal, sometimes the wax. But this should be understood merely as an analogy, for nothing quite like this power is to be found in corporeal things. It is one and the

416   same power: when applying itself along with imagination to the 'common' sense, it is said to see, touch etc.; when addressing itself to the imagination alone, in so far as the latter is invested with various figures, it is said to remember; when applying itself to the imagination in order to form new figures, it is said to imagine or conceive; and lastly, when it acts on its own, it is said to understand. How understanding comes about I shall explain at greater length in the appropriate place. According to its different functions, then, the same power is called either pure intellect, or imagination, or memory, or sense-perception. But when it forms new ideas in the corporeal imagination, or concentrates on those already formed, the proper term for it is 'native intelligence'. We are

regarding it as being capable of performing these different operations; and the distinction between these terms will have to be kept in mind in what follows. If all these matters are conceived along such lines, the attentive reader will have no difficulty in gathering what aids we should seek to obtain from each of these faculties and the lengths to which human endeavour can be stretched in supplementing the shortcomings of our native intelligence.

The intellect can either be stimulated by the imagination or act upon it. Likewise the imagination can act upon the senses through the motive force, by directing them to objects, while the senses in their turn can act upon the imagination, by depicting the images of bodies upon it. But memory is no different from imagination – at least the memory which is corporeal and similar to the one which animals possess. So we can conclude with certainty that when the intellect is concerned with matters in which there is nothing corporeal or similar to the corporeal, it cannot receive any help from those faculties; on the contrary, if it is not to be hampered by them, the senses must be kept back and the imagination must, as far as possible, be divested of every distinct impression. If, however, the intellect proposes to examine something which can be referred to the body, the idea of that thing must be formed as distinctly as 417 possible in the imagination. In order to do this properly, the thing itself which this idea is to represent should be displayed to the external senses. A plurality of things cannot be of assistance to the intellect in distinctly intuiting individual things. Rather, in order to deduce a single thing from a collection of things – a frequent task – we must discard from the ideas of the things whatever does not demand our present attention, so that the remaining features can be retained more readily in the memory. In the same way, it is not the things themselves which should be displayed to the external senses, but rather certain abbreviated representations of them; and the more compact these are, the handier they are, provided they act as adequate safeguards against lapses of memory. If we observe all these points, then I think we shall omit nothing which pertains to this part of the Rule.

Let us now take up the second factor.[1] Our aim here is to distinguish carefully the notions of simple things from those which are composed of them, and in both cases to try to see where falsity can come in, so that we may guard against it, and to see what can be known with certainty, so that we may concern ourselves exclusively with that. To this end, as before, certain assumptions must be made in this context which perhaps not everyone will accept. But even if they are thought to be no more real than the imaginary circles which astronomers use to describe the

1 I.e. the objects of knowledge. See above, p. 39.

phenomena they study, this matters little, provided they help us to pick out the kind of apprehension of any given thing that may be true and to distinguish it from the kind that may be false.

418   We state our view, then, in the following way. First, when we consider things in the order that corresponds to our knowledge of them, our view of them must be different from what it would be if we were speaking of them in accordance with how they exist in reality. If, for example, we consider some body which has extension and shape, we shall indeed admit that, with respect to the thing itself, it is one single and simple entity. For, viewed in that way, it cannot be said to be a composite made up of corporeal nature, extension and shape, since these constituents have never existed in isolation from each other. Yet with respect to our intellect we call it a composite made up of these three natures, because we understood each of them separately before we were in a position to judge that the three of them are encountered at the same time in one and the same subject. That is why, since we are concerned here with things only in so far as they are perceived by the intellect, we term 'simple' only those things which we know so clearly and distinctly that they cannot be divided by the mind into others which are more distinctly known. Shape, extension and motion, etc. are of this sort; all the rest we conceive to be in a sense composed out of these. This point is to be taken in a very general sense, so that not even the things that we occasionally abstract from these simples are exceptions to it. We are abstracting, for example, when we say that shape is the limit of an extended thing, conceiving by the term 'limit' something more general than shape, since we can talk of the limit of a duration, the limit of a motion, etc. But, even if the sense of the term 'limit' is derived by abstraction from the notion of shape, that is

419   no reason to regard it as simpler than shape. On the contrary, since the term 'limit' is also applied to other things – such as the limit of a duration or a motion, etc., things totally different in kind from shape – it must have been abstracted from these as well. Hence, it is something compounded out of many quite different natures, and the term 'limit' does not have a univocal application in all these cases.

Secondly, those things which are said to be simple with respect to our intellect are, on our view, either purely intellectual or purely material, or common to both. Those simple natures which the intellect recognizes by means of a sort of innate light, without the aid of any corporeal image, are purely intellectual. That there is a number of such things is certain: it is impossible to form any corporeal idea which represents for us what knowledge or doubt or ignorance is, or the action of the will, which may be called 'volition', and the like; and yet we have real knowledge of all of these, knowledge so easy that in order to possess it all we need is some degree of rationality. Those simple natures, on the other hand, which are recognized to be present only in bodies – such as shape, extension and motion, etc. – are purely material. Lastly, those simples are to be termed 'common' which are ascribed indifferently, now to corporeal things, now to spirits – for instance, existence, unity, duration and the like. To this class we must also refer those common notions which are, as it were, links which connect other simple natures together, and whose self-evidence is the basis for all the rational inferences we make. Examples of these are: 'Things that are the same as a third thing are the same as each other'; 'Things that cannot be related in the same way to a third thing are different in some respect.' These common notions can be known either by the pure intellect or by the intellect as it intuits the images of material 420 things.

Moreover, it is as well to count among the simple natures the corresponding privations and negations, in so far as we understand these. For when I intuit what nothing is, or an instant, or rest, my apprehension is as much genuine knowledge as my understanding what existence is, or duration, or motion. This way of conceiving things will be helpful later on in enabling us to say that all the rest of what we know is put together out of these simple natures. Thus, if I judge that a certain shape is not moving, I shall say that my thought is in some way composed of shape and rest; and similarly in other cases.

Thirdly, these simple natures are all self-evident and never contain any falsity. This can easily be shown if we distinguish between the faculty by which our intellect intuits and knows things and the faculty by which it makes affirmative or negative judgements. For it can happen that we think we are ignorant of things we really know, as for example when we suspect that they contain something else which eludes us, something beyond what we intuit or reach in our thinking, even though we are mistaken in thinking this. For this reason, it is evident that we are mistaken if we ever judge that we lack complete knowledge of any one of these simple natures. For if we have even the slightest grasp of it in our mind – which we surely must have, on the assumption that we are making a judgement about it – it must follow that we have complete knowledge of it. Otherwise it could not be said to be simple, but a 421 composite made up of that which we perceive in it and that of which we judge we are ignorant.

Fourthly, the conjunction between these simple things is either neces-sary or contingent. The conjunction is necessary when one of them is somehow implied (albeit confusedly) in the concept of the other so that we cannot conceive either of them distinctly if we judge them to be separate from each other. It is in this way that shape is conjoined with extension, motion with duration or time, etc., because we cannot conceive of a shape which is completely lacking in extension, or a motion wholly lacking in duration. Similarly, if I say that 4 and 3 make 7, the composition is a necessary one, for we do not have a distinct conception of the number 7 unless in a confused sort of way we include 3 and 4 in it. In the same way, whatever we demonstrate concerning figures or numbers necessarily links up with that of which it is affirmed. This necessity applies not just to things which are perceivable by the senses but to others as well. If, for example, Socrates says that he doubts everything, it necessarily follows that he understands at least that he is doubting, and hence that he knows that something can be true or false, etc.; for there is a necessary connection between these facts and the nature of doubt. The union between such things, however, is contingent when the relation conjoining them is not an inseparable one. This is the case when we say that a body is animate, that a man is dressed, etc. Again, there are many instances of things which are necessarily conjoined, even though most people count them as contingent, failing to notice the relation between them: for example the proposition, 'I am, therefore God exists', or 'I understand, therefore I have a mind distinct from my body.' Finally, we must note that very many necessary propositions, when converted, are contingent. Thus from the fact that I exist I may conclude with certainty that God exists, but from the fact that God exists I cannot legitimately assert that I too exist.

Fifthly, it is not possible for us ever to understand anything beyond those simple natures and a certain mixture or compounding of one with another. Indeed, it is often easier to attend at once to several mutually conjoined natures than to separate one of them from the others. For example, I can have knowledge of a triangle, even though it has never occurred to me that this knowledge involves knowledge also of the angle, the line, the number three, shape, extension, etc. But that does not preclude our saying that the nature of a triangle is composed of these other natures and that they are better known than the triangle, for it is just these natures that we understand to be present in it. Perhaps there are many additional natures implicitly contained in the triangle which escape our notice, such as the size of the angles being equal to two right angles, the innumerable relations between the sides and the angles, the size of its surface area, etc.

Sixthly, those natures which we call 'composite' are known by us either because we learn from experience what sort they are, or because we ourselves put them together. Our experience consists of whatever we perceive by means of the senses, whatever we learn from others, and in general whatever reaches our intellect either from external sources or

from its own reflexive self-contemplation. We should note here that the 423
intellect can never be deceived by any experience, provided that when the
object is presented to it, it intuits it in a fashion exactly corresponding to
the way in which it possesses the object, either within itself or in the
imagination. Furthermore, it must not judge that the imagination
faithfully represents the objects of the senses, or that the senses take on
the true shapes of things, or in short that external things always are just
as they appear to be. In all such cases we are liable to go wrong, as we do
for example when we take as gospel truth a story which someone has told
us; or as someone who has jaundice does when, owing to the yellow tinge
of his eyes, he thinks everything is coloured yellow; or again, as we do
when our imagination is impaired (as it is in depression) and we think
that its disordered images represent real things. But the understanding of
the wise man will not be deceived in such cases: while he will judge that
whatever comes to him from his imagination really is depicted in it, he
will never assert that it passes, complete and unaltered, from the external
world to his senses, and from his senses to the corporeal imagination,
unless he already has some other grounds for claiming to know this. But
whenever we believe that an object of our understanding contains
something of which the mind has no immediate perceptual experience,
then it is we ourselves who are responsible for its composition. In the
same way, when someone who has jaundice is convinced that the things
he sees are yellow, this thought of his will be composite, consisting partly
of what his corporeal imagination represents to him and partly of the
assumption he is making on his own account, *viz.* that the colour looks
yellow not owing to any defect of vision but because the things he sees
really are yellow. It follows from this that we can go wrong only when
we ourselves compose in some way the objects of our belief.

Seventhly, this composition can come about in three ways: through 424
impulse, through conjecture or through deduction. It is a case of
composition through impulse when, in forming judgements about things,
our mind leads us to believe something, not because good reasons
convince us of it, but simply because we are caused to believe it, either by
some superior power, or by our free will, or by a disposition of the
corporeal imagination. The first cause is never a source of error, the
second rarely, the third almost always; but the first of these is irrelevant
in this context, since it does not come within the scope of method. An
example of composition by way of conjecture would be our surmising
that above the air there is nothing but a very pure ether, much thinner
than air, on the grounds that water, being further from the centre of the
globe than earth, is a thinner substance than earth, and air, which rises to
greater heights than water, is thinner still. Nothing that we put together

in this way really deceives us, so long as we judge it to be merely probable, and never assert it to be true; nor for that matter does it make us any the wiser.[1]

Deduction, therefore, remains as our sole means of compounding things in a way that enables us to be certain of their truth. Yet even with deduction there can be many drawbacks. If, say, we conclude that a given space full of air is empty, on the grounds that we do not perceive anything in it, either by sight, touch, or any other sense, then we are incorrectly conjoining the nature of a vacuum with the nature of this space. This is just what happens when we judge that we can deduce something general and necessary from something particular and contingent. But it is within our power to avoid this error, *viz.* by never conjoining things unless we intuit that the conjunction of one with the other is wholly necessary, as we do for example when we deduce that nothing which lacks extension can have a shape, on the grounds that there is a necessary connection between shape and extension, and so on.

From all these considerations we may draw several conclusions. First, we have explained distinctly and, I think, by an adequate enumeration, what at the outset we were able to present only in a confused and rough-and-ready way, *viz.* that there are no paths to certain knowledge of the truth accessible to men save manifest intuition and necessary deduction. We have also explained what the simple natures are which were mentioned in Rule Eight. It is clear that mental intuition extends to all these simple natures and to our knowledge of the necessary connections between them, and in short to everything else which the intellect finds to be present exactly within itself or in the corporeal imagination. But I shall have more to say about deduction below.[2]

Second, we need take no great pains to discover these simple natures, because they are self-evident enough. What requires effort is distinguishing one from another, and intuiting each one separately with steadfast mental gaze. There is no one so dull-witted that he fails to perceive that when sitting he is to some extent different from what he is when standing; but it is not everyone who can distinguish just as distinctly the nature of posture from the other notions which this thought contains, or who can assert that it is only the posture which alters in these two cases. There is good reason for our urging this point here, because the learned are often inclined to be so clever that they find ways of blinding themselves even to facts which are self-evident and which every peasant knows. This is what happens whenever they try and explain

425

426

---

1 Following Crapulli's reading of A and H, *non facit* ('does not make'). AT read *nos facit* ('makes us') without giving any variant reading.
2 See point eight below, p. 50.

things which are self-evident in terms of something even more evident: what they do is to explain something else or nothing at all. For example, can anyone fail to perceive all the respects in which change occurs[1] when we change our place? And when told that 'place is the surface of the surrounding body',[2] would anyone conceive of the matter in the same way? For the surface of the 'surrounding body' can change, even though I do not move or change my place; conversely, it may move along with me, so that, although it still surrounds me, I am no longer in the same place. Again, when people say that motion, something perfectly familiar to everyone, is 'the actuality of a potential being, in so far as it is potential',[3] do they not give the impression of uttering magic words which have a hidden meaning beyond the grasp of the human mind? For who can understand these expressions? Who does not know what motion is? Who would deny that these people are finding a difficulty where none exists? It must be said, then, that we should never explain things of this sort by definitions,[4] in case we take hold of composite things instead of simple ones. Rather, each of us, according to the light of his own mind, must attentively intuit only those things which are distinguished from all others. 427

Third, the whole of human knowledge[5] consists uniquely in our achieving a distinct perception of how all these simple natures contribute to the composition of other things. This is a very useful point to note, since whenever some difficulty is proposed for investigation, almost everyone gets stuck right at the outset, uncertain as to which thoughts he ought to concentrate his mind on, yet quite convinced that he ought to seek some new kind of entity previously unknown to him. Thus, if the question concerns the nature of the magnet, foreseeing that the topic will prove inaccessible and difficult, he turns his mind away from everything that is evident, and immediately directs it at all the most difficult points, in the vague expectation that by rambling through the barren field of manifold causes he will hit upon something new. But take someone who thinks that nothing in the magnet can be known which does not consist of certain self-evident, simple natures: he is in no doubt about how he should proceed. First he carefully gathers together all the available observations[6] concerning the stone in question; then he tries to deduce from this what sort of mixture of simple natures is necessary for producing all the effects which the magnet is found to have. Once he has

1 Reading *immutatur*, A, H (following Crapulli). AT adopt Leibniz's emendation, *immutamur* ('we change').
2 Cf. Aristotle, *Physics*, IV, 4, 212ᵃ5. 3 Cf. Aristotle, *Physics*, III, 1, 201ᵃ10.
4 Cf. *Principles*, Part I, art. 10, p. 195 below.
5 Lat. *scientia*; see footnote on p. 10 above.
6 Lat. *experimenta*; see footnote on the equivalent French term *expériences*, p. 143 below.

discovered this mixture, he is in a position to make the bold claim that he has grasped the true nature of the magnet, so far as it is humanly possible to discover it on the basis of given observations.

Lastly, from what has been said it follows that we should not regard some branches of our knowledge of things as more obscure than others, since they are all of the same nature and consist simply in the putting together of self-evident facts. Very few people are aware of this point. Prepossessed by the opposite view, the more confident among them do not hesitate to proclaim their own conjectures as true demonstrations: in matters about which they are completely ignorant they pronounce that they see, as if through a cloud, truths which are often obscure; and they have no qualms about making such claims. They tie their concepts up in various technical terms and, fortified with these, are inclined to discuss, coherently enough, many matters which neither they themselves nor their listeners really understand. But the more modest among them often refrain from investigating many matters – even though they are not difficult and are quite essential for life – simply because they deem themselves unequal to the task. And since they think that such matters can best be understood by others who are more intellectually gifted, they embrace the views of those in whose authority they have more confidence.

Eighthly,[1] deduction can only proceed from words to things, from effects to causes or from causes to effects, from like to like, from parts to parts or to the whole . . .[2]

For the rest, in case anyone should fail to see the interconnection between our Rules, we divide everything that can be known into simple propositions and problems. As for simple propositions, the only rules we provide are those which prepare our cognitive powers for a more distinct intuition of any given object and for a more discerning examination of it. For these simple propositions must occur to us spontaneously; they cannot be sought out. We have covered simple propositions in the preceding twelve Rules, and everything that might in any way facilitate the exercise of reason has, we think, been presented in them. As for problems, however, some can be understood perfectly, even though we do not know the solutions to them, while others are not perfectly understood. We shall deal solely with the former sort of problems in the following twelve Rules, and shall postpone discussion of the latter until

___

1 Reading *octavo* A, following Crapulli. The variant, *5to*, in H is a misreading of *8to*. This is the eighth 'assumption', following on naturally from the seventh (p. 47 above). Conclusions one to four (pp. 48ff) are a long digression between 'assumptions' seven and eight.

2 There is a lacuna in the texts of A and H at this point. The topic is taken up again below, pp. 53f.

the final set of twelve Rules.[1] The division between perfectly understood and imperfectly understood problems is one that we have introduced quite deliberately: its purpose is partly to save us from having to mention anything which presupposes an acquaintance with what follows, and partly to enable us to set forth first those matters which in our view have to be tackled first if we are to cultivate our mental powers. We must note that a problem is to be counted as perfectly understood only if we have a distinct perception of the following three points: first, what the criteria are which enable us to recognize what we are looking for when we come upon it; second, what exactly is the basis from which we ought to deduce it; third, how it is to be proved that the two are so mutually dependent that the one cannot alter in any respect without there being a corresponding alteration in the other. So now that we possess all the premisses, the only thing that remains to be shown is how the conclusion is to be found. This is not a matter of drawing a single deduction from a single, simple fact, for, as we have already pointed out, that can be done without the aid of rules; it is, rather, a matter of deriving a single fact which depends on many interconnected facts, and of doing this in such a methodical way that no greater intellectual capacity is required than is needed for the simplest inference. Problems of this sort are for the most part abstract, and arise almost exclusively in arithmetic and geometry, which is why they will seem to ignorant people to be of little use. But those who desire a perfect mastery of the latter part of my method (which deals with the other sort of problem) should be advised that a long period of study and practice is needed in order to acquire this technique.

430

Rule Thirteen

If we perfectly understand a problem we must abstract it from every superfluous conception, reduce it to its simplest terms and, by means of an enumeration, divide it up into the smallest possible parts.

This is the sole respect in which we imitate the dialecticians: when they expound the forms of the syllogisms, they presuppose that the terms or subject-matter of the syllogisms are known; similarly, we are making it a prerequisite here that the problem under investigation is perfectly understood. But we do not distinguish, as they do, a middle term and two extreme terms.[2] We view the whole matter in the following way. First, in every problem there must be something unknown; otherwise there would

---

1 The final set of twelve Rules was not completed. See Translator's preface, p. 7 above.
2 The middle term of a categorical syllogism is the term which occurs in both premisses but not in the conclusion; the extreme terms are the two terms each of which occurs in one premiss only, and which are connected in the conclusion.

be no point in posing the problem. Secondly, this unknown something must be delineated in some way, otherwise there would be nothing to point us to one line of investigation as opposed to any other. Thirdly, the unknown something can be delineated only by way of something else which is already known. These conditions hold also for imperfect problems. If, for example, the problem concerns the nature of the

431 magnet, we already understand what is meant by the words 'magnet' and 'nature', and it is this knowledge which determines us to adopt one line of inquiry rather than another, etc. But if the problem is to be perfect, we want it to be determinate in every respect, so that we are not looking for anything beyond what can be deduced from the data. For example, someone may ask me what conclusions are to be drawn about the nature of the magnet simply from the experiments which Gilbert claims to have performed, be they true or false.[1] Or again I may be asked to determine what the nature of sound is, solely and precisely from the following data: three strings, A, B and C emit the same sound; B is twice as thick as A, but no longer, and is tensioned by a weight which is twice as heavy: C is twice as long as A, though not so thick, and is tensioned by a weight four times as heavy. It is easy to see from such examples how imperfect problems can all be reduced to perfect ones – as I shall explain at greater length in the appropriate place.[2] We can also see how, by following this Rule, we can abstract a problem which is well understood from every irrelevant conception and reduce it to such a form that we are no longer aware of dealing with this or that subject-matter but only with certain magnitudes in general and the comparison between them.[3] For example, once we have decided to investigate specific observations relating solely to the magnet, we no longer have any difficulty in dismissing all other observations from our mind.

432   Furthermore, the problem should be reduced to the simplest terms according to Rules Five and Six, and it should be divided up according to Rule Seven. Thus if I carry out many observations in my research on the magnet, I shall run through them separately one after another. Again, if the subject of my research is sound, as in the case above, I shall make separate comparisons between strings A and B, then between A and C, etc., with a view to including all of them together in a sufficient enumeration. With respect to the terms of a given problem, these three points are the only ones which the pure intellect has to observe before embarking on the final solution of the problem, for which the following

1 William Gilbert, the English physicist (1540–1603), author of *De Magnete* (1600).
2 Descartes did not complete this task.
3 Reading *comparandas*, H (*componendas*, A, 'composition').

eleven Rules may be required. How this is to be done will be made clearer in the third part of the treatise. By 'problems', moreover, we mean everything in which there lies truth or falsity. We must enumerate the different kinds of problems, so that we may determine what we have the power to achieve in each kind.

As we have already said, there can be no falsity in the mere intuition of things, be they simple or conjoined. In that respect they are not called 'problems'; but they acquire that name as soon as we decide to make a definite judgement about them. Indeed, it is not just the puzzles which others set that we count as problems. Socrates posed a problem about his own ignorance, or rather doubt: when he became aware of his doubt, he began to ask whether it was true that he was in doubt about everything, and his answer was affirmative.

Now, we are seeking to derive things from words, or causes from   433
effects, or effects from causes, or a whole from parts or parts from other parts, or several of these at once.

We say that we are seeking to derive things from words whenever the difficulty lies in the obscurity of the language employed. Riddles all belong to this class of problem: for example the riddle of the Sphinx about the animal which is four-footed to begin with, then two-footed, and later on becomes three-footed; or the one about the anglers standing on the shore with rod and line, maintaining that they no longer have the ones they caught but do have those which they have not yet managed to catch, etc.[1] Moreover, in the vast majority of issues about which the learned dispute, the problem is almost always one of words. There is no need, however, to have such a low opinion of great minds as to think that they have a wrong conception of the things themselves when they fail to explain them in terms which are quite appropriate. When, for example, they define place as 'the surface of the surrounding body', they are not really conceiving anything false, but are merely misusing the word 'place', which in its ordinary use denotes the simple and self-evident nature in virtue of which something is said to be here or there. This nature consists entirely in a certain relation between the thing said to be at the place and the parts of extended[2] space. Some, seeing that the term 'place' has been used to denote the surrounding surface, have improperly called this nature 'intrinsic place',[3] and the same goes for other cases of   434

---

1 See below, p. 55.
2 Lat. *extensi*, A, H. AT unnecessarily emend to *exterioris* ('exterior'); Crapulli emends to *externi* ('external').
3 In scholastic physics 'intrinsic' place is the space which a body occupies. Cf. *Principles*, pp. 227f below.

this sort. These questions about words arise so frequently that, if philosophers always agreed about the meanings of words, their controversies would almost all be at an end.

It is a problem of deriving causes from effects when in our investigation into something we ask whether it exists, or what it is . . .[1]

Moreover, when we are given a problem to solve, we are often unable to recognize immediately what sort of problem it is, and whether it is a matter of deriving things from words, or causes from effects, etc. Hence it would, I think, be quite pointless to give a lengthy account of the different kinds of problem. It will be less time-consuming and more convenient if instead we make a general and orderly survey of all the points which have to be covered in the solution of any difficulty whatever. Accordingly, no matter what the problem is, we must above all strive to understand distinctly what is being sought.

Frequently people are in such a hurry in their investigation of problems that they set about solving them with their minds blank – without first taking account of the criteria which will enable them to recognize distinctly the thing they are seeking, should they come across it. They are thus behaving like a foolish servant who, sent on some errand by his master, is so eager to obey that he dashes off without instructions and without knowing where he is to go.

In every problem, of course, there has to be something unknown – otherwise the inquiry would be pointless. Nevertheless this unknown 435   something must be delineated by definite conditions, which point us decidedly in one direction of inquiry rather than another. These conditions should, in our view, be gone into right from the very outset. We shall do this if we concentrate our mind's eye on intuiting each individual condition distinctly, looking carefully to see to what extent each condition delimits the unknown object of our inquiry. For in this context the human mind is liable to go wrong in one or other of two ways: it may assume something beyond the data required to define the problem, or on the other hand it may leave something out.

We must take care not to assume more than the data, and not to take the data in too narrow a sense. This is especially true in the case of riddles and other enigmas ingeniously contrived to tax our wits. But it applies sometimes to other problems as well, as for example, when for the sake of a solution we apparently take something as if it were certain, although

---

1 A lacuna in the texts of A and H. The lost matter is perhaps partially reproduced by Arnauld in the second edition of his *Logic* (the 'Port-Royal Logic'), an extract from which is given in the Appendix below, p. 77.

our confidence in it is due more to ingrained prejudice than to any certain reason. In the riddle of the Sphinx, for example, there is no need to think that the word 'footed' refers exclusively to real feet – to animals' feet. Rather, we should try and see whether it can be applied figuratively to other things as well, as it sometimes is to a baby's hands or an old man's walking-stick, since these are both used, like feet, for getting about. Likewise, in the conundrum about the anglers, we must try not to let the thought of fish so preoccupy our minds that it distracts us from thinking of those tiny creatures which the poor often unwillingly carry about their person and throw away when caught. Again, the question may concern the way in which a certain vessel is constructed, such as the bowl we once saw, which had a column in the centre of it, on top of which was a figure 436 of Tantalus looking as if he was longing to have a drink: water which was poured into the bowl remained within it, as long as the level was below Tantalus' mouth; but as soon as the water reached the unfortunate man's lips, it all ran out. At first glance it might seem that the artistry here lay entirely in the construction of the figure of Tantalus, when in fact that is merely a coincidental feature and by no means a factor which defines the problem. The whole difficulty is this: how must the bowl be constructed if it lets out all the water as soon as, but not before, it reaches a fixed height? One last example: say the question is, 'What can we assert about the motion of the stars, given all the observational data we have relating to them?' In this case we must not freely assume, as the ancients did, that the earth is motionless and fixed at the centre of the universe, just because from our infancy that is how it appeared to us to be. That assumption should be called in doubt so that we may then consider what in the way of certainty our judgement may attain on this matter. And the same goes for other cases of this sort.

On the other hand it is a sin of omission when we fail to take account of some condition necessary for defining a problem, a factor which is either explicitly stated in it or is in some way implied by it. Consider for example the question of perpetual motion – not the natural variety present in the stars and in springs, but the man-made variety. Some have believed that it is possible to achieve perpetual motion of this sort. Regarding the earth as being in perpetual circular motion about its own 437 axis, and the magnet as having all the properties of the earth, they think that they could invent perpetual motion if they could set up a lodestone to move in a circle or at least get it to transfer its motion, along with its other powers, to a piece of iron. Yet even if this were done, what they produced would not be artificial perpetual motion; it would simply be a natural motion which they had harnessed, and would be no different from the continuous motion produced by placing a wheel in a mill-race.

They would therefore be failing to take notice of a condition which is essential for defining the problem, etc.[1]

Once we have sufficiently understood the problem, we should try and see exactly where the difficulty lies, so that by abstracting it from everything else, the problem may be the more easily solved.

In order to find out where the difficulty lies, it is not always sufficient simply to understand the problem; we must also give thought to the particular factors which are essential to it. If any considerations should occur to us which are easy to discover, we shall put these aside; and once these have been eliminated, what we are left with will be just the point we are looking for. Thus in the case described above, it is easy to see how the bowl must be constructed. Once we have set aside, as irrelevant to the issue, such features as the column in the middle, the picture of the bird, etc., the problem is laid bare, which is to explain why it is that all the water flows out of the bowl when it reaches a certain level.

438   The only thing worth doing, then, in our view is to scrutinize in due order all the factors given in the problem at hand, to dismiss those which we plainly see are irrelevant to the issue, to hold onto those which are essential, and to submit the doubtful ones to a more careful examination.

Rule Fourteen

The problem should be re-expressed in terms of the real extension of bodies and should be pictured in our imagination entirely by means of bare figures. Thus it will be perceived much more distinctly by our intellect.

If, moreover, we are to make use of the imagination as an aid we should note that whenever we deduce something unknown from something already known, it does not follow that we are discovering some new kind of entity, but merely that we are extending our entire knowledge of the topic in question to the point where we perceive that the thing we are looking for participates in this way or that way in the nature of the things given in the statement of the problem. For example, if someone is blind from birth, we should not expect to be able by force of argument to get him to have true ideas of colours just like the ones we have, derived as they are from the senses. But if someone at some time has seen the primary colours, though not the secondary or mixed colours, then by

---

1 This passage follows the text of A. The text of AT is based on H, and contains several minor emendations.

means of a deduction of sorts it is possible for him to form images even of those he has not seen, in virtue of their similarity to those he has seen.[1] In the same way, if the magnet contains some kind of entity the like of which our intellect has never before perceived, it is pointless to hope that we shall ever get to know it simply by reasoning; in order to do that, we should need to be endowed with some new sense, or with a divine mind. But if we perceive very distinctly that combination of familiar entities or natures which produces the same effects which appear in the magnet, then we shall credit ourselves with having achieved whatever it is possible for the human mind to attain in this matter.

Indeed, it is by means of one and the same idea that we recognize in different subjects[2] each of these familiar entities, such as extension, shape, motion and the like (which we need not enumerate here). The question whether a crown is made of silver or of gold makes no difference to the way we imagine its shape. This common idea is carried over from one subject to the other solely by means of a simple comparison, which enables us to state that the thing we are seeking is in this or that respect similar to, or identical with, or equal to, some given thing. Accordingly, in all reasoning it is only by means of comparison that we attain an exact knowledge of the truth. Consider, for example, the inference: all A is B, all B is C, therefore all A is C. In this case the thing sought and the thing given, A and C, are compared with respect to their both being B, etc. But, as we have frequently insisted,[3] the syllogistic forms are of no help in grasping the truth of things. So it will be to the reader's advantage to reject them altogether and to think of all knowledge whatever – save knowledge obtained through simple and pure intuition of a single, solitary thing – as resulting from a comparison between two or more things. In fact the business of human reason consists almost entirely in preparing for this operation. For when the operation is straightforward and simple, we have no need of a technique to help us intuit the truth which the comparison yields; all we need is the light of nature.

We should note that comparisons are said to be simple and straightforward only when the thing sought and the initial data participate equally in a certain nature. The reason why preparation is required for other sorts of comparison is simply that the common nature in question is not present equally in both, but only by way of other relations or

439

440

1 H contains the note (in the margin), 'This example is not absolutely true, but I did not have a better one for explicating what is true.'
2 I.e. subjects of which attributes are predicated – the sense which 'subject' generally bears in the *Rules*.
3 See above, pp. 12, 16, 36.

proportions which imply it. The chief part of human endeavour is simply to reduce these proportions to the point where an equality between what we are seeking and what we already know is clearly visible.

We should note, moreover, that nothing can be reduced to such an equality except what admits of differences of degree, and everything covered by the term 'magnitude'. Consequently, when the terms of a problem have been abstracted from every subject in accordance with the preceding Rule, then we understand that all we have to deal with here are magnitudes in general.

The final point to note is this: if we are to imagine something, and are to make use, not of the pure intellect, but of the intellect aided by images 441 depicted in the imagination, then nothing can be ascribed to magnitudes in general which cannot also be ascribed to any species of magnitude.

It is easy to conclude from this that it will be very useful if we transfer what we understand to hold for magnitudes in general to that species of magnitude which is most readily and distinctly depicted in our imagination. But it follows from what we said in Rule Twelve[1] that this species is the real extension of a body considered in abstraction from everything else about it save its having a shape. In that Rule we conceived of the imagination, along with the ideas existing in it, as being nothing but a real body with a real extension and shape. That indeed is self-evident, since no other subject displays more distinctly all the various differences in proportions. One thing can of course be said to be more or less white than another, one sound more or less sharp than another, and so on; but we cannot determine exactly whether the greater exceeds the lesser by a ratio of 2 to 1 or 3 to 1 unless we have recourse to a certain analogy with the extension of a body that has shape. Let us then take it as firmly settled that perfectly determinate problems present hardly any difficulty at all, save that of expressing proportions in the form of equalities, and also that everything in which we encounter just this difficulty can easily be, and ought to be, separated from every other subject and then expressed in terms of extension and figures. Accordingly, we shall dismiss everything else from our thoughts and deal exclusively with these until we reach Rule Twenty-five.

442 At this point we should be delighted to come upon a reader favourably disposed towards arithmetic and geometry, though I would rather that he had not yet embarked upon these studies than that he had been taught them in the usual manner. For the Rules which I am about to expound are much more readily employed in the study of these sciences (where they are all that is needed) than in any other sort of problem. Moreover,

1 See above, pp. 40f, 43.

these Rules are so useful in the pursuit of deeper wisdom that I have no hesitation in saying that this part of our method was designed not just for the sake of mathematical problems; our intention was, rather, that the mathematical problems should be studied almost exclusively for the sake of the excellent practice which they give us in the method. I shall not assume anything drawn from the aforementioned disciplines, save perhaps certain facts which are self-evident and accessible to everyone. But the usual sort of knowledge of these subjects which others have, even if not vitiated by any glaring errors, is nevertheless obscured by many vague and ill-conceived principles, which from time to time we shall endeavour to correct in the following pages.

By 'extension' we mean whatever has length, breadth and depth, leaving aside the question whether it is a real body or merely a space. This notion does not, I think, need any further elucidation, for there is nothing more easily perceived by our imagination. Of course the learned often employ distinctions so subtle that they disperse the natural light, and they detect obscurities even in matters which are perfectly clear to peasants. So we must point out to such people that by the term 'extension' we do not mean here something distinct and separate from the subject itself, and that we generally do not recognize philosophical entities of the sort that are not genuinely imaginable. For although someone may convince himself that it is not self-contradictory for 443 extension *per se* to exist all on its own even if everything extended in the universe were annihilated, he would not be employing a corporeal idea in conceiving this, but merely an incorrect judgement of the intellect alone. He will admit this himself if he carefully reflects on the image of extension which he tries to form in his imagination. He will realize that he does not perceive it in isolation from every subject, and that his imagination of it is quite different from his judgement about it. Consequently, whatever our intellect believes about the truth of the matter, these abstract entities are never formed in the imagination in isolation from subjects.

But since henceforth we shall not be undertaking anything without the aid of the imagination, it will be worthwhile to distinguish carefully those ideas by means of which the individual meanings of our words are to be conveyed to our intellect. To this end we suggest for consideration the following three ways of talking: 'Extension occupies a place', 'Body possesses extension', and 'Extension is not body'.

The first sentence shows how 'extension' may be taken to mean 'that which is extended'. Whether I say 'Extension occupies a place' or 'That which is extended occupies a place', my conception is clearly the same in each case. But it does not follow that it is better to use the expression, 'that which is extended', for the sake of avoiding ambiguity, for the latter expression would not convey so distinctly what we are conceiving, *viz.* that some subject occupies a place in virtue of its being extended. The sentence could be taken to mean simply 'That which is extended is a subject occupying a place', with a sense similar to that of the statement 'That which is animate occupies a place.' It is for this reason that we said that here we would be concerned with extension rather than with that which is extended, even though we think that there ought to be no difference in conception between extension and that which is extended.

444   Let us now proceed to the sentence, 'Body possesses extension.' Here we understand the term 'extension' to denote something other than 'body'; yet we do not form two distinct ideas in our imagination, one of extension, the other of body, but just the single idea of extended body. So far as the fact of the matter is concerned I might just as well have said 'Body is extended', or better still 'That which is extended is extended.' This is a peculiarity of those entities which exist only in something else, and which can never be conceived apart from a subject. But when it comes to entities which are really distinguishable from their subjects, the situation is quite different. If, for example, I were to say 'Peter has wealth', my idea of Peter would be quite different from my idea of wealth. Again, if I said 'Paul is wealthy', the content of my imagination would be entirely different from what it would be if I said 'The wealthy man is wealthy.' Many fail to recognize this difference and make the mistake of thinking that extension contains something distinct from that which is extended, in the same way as Paul's wealth is distinct from Paul.

Finally, take the sentence, 'Extension is not body.' The term 'extension' here is understood in a sense quite different from the one above: in this sense there is no specific idea corresponding to it in the imagination. In fact this expression is entirely the work of the pure intellect: it alone has the ability to distinguish between abstract entities of this sort. This is a source of error for many who, not realizing that extension taken in this sense cannot be grasped by the imagination, represent it by means of a real idea. Now such an idea necessarily involves the concept of body. So if they say that extension so conceived is
445   not body, they are unwittingly ensnared into saying 'The same thing is at once body and not body.' It is very important to distinguish utterances in which such terms as 'extension', 'shape', 'number', 'surface', 'line', 'point', 'unity', etc. are given such a narrow sense that they exclude something which is not really distinct from what they signify, as for example in the statements: 'Extension or shape is not body', 'A number is not the thing numbered', 'A surface is the limit of a body', 'A line is the limit of a surface', 'A point is the limit of a line', 'Unity is not a quantity',

etc. All these and similar propositions should be removed completely from the imagination if they are to be true. That is why we shall not be concerned with them in what follows.

We must carefully note the following point with respect to all other propositions in which these terms retain the same meaning and are used in abstraction from subjects, yet do not exclude or deny anything which is not really distinct from what they denote: in these cases we can and should employ the terms with the help of the imagination. For, even if the intellect attends solely and precisely to what the word denotes, the imagination nonetheless ought to form a real idea of the thing, so that the intellect, when required, can be directed towards the other features of the thing which are not conveyed by the term in question, and so that it may never injudiciously take these features to be excluded. Thus, when the problem concerns number, we imagine some subject which is measurable in terms of a set of units. The intellect of course may for the moment confine its attention to this set; nevertheless we must see to it that, in doing so, it does not draw a conclusion which implies that the thing numbered has been excluded from our conception. Those who attribute wonderful and mysterious properties to numbers do just that. They would surely not believe so firmly in such sheer nonsense, if they did not think that number is something distinct from things numbered. Likewise, when we are concerned with a figure, we should bear in mind that we are dealing with an extended subject, conceived simply with respect to its having a shape. When we are concerned with a body, we should bear in mind that it is the same thing we are dealing with, in that it is something which has length, breadth and depth. In the case of a surface, we should conceive of the same thing, as being something with length and breadth – this time leaving out depth, though not denying it. In the case of a line, let us think of it as having just length; and in the case of a point, the same will apply, though this time we should leave out every other property save its being an entity.

Although I am explaining these points at some length here, the minds of mortals are so prejudiced that very few, I fear, are in no danger of losing their way in this area, and most will find that my long discourse gives too brief an account of my meaning. Even arithmetic and geometry lead us astray here in spite of their being the most certain of all the arts. For does not every arithmetician think that numbers are abstracted from every subject by means of the intellect and that they are even to be really distinguished from every subject by means of the imagination? Is there a geometer who does not muddy the manifest clarity of his subject-matter by employing inconsistent principles? The geometer judges that lines have no breadth, surfaces no depth, yet he goes on to construct the one

446

from the other, not realizing that a line, whose flowing motion he conceives as creating a surface, is a real body, whereas that which lacks breadth is simply a mode of body. But in order not to prolong our account of these matters, it will save time if we explain how we are supposing our object is to be conceived, our aim being to provide the easiest possible demonstration of such truth as may be found in arithmetic and geometry.

In this context, then, we are concerned with an extended object, thinking of it exclusively in terms of its extension, and deliberately refraining from using the term 'quantity'; for there are some philosophers so subtle that they have even distinguished quantity from extension. We are assuming that every problem has been reduced to the point where our sole concern is to discover a certain extension on the basis of a comparison with some other extension which we already know. For in this context we are not expecting to obtain knowledge of any new entity; our intention, rather, is simply to reduce the proportions, however complicated, to the point where we can discover some equality between that which is unknown and something known. Thus it is certain that whatever differences of proportion obtain in other subjects, the same differences can also be found to hold between two or more extensions. Hence it is enough for our purposes if we consider all the characteristics of extension itself which may assist us in elucidating differences in proportion. There are only three such characteristics, *viz.* dimension, unity and shape.

By 'dimension' we mean simply a mode or aspect in respect of which some subject is considered to be measurable. Thus length, breadth and depth are not the only dimensions of a body: weight too is a dimension – the dimension in terms of which objects are weighed. Speed is a dimension – the dimension of motion; and there are countless other instances of this sort. For example, division into several equal parts, whether it be a real or merely intellectual division is, strictly speaking, the dimension in terms of which we count things. The mode which gives rise to number is strictly speaking a species of dimension, though there is some difference between the meanings of the two terms. If we consider the order of the parts in relation to the whole, we are then said to be counting; if on the other hand we regard the whole as being divided up into parts, we are measuring it. For example, we measure centuries in terms of years, days, hours, minutes; if on the other hand we count minutes, hours, days and years, we end up with centuries.

It is clear from this that there can be countless different dimensions within the same subject, that these add absolutely nothing to the things which possess them, and that they are understood in the same way whether they have a real basis in the objects themselves or are arbitrary inventions of our mind. The weight of a body is something real; so too is the speed of a motion, or the division of a century into years and days; but the division of the day into hours and minutes is not. Yet these all function in the same way from the point of view simply of dimension, which is how they ought to be viewed here and in the mathematical disciplines. Whether dimensions have a real basis is something for the physicists to consider.

Recognition of this fact throws much light on geometry, for in that discipline almost everyone misconceives the three species of quantity: the line, the surface and the solid. We have already pointed out that the line and the surface are not conceived as being really distinct from the solid or   449
from one another. Indeed, if they are thought of without respect to anything else, as abstractions of the intellect, then they are no more different species of quantity than 'animal' and 'living' in man are different species of substances. We should note incidentally that there is merely a nominal difference between the three dimensions of body – length, breadth and depth; for in any given solid it is quite immaterial which aspect of its extension we take as its length, which as its breadth, etc. Although these three dimensions have a real basis at any rate in every extended thing simply *qua* extended, we are no more concerned with them here than with countless others which are either intellectual fictions or have some other basis in things. Thus in the case of a triangle, if we wish to measure it exactly, there are three real aspects of it which we need to know, *viz.* its three sides, or two sides and one angle, or two angles and its area. Again, in the case of a trapezium there are five factors we need to know; in the case of a tetrahedron, six, etc. These can all be termed 'dimensions'. But if we are to select those dimensions which will be of the greatest assistance to our imagination, we should never attend to more than one or two of them as depicted in our imagination, even though we are well aware that there is an indefinite number involved in the problem at issue. It is part of the method to distinguish as many dimensions as possible, so that, while attending to as few as possible at the same time, we nevertheless proceed to take in all of them one by one.

Unity is the common nature which, we said above,[1] all the things which we are comparing must participate in equally. If no determinate unit is specified in the problem, we may adopt as unit either one of the   450
magnitudes already given or any other magnitude, and this will be the common measure of all the others. We shall regard it as having as many

---

1 See above, pp. 57f.

dimensions as the extreme terms which are to be compared. We shall conceive of it either simply as something extended, abstracting it from everything else – in which case it will be the same as a geometrical point (the movement of which makes up a line, according to the geometers), or as some sort of line, or as a square.

As for figures, we have already shown how ideas of all things can be formed by means of these alone. We have still to point out in this context that, of the innumerable different species of figure, we are to use here only those which most readily express all the various relations or proportions. There are but two kinds of things which are compared with each other: sets[1] and magnitudes. We also have two kinds of figures which we may use to represent these conceptually: for example, the points,

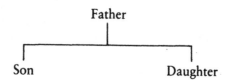

which represent a triangular number;[2] or the diagram which represents someone's family tree,

Father

Son   Daughter

451   Figures such as these represent sets; while those which are continuous and unbroken, such as △, ☐ etc., illustrate magnitudes.

Moreover, if we are to explain which of all the available figures we are going to make use of here, we should know that all the relations which may possibly obtain between entities of the same kind should be placed under one or other of two categories, *viz.* order or measure.

We must know, furthermore, that to work out an order is no mean feat, as our method makes clear throughout, that being virtually its entire message. But there is no difficulty whatever in recognizing an order once we have come upon one. By following Rule Seven we can easily survey in our mind the individual parts which we have ordered, because in

1 Lit. 'multitudes' (*multitudines*).
2 Triangular numbers are those which, like 3, 6, 10, 15 etc., can be arranged in the form of a triangle when expressed as a set of points.

relations of this kind the parts are related to one another with respect to themselves alone and not by way of an intermediary third term, as is the case with measures, which it is our sole concern to explicate here. I can recognize what the order between A and B is without considering anything over and above these two terms. But I cannot get to know what the proportion of magnitude between 2 and 3 is without considering some third term, *viz.* the unit which is the common measure of both.

Again, we should realize that, with the aid of the unit we have adopted, 452 it is sometimes possible completely to reduce continuous magnitudes to a set and that this can always be done partially at least. The set of units can then be arranged in such an order that the difficulty involved in discerning a measure becomes simply one of scrutinizing the order. The greatest advantage of our method lies in this progressive ordering.

The final point we should bear in mind is that among the dimensions of a continuous magnitude none is more distinctly conceived than length and breadth, and if we are to compare two different things with each other, we should not attend at the same time to more than these two dimensions in any given figure. For when we have more than two different things to compare, our method demands that we survey them one by one and concentrate on no more than two of them at once.

It is easy to see what conclusions follow from these observations. We have as much reason to abstract propositions from geometrical figures, if the problem has to do with these, as we have from any other subject-matter. The only figures that we need to reserve for this purpose are rectilinear and rectangular surfaces, or straight lines, which we also call figures, because, as we said above,[1] these are just as good as surfaces in assisting us to imagine an object that is really extended. Lastly, these same figures must serve to represent sometimes continuous magnitudes, sometimes a set or a number. To find a simpler way of expressing differences in relation would be beyond the bounds of human endeavour.

Rule Fifteen 453

It is generally helpful if we draw these figures and display them before our external senses. In this way it will be easier for us to keep our mind alert.

If we wish to form more distinct images of these figures in our imagination with the aid of a visual display, then it is self-evident how they should be drawn. For example, we shall depict the unit in three ways, *viz.* by means of a square, □, if we think of it only as having length and breadth; by a line, —, if we regard it as having just length; or, lastly,

---

1 See pp. 61f.

by a point, . , if we view it as the element which goes to make up a set. But however it is depicted and conceived, we shall always understand the unit to be in every sense an extended subject and one susceptible of countless dimensions. The same goes for the terms of the proposition at issue: if we have to attend simultaneously to two different magnitudes belonging to the terms, we shall display them visually as a rectangle, two sides of which will be the two magnitudes in question. If they are incommensurable with the unit, we shall represent them thus:

If commensurable, thus:

or thus:

454   Nothing more is needed, except where the problem concerns a set of units. If, lastly, we are dealing with just one of the magnitudes of the terms, we shall draw a line either in the form of a rectangle, one side of which is the magnitude in question and another is the unit, thus:

(this is what we do when the same line is to be compared with some surface); or simply in the form of a length, thus, ———, if we view it simply as an incommensurable length; or thus, ... , if it is a set.[1]

Rule Sixteen

As for things which do not require the immediate attention of the mind, however necessary they may be for the conclusion, it is better to represent them by very concise symbols rather than by complete figures. It will thus be impossible for our memory to go wrong, and our mind will not be distracted by having to retain these while it is taken up with deducing other matters.

Moreover, as we said,[2] we should not contemplate, in one and the same visual or mental gaze, more than two of the innumerable different

---

1   The translation of this sentence adheres to the text of A and H (following Crapulli). AT emend the text in such a way that the phrase 'draw a line' becomes 'draw it', and 'when the same line' becomes 'when it'.

2   See above, p. 65.

dimensions which it is possible to depict in the imagination. It is therefore important to retain all the others in such a way that they readily
come to mind whenever we need to recall them. It seems that memory has
been ordained by nature for this very purpose. But because memory is
often unreliable, and in order not to have to squander one jot of our
attention on refreshing it while engaged with other thoughts, human
ingenuity has given us that happy invention – the practice of writing.
Relying on this as an aid, we shall leave absolutely nothing to memory   455
but put down on paper whatever we have to retain, thus allowing the
imagination to devote itself freely and completely to the ideas immediately before it. We shall do this by means of very concise symbols, so that
after scrutinizing each item (in accordance with Rule Nine), we may be
able (in accordance with Rule Eleven) to run through all of them with the
swiftest sweep of thought and intuit as many as possible at the same time.

Therefore, whatever is to be viewed as one thing from the point of view
of the problem we shall represent by a unique symbol, which can be
formed in any way we like. But for the sake of convenience, we shall
employ the letters a, b, c, etc. to express magnitudes already known, and
A, B, C, etc. for ones that are unknown. To these we shall often prefix the
numerals, 1, 2, 3, 4, etc. to indicate how many of them there are; again,
we shall also append these as suffixes to indicate the number of the
relations which they are to be understood to contain. Thus if I write '$2a^3$',
that will mean 'twice the magnitude symbolized by the letter a, which
contains three relations'. With this device we shall not just be economiz-
ing with words but, and this is the important point, we shall also be
displaying the terms of the problem in such a pure and naked light that,
while nothing useful will be omitted, nothing superfluous will be
included – nothing, that is, which might needlessly occupy our mental
powers when our mind is having to take in many things at once.

For a clearer understanding of these points, we should note first
that arithmeticians usually represent individual magnitudes by means of
several units or by some number, whereas in this context we are
abstracting just as much from numbers as we did from geometrical
figures a little while back[1] – or from any matter whatever. We do this,   456
both to avoid the tedium of long and unnecessary calculation and, most
importantly, to see that the parts of the subject relevant to the nature of
the problem are kept separate at all times and are not bogged down with
pointless numerical expressions. Thus if the problem is to find the
hypotenuse of a right-angled triangle whose sides are 9 and 12, the
arithmetician will say that it is $\sqrt{225}$ or 15. We on the other hand will

---

1 See above, p. 63.

substitute *a* and *b* for 9 and 12, and will find the hypotenuse to be $\sqrt{a^2+b^2}$, which keeps distinct the two parts a^2 and b^2 which the numerical expression conflates.

We should note also that those proportions which form a continuing sequence are to be understood in terms of a number of relations; others endeavour to express these proportions in ordinary algebraic terms by means of many dimensions and figures. The first of these they call 'the root', the second 'the square', the third 'the cube', the fourth 'the square of the square'. I confess that I have for a long time been misled by these expressions. For, after the line and the square, nothing, it seemed, could be represented more clearly in my imagination than the cube and other figures modelled on these. Admittedly, I was able to solve many a problem with the help of these. But through long experience I came to realize that by conceiving things in this way I had never discovered anything which I could not have found much more easily and distinctly without it. I realized that such terminology was a source of conceptual confusion and ought to be abandoned completely. For a given magnitude, even though it is called a cube or the square of the square, should never be represented in the imagination otherwise than as a line or a surface, in accordance with the preceding Rule. So we must note above all that the root, the square, the cube, etc. are nothing but magnitudes in continued proportion which, it is always supposed, are preceded by the arbitrary unit mentioned above.[1] The first proportional is related to this unit immediately and by a single relation; the second proportional is related to it by way of the first proportional, and hence by way of two relations; the third proportional by way of the first and the second, and so by way of three relations, etc.[2] From now on, then, the magnitude referred to in algebra as 'the root' we shall term 'the first proportional'; the magnitude referred to as 'the square' we shall call 'the second proportional', and the same goes for the other cases.

Finally, we must note that, even though we are abstracting the terms of a problem from certain numbers in order to investigate its nature, yet it often turns out that the problem can be solved in a simpler way by employing the given numbers than by abstracting from them. This is due to the dual function which numbers have, which is, as we have already mentioned,[3] sometimes to express order, sometimes measure. Accordingly, once we have investigated the problem expressed in general terms, we should re-express it in terms of given numbers, to see whether these

457

1 Cf. above pp. 63ff.
2 Descartes' idea here is to express, for example, the series, a, a^2, a^3, etc. as $1 \times a$, $a \times a$, $a^2 \times a$, etc.
3 See above, p. 64.

might provide us with a simpler solution. For example, once we have seen that the hypotenuse of a right-angled triangle with sides a and b is $\sqrt{a^2+b^2}$, we should substitute 81 for a^2 and 144 for b^2, the addition of which gives us 225. The root of 225, or the mean proportional between the unit and 225, is 15. We shall see from this that the length of the hypotenuse, 15, is commensurable with the lengths of the other sides, 9 and 12; we shall not generally recognize this from the fact that it is the hypotenuse of a right-angled triangle, two sides of which are in the ratio of 3 to 4. We insist on these distinctions, seeking as we do a knowledge of things that is evident and distinct. The arithmeticians, however, make no such distinctions: they are quite content if the sum they are seeking comes to light, even though they have no idea how it depends on the data; yet that, quite simply, is what knowledge[1] strictly speaking consists in.

But in general we should bear in mind that if we can set it down on paper, we need never commit to memory anything that does not demand our constant attention; otherwise a part of our mind may be distracted by needless recollection from its awareness of the object before it. We ought to write down a list of the terms of the problem as they were stated in the first place; then we should note down the way in which they may be abstracted, and the symbols we might use to represent them. The purpose of this is that once we have found the solution in terms of these symbols, we shall be able to apply it easily to the particular subject we are dealing with, without having recourse to memory. For we always abstract something more general from something less general. So I shall write down the problem in the following way:

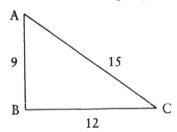

The question being to find the hypotenuse, AC, of the right-angled triangle ABC, I first make an abstraction of the problem, so that the question becomes the general one of finding the magnitude of the hypotenuse from the magnitudes of the other sides. I then substitute a for AB, which is 9, and b for BC, which is 12; and so on in other cases.

We should point out that further use will be made of these latter four Rules in the third part of the treatise, though they will be taken in a

458

459

---

somewhat broader sense than they have been given in the present exposition. But all this will be made clear in due course.

Rule Seventeen

We should make a direct survey of the problem to be solved, disregarding the fact that some of its terms are known and others unknown, and intuiting, through a train of sound reasoning, the dependence of one term on another.

The preceding four Rules have shown us how to abstract determinate and perfectly understood problems from particular subjects and to reduce them to the point where the question becomes simply one of discovering certain magnitudes on the basis of the fact that they bear such and such a relation to certain given magnitudes. Now in the following five Rules we shall explain the method of dealing with these difficulties, so that no matter how many unknown magnitudes there are in a single proposition they can all be arranged in a serial order: the first will stand to the unit as the second to the first, and the third to the second as the fourth to the third, and so on in due sequence. Thus no matter how many of them there are, they will yield a sum equal to some known magnitude. So reliable is our method of doing this that we may safely assert that, however strenuous our efforts, it would be impossible to reduce the magnitudes to simpler terms.

460   For the present, however, we should note that in every problem to be solved through deduction there is a way of passing from one term to another that is plain and direct: it is the easiest way of all, the others being more difficult and round-about. In order to understand this point we must remember what was said in Rule Eleven, where we explained the nature of that sequence of interlinked propositions which enabled us to see easily,[1] when comparing individual propositions, how the first and the last ones are interrelated, even if we cannot deduce the intermediate ones so easily from the first and last ones. Now if, in order to deduce the way in which the last one depends on the first, we intuit the interdependence between the individual propositions without ever interrupting the order, we are going through the problem in a direct way. If on the other hand we know the first and last propositions to be interconnected in a definite way, and we wish to deduce from this the intermediate ones connecting them, the order we follow will be completely indirect and the reverse of the previous one.[2] Now we are concerned here only with

---

1 See above, pp. 37f.   2 Cf. above, pp. 24, 38.

complicated questions where the problem is to discern, albeit in a complicated order, certain intermediate propositions, on the basis of our knowledge of the first and last propositions in the series. So the trick here is to treat the unknown ones as if they were known. This may enable us to adopt the easy and direct method of inquiry even in the most complicated of problems. There is no reason why we should not always do this, since from the outset of this part of the treatise[1] our assumption has been that we know that the unknown terms in the problem are so 461 dependent on the known ones that they are wholly determined by them. Accordingly, we shall be carrying out everything this Rule prescribes if, recognizing that the unknown is determined by the known, we reflect on the terms which occur to us first and count the unknown ones among the known, so that by reasoning soundly step by step we may deduce from these all the rest, even the known terms as if they are unknown. We shall postpone illustrating this point (and most of the points to be dealt with below) until Rule Twenty-four:[2] it will be more convenient to expound them there.

Rule Eighteen

For this purpose only four operations are required: addition, subtraction, multiplication and division. The latter two operations should seldom be employed here, for they may lead to needless complication, and they can be carried out more easily later.

A large number of rules is often the result of inexperience in the teacher. Things are much clearer when they are brought under one single general precept rather than split up among many particular ones. For this reason we are bringing under just four heads all the operations needed for working out a problem, i.e. for deducing some magnitudes from others. How it is that these are all we need will become clearer from our account of them.

When we come to know one magnitude on the basis of our prior 462 knowledge of the parts which make it up, the process is one of addition. When we discover a part on the basis of our prior knowledge of the whole and the extent to which the whole exceeds the part, the process is one of subtraction: there is no other possible way of deriving one magnitude from other magnitudes, taken in an absolute sense, which somehow contain it. But if we are to derive some magnitude from others which are quite different from it and which in no way contain it, it is

---

1 I.e. from Rule Thirteen.
2 The *Rules* in fact end at Rule Twenty-one; see Translator's preface, p. 7 above.

necessary to find some way of relating it to them. If this relation or connection is to be made in a direct way, then we must use multiplication; if in an indirect way, then division.

In order to give a clear account of the latter two operations, we must be apprised of the fact that the unit, which we have spoken about earlier,[1] is here the basis and foundation of all the relations, and occupies the first place in a series of magnitudes which are in continued proportion. The given magnitudes occupy the second place in the series, while those to be discovered occupy the third, fourth, and the remaining places, if the problem in question[2] is a direct one. If, however, the problem is an indirect one, the given magnitude comes last, and the magnitude sought comes in the second place or in other intermediate places.

463   Thus if we are told that as the unit stands to a given magnitude a (5, say), so b (7, say) stands to the number we are seeking, which is ab (i.e. 35), then a and b occupy the second place, and their product, ab, comes in the third place.[3] Again, if we are told that as the unit is to c (e.g. 9), so ab (e.g. 35) is to the number sought, abc (i.e. 315), then abc occupies the fourth place, and is the product of the two multiplications with respect to ab, and c, which occupy the second place;[4] the same holds for other cases. Again, as the unit is to a (i.e. 5), so a is to a^2 (i.e. 25); likewise as the unit is to a (i.e. 5), so a^2 (i.e. 25) is to a^3 (i.e. 125); and lastly as the unit is to a (i.e. 5), so a^3 (i.e. 125) is to a^4 (i.e. 625), etc. For whether a magnitude is multiplied by itself or by a quite different magnitude, the process of multiplication is the same.

If, however, we are told that as the unit is to a given divisor, a (e.g. 5), so the magnitude we are seeking, B (e.g. 7) is to the given dividend, ab (i.e. 35), then the order is confused and indirect,[5] for B can be obtained only by dividing the datum ab by the datum a. The case is the same if the statement is that as the unit is to A (e.g. 5), the number sought, so A is to the datum, a^2 (i.e. 25); or as the unit is to A (5), the number sought, so is A^2 (25) to the datum, a^3 (i.e. 125). And the same is true in other cases. These examples are all included under the term 'division', although we should note that the latter two instances of division are more difficult than the former, since there are more occurrences of the magnitude sought, which therefore involves a greater number of relations. The significance of the latter examples would be the same if we were to employ expressions

464   commonly used by arithmeticians, such as, 'Extract the square root of a^2

---

1 Cf. above pp. 63, 68.
2 Reading *propositio*, A, H. AT unnecessarily emend to *proportio* ('proportion').
3 The formula here is $1/a = a/x$.   4 The formula here is $1/c = ab/x$.
5 Henceforth Descartes uses capital letters to denote the unknown magnitudes. See above, p. 67.

(e.g. 25)', or 'Extract the cube root of a^3 (e.g. 125)' – and similarly in the other cases. Alternatively, the problems may be couched in geometrical terms: it amounts to the same thing whether we say 'Find the mean proportional between the arbitrary magnitude called "the unit" and that denoted by the expression a^2', or 'Find two mean proportionals between the unit and a^3', etc.

From these considerations it is easy to see how these two operations are all we need for the purpose of discovering whatever magnitudes we are required to deduce from others on the basis of some relation. Once we have understood these operations, the next thing to do is to explain how to present them to the imagination for examination, and how to display them visually, so that later on we may explain their uses or applications.

If addition or subtraction is to be used, we conceive the subject in the form of a line, or in the form of an extended magnitude in which length alone[1] is to be considered. For if we are to add line a to line b,

we add the one to the other, in the following way,

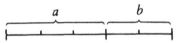

and the result is c:

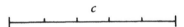

But if the smaller magnitude is to be taken away from the larger, *viz. b* 465 from a,

we place the one above the other thus:

$$b \vdash\!\!-\!\!-\!\dashv$$

$$a \vdash\!\!-\!\!-\!\!-\!\!-\!\dashv$$

and this will give us that segment of the larger one which the smaller one cannot cover, *viz.*,

$$c \vdash\!\!-\!\dashv$$

1 Reading *in quâ sola*, H (following Crapulli). AT read *in quâ solâ*. A, 'in which thing alone'.

In multiplication we also conceive the given magnitudes in the form of lines; though in this case we imagine them as forming a rectangle. For if we multiply a by b,

we fit one line at right angles to the other, thus:

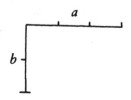

to make the rectangle:

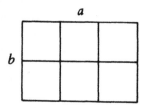

466   Again, if we wish to multiply ab by c,

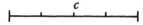

we ought to conceive ab as a line, viz.,

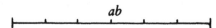

in order to obtain for abc the following figure:

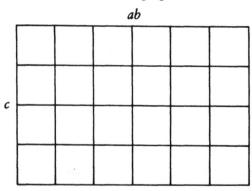

Lastly, in division, where the divisor is given, we imagine the magnitude to be divided as being a rectangle, one side of which is the divisor and the other the quotient. Thus if the rectangle *ab* is to be divided by *a*,

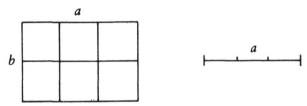

we take away from it the breadth *a*, and are left with *b* as the quotient:

If, on the other hand, we divide the same rectangle by *b*, we take away   467
the height *b*, and the quotient will be *a*:

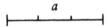

As for those divisions in which the divisor is not given but only indicated by some relation, as when we are required to extract the square root or the cube root etc., in these cases we must note that the term to be divided, and all the other terms, are always to be conceived as lines which form a series of continued proportionals, the first member of which is the unit, and the last the magnitude to be divided.[1] We shall explain in due course how to find any number of mean proportionals between the latter two magnitudes. For the moment we must be content to point out that we are assuming that we have not yet quite done with these operations, since in order to be performed they require indirect and reverse movements of the imagination, and at present we are dealing only with problems which are to be treated in the direct manner.

As for the other operations, we can easily dispose of these if we conceive them along the lines recommended above. But we have still to show how their terms are initially to be set out. For although, on first dealing with a problem, we are free to conceive of its terms as if they were lines or rectangles, without assigning any other figures to them (as stated in Rule Fourteen),[2] nevertheless in the course of the operation it frequently turns out that a rectangle, which has been produced by the   468
multiplication of two lines, has to be conceived as a line, for the sake of some further operation. Or again, the same rectangle, or a line resulting

1 Cf. above, pp. 72f.   2 Cf. above, p. 65.

from an addition or subtraction, has to be conceived as a different rectangle drawn above the line which has been designated as its divisor.

It is therefore important to explain here how every rectangle can be transformed into a line, and conversely how a line or even a rectangle can be transformed into another rectangle, one side of which is specified. Geometers can do this very easily, provided they recognize that in comparing lines with some rectangle (as we are now doing), we always conceive the lines as rectangles, one side of which is the length which we adopted as our unit. In this way, the entire business is reduced to the following problem: given a rectangle, to construct upon a given side another rectangle equal to it.

The merest beginner in geometry is of course perfectly familiar with this; nevertheless I want to make the point, in case it should seem that I have omitted something.

Rule Nineteen

Using this method of reasoning, we must try to find as many magnitudes, expressed in two different ways, as there are unknown terms, which we treat as known in order to work out the problem in the direct way. That will give us as many comparisons between two equal terms.[1]

469

Rule Twenty

Once we have found the equations, we must carry out the operations which we have left aside,[2] *never using multiplication when division is in order.*

Rule Twenty-one

If there are many equations of this sort, they should all be reduced to a single one, viz. to the equation whose terms occupy fewer places in the series of magnitudes which are in continued proportion, i.e. the series in which the order of the terms is to be arranged.

THE END[3]

---

1 Descartes' *Geometry* suggests that by the phrase 'expressed in two different ways' he means 'expressed in equations'. The point seems to be that if a problem is to be determinate, there must be as many equations as there are unknowns. Cf. *Geometry*, AT VI 373.
2 I.e. multiplication and division.
3 As far as we know, Descartes did not complete Rules Nineteen to Twenty-one. 'THE END' occurs in A and H.

Appendix

[The extract which follows is from the second edition of Antoine Arnauld and Pierre Nicole's *Logic or the Art of Thinking* (1664).[1] It is known that the authors made use of Descartes' *Rules* when preparing the second edition of their work. In chapter 2 of part 4 they provide a loose paraphrase of the latter part of Rule Thirteen.[2] The paraphrase contains an additional passage which occupies a place corresponding to a lacuna in Rule Thirteen, and it may possibly be a paraphrase of some of the missing material.]

AT X
471

Problems concerning things can be reduced to four main sorts.

In the first sort of problem causes are sought by way of effects. We know, for example, the various effects of the magnet, and we try to find the causes of these effects. We know the various effects which are usually attributed to nature's abhorrence of a vacuum; we inquire whether the latter is the true cause of these effects, and have discovered that it is not.[3] We are familiar with the ebb and flow of the tide, and we want to know what can cause such a great and regular movement.

In the second sort of problem we try to discover effects by way of causes. It has always been known, for example, that wind and water can move bodies with great force; but the ancients did not sufficiently investigate what the effects of these causes could be, and so did not apply them, as they have since been applied in mills, to many things which are very useful to human society and notably ease the burden of human labour, and which ought to be the harvest of true physics. Consequently we can say that the first sort of problem, in which causes are sought by 472 way of their effects, constitutes the entire speculative side of physics, while the second sort of problem, in which effects are sought by way of causes, constitutes the entire practical side.

In the third sort of problem a whole is sought by way of its parts, as for example when we try to find the sum of several numbers by adding them together, or when, given two numbers, we try to find their product by multiplying them together.

In the fourth sort of problem we try to find a part of a whole, given the

---

1 From ch. 2, part 4, pp. 391ff (AT x 471ff).   2 See above, pp. 54ff.
3 Perhaps a tacit reference to Pascal's *Treatise on the Equilibrium of Liquids and the Weight of the Atmosphere*. Since the latter work was published in 1663 (after Descartes death), some of the content of the above extract (perhaps all) may be due to Arnauld.

whole and some other part of it, as when, given a number and another number to be subtracted from it, we try to find the remainder; or when, given a number, we try to find such and such a part of it.

But in order to extend the scope of the latter two sorts of problem, so that they include what could not properly be brought under the former two sorts, we must note that the word 'part' has to be taken in a very wide sense, as signifying everything that goes to make up a thing – its modes, its extremities, its accidents, its properties, and in general all its attributes. Accordingly we shall be seeking a whole by way of its parts when we try to find the area of a triangle, given its height and its base. On the other hand we shall be seeking a part by way of the whole together with another part when we try to find a side of a rectangle on the basis of our knowledge of its area and one of its sides.

The World and Treatise on Man

Translator's Preface

The World and Treatise on Man are two parts of a work which Descartes wrote in French during the years 1629–33, and which the condemnation of Galileo by the Roman Inquisition caused him not to publish. They were published posthumously.

The World first appeared at Paris in 1664, under the title Le Monde de M. Descartes ou le Traité de la Lumière. But this edition was based only on a copy of the original manuscript, and in 1677 Clerselier produced a version based on the original. The Treatise on Man was published at Paris in 1664 under the title L'Homme de René Descartes, again edited by Clerselier and based on the original manuscript (a Latin translation based on a copy of the original having appeared at Leiden in 1662).

Although published separately, the works are part of a single treatise. In this treatise, Descartes tells Mersenne in November 1629, 'instead of explaining only one phenomenon, I have resolved to explain all the phenomena of nature, i.e. all of physics'. And on 22 July 1633 Descartes announced to Mersenne that his treatise was almost finished, needing only to be corrected and recopied. While revising the work, however, Descartes learned that the Church had condemned Galileo for publishing his views about the motion of the earth, and in November 1633 he informed Mersenne that he had decided not to publish the treatise. 'For', he wrote, 'I would not for all the world want a discourse to issue from me that contained the least word of which the Church would disapprove, and so I would prefer to suppress it than to have it appear in a mangled form.'

From the contents of the published works and Descartes' account of them in his correspondence and in the Discourse, it appears that the suppressed treatise began with the work published as The World, continued with two chapters (now lost) linking this material with the contents of the Treatise on Man, and concluded with the latter work. But the published Treatise on Man is itself incomplete, containing frequent references to subsequent discussions of the rational soul and its relation to the body, which have been lost or were incorporated by Descartes in his later writings. In addition, it may be conjectured that the suppressed treatise contained material later published in the *Meteorology* and the *Principles of Philosophy.*

The present translation, consisting of Chapters 1, 2, 3 (in part), 4, 5 (in part), 6 and 7 (with an omission) from *The World*, and substantial extracts from the *Treatise on Man*, is based on the text in Volume XI of Adam and Tannery.[1] Thus it follows the 1677 version of *The World* (though, as Adam notes, the chapter headings were probably added by Clerselier) and the 1664 version of the *Treatise on Man* (but without Clerselier's division of the work into chapters).

R.S.

1 See General Introduction, p. x above.

Chapter 1   *The difference between our sensations and the things that produce them*

The subject I propose to deal with in this treatise is light, and the first point I want to draw to your attention is that there may be a difference between the sensation we have of light (i.e. the idea of light which is formed in our imagination by the mediation of our eyes) and what it is in the objects that produces this sensation within us (i.e. what it is in a flame or the sun that we call by the name 'light'). For although everyone is commonly convinced that the ideas we have in our mind are wholly similar to the objects from which they proceed, nevertheless I cannot see any reason which assures us that this is so. On the contrary, I note many   4
observations which should make us doubt it.

Words, as you well know, bear no resemblance to the things they signify, and yet they make us think of these things, frequently even without our paying attention to the sound of the words or to their syllables. Thus it may happen that we hear an utterance whose meaning we understand perfectly well, but afterwards we cannot say in what language it was spoken. Now if words, which signify nothing except by human convention, suffice to make us think of things to which they bear no resemblance, then why could nature not also have established some sign which would make us have the sensation of light, even if the sign contained nothing in itself which is similar to this sensation? Is it not thus that nature has established laughter and tears, to make us read joy and sadness on the faces of men?

But perhaps you will say that our ears really cause us to perceive only the sound of the words, and our eyes only the countenance of the person who is laughing or weeping, and that it is our mind which, recollecting what the words and the countenance signify, represents their meaning to us at the same time. I could reply that by the same token it is our mind which represents to us the idea of light each time our eye is affected by the action which signifies it. But rather than waste time debating the   5
question, I prefer to bring forward another example.

Suppose we hear only the sound of some words, without attending to their meaning. Do you think the idea of this sound, as it is formed in our mind, is anything like the object which is its cause? A man opens his mouth, moves his tongue, and breathes out: I do not see anything in these actions which is not very different from the idea of the sound which they make us imagine. Most philosophers maintain that sound is nothing but a certain vibration of air which strikes our ears. Thus, if the sense of hearing transmitted to our mind the true image of its object then, instead of making us conceive the sound, it would have to make us conceive the motion of the parts of the air which is then vibrating against our ears. But not everyone will wish to believe what the philosophers say, and so I shall bring forward yet another example.

Of all our senses, touch is the one considered the least deceptive and most certain. Thus, if I show you that even touch makes us conceive many ideas which bear no resemblance to the objects which produce them, I do not think you should find it strange if I say that sight can do likewise. Now, everyone knows that the ideas of tickling and of pain,
6 which are formed in our mind on the occasion of our being touched by external bodies, bear no resemblance to these bodies. Suppose we pass a feather gently over the lips of a child who is falling asleep, and he feels himself being tickled. Do you think the idea of tickling which he conceives resembles anything present in this feather? A soldier returns from battle; in the heat of combat he might have been wounded without being aware of it. But now, as he begins to cool off, he feels pain and believes himself wounded. We call a surgeon, who examines the soldier after we remove his armour, and we find in the end that what he was feeling was nothing but a buckle or strap caught under his armour, which was pressing on him and causing his discomfort. If his sense of touch, in making him feel this strap, had imprinted an image of it in his mind, there would have been no need for a surgeon to inform him of what he was feeling.

Now, I see no reason which compels us to believe that what it is in objects that gives rise to the sensation of light is any more like this sensation than the actions of a feather and a strap are like a tickling sensation and pain. And yet I have not brought up these examples to make you believe categorically that the light in the objects is something different from what it is in our eyes. I merely wanted you to suspect that there might be a difference, so as to keep you from assuming the opposite, and to make you better able to help me in examining the matter further.

Chapter 2   What the heat and the light of fire consist in   7

I know of only two sorts of bodies in the world in which light is present, namely the stars and flame or fire. And because the stars are undoubtedly less accessible to human knowledge than fire or flame, I shall try first to explain what I observe regarding flame.

When flame burns wood or some other similar material, we can see with the naked eye that it sets the minute parts of the wood in motion and separates them from one another, thus transforming the finer parts into fire, air and smoke, and leaving the coarser parts as ashes. Others may, if they wish, imagine the form of fire, the quality of heat, and the process of burning to be completely different things in the wood. For my part, I am afraid of mistakenly supposing there is anything more in the wood than what I see must necessarily be in it, and so I am content to limit my conception to the motion of its parts. For you may posit 'fire' and 'heat' in the wood, and make it burn as much as you please: but if you do not suppose in addition that some of its parts move about and detach themselves from their neighbours, I cannot imagine it undergoing any alteration or change. On the other hand, if you take away the 'fire', take away the 'heat', and keep the wood from 'burning'; then, provided only that you grant me there is some power which puts its finer parts into violent motion and separates them from the coarser parts, I consider that   8 this power alone will be able to bring about all the same changes that we observe in the wood when it burns.

Now since it does not seem possible to conceive how one body could move another except through its own movement, I conclude that the body of the flame which acts upon the wood is composed of minute parts, which move about independently of one another with a very rapid and very violent motion. As they move about in this way they push against the parts of the bodies they are touching and move those which do not offer them too much resistance. I say that the flame's parts move about individually, for although many of them often work together to bring about a single effect, we see nevertheless that each of them acts on its own upon the bodies they touch. I say, too, that their motion is very rapid and very violent, for they are so minute that we cannot distinguish them by sight, and so they would not have the force they have to act upon the other bodies if the rapidity of their movement did not compensate for their lack of size.

I add nothing about the direction in which each part moves. For the power to move and the power that determines in what direction the motion must take place are completely different things, and can exist one   9 without the other (as I have explained in the *Optics*).[1] If you consider this fact, you will easily recognize that each part moves in the manner made least difficult for it by the disposition of the bodies surrounding it. In the same flame there may be some parts going up, others going down, some going in straight lines, others in circles, and some in every direction, all without any variation in the flame's nature. Thus if you see almost all the parts tending upward you need not think this is happening for any reason except that the other bodies touching them are almost always disposed to offer them more resistance in all the other directions.

But now that we have recognized that the parts of a flame move in this manner, and that it suffices to conceive of their motions in order to understand how the flame has the power to consume the wood and to burn, I suggest that we ask whether the same will not also suffice to make us understand how the flame provides us with heat and light. For if that is the case, it will not be necessary for the flame to possess any other quality, and we shall be able to say that it is this motion alone which is called now 'heat' and now 'light', according to the different effects it produces.

As regards heat, the sensation we have of it may, I think, be taken for a kind of pain when the motion is violent, and sometimes for a kind of tickling when the motion is moderate. And since we have already said that there is nothing outside our thought which is similar to the ideas we conceive of tickling and pain, we may well believe also that there is nothing which is similar to the idea we conceive of heat; rather, this sensation may be produced in us by anything that can set up various motions in the minute parts of our hands or of any other place in our body. This view is supported by many observations.[2] For we can heat our hands merely by rubbing them together, and any other body can also be heated without being placed near a fire, provided only that it is agitated and shaken so that many of its minute parts move about and thereby can move the minute parts of our hands.

As regards light, we can also conceive that this same motion in the flame is sufficient to cause our sensation of it. But since this forms the main part of my project, I shall try to explain it at some length when I resume discussion of this matter.

Chapter 3   Hardness and fluidity

I believe that countless different motions go on perpetually in the world. After noting the greatest of these (which bring about the days, months and years), I take note that terrestrial vapours constantly rise to the clouds and descend from them, that the air is forever agitated by the

---

1 Cf. pp. 155ff below.   2 See note on p. 143 below.

winds, that the sea is never at rest, that springs and rivers flow ceaselessly, that the strongest buildings eventually fall into decay, that plants and animals are always growing or decaying – in short, that there is nothing anywhere which is not changing. From this I know clearly that a flame is not the only thing in which there are a number of minute parts in ceaseless motion, but that every other body has such parts, even though their actions are not so violent and they are so minute that they cannot be perceived by any of our senses.

I shall not pause to seek the cause of their motions, for it suffices for me to suppose that they began to move as soon as the world began to exist. That being the case, I find by my reasoning that their motions cannot possibly ever cease, or even change in any way except in respect of their subject. That is to say, the virtue or power of self-movement found in one body may indeed pass wholly or partially into another and thus be no longer present in the first; but it cannot entirely cease to exist in the world. My arguments, I say, are enough to satisfy me on this point; but I have not yet had occasion to relate them to you. In the meantime you may imagine if you wish (as do most of the learned) that there is some prime mover which, travelling about the world at a speed beyond comprehension, is the origin and source of all the other motions found in it . . .[1]

Chapter 4 The void, and how it happens that our senses do not perceive certain bodies (16)

But we must examine in greater detail why air, although it too is a body, cannot be perceived by the senses as well as other bodies. In this way we shall free ourselves from an error that has gripped all of us since our childhood, when we came to believe that there are no bodies around us except those capable of being perceived by the senses, and therefore that if air were one of them (because we perceive it to some extent) it could not be so material or solid as those we perceive to a greater extent.

On this subject I should first like you to note that all bodies, both hard and fluid, are made from the same matter, and that it is impossible to conceive of the parts of this matter ever composing a more solid body, or one occupying less space, than they do when each of them is touched on all sides by the other surrounding parts. It follows, on my view, that if a vacuum can exist anywhere, it must be in hard bodies rather than in fluid

1 Descartes goes on to explain the difference between hard bodies and fluid bodies in terms of the motion of their parts. The hardest body imaginable is one whose parts, in a state of complete rest, touch each other with no space between any two; and the most fluid body is one whose smallest parts are constantly moving away from each other in rapid and random motion, while still touching each other on all sides. Cf. *Principles*, Part 2, art. 54–5, pp. 245f below. For an English version of material omitted here and below, see *René Descartes: The World*, tr. M. S. Mahoney (N.Y.: Abaris, 1979).

ones. For obviously it is easier for the parts of hard bodies to press and arrange themselves against one another than for the parts of fluid bodies to do so, since the latter are moving about while the former are motionless.

For example, when you put powder into a jar, you shake the jar and tap it to make room for more powder. But if you pour some liquid into a jar, it immediately settles down automatically into the smallest place you could put it. And indeed, if you consider some of the experiments which 18 philosophers commonly use to show that there is no vacuum in nature, you will readily recognize that all those spaces which people consider empty, where we perceive only air, are at least as full, and filled with the same matter, as the spaces where we perceive other bodies.

We know from observations of certain machines that nature causes the heaviest bodies to rise and the hardest to shatter, rather than permitting any of their parts to stop touching one another or to come into contact with any other bodies. Tell me, if you please, how likely it is that nature would do this while yet allowing the parts of air, which are so easy to bend and to arrange in all ways, to remain next to each other without being touched on all sides, or without there being any other body between them which they touch? Could one really believe that the water in a well has to rise, contrary to its natural inclination, merely in order that the pipe of a pump may be filled, or think that the water in clouds does not have to fall in order to fill the spaces here on earth, if there were even the least vacuum between the parts of the bodies they contain?

But here you might bring forward a difficulty which is rather important – namely, that the component parts of fluid bodies cannot, it seems, 19 move about incessantly as I have said they do, unless there is empty space between them, at least in the places which the parts vacate as they move about. I would have difficulty in replying if I had not learned, through various observations, that all the motions which take place in the world are in some way circular. That is, when a body leaves its place, it always enters into the place of some other body, and so on to the last body, which at the same instant occupies the place vacated by the first. Thus there is no more of a vacuum between bodies when they are moving about than when they are at rest. And note here that in order for this to happen it is not necessary that all the parts of bodies moving together should be arranged exactly in a ring, as in a true circle, nor even that they should be of equal size and shape. For any such inequalities can easily be counter-balanced by other inequalities in their speed.

We do not usually notice these circular motions when bodies are moving in the air, because we are accustomed to conceiving of the air only as an empty space. But look at fish swimming in the pool of a fountain: if they do not come too near the surface of the water, they cause no motion in it at all, even though they are passing beneath it with great speed. From this it clearly appears that the water they push before them does not push all the water in the pool indiscriminately: it pushes only the water which can best serve to perfect the circle of their movement and to occupy the place which they vacate.

This observation is enough to show the ease and familiarity with which these circular motions occur in nature. But I want now to adduce another observation, in order to show that no motion ever takes place which is not circular. When the wine in a cask does not flow from the bottom opening because the top is completely closed, it is improper to say, as they ordinarily do, that this takes place through 'fear of a vacuum'. We are well aware that the wine has no mind to fear anything; and even if it did, I do not know for what reason it could be apprehensive of this vacuum, which indeed is nothing but a chimera. Instead we must say that the wine cannot leave the cask because outside everything is as full as can be, and the part of the air whose place the wine would occupy if it were to flow out can find no other place to occupy in all the rest of the universe unless we make an opening in the top of the cask through which the air can rise by a circular path into its place.

For all that, I do not wish to insist that there is no vacuum at all in nature. My treatise would, I fear, become too long if I undertook to explain the matter at length, and the observations of which I have spoken are not sufficient to prove my point, although they are enough to confirm that the spaces in which we perceive nothing by our senses are filled with the same matter as those occupied by the bodies that we do perceive, and contain at least as much of this matter as the latter spaces. Thus, for example, when a vessel is full of gold or lead, it contains no more matter than when we think it is empty. This may seem very strange to many people, whose reason extends no further than their fingertips, and who suppose that there is nothing in the world except what they touch. But when you have given a little consideration to what makes us perceive a body by our senses, or not perceive it, I am sure that you will find nothing incredible in this. For you will recognize it as evident that, so far from all the things around us being perceivable, on the contrary those that usually are there are the least perceivable, and those that are always there can never be perceived at all.

The heat of our heart is very great, but we do not feel it because it is usually there. The weight of our body is not small, but it does not discomfort us. We do not even feel the weight of our clothes, because we are accustomed to wearing them. The reason for this is clear enough: for it is certain that we cannot perceive any body by our senses unless it is the

22 cause of some change in our sense organs – that is, unless it somehow moves the minute parts of the matter of which these organs are composed. Objects which are not always present can indeed do this, provided they have enough force; for if they damage something in the sense organs while acting on them, that can be repaired afterwards by nature, when they are no longer acting. But regarding the objects which continually touch us, if they ever had the power to produce any change in our senses and to move some parts of their matter, they must have moved these parts, and thereby separated them entirely from the others, at the outset of our life; and in this way they can have left there only the parts which completely resist their action and by means of which they cannot be perceived by our senses in any way. From this you can see that it is no wonder that there are many spaces about us in which we do not perceive any body by our senses, even though they contain no fewer bodies than the spaces in which we perceive the most.

It must not be thought, however, that the ordinary air which we draw into our lungs while breathing – the air which turns into wind when set in motion, which seems hard when enclosed in a balloon, and which is composed only of exhalations and fumes – is as solid as water or earth. Here we must follow the common opinion of the philosophers, who all maintain that it is rarer. This can easily be known through observation. For when the parts of a drop of water are separated from one another by the agitation of heat, they can make up much more of this ordinary air 23 than could be contained in the space that held the water. From this it follows with certainty that there are a great number of tiny gaps between the parts of which the air is composed, for there is no other way to conceive of a rare body. But since these gaps cannot be empty, as I have said above, I conclude that there are necessarily some other bodies, one or many, mixed in with the air, and these bodies fill as tightly as possible the tiny gaps left between its parts. It now only remains for me to consider what these other bodies can be; after that, I hope it will not be difficult to understand what the nature of light can be.

Chapter 5   *The number of elements and their qualities*

The philosophers maintain that above the clouds there is a kind of air much finer than ours, which is not composed of terrestrial vapours, as our air is, but constitutes a separate element. They say too that above this air there is yet another body, much finer again, which they call the element of fire. They add, moreover, that these two elements are mixed with water and earth to make up all the bodies below. Thus I shall merely be following their opinion if I say that this finer air and this element of fire fill the gaps which are between the parts of the ordinary air we 24 breathe, so that these bodies, interlaced with one another, make up a mass which is as solid as any body can be.

But in order to get you to understand my thought on this subject, and so that you will not think I want to compel you to believe all that the philosophers tell you about the elements, I must describe them to you in my own fashion . . .[1]

If you find it strange that in explaining these elements I do not use the (25) qualities called 'heat', 'cold', 'moisture' and 'dryness' – as the philosophers do – I shall say to you that these qualities themselves seem to me 26 to need explanation. Indeed, unless I am mistaken, not only these four qualities but all the others as well, including even the forms of inanimate bodies, can be explained without the need to suppose anything in their matter other than the motion, size, shape, and arrangement of its parts. In consequence I shall easily be able to get you to understand why I do not acknowledge any elements other than the three I have described. For the difference that must exist between them and the other bodies, which philosophers call 'mixed' or 'composite', consists in the fact that the forms of these mixed bodies always contain some qualities which oppose and counteract one another, or which at least do not tend to the preservation of one another. But in fact the forms of the elements must be simple and must not have any qualities which do not accord so perfectly with one another that each contributes to the preservation of all the others.

Now I cannot find any such forms in the world except the three I have described. For the form I have attributed to the first element consists in its parts moving so extremely rapidly and being so minute that there are no other bodies capable of stopping them; and in addition they need not have any determinate size, shape, or position. The form of the second element consists in its parts being so moderate in their motion and size 27 that if there are many causes in the world which may increase their motion and decrease their size, there are just as many others which can do exactly the opposite; and so they always remain balanced as it were in the same moderate condition. And the form of the third element consists in its parts being so large or so closely joined together that they always have the force to resist the motions of the other bodies.

Examine as much as you please all the forms that can be given to mixed bodies by the various motions, the various shapes and sizes, and the different arrangement of the parts of matter: I am sure you will find none that does not contain in itself qualities which tend to bring it about

1 There follows a brief description of the three elements *fire, air* and *earth*, which Descartes distinguishes solely in terms of the size, shape and motion of their parts.

that matter undergoes change and, in changing, reduces to one of the forms of the elements . . .[1]

(31)   Many other things remain for me to explain here, and I would myself be happy to add several arguments to make my opinions more plausible. But in order to make this long discourse less boring for you, I want to clothe part of it in the guise of a fable, in the course of which I hope the truth will not fail to become sufficiently clear, and will be no less pleasing to see than if I were to set it forth wholly naked.

Chapter 6   *Description of a new world; and the qualities of the matter of which it is composed*

For a while, then, allow your thought to wander beyond this world to view another world – a wholly new one which I shall bring into being before your mind in imaginary spaces. The philosophers tell us that such

32   spaces are infinite, and they should certainly be believed, since it is they themselves who invented them. But in order to keep this infinity from hampering and confusing us, let us not try to go right to the end: let us enter it only far enough to lose sight of all the creatures that God made five or six thousand years ago; and after stopping in some definite place, let us suppose that God creates anew so much matter all around us that in whatever direction our imagination may extend, it no longer perceives any place which is empty.

Even though the sea is not infinite, people on some vessel in the middle of it may stretch their view seemingly to infinity; and yet there is more water beyond what they see. Likewise, although our imagination seems able to stretch to infinity, and this new matter is not supposed to be infinite, yet we can suppose that it fills spaces much greater than all those we have imagined. And just to ensure that this supposition contains nothing you might find objectionable, let us not allow our imagination to extend as far as it could; let us intentionally confine it to a determinate space which is no greater, say, than the distance between the earth and the principal stars in the heavens, and let us suppose that the matter which God has created extends indefinitely far beyond in all directions.

33   For it is much more reasonable to prescribe limits to the action of our mind than to the works of God, and we are much better able to do so.

Now since we are taking the liberty of fashioning this matter as we fancy, let us attribute to it, if we may, a nature in which there is absolutely nothing that everyone cannot know as perfectly as possible.

---

1 Descartes goes on to show why the bodies about us must be 'mixed', or composed of parts of the three elements. He likens these bodies to sponges, their 'pores' being filled with parts of the first and second elements, which cannot be perceived by the senses. Cf. *Principles*, Part 2, art. 6, p. 225 below.

To this end, let us expressly suppose that it does not have the form of earth, fire, or air, or any other more specific form, like that of wood, stone, or metal. Let us also suppose that it lacks the qualities of being hot or cold, dry or moist, light or heavy, and of having any taste, smell, sound, colour, light, or other such quality in the nature of which there might be said to be something which is not known clearly by everyone.

On the other hand, let us not also think that this matter is the 'prime matter' of the philosophers, which they have stripped so thoroughly of all its forms and qualities that nothing remains in it which can be clearly understood. Let us rather conceive it as a real, perfectly solid body which uniformly fills the entire length, breadth and depth of this huge space in the midst of which we have brought our mind to rest. Thus, each of its parts always occupies a part of that space which it fits so exactly that it could neither fill a larger one nor squeeze into a smaller; nor could it, while remaining there, allow another body to find a place there.

Let us add that this matter may be divided into as many parts having as many shapes as we can imagine, and that each of its parts is capable of taking on as many motions as we can conceive. Let us suppose, moreover, that God really divides it into many such parts, some larger and some smaller, some of one shape and some of another, however we care to imagine them. It is not that God separates these parts from one another so that there is some void between them: rather, let us regard the differences he creates within this matter as consisting wholly in the diversity of the motions he gives to its parts. From the first instant of their creation, he causes some to start moving in one direction and others in another, some faster and others slower (or even, if you wish, not at all); and he causes them to continue moving thereafter in accordance with the ordinary laws of nature. For God has established these laws in such a marvellous way that even if we suppose he creates nothing beyond what I have mentioned, and sets up no order or proportion within it but composes from it a chaos as confused and muddled as any the poets could describe, the laws of nature are sufficient to cause the parts of this chaos to disentangle themselves and arrange themselves in such good order that they will have the form of a quite perfect world – a world in which we shall be able to see not only light but also all the other things, general as well as particular, which appear in the real world.

But before I explain this at greater length, pause again for a bit to consider this chaos, and observe that it contains nothing which you do not know so perfectly that you could not even pretend to be ignorant of it. For, as regards the qualities I have put into it, you may have noticed that I supposed them to be only of such a kind that you could imagine them. And, as regards the matter from which I have composed it, there is nothing simpler or easier to know in inanimate creatures. The idea of this matter is included to such an extent in all the ideas that our imagination can form that you must necessarily conceive it or else you can never imagine anything at all.

Nevertheless, the philosophers are so subtle that they can find difficulties in things which seem extremely clear to other men, and the memory of their 'prime matter', which they know to be rather hard to conceive, may divert them from knowledge of the matter of which I am speaking. Thus I must tell them at this point that, unless I am mistaken, the whole difficulty they face with their matter arises simply from their wanting to distinguish it from its own quantity and from its external extension – that is, from the property it has of occupying space. In this, however, I am quite willing for them to think they are right, for I have no intention of
36 stopping to contradict them. But they should also not find it strange if I suppose that the quantity of the matter I have described does not differ from its substance any more than number differs from the things numbered. Nor should they find it strange if I conceive its extension, or the property it has of occupying space, not as an accident, but as its true form and essence. For they cannot deny that it can be conceived quite easily in this way. And my purpose is not to explain, as they do, the things which are in fact in the real world, but only to make up, as I please, a world in which there is nothing that the dullest minds are incapable of conceiving, and which nevertheless could be created exactly as I have imagined it.

Were I to put into this new world the least thing that is obscure, this obscurity might well conceal some hidden contradiction I had not perceived, and hence, without thinking, I might be supposing something impossible. Instead, since everything I propose here can be distinctly imagined, it is certain that even if there were nothing of this sort in the old world, God can nevertheless create it in a new one. For it is certain that he can create everything we can imagine.

Chapter 7   *The laws of nature of this new world*

But I do not want to delay any longer telling you by what means nature alone can untangle the confusion of the chaos of which I have spoken, and what the laws are that God has imposed on it.
37   Note, in the first place, that by 'nature' here I do not mean some goddess or any other sort of imaginary power. Rather, I am using this word to signify matter itself, in so far as I am considering it taken together with all the qualities I have attributed to it, and under the condition that God continues to preserve it in the same way that he created it. For it follows of necessity, from the mere fact that he continues

thus to preserve it, that there must be many changes in its parts which cannot, it seems to me, properly be attributed to the action of God (because that action never changes), and which therefore I attribute to nature. The rules by which these changes take place I call the 'laws of nature'.

In order to understand this better, recall that among the qualities of matter, we have supposed that its parts have had various different motions from the moment they were created, and furthermore that they are all in contact with each other on all sides without there being any void between any two of them. From this it follows necessarily that from the time they began to move, they also began to change and diversify their motions by colliding with one another. So if God subsequently preserves them in the same way that he created them, he does not preserve them in the same state. That is to say, with God always acting in the same way and consequently always producing substantially the same effect, there are, as if by accident, many differences in this effect. And it is easy to accept that God, who is, as everyone must know, immutable, always acts in the same way. But without involving myself any further in these metaphysical considerations, I shall set out two or three of the principal rules according to which it must be thought that God causes the nature of this new world to operate. These, I believe, will suffice to acquaint you with all the others.

The first is that each individual part of matter continues always to be in the same state so long as collision with others does not force it to change that state. That is to say, if the part has some size, it will never become smaller unless others divide it; if it is round or square, it will never change that shape unless others force it to; if it is brought to rest in some place, it will never leave that place unless others drive it out; and if it has once begun to move, it will always continue with an equal force until others stop or retard it.[1]

There is no one who does not believe that this same rule holds in the old world with respect to size, shape, rest and numerous other such things. But the philosophers have excluded motion from the rule – which is just the thing I most definitely wish to include in it. Do not think, however, that I intend to contradict them: the motion they speak of is so very different from the one I conceive that it may very easily happen that what is true of the one is not true of the other.

They admit themselves that the nature of their motion is very little understood. To render it in some way intelligible they have not yet been able to explain it more clearly than in these terms: *Motus est actus entis in*

---

1 See *Principles*, Part 2, art. 37 (below, p. 240) for Descartes' later formulation of this law.

potentia, prout in potentia est.[1] For me these words are so obscure that I am compelled to leave them in Latin because I cannot interpret them. (And in fact the sentence 'Motion is the actuality of a potential being in so far as it is potential' is no clearer for being translated.) By contrast, the nature of the motion I mean to speak of here is so easy to know that the geometers themselves, who among all men are the most concerned to conceive very distinctly the things they study, have judged it simpler and more intelligible than the nature of their surfaces and lines – as is shown by the fact that they have explained 'line' as the motion of a point and 'surface' as the motion of a line.

The philosophers also posit many motions which they think can take place without any body's changing place, like those they call *motus ad formam, motus ad calorem, motus ad quantitatem* ('motion with respect to form', 'motion with respect to heat', 'motion with respect to quantity') and numerous others. For my part, I am not acquainted with any motion except that which is easier to conceive than the lines of the geometers – the motion which makes bodies pass from one place to another and successively occupy all the spaces which exist in between.

In addition, the philosophers attribute to the least of these motions a being much more solid and real than they attribute to rest, which they say is nothing but the privation of motion. For my part, I conceive of rest as a quality too, which should be attributed to matter while it remains in one place, just as motion is a quality attributed to matter while it is changing place.

Finally, the motion of which they speak has a very strange nature; for whereas all other things have their perfection as an end and strive only to preserve themselves, it has no other end and no other goal than rest and, contrary to all the laws of nature, it strives of its own accord to destroy itself. By contrast, the motion which I posit follows the same laws of nature as do generally all the dispositions and qualities found in matter – including those which the Schoolmen call *modos et entia rationis cum fundamento in re* ('conceptual modes and entities founded in things') as well as those they call *qualitates reales* (their 'real qualities', in which I confess frankly that I can find no more reality than in the others).

I suppose as a second rule that when one body pushes another it cannot give the other any motion unless it loses as much of its own motion at the same time; nor can it take away any of the other's motion unless its own is increased by as much.[2] This rule, together with the

---

1 Aristotle, *Physics*, III, 1, 201ª10. Descartes criticizes this definition also in Rule Twelve of the *Rules* (see above, p. 49).
2 See *Principles*, part 2, art. 40 (below, p. 242) where this appears as the third law of nature.

preceding, agrees very well with all the observations in which we see one body begin or cease to move because it is pushed or stopped by another one. For, having supposed the preceding rule, we are free from the difficulty in which the Schoolmen find themselves when they wish to explain why a stone continues to move for some time after leaving the hand of the one who threw it. For we should ask, instead, why does the stone not continue to move forever? Yet the reason is easy to give. For who can deny that the air in which it is moving offers it some resistance? We hear it whistle when it cuts through the air; and if a fan, or some other very light and extensive body, is moved through the air, we shall even be able to feel by the weight in our hand that the air is impeding its motion rather than keeping it moving, as some have wanted to say. But suppose we refuse to explain the effects of the air's resistance in accordance with our second rule, and we think that the more resistance a body can offer the greater its capacity to check the motion of other bodies (as perhaps we might be persuaded at first). In this case we shall have great difficulty explaining why the motion of the stone is reduced more in 42 colliding with a soft body which offers moderate resistance than when it collides with a harder body which resists it more. Likewise, we shall find it difficult to explain why, as soon as it has encountered some resistance in the latter, it immediately turns in its tracks rather than stopping or interrupting its motion on that account. On the other hand, if we accept this rule, there is no difficulty at all. For it tells us that the motion of one body is retarded by its collision with another not in proportion to how much the latter resists it, but only in proportion to how much the latter's resistance is overcome, and to the extent that the latter obeys the rule by taking on the force of motion that the former gives up.

Now, in most of the motions we see in the real world we cannot perceive that the bodies which begin or cease to move are pushed or stopped by some other bodies. But that gives us no reason to think that these two rules are not being followed exactly. For it is certain that such bodies can often receive their agitation from the two elements, air and fire, which are always present among them without being perceivable by the senses (as has just been said), or they may receive it even from the ordinary air, which also cannot be perceived by the senses. It is certain too that they can transfer this agitation sometimes to the ordinary air, and sometimes to the whole mass of the earth; and when dispersed in the latter, it also cannot be perceived.

But even if everything our senses ever experienced in the real world 43 seemed manifestly contrary to what is contained in these two rules, the reasoning which has taught them to me seems so strong that I cannot help believing myself obliged to posit them in the new world I am describing to you. For what more firm and solid foundation could one find for establishing a truth, even if one wished to choose it at will, than the very firmness and immutability which is in God?

So it is that these two rules follow manifestly from the mere fact that God is immutable and that, acting always in the same way, he always produces the same effect. For, supposing that God placed a certain quantity of motion in all matter in general at the first instant he created it, we must either admit that he always preserves the same amount of motion in it, or not believe that he always acts in the same way. Suppose, in addition, that from this first instant the various parts of matter, in which these motions are found unequally dispersed, began to retain them or transfer them from one to another, according as they had the force to do so. Then we must necessarily think that God causes them to continue always doing so. And that is what these two rules contain.

I shall add, as a third rule, that when a body is moving, even though its
44 motion for the most part takes place along a curved path and, as we said above, it can never make any movement which is not in some way circular, yet each of its parts individually tends always to continue moving along a straight line.[1] And so the action of these parts – i.e. the tendency they have to move – is different from their motion.

For example, if we make a wheel turn on its axle, even though all its parts go in a circle (because, being joined to one another, they cannot do otherwise), their tendency is to go straight ahead. This is obvious if one part happens to get detached from the others, for as soon as it is free its motion ceases to be circular and continues in a straight line.

Likewise, when you swing a stone in a sling, not only does it fly straight out as soon as it leaves the sling, but also while it is in the sling it presses against the middle of it and causes the cord to stretch. This makes it obvious that it always has a tendency to go in a straight line and that it goes in a circle only under constraint.

This rule is based on the same foundation as the other two: it depends solely on God's preserving each thing by a continuous action, and consequently on his preserving it not as it may have been some time earlier but precisely as it is at the very instant that he preserves it. So it is
45 that of all motions, only motion in a straight line is entirely simple and has a nature which may be wholly grasped in an instant. For in order to conceive such motion it suffices to think that a body is in the process of moving in a certain direction, and that this is the case at each determinable instant during the time it is moving. By contrast, in order to conceive circular motion, or any other possible motion, it is necessary to consider

---

1 See *Principles*, Part 2, art. 39, p. 241 below.

at least two of its instants, or rather two of its parts, and the relation between them. But so that the philosophers (or rather the sophists) do not find occasion here to exercise their useless subtleties, note that I am not saying that rectilinear motion can take place in an instant, but only that everything required to produce it is present in bodies at each instant which might be determined while they are moving, whereas not everything required to produce circular motion is present . . .

According to this rule, then, it must be said that God alone is the (46) author of all the motions in the world in so far as they exist and in so far as they are rectilinear; but it is the various dispositions of matter which render them irregular and curved. Likewise, the theologians teach us that God is also the author of all our actions, in so far as they exist and in so 47 far as they have some goodness, but it is the various dispositions of our wills that can render them evil.

I could set out many further rules here for determining in detail when, how, and by how much the motion of each body can be changed and increased or decreased by colliding with others – in sum, rules which comprehend in a concise way all the effects of nature. But I shall be content with telling you that apart from the three laws I have expounded, I do not wish to suppose any others but those which follow inevitably from the eternal truths on which mathematicians have usually based their most certain and most evident demonstrations – the truths, I say, according to which God himself has taught us that he has arranged all things in number, weight and measure. The knowledge of these truths is so natural to our souls that we cannot but judge them infallible when we conceive them distinctly, nor doubt that if God had created many worlds, they would be as true in each of them as in this one. Thus those who are able to examine sufficiently the consequences of these truths and of our rules will be able to recognize effects by their causes. To express myself in scholastic terms, they will able to have *a priori* demonstrations of everything that can be produced in this new world.

In order to eliminate any exception that may prevent this, we shall, if 48 you please, suppose in addition that God will never perform any miracle in the new world, and that the intelligences, or the rational souls, which we might later suppose to be there, will not disrupt in any way the ordinary course of nature. In consequence of this, however, I do not promise to set out exact demonstrations of everything I shall say. It will be enough if I open the way which will enable you to discover them yourselves, when you take the trouble to look for them. Most minds lose interest when things are made too easy for them. And to present a picture which pleases you, I need to use shadow as well as bright colours. So I shall be content to continue with the description I have begun, as if my intention was simply to tell you a fable.[1]

1 The remaining chapters of *The World* deal with topics indicated in the chapter headings:

These men will be composed, as we are, of a soul and a body.[1] First I must describe the body on its own; then the soul, again on its own; and 120 finally I must show how these two natures would have to be joined and united in order to constitute men who resemble us.

I suppose the body to be nothing but a statue or machine made of earth,[2] which God forms with the explicit intention of making it as much as possible like us. Thus God not only gives it externally the colours and shapes of all the parts of our bodies, but also places inside it all the parts required to make it walk, eat, breathe, and indeed to imitate all those of our functions which can be imagined to proceed from matter and to depend solely on the disposition of our organs.

We see clocks, artificial fountains, mills, and other such machines which, although only man-made, have the power to move of their own accord in many different ways. But I am supposing this machine to be made by the hands of God, and so I think you may reasonably think it capable of a greater variety of movements than I could possibly imagine in it, and of exhibiting more artistry than I could possibly ascribe to it.

Now I shall not pause to describe the bones, nerves, muscles, veins, arteries, stomach, liver, spleen, heart, brain, or any of the various other parts from which this machine must be composed. For I am supposing that they are entirely like the parts of our own bodies which have the same names, and I assume that if you do not already have sufficient first-hand knowledge of them, you can get a learned anatomist to show them to you – at any rate, those which are large enough to be seen with 121 the naked eye. As for the parts which are too small to be seen, I can inform you about them more easily and clearly by speaking of the movements which depend on them. Thus I need only give an orderly

---

1 By 'these men', Descartes means the fictional men he introduced in an earlier (lost) part of the work. Their description is intended to cast light on the nature of real men in the same way that the description of a 'new world' in *The World*, ch. 6, is intended to cast light on the real world. See also *Discourse*, part 5, pp. 132ff below.
2 By 'earth' Descartes means the third 'element', which he had discussed in *The World*, ch. 5 (cf. p. 89 above).

account of these movements in order to tell you which of our functions they represent . . .[1]

129   The parts of the blood which penetrate as far as the brain serve not only to nourish and sustain its substance, but also and primarily to produce in it a certain very fine[2] wind, or rather a very lively and pure flame, which is called the *animal spirits*. For it must be noted that the arteries which carry blood to the brain from the heart, after dividing into countless tiny branches which make up the minute tissues that are stretched like tapestries at the bottom of the cavities of the brain, come together again around a certain little *gland*[3] situated near the middle of the substance of the brain, right at the entrance to its cavities. The arteries in this region have a great many little holes through which the
(130)   finer parts of the blood can flow into this gland . . . These parts of the blood, without any preparation or alteration except for their separation from the coarser parts and their retention of the extreme rapidity which the heat of the heart has given them, cease to have the form of blood, and are called the 'animal spirits'.

Now in the same proportion as the animal spirits enter the cavities of the brain, they pass from there into the pores of its substance, and from these pores into the nerves. And depending on the varying amounts which enter (or merely tend to enter) some nerves more than others, the spirits have the power to change the shape of the muscles in which the nerves are embedded, and by this means to move all the limbs. Similarly you may have observed in the grottos and fountains in the royal gardens that the mere force with which the water is driven as it emerges from its source is sufficient to move various machines, and even to make them play certain instruments or utter certain words depending on the various arrangements of the pipes through which the water is conducted.

131   Indeed, one may compare the nerves of the machine I am describing with the pipes in the works of these fountains, its muscles and tendons with the various devices and springs which serve to set them in motion, its animal spirits with the water which drives them, the heart with the source of the water, and the cavities of the brain with the storage tanks. Moreover, breathing and other such activities which are normal and

---

1   There follows a description of digestion, the formation and circulation of the blood, the action of the heart, and respiration. Cf. *Discourse*, part 5, pp. 132ff below, and *Passions*, Part 1, art. 3–10, pp. 329ff, and *Description of the Human Body*, pp. 316ff, below. For an English version of material omitted here and below, see *Descartes: Treatise on Man*, tr. T. S. Hall (Cambridge: Harvard U.P., 1972).

2   Fr. *subtil*, by which Descartes means 'composed of very small, fast-moving particles'.

3   The pineal gland, which Descartes later identifies as the seat of the imagination and the 'common' sense (p. 106 below). See also *Passions* (pp. 340ff, below), where the gland is identified as the seat of the soul.

natural to this machine, and which depend on the flow of the spirits, are like the movements of a clock or mill, which the normal flow of water can render continuous. External objects, which by their mere presence stimulate its sense organs and thereby cause them to move in many different ways depending on how the parts of its brain are disposed, are like visitors who enter the grottos of these fountains and unwittingly cause the movements which take place before their eyes. For they cannot enter without stepping on certain tiles which are so arranged that if, for example, they approach a Diana who is bathing they will cause her to hide in the reeds, and if they move forward to pursue her they will cause a Neptune to advance and threaten them with his trident; or if they go in another direction they will cause a sea-monster to emerge and spew water onto their faces; or other such things according to the whim of the engineers who made the fountains. And finally, when a *rational soul* is present in this machine it will have its principal seat in the brain, and reside there like the fountain-keeper who must be stationed at the tanks to which the fountain's pipes return if he wants to produce, or prevent, or change their movements in some way . . .[1] 132

Next, to understand how the external objects which strike the sense organs can prompt this machine to move its limbs in numerous different ways, you should consider that the tiny fibres (which, as I have already told you, come from the innermost region of its brain and compose the marrow of the nerves) are so arranged in each part of the machine that serves as the organ of some sense that they can easily be moved by the objects of that sense. And when they are moved, with however little force, they simultaneously pull the parts of the brain from which they come, and thereby open the entrances to certain pores in the internal surface of the brain. Through these pores the animal spirits in the cavities of the brain immediately begin to make their way into the nerves and so to the muscles which serve to cause movements in the machine quite similar to those we are naturally prompted to make when our senses are affected in the same way. (141)

Thus, for example [in Fig. 1], if fire A is close to foot B, the tiny parts of this fire (which, as you know, move about very rapidly) have the power also to move the area of skin which they touch. In this way they pull the tiny fibre *cc* which you see attached to it, and simultaneously open the entrance to the pore *de*, located opposite the point where this fibre terminates – just as when you pull one end of a string, you cause a bell hanging at the other end to ring at the same time. 142

When the entrance to the pore or small tube *de* is opened in this way,

1 There follows a description of the way in which the animal spirits bring about muscular movements, breathing, swallowing, etc. See *Passions*, Part 1, pp. 334ff below.

Fig. 1

the animal spirits from cavity *F* enter and are carried through it – some to muscles which serve to pull the foot away from the fire, some to muscles which turn the eyes and head to look at it, and some to muscles which make the hands move and the whole body turn in order to protect it . . .

(143)   Now I maintain that when God unites a rational soul to this machine (in a way that I intend to explain later) he will place its principal seat in the brain, and will make its nature such that the soul will have different sensations corresponding to the different ways in which the entrances to the pores in the internal surface of the brain are opened by means of the nerves.

Suppose, firstly, that the tiny fibres which make up the marrow of the nerves are pulled with such force that they are broken and separated from the part of the body to which they are joined, with the result that 144   the structure of the whole machine becomes somehow less perfect. Being pulled in this way, the fibres cause a movement in the brain which gives occasion for the soul (whose place of residence must remain constant) to have the sensation of *pain*.

Now suppose the fibres are pulled with a force almost as great as the one just mentioned, but without their being broken or separated from the parts to which they are attached. Then they will cause a movement in the brain which, testifying to the good condition of the other parts of the body, will give the soul occasion to feel a certain bodily pleasure which we call '*titillation*'. This, as you see, is very close to pain in respect of its cause but quite opposite in its effect.

Again, if many of these tiny fibres are pulled equally and all together, they will make the soul perceive that the surface of the body touching the limb where they terminate is *smooth*; and if the fibres are pulled unequally they will make the soul feel the surface to be uneven and *rough*.

And if the fibres are disturbed only slightly and separately from one another, as they constantly are by the heat which the heart transmits to the other parts of the body, the soul will have no more sensation of this than of any other normal function of the body. But if this stimulation is increased or decreased by some unusual cause, its increase will make the soul have a sensation of *heat*, and its decrease a sensation of *cold*. Finally, according to the various other ways in which they are stimulated, the fibres will cause the soul to perceive all the other qualities belonging to touch in general, such as *moisture, dryness, weight* and the like. 145

It must be observed, however, that despite the extreme thinness and mobility of these fibres, they are not thin and mobile enough to transmit to the brain all the more subtle motions that take place in nature. In fact the slightest motions they transmit are ones involving the coarser parts of terrestrial bodies. And even among these bodies there may be some whose parts, although rather coarse, can slide against the fibres so gently that they compress them or cut right through them without their action passing to the brain. In just the same way there are certain drugs which have the power to numb or even destroy the parts of the body to which they are applied without causing us to have any sensation of them at all . . .[1]

It is time for me to begin to explain how the animal spirits make their (165) way through the cavities and pores of the brain of this machine, and which of the machine's functions depend on these spirits.

[1] There follows an account of the other external senses (taste, smell, hearing and sight) and of internal sensations (hunger, thirst, joy and sadness). For Descartes' theory of vision, see *Optics* (pp. 167ff below), for the other external senses, see *Principles*, Part 4, art. 192–4 (pp. 282ff below) and for the internal sensations, see *Passions, passim*.

If you have ever had the curiosity to examine the organs in our churches, you know how the bellows push the air into certain receptacles (which are called, presumably for this reason, wind-chests). And you know how the air passes from there into one or other of the pipes, depending on the different ways in which the organist moves his fingers on the keyboard. You can think of our machine's heart and arteries, which push the animal spirits into the cavities of its brain, as being like the bellows of an organ, which push air into the wind-chests; and you can think of external objects, which stimulate certain nerves and cause spirits contained in the cavities to pass into some of the pores, as being like the fingers of the organist, which press certain keys and cause the air to pass from the wind-chests into certain pipes. Now the harmony of an organ does not depend on the externally visible arrangement of the pipes or on the shape of the wind-chests or other parts. It depends solely on

166   three factors: the air which comes from the bellows, the pipes which make the sound, and the distribution of the air in the pipes. In just the same way, I would point out, the functions we are concerned with here do not depend at all on the external shape of the visible parts which anatomists distinguish in the substance of the brain, or on the shape of the brain's cavities, but solely on three factors: the spirits which come from the heart, the pores of the brain through which they pass, and the way in which the spirits are distributed in these pores. Thus my sole task here is to give an orderly account of the most important features of these three factors . . .[1]

(173)   Now, the substance of the brain being soft and pliant, its cavities would be very narrow and almost all closed (as they appear in the brain of a corpse) if no spirits entered them. But the source which produces these spirits is usually so abundant that they enter these cavities in sufficient quantity to have the force to push out against the surrounding matter and make it expand, thus tightening all the tiny nerve-fibres which come from it (in the way that a moderate wind can inflate the sails of a ship and tighten all the ropes to which the sails are attached.) It follows that at such times the machine is disposed to respond to all the actions of the spirits, and hence it represents the body of a man who is *awake*. Or at least the spirits have enough force to push against some parts of the surrounding matter in this way, and so make it tight, while the other parts remain free and relaxed (as happens in parts of a sail when the wind is a little too weak to fill it). At such times the machine represents the body of a man who is *asleep* and who has *various dreams* as he sleeps . . .

1   There follows a description of the animal spirits and how their state is affected by digestion, respiration, and other bodily functions; of the pores of the brain; and of the movement of the spirits through the pores.

But before I speak in greater detail about *sleep* and *dreams*, I must have (174)
you consider the most noteworthy events that take place in the brain
during the time of waking: namely, how ideas of objects are formed in
the place assigned to the *imagination* and to the '*common*' *sense*,[1] how
the ideas are retained in the *memory*, and how they cause *movement in
all the parts of the body* . . .

In order . . . to see clearly how ideas are formed of the objects which
strike the senses, observe in this diagram [Fig. 2] the tiny fibres 12, 34, 175
56, and the like, which make up the optic nerve and stretch from the back
of the eye at 1, 3, 5 to the internal surface of the brain at 2, 4, 6. Now
assume that these fibres are so arranged that if the rays coming, for
example, from point A of the object happen to press upon the back of the
eye at point 1, they pull the whole of fibre 12 and enlarge the opening of
the tiny tube marked 2. In the same way, the rays which come from point
B enlarge the opening of the tiny tube 4, and likewise for the others. We
have already described how, depending on the different ways in which
the points 1, 3, 5 are pressed by these rays, a figure is traced on the back

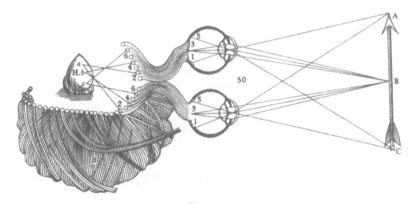

Fig. 2

of the eye corresponding to that of the object ABC. Similarly, it is
obvious that, depending on the different ways in which the tiny tubes 2,
4, 6 are opened by the fibres 12, 34, 56, etc., a corresponding figure must
also be traced on the internal surface of the brain.

Suppose next that the spirits which tend to enter each of the tiny tubes
2, 4, 6, and the like, do not come indifferently from all points on the
surface of gland H, but only from certain of these points: those coming
from point *a* on this surface, for example, tend to enter tube 2, those
from points *b* and *c* tend to enter tubes 4 and 6, and likewise for the

1 See footnote 1, p. 41 above.

176   others. As a result, at the same instant that the openings to these tubes
expand, the spirits begin to leave the corresponding points on the gland
more freely and more rapidly than they did previously. Thus, just as a
figure corresponding to that of the object ABC is traced on the internal
surface of the brain according to the different ways in which tubes 2, 4, 6
are opened, likewise that figure is traced on the surface of the gland
according to the ways in which the spirits leave from points *a, b, c*.

And note that by 'figures' I mean not only things which somehow
represent the position of the edges and surfaces of objects, but also
anything which, as I said above, can give the soul occasion to perceive
movement, size, distance, colours, sounds, smells and other such qualities. And I also include anything that can make the soul feel pleasure,
pain, hunger, thirst, joy, sadness and other such passions. For it is easy to
understand that tube 2, for example, may be opened in different ways —
in one way by the action which I said causes sensory perception of the
colour red, or of tickling, and in another way by the action which I said
causes sensory perception of the colour white, or of pain; and the spirits
which leave from point *a* will tend to move towards this tube in a
different manner according to differences in its manner of opening, and
likewise for the others.

Now among these figures, it is not those imprinted on the external
sense organs, or on the internal surface of the brain, which should be
taken to be ideas — but only those which are traced in the spirits on the
surface of the gland H (*where the seat of the imagination and the*
177   '*common' sense is located*).[1] That is to say, it is only the latter figures
which should be taken to be the forms or images which the rational soul
united to this machine will consider directly when it imagines some
object or perceives it by the senses.

And note that I say 'imagines or perceives by the senses'. For I wish to
apply the term 'idea' generally to all the impressions which the spirits can
receive as they leave gland H. These are to be attributed to the 'common'
sense when they depend on the presence of objects; but they may also
proceed from many other causes (as I shall explain later), and they should
then be attributed to the imagination.

Here I could add something about how the traces of these ideas pass
through the arteries to the heart, and thus radiate through all the blood;
and about how certain actions of a mother may sometimes even cause
such traces to be imprinted on the limbs of the child being formed in her
womb. But I shall content myself with telling you more about how the
traces are imprinted on the internal part of the brain [marked B on Fig. 2]
which is the seat of the *memory*.

1 See note 3, p. 100 above.

To this end, suppose that after the spirits leaving gland H have received the impression of some idea, they pass through tubes 2, 4, 6, and the like, into the pores or gaps lying between the tiny fibres which make up part B of the brain. And suppose that the spirits are strong enough to enlarge these gaps somewhat, and to bend and arrange in various ways any fibres they encounter, according to the various ways in which the spirits are moving and the different openings of the tubes into which they pass. 178 Thus they also trace figures in these gaps, which correspond to those of the objects. At first they do this less easily and perfectly than they do on gland H, but gradually they do it better and better, as their action becomes stronger and lasts longer, or is repeated more often. That is why these figures are no longer so easily erased, and why they are preserved in such a way that the ideas which were previously on the gland can be formed again long afterwards without requiring the presence of the objects to which they correspond. And this is what *memory* consists in ...[1]

But before going on to describe the rational soul, I should like you (200) once again to give a little thought to everything I have said about this machine. Consider, in the first place, that I have supposed in it only organs and mechanisms of such a type that you may well believe very similar ones to be present both in us and in many animals which lack reason as well. Regarding those which can be seen clearly with the naked eye, the anatomists have already observed them all. And as for what I have said about the way in which the arteries carry the spirits into the head, and about the difference between the internal surface of the brain and its central substance, the anatomists will, if they simply make closer observations, be able to see sufficient indications of this to allay any doubts about these matters too. Nor will they be able to have doubts about the tiny doors or valves which I have placed in the nerves where they enter each muscle, if they take care to note that nature generally has 201 formed such valves at all the places in our bodies where some matter regularly goes in and may tend to come out, as at the entrances to the heart, gall-bladder, throat, and large intestine, and at the main divisions of all the veins. Again, regarding the brain, they will not be able to imagine anything more plausible than that it is composed of many tiny fibres variously interlaced; for, in view of the fact that every type of skin and flesh appears to be similarly composed of many fibres or threads, and that the same thing is observed in all plants, such fibrous composition is apparently a common property of all bodies that can grow and be

---

1 There follows an account of the way in which the animal spirits form ideas on the surface of the pineal gland, and produce bodily movements like those of real men, despite the absence of any soul. See *Passions*, Part 1, art. 13–16, 21–4, pp. 333ff, 336f below.

nourished by the union and joining together of the minute parts of other bodies. Finally, as for the rest of the things I have assumed which cannot be perceived by any sense, they are all so simple and commonplace, and also so few in number, that if you compare them with the diverse composition and marvellous artistry which is evident in the structure of the visible organs, you will have more reason to think I have omitted many that are in us than to think I have introduced any that are not. And, knowing that nature always acts by the simplest and easiest means, you will perhaps conclude that it is possible to find some which are more similar to the ones she in fact uses than to those proposed here.

202   I should like you to consider, after this, all the functions I have ascribed to this machine – such as the digestion of food, the beating of the heart and arteries, the nourishment and growth of the limbs, respiration, waking and sleeping, the reception by the external sense organs of light, sounds, smells, tastes, heat and other such qualities, the imprinting of the ideas of these qualities in the organ of the 'common' sense and the imagination, the retention or stamping of these ideas in the memory, the internal movements of the appetites and passions, and finally the external movements of all the limbs (movements which are so appropriate not only to the actions of objects presented to the senses, but also to the passions and the impressions found in the memory, that they imitate perfectly the movements of a real man). I should like you to consider that these functions follow from the mere arrangement of the machine's organs every bit as naturally as the movements of a clock or other automaton follow from the arrangement of its counter-weights and wheels. In order to explain these functions, then, it is not necessary to conceive of this machine as having any vegetative or sensitive soul or other principle of movement and life, apart from its blood and its spirits, which are agitated by the heat of the fire burning continuously in its heart–a fire which has the same nature as all the fires that occur in inanimate bodies.

Discourse and Essays

Translator's preface

Descartes' first published writings, the *Discourse and Essays* appeared anonymously at Leiden in June 1637, under the full title *Discourse on the Method of rightly conducting one's reason and seeking the truth in the sciences, and in addition the Optics, the Meteorology and the Geometry, which are essays in this Method (Discours de la Méthode pour bien conduire sa raison, et chercher la vérité dans les sciences. Plus la Dioptrique, les Météores et la Géométrie qui sont des essais de cette Méthode).*

This title is an abbreviated form of the more elaborate title that Descartes proposed in a letter to Mersenne of March 1636, where he speaks of 'four treatises, all in French, with the general title: *The Plan of a universal Science which is capable of raising our nature to its highest degree of perfection. In addition, the Optics, the Meteorology and the Geometry, in which the Author, in order to give proof of his universal Science, explains the most abstruse Topics he could choose, and does so in such a way that even persons who have never studied can understand them.'* When Mersenne raised questions about the title of the published work, Descartes replied (in a letter of February 1637):

I have not put *Treatise on the Method* but *Discourse on the Method*, which amounts to the same as *Preface* or *Note concerning the Method*, in order to show that I do not intend to teach the method but only to speak about it. For, as can be seen from what I say, it consists much more in practice than in theory. I call the treatises following it *Essays in this Method* because I claim that what they contain could not have been discovered without it, and they enable us to recognize its value. And I have included a certain amount of metaphysics, physics and medicine in the introductory *Discourse* in order to show that the method extends to every kind of subject-matter.

The *Essays* were all written or conceived well before the *Discourse*. Thus, Descartes announces his intention to write the *Meteorology* in a letter to Mersenne of 8 October 1629, and in the same letter he also indicates his wish to publish anonymously, with the author 'hidden behind the picture so as to hear what is said of it'. The *Optics* is mentioned in a letter of 1630, and Descartes sent a part of it (probably the section on refraction) to a correspondent in 1632. He refers to it in *The World*, which was completed in 1633, and in 1635 he showed it to Huygens, to whom he wrote in November of his plan to publish the *Meteorology* with the *Optics*, and to add to them a 'preface'. As for the *Geometry*, Descartes claimed (in a letter of 22 February 1638) that it was written out, and even in part devised, while the *Meteorology* was being printed (i.e. in the spring of 1636). But he also maintains that he had known one of its results 'for twenty years' (letter to Mersenne, 29 June 1638), and his correspondence confirms that the *Geometry* contains discoveries made prior to 1630.

In 1644 a Latin translation of the *Discourse and Essays* (omitting the *Geometry*) was published at Amsterdam. This translation incorporates changes made by Descartes himself, but none of them indicates any important modification of his philosophical views. Hence the present translation, which comprises the whole of the *Discourse* and substantial excerpts from the *Optics*, follows only Adam and Tannery's edition of the French original.[1]

R.S.

1 See General Introduction, p. x above.

DISCOURSE ON THE METHOD

of rightly conducting one's reason and seeking the truth in the sciences

If this discourse seems too long to be read at a sitting you may divide it into six parts. In the first you will find various considerations regarding the sciences; in the second, the principal rules of the method which the author has sought; in the third, some of the moral rules he has derived from this method; in the fourth, the arguments by which he proves the existence of God and the human soul, which are the foundations of his metaphysics; in the fifth, the order of the questions in physics that he has investigated, particularly the explanation of the movement of the heart and of some other difficulties pertaining to medicine, and also the difference between our soul and that of the beasts; and in the last, the things he believes necessary in order to make further progress in the investigation of nature than he has made, and the reasons which made him write this discourse.

Part One

Good sense is the best distributed thing in the world: for everyone thinks himself so well endowed with it that even those who are the hardest to please in everything else do not usually desire more of it than they possess. In this it is unlikely that everyone is mistaken. It indicates rather that the power of judging well and of distinguishing the true from the false – which is what we properly call 'good sense' or 'reason' – is naturally equal in all men, and consequently that the diversity of our opinions does not arise because some of us are more reasonable than others but solely because we direct our thoughts along different paths and do not attend to the same things. For it is not enough to have a good mind; the main thing is to apply it well. The greatest souls are capable of the greatest vices as well as the greatest virtues; and those who proceed but very slowly can make much greater progress, if they always follow the right path, than those who hurry and stray from it.

For my part, I have never presumed my mind to be in any way more perfect than that of the ordinary man; indeed, I have often wished to have as quick a wit, or as sharp and distinct an imagination, or as ample or prompt a memory as some others. And apart from these, I know of no other qualities which serve to perfect the mind; for, as regards reason or sense, since it is the only thing that makes us men and distinguishes us from the beasts, I am inclined to believe that it exists whole and complete in each of us. Here I follow the common opinion of the philosophers,

3   who say there are differences of degree only between the *accidents*, and not between the *forms* (or natures) of *individuals* of the same *species*.

But I say without hesitation that I consider myself very fortunate to have happened upon certain paths in my youth which led me to considerations and maxims from which I formed a method whereby, it seems to me, I can increase my knowledge gradually and raise it little by little to the highest point allowed by the mediocrity of my mind and the short duration of my life. Now I always try to lean towards diffidence rather than presumption in the judgements I make about myself; and when I cast a philosophical eye upon the various activities and undertakings of mankind, there are almost none which I do not consider vain and useless. Nevertheless I have already reaped such fruits from this method that I cannot but feel extremely satisfied with the progress I think I have already made in the search for truth, and I cannot but entertain such hopes for the future as to venture the opinion that if any purely human occupation has solid worth and importance, it is the one I have chosen.

Yet I may be wrong: perhaps what I take for gold and diamonds is nothing but a bit of copper and glass. I know how much we are liable to err in matters that concern us, and also how much the judgements of our friends should be distrusted when they are in our favour. I shall be glad,

4   nevertheless, to reveal in this discourse what paths I have followed, and to represent my life in it as if in a picture, so that everyone may judge it for himself; and thus, learning from public response the opinions held of it, I shall add a new means of self-instruction to those I am accustomed to using.

My present aim, then, is not to teach the method which everyone must follow in order to direct his reason correctly, but only to reveal how I have tried to direct my own. One who presumes to give precepts must think himself more skilful than those to whom he gives them; and if he makes the slightest mistake, he may be blamed. But I am presenting this work only as a history or, if you prefer, a fable in which, among certain examples worthy of imitation, you will perhaps also find many others that it would be right not to follow; and so I hope it will be useful for some without being harmful to any, and that everyone will be grateful to me for my frankness.

From my childhood I have been nourished upon letters, and because I was persuaded that by their means one could acquire a clear and certain knowledge of all that is useful in life, I was extremely eager to learn them. But as soon as I had completed the course of study at the end of which one is normally admitted to the ranks of the learned, I completely changed my opinion. For I found myself beset by so many doubts and errors that I came to think I had gained nothing from my attempts to become educated but increasing recognition of my ignorance. And yet I 5 was at one of the most famous schools in Europe, where I thought there must be learned men if they existed anywhere on earth. There I had learned everything that the others were learning; moreover, not content with the subjects they taught us, I had gone through all the books that fell into my hands concerning the subjects that are considered most abstruse and unusual. At the same time, I knew how the others judged me, and I saw that they did not regard me as inferior to my fellow students, even though several among them were already destined to take the place of our teachers. And finally, the age in which we live seemed to me to be as flourishing, and as rich in good minds, as any before it. This made me feel free to judge all others by reference to myself and think there was no knowledge in the world such as I had previously been led to hope for.

I did not, however, cease to value the exercises done in the Schools. I knew that the languages learned there are necessary for understanding the works of the ancients; that the charm of fables awakens the mind, while the memorable deeds told in histories uplift it and help to shape one's judgement if they are read with discretion; that reading good books is like having a conversation with the most distinguished men of past ages – indeed, a rehearsed conversation in which these authors reveal to us only the best of their thoughts; that oratory has incomparable powers and beauties; that poetry has quite ravishing delicacy and sweetness; that 6 mathematics contains some very subtle devices which serve as much to satisfy the curious as to further all the arts and lessen man's labours; that writings on morals contain many very useful teachings and exhortations to virtue; that theology instructs us how to reach heaven; that philosophy gives us the means of speaking plausibly about any subject and of winning the admiration of the less learned; that jurisprudence, medicine, and other sciences bring honours and riches to those who cultivate them; and, finally, that it is good to have examined all these subjects, even those full of superstition and falsehood, in order to know their true value and guard against being deceived by them.

But I thought I had already given enough time to languages and likewise to reading the works of the ancients, both their histories and their fables. For conversing with those of past centuries is much the same as travelling. It is good to know something of the customs of various peoples, so that we may judge our own more soundly and not think that everything contrary to our own ways is ridiculous and irrational, as those who have seen nothing of the world ordinarily do. But one who spends too much time travelling eventually becomes a stranger in his own country; and one who is too curious about the practices of past ages usually remains quite ignorant about those of the present. Moreover,

7   fables make us imagine many events as possible when they are not. And even the most accurate histories, while not altering or exaggerating the importance of matters to make them more worthy of being read, at any rate almost always omit the baser and less notable events; as a result, the other events appear in a false light, and those who regulate their conduct by examples drawn from these works are liable to fall into the excesses of the knights-errant in our tales of chivalry, and conceive plans beyond their powers.

I valued oratory and was fond of poetry; but I thought both were gifts of the mind rather than fruits of study. Those with the strongest reasoning and the most skill at ordering their thoughts so as to make them clear and intelligible are always the most persuasive, even if they speak only low Breton and have never learned rhetoric. And those with the most pleasing conceits and the ability to express them with the most embellishment and sweetness would still be the best poets, even if they knew nothing of the theory of poetry.

Above all I delighted in mathematics, because of the certainty and self-evidence of its reasonings. But I did not yet notice its real use; and since I thought it was of service only in the mechanical arts, I was surprised that nothing more exalted had been built upon such firm and solid foundations. On the other hand, I compared the moral writings of

8   the ancient pagans to very proud and magnificent palaces built only on sand and mud. They extol the virtues, and make them appear more estimable than anything else in the world; but they do not adequately explain how to recognize a virtue, and often what they call by this fine name is nothing but a case of callousness, or vanity, or desperation, or parricide.

I revered our theology, and aspired as much as anyone else to reach heaven. But having learned as an established fact that the way to heaven is open no less to the most ignorant than to the most learned, and that the revealed truths which guide us there are beyond our understanding, I would not have dared submit them to my weak reasonings; and I thought that to undertake an examination of them and succeed, I would need to have some extraordinary aid from heaven and to be more than a mere man.

Regarding philosophy, I shall say only this: seeing that it has been cultivated for many centuries by the most excellent minds and yet there is still no point in it which is not disputed and hence doubtful, I was not so presumptuous as to hope to achieve any more in it than others had done. And, considering how many diverse opinions learned men may maintain on a single question – even though it is impossible for more than one to be true – I held as well-nigh false everything that was merely probable.

As for the other sciences, in so far as they borrow their principles from philosophy I decided that nothing solid could have been built upon such 9 shaky foundations. Neither the honour nor the riches they offered was enough to induce me to learn them. For my circumstances did not, thanks to God, oblige me to augment my fortune by making science my profession; and although I did not profess to scorn glory, like a Cynic, yet I thought very little of the glory which I could hope to acquire only through false pretences. Finally, as for the false sciences, I thought that I already knew their worth well enough not to be liable to be deceived by the promises of an alchemist or the predictions of an astrologer, the tricks of a magician or the frauds and boasts of those who profess to know more than they do.

That is why, as soon as I was old enough to emerge from the control of my teachers, I entirely abandoned the study of letters. Resolving to seek no knowledge other than that which could be found in myself or else in the great book of the world, I spent the rest of my youth travelling, visiting courts and armies, mixing with people of diverse temperaments and ranks, gathering various experiences, testing myself in the situations which fortune offered me, and at all times reflecting upon whatever came my way so as to derive some profit from it. For it seemed to me that much more truth could be found in the reasonings which a man makes concerning matters that concern him than in those which some scholar makes in his study about speculative matters. For the consequences of the 10 former will soon punish the man if he judges wrongly, whereas the latter have no practical consequences and no importance for the scholar except that perhaps the further they are from common sense the more pride he will take in them, since he will have had to use so much more skill and ingenuity in trying to render them plausible. And it was always my most earnest desire to learn to distinguish the true from the false in order to see clearly into my own actions and proceed with confidence in this life.

It is true that, so long as I merely considered the customs of other men, I found hardly any reason for confidence, for I observed in them almost as much diversity as I had found previously among the opinions of philosophers. In fact the greatest benefit I derived from these observations was that they showed me many things which, although seeming very extravagant and ridiculous to us, are nevertheless commonly accepted and approved in other great nations; and so I learned not to believe too firmly anything of which I had been persuaded only by example and custom. Thus I gradually freed myself from many errors which may obscure our natural light and make us less capable of heeding reason. But after I had spent some years pursuing these studies in the book of the world and trying to gain some experience, I resolved one day to undertake studies within myself too and to use all the powers of my mind in choosing the paths I should follow. In this I have had much more success, I think, than I would have had if I had never left my country or my books.

11

Part Two

At that time I was in Germany, where I had been called by the wars that are not yet ended there. While I was returning to the army from the coronation of the Emperor, the onset of winter detained me in quarters where, finding no conversation to divert me and fortunately having no cares or passions to trouble me, I stayed all day shut up alone in a stove-heated room, where I was completely free to converse with myself about my own thoughts.[1] Among the first that occurred to me was the thought that there is not usually so much perfection in works composed of several parts and produced by various different craftsmen as in the works of one man. Thus we see that buildings undertaken and completed by a single architect are usually more attractive and better planned than those which several have tried to patch up by adapting old walls built for different purposes. Again, ancient cities which have gradually grown from mere villages into large towns are usually ill-proportioned, compared with those orderly towns which planners lay out as they fancy on level ground. Looking at the buildings of the former individually, you will often find as much art in them, if not more, than in those of the latter; but in view of their arrangement – a tall one here, a small one there – and the way they make the streets crooked and irregular, you would say it is chance, rather than the will of men using reason, that placed them so. And when you consider that there have always been certain officials whose job is to see that private buildings embellish public places, you will understand how difficult it is to make something perfect by working only on what others have produced. Again, I thought, peoples who have grown gradually from a half-savage to a civilized state, and have made their laws only in so far as they were forced to by the

12

---

1 In 1619 Descartes attended the coronation of Ferdinand II in Frankfurt, which took place from 20 July to 9 September. The mentioned army was that of the Catholic Duke Maximilian of Bavaria. It is thought that Descartes was detained in a village near Ulm. His day of solitary reflection in a stove-heated room was, according to Baillet, 10 November 1619. See above, p. 4.

inconvenience of crimes and quarrels, could not be so well governed as those who from the beginning of their society have observed the basic laws laid down by some wise law-giver. Similarly, it is quite certain that the constitution of the true religion, whose articles have been made by God alone, must be incomparably better ordered than all the others. And to speak of human affairs, I believe that if Sparta was at one time very flourishing, this was not because each of its laws in particular was good (seeing that some were very strange and even contrary to good morals), but because they were devised by a single man and hence all tended to the same end.[1] And so I thought that since the sciences contained in books – at least those based upon merely probable, not demonstrative, reasoning – is compounded and amassed little by little from the opinions of many different persons, it never comes so close to the truth as the simple reasoning which a man of good sense naturally makes concerning 13 whatever he comes across. So, too, I reflected that we were all children before being men and had to be governed for some time by our appetites and our teachers, which were often opposed to each other and neither of which, perhaps, always gave us the best advice; hence I thought it virtually impossible that our judgements should be as unclouded and firm as they would have been if we had had the full use of our reason from the moment of our birth, and if we had always been guided by it alone.

Admittedly, we never see people pulling down all the houses of a city for the sole purpose of rebuilding them in a different style to make the streets more attractive; but we do see many individuals having their houses pulled down in order to rebuild them, some even being forced to do so when the houses are in danger of falling down and their foundations are insecure. This example convinced me that it would be unreasonable for an individual to plan to reform a state by changing it from the foundations up and overturning it in order to set it up again; or again for him to plan to reform the body of the sciences or the established order of teaching them in the schools. But regarding the opinions to which I had hitherto given credence, I thought that I could not do better than undertake to get rid of them, all at one go, in order to replace them afterwards with better ones, or with the same ones once I had squared 14 them with the standards of reason. I firmly believed that in this way I would succeed in conducting my life much better than if I built only upon old foundations and relied only upon principles that I had accepted in my youth without ever examining whether they were true. For although I noted various difficulties in this undertaking, they were not insurmountable. Nor could they be compared with those encountered in the reform

---

1 By tradition the constitution of Sparta was attributed to Lycurgus.

of even minor matters affecting public institutions. These large bodies are too difficult to raise up once overthrown, or even to hold up once they begin to totter, and their fall cannot but be a hard one. Moreover, any imperfections they may possess – and their very diversity suffices to ensure that many do possess them – have doubtless been much smoothed over by custom; and custom has even prevented or imperceptibly corrected many imperfections that prudence could not so well provide against. Finally, it is almost always easier to put up with their imperfections than to change them, just as it is much better to follow the main roads that wind through mountains, which have gradually become smooth and convenient through frequent use, than to try to take a more direct route by clambering over rocks and descending to the foot of precipices.

   That is why I cannot by any means approve of those meddlesome and restless characters who, called neither by birth nor by fortune to the management of public affairs, are yet forever thinking up some new 15 reform. And if I thought this book contained the slightest ground for suspecting me of such folly, I would be very reluctant to permit its publication. My plan has never gone beyond trying to reform my own thoughts and construct them upon a foundation which is all my own. If I am sufficiently pleased with my work to present you with this sample of it, this does not mean that I would advise anyone to imitate it. Those on whom God has bestowed more of his favours will perhaps have higher aims; but I fear that even my aim may be too bold for many people. The simple resolution to abandon all the opinions one has hitherto accepted is not an example that everyone ought to follow. The world is largely composed of two types of minds for whom it is quite unsuitable. First, there are those who, believing themselves cleverer than they are, cannot avoid precipitate judgements and never have the patience to direct all their thoughts in an orderly manner; consequently, if they once took the liberty of doubting the principles they accepted and of straying from the common path, they could never stick to the track that must be taken as a short-cut, and they would remain lost all their lives. Secondly, there are those who have enough reason or modesty to recognize that they are less capable of distinguishing the true from the false than certain others by whom they can be taught; such people should be content to follow the opinions of these others rather than seek better opinions themselves.

16   For myself, I would undoubtedly have been counted among the latter if I had had only one teacher or if I had never known the differences that have always existed among the opinions of the most learned. But in my college days I discovered that nothing can be imagined which is too strange or incredible to have been said by some philosopher; and since

then I have recognized through my travels that those with views quite contrary to ours are not on that account barbarians or savages, but that many of them make use of reason as much or more than we do. I thought, too, how the same man, with the same mind, if brought up from infancy among the French or Germans, develops otherwise than he would if he had always lived among the Chinese or cannibals; and how, even in our fashions of dress, the very thing that pleased us ten years ago, and will perhaps please us again ten years hence, now strikes us as extravagant and ridiculous. Thus it is custom and example that persuade us, rather than any certain knowledge. And yet a majority vote is worthless as a proof of truths that are at all difficult to discover; for a single man is much more likely to hit upon them than a group of people. I was, then, unable to choose anyone whose opinions struck me as preferable to those of all others, and I found myself as it were forced to become my own guide.

But, like a man who walks alone in the dark, I resolved to proceed so slowly, and to use such circumspection in all things, that even if I made 17 but little progress I should at least be sure not to fall. Nor would I begin rejecting completely any of the opinions which may have slipped into my mind without having been introduced there by reason, until I had first spent enough time in planning the work I was undertaking and in seeking the true method of attaining the knowledge of everything within my mental capabilities.

When I was younger, my philosophical studies had included some logic, and my mathematical studies some geometrical analysis and algebra. These three arts or sciences, it seemed, ought to contribute something to my plan. But on further examination I observed with regard to logic that syllogisms and most of its other techniques are of less use for learning things than for explaining to others the things one already knows or even, as in the art of Lully, for speaking without judgement about matters of which one is ignorant.[1] And although logic does contain many excellent and true precepts, these are mixed up with so many others which are harmful or superfluous that it is almost as difficult to distinguish them as it is to carve a Diana or a Minerva from an unhewn block of marble. As to the analysis of the ancients and the algebra of the moderns, they cover only highly abstract matters, which seem to have no use. Moreover the former is so closely tied to the examination of figures that it cannot exercise the intellect without greatly tiring the imagination; 18 and the latter is so confined to certain rules and symbols that the end result is a confused and obscure art which encumbers the mind, rather

1 Raymond Lully (1232–1315) was a Catalan theologian whose *Ars Magna* purported to provide a universal method of discovery.

than a science which cultivates it. For this reason I thought I had to seek some other method comprising the advantages of these three subjects but free from their defects. Now a multiplicity of laws often provides an excuse for vices, so that a state is much better governed when it has but few laws which are strictly observed; in the same way, I thought, in place of the large number of rules that make up logic, I would find the following four to be sufficient, provided that I made a strong and unswerving resolution never to fail to observe them.

The first was never to accept anything as true if I did not have evident knowledge of its truth: that is, carefully to avoid precipitate conclusions and preconceptions, and to include nothing more in my judgements than what presented itself to my mind so clearly and so distinctly that I had no occasion to doubt it.

The second, to divide each of the difficulties I examined into as many parts as possible and as may be required in order to resolve them better.

The third, to direct my thoughts in an orderly manner, by beginning with the simplest and most easily known objects in order to ascend little by little, step by step, to knowledge of the most complex, and by supposing some order even among objects that have no natural order of precedence.

And the last, throughout to make enumerations so complete, and reviews so comprehensive, that I could be sure of leaving nothing out.

Those long chains composed of very simple and easy reasonings, which geometers customarily use to arrive at their most difficult demonstrations, had given me occasion to suppose that all the things which can fall under human knowledge are interconnected in the same way. And I thought that, provided we refrain from accepting anything as true which is not, and always keep to the order required for deducing one thing from another, there can be nothing too remote to be reached in the end or too well hidden to be discovered. I had no great difficulty in deciding which things to begin with, for I knew already that it must be with the simplest and most easily known. Reflecting, too, that of all those who have hitherto sought after truth in the sciences, mathematicians alone have been able to find any demonstrations – that is to say, certain and evident reasonings – I had no doubt that I should begin with the very things that they studied. From this, however, the only advantage I hoped to gain was to accustom my mind to nourish itself on truths and not to be satisfied with bad reasoning. Nor did I have any intention of trying to learn all the special sciences commonly called 'mathematics'.[1] For I saw that, despite the diversity of their objects, they agree in considering nothing but the various relations or proportions that hold between these objects. And so I

1 These are subjects with a theoretical basis in mathematics, such as astronomy, music and optics.

thought it best to examine only such proportions in general, supposing them to hold only between such items as would help me to know them more easily. At the same time I would not restrict them to these items, so that I could apply them the better afterwards to whatever others they might fit. Next I observed that in order to know these proportions I would need sometimes to consider them separately, and sometimes merely to keep them in mind or understand many together. And I thought that in order the better to consider them separately I should suppose them to hold between lines, because I did not find anything simpler, nor anything that I could represent more distinctly to my imagination and senses. But in order to keep them in mind or understand several together, I thought it necessary to designate them by the briefest possible symbols. In this way I would take over all that is best in geometrical analysis and in algebra, using the one to correct all the defects of the other.

In fact, I venture to say that by strictly observing the few rules I had chosen, I became very adept at unravelling all the questions which fall under these two sciences. So much so, in fact, that in the two or three months I spent in examining them – beginning with the simplest and most general and using each truth I found as a rule for finding further 21 truths – not only did I solve many problems which I had previously thought very difficult, but also it seemed to me towards the end that even in those cases where I was still in the dark I could determine by what means and to what extent it was possible to find a solution. This claim will not appear too arrogant if you consider that since there is only one truth concerning any matter, whoever discovers this truth knows as much about it as can be known. For example, if a child who has been taught arithmetic does a sum following the rules, he can be sure of having found everything the human mind can discover regarding the sum he was considering. In short, the method which instructs us to follow the correct order, and to enumerate exactly all the relevant factors, contains everything that gives certainty to the rules of arithmetic.

But what pleased me most about this method was that by following it I was sure in every case to use my reason, if not perfectly, at least as well as was in my power. Moreover, as I practised the method I felt my mind gradually become accustomed to conceiving its objects more clearly and distinctly; and since I did not restrict the method to any particular subject-matter, I hoped to apply it as usefully to the problems of the other sciences as I had to those of algebra. Not that I would have dared to try at the outset to examine every problem that might arise, for that would itself have been contrary to the order which the method prescribes. But observing that the principles of these sciences must all be derived from

22 philosophy, in which I had not yet discovered any certain ones, I thought that first of all I had to try to establish some certain principles in philosophy. And since this is the most important task of all, and the one in which precipitate conclusions and preconceptions are most to be feared, I thought that I ought not try accomplish it until I had reached a more mature age than twenty-three, as I then was, and until I had first spent a long time in preparing myself for it. I had to uproot from my mind all the wrong opinions I had previously accepted, amass a variety of experiences to serve as the subject-matter of my reasonings, and practise constantly my self-prescribed method in order to strengthen myself more and more in its use.

Part Three

Now, before starting to rebuild your house, it is not enough simply to pull it down, to make provision for materials and architects (or else train yourself in architecture), and to have carefully drawn up the plans; you must also provide yourself with some other place where you can live comfortably while building is in progress. Likewise, lest I should remain indecisive in my actions while reason obliged me to be so in my judgements, and in order to live as happily as I could during this time, I formed for myself a provisional moral code consisting of just three or four maxims, which I should like to tell you about.

23   The first was to obey the laws and customs of my country, holding constantly to the religion in which by God's grace I had been instructed from my childhood, and governing myself in all other matters according to the most moderate and least extreme opinions – the opinions commonly accepted in practice by the most sensible of those with whom I should have to live. For I had begun at this time to count my own opinions as worthless, because I wished to submit them all to examination, and so I was sure I could do no better than follow those of the most sensible men. And although there may be men as sensible among the Persians or Chinese as among ourselves, I thought it would be most useful for me to be guided by those with whom I should have to live. I thought too that in order to discover what opinions they really held I had to attend to what they did rather than what they said. For with our declining standards of behaviour, few people are willing to say everything that they believe; and besides, many people do not know what they believe, since believing something and knowing that one believes it are different acts of thinking, and the one often occurs without the other. Where many opinions were equally well accepted, I chose only the most moderate, both because these are always the easiest to act upon and

probably the best (excess being usually bad), and also so that if I made a mistake, I should depart less from the right path than I would if I chose one extreme when I ought to have pursued the other. In particular, I 24 counted as excessive all promises by which we give up some of our freedom. It was not that I disapproved of laws which remedy the inconstancy of weak minds by allowing us to make vows or contracts that oblige perseverance in some worthy project (or even, for the security of commerce, in some indifferent one). But I saw nothing in the world which remained always in the same state, and for my part I was determined to make my judgements more and more perfect, rather than worse. For these reasons I thought I would be sinning against good sense if I were to take my previous approval of something as obliging me to regard it as good later on, when it had perhaps ceased to be good or I no longer regarded it as such.

My second maxim was to be as firm and decisive in my actions as I could, and to follow even the most doubtful opinions, once I had adopted them, with no less constancy than if they had been quite certain. In this respect I would be imitating a traveller who, upon finding himself lost in a forest, should not wander about turning this way and that, and still less stay in one place, but should keep walking as straight as he can in one direction, never changing it for slight reasons even if mere chance made him choose it in the first place; for in this way, even if he does not go exactly where he wishes, he will at least end up in a place where he is 25 likely to be better off than in the middle of a forest. Similarly, since in everyday life we must often act without delay, it is a most certain truth that when it is not in our power to discern the truest opinions, we must follow the most probable. Even when no opinions appear more probable than any others, we must still adopt some; and having done so we must then regard them not as doubtful, from a practical point of view, but as most true and certain, on the grounds that the reason which made us adopt them is itself true and certain. By following this maxim I could free myself from all the regrets and remorse which usually trouble the consciences of those weak and faltering spirits who allow themselves to set out on some supposedly good course of action which later, in their inconstancy, they judge to be bad.

My third maxim was to try always to master myself rather than fortune, and change my desires rather than the order of the world. In general I would become accustomed to believing that nothing lies entirely within our power except our thoughts, so that after doing our best in dealing with matters external to us, whatever we fail to achieve is absolutely impossible so far as we are concerned. This alone, I thought, would be sufficient to prevent me from desiring in future something I

could not get, and so to make me content. For our will naturally tends to
26 desire only what our intellect represents to it as somehow possible; and
so it is certain that if we consider all external goods as equally beyond
our power, we shall not regret the absence of goods which seem to be our
birthright when we are deprived of them through no fault of our own,
any more than we regret not possessing the kingdom of China or of
Mexico. Making a virtue of necessity, as they say, we shall not desire to
be healthy when ill or free when imprisoned, any more than we now
desire to have bodies of a material as indestructible as diamond or wings
to fly like the birds. But I admit that it takes long practice and repeated
meditation to become accustomed to seeing everything in this light. In
this, I believe, lay the secret of those philosophers who in earlier times
were able to escape from the dominion of fortune and, despite suffering
and poverty, rival their gods in happiness. Through constant reflection
upon the limits prescribed for them by nature, they became perfectly
convinced that nothing was in their power but their thoughts, and this
alone was sufficient to prevent them from being attracted to other things.
Their mastery over their thoughts was so absolute that they had reason to
count themselves richer, more powerful, freer and happier than other
men who, because they lack this philosophy, never achieve such mastery
27 over all their desires, however favoured by nature and fortune they may
be.

Finally, to conclude this moral code, I decided to review the various
occupations which men have in this life, in order to try to choose the best.
Without wishing to say anything about the occupations of others, I
thought I could do no better than to continue with the very one I was
engaged in, and devote my whole life to cultivating my reason and
advancing as far as I could in the knowledge of the truth, following the
method I had prescribed for myself. Since beginning to use this method I
had felt such extreme contentment that I did not think one could enjoy
any sweeter or purer one in this life. Every day I discovered by its means
truths which, it seemed to me, were quite important and were generally
unknown by other men; and the satisfaction they gave me so filled my
mind that nothing else mattered to me. Besides, the sole basis of the
foregoing three maxims was the plan I had to continue my self-
instruction. For since God has given each of us a light to distinguish truth
from falsehood, I should not have thought myself obliged to rest content
with the opinions of others for a single moment if I had not intended in
due course to examine them using my own judgement; and I could not
have avoided having scruples about following these opinions, if I had not
28 hoped to lose no opportunity to discover better ones, in case there were
any. Lastly, I could not have limited my desires, or been happy, had I not

been following a path by which I thought I was sure to acquire all the knowledge of which I was capable, and in this way all the true goods within my reach. For since our will tends to pursue or avoid only what our intellect represents as good or bad, we need only to judge well in order to act well, and to judge as well as we can in order to do our best – that is to say, in order to acquire all the virtues and in general all the other goods we can acquire. And when we are certain of this, we cannot fail to be happy.

Once I had established these maxims and set them on one side together with the truths of faith, which have always been foremost among my beliefs, I judged that I could freely undertake to rid myself of all the rest of my opinions. As I expected to be able to achieve this more readily by talking with other men than by staying shut up in the stove-heated room where I had had all these thoughts, I set out on my travels again before the end of winter. Throughout the following nine years I did nothing but roam about in the world, trying to be a spectator rather than an actor in all the comedies that are played out there. Reflecting especially upon the points in every subject which might make it suspect and give occasion for us to make mistakes, I kept uprooting from my mind any errors that might previously have slipped into it. In doing this I was not copying the 29 sceptics, who doubt only for the sake of doubting and pretend to be always undecided; on the contrary, my whole aim was to reach certainty – to cast aside the loose earth and sand so as to come upon rock or clay. In this I think I was quite successful. For I tried to expose the falsity or uncertainty of the propositions I was examining by clear and certain arguments, not by weak conjectures; and I never encountered any proposition so doubtful that I could not draw from it some quite certain conclusion, if only the conclusion that it contained nothing certain. And, just as in pulling down an old house we usually keep the remnants for use in building a new one, so in destroying all those opinions of mine that I judged ill-founded I made various observations and acquired many experiences which I have since used in establishing more certain opinions. Moreover, I continued practising the method I had prescribed for myself. Besides taking care in general to conduct all my thoughts according to its rules, I set aside some hours now and again to apply it more particularly to mathematical problems. I also applied it to certain other problems which I could put into something like mathematical form by detaching them from all the principles of the other sciences, which I did not find sufficiently secure (as you will see I have done in many problems discussed later in this book). Thus, while appearing to live like 30 those concerned only to lead an agreeable and blameless life, who take care to keep their pleasures free from vices, and who engage in every honest pastime in order to enjoy their leisure without boredom, I never stopped pursuing my project, and I made perhaps more progress in the knowledge of the truth than I would have if I had done nothing but read books or mix with men of letters.

Those nine years passed by, however, without my taking any side regarding the questions which are commonly debated among the learned, or beginning to search for the foundations of any philosophy more certain than the commonly accepted one. The example of many fine intellects who had previously had this project, but had not, I thought, met with success, made me imagine the difficulties to be so great that I would not have dared to embark upon it so soon if I had not noticed that some people were spreading the rumour that I had already completed it. I cannot say what basis they had for this opinion. If I contributed anything to it by my conversation, it must have been because I confessed my ignorance more ingenuously than is customary for those with a little learning, and perhaps also because I displayed the reasons I had for doubting many things which others regard as certain, rather than because I boasted of some learning. But as I was honest enough not to wish to be taken for what I was not, I thought I had to try by every means to become

31   worthy of the reputation that was given me. Exactly eight years ago this desire made me resolve to move away from any place where I might have acquaintances and retire to this country, where the long duration of the war has led to the establishment of such order that the armies maintained here seem to serve only to make the enjoyment of the fruits of peace all the more secure.[1] Living here, amidst this great mass of busy people who are more concerned with their own affairs than curious about those of others, I have been able to lead a life as solitary and withdrawn as if I were in the most remote desert, while lacking none of the comforts found in the most populous cities.

Part Four

I do not know whether I should tell you of the first meditations that I had there, for they are perhaps too metaphysical and uncommon for everyone's taste. And yet, to make it possible to judge whether the foundations I have chosen are firm enough, I am in a way obliged to speak of them. For a long time I had observed, as noted above, that in practical life it is sometimes necessary to act upon opinions which one knows to be quite uncertain just as if they were indubitable. But since I now wished to devote myself solely to the search for truth, I thought it necessary to do

1 Descartes settled in Holland in 1629. The war was that conducted by the United Provinces against Spain from 1572 to 1648.

the very opposite and reject as if absolutely false everything in which I could imagine the least doubt, in order to see if I was left believing anything that was entirely indubitable. Thus, because our senses some- 32 times deceive us, I decided to suppose that nothing was such as they led us to imagine. And since there are men who make mistakes in reasoning, committing logical fallacies concerning the simplest questions in geometry, and because I judged that I was as prone to error as anyone else, I rejected as unsound all the arguments I had previously taken as demonstrative proofs. Lastly, considering that the very thoughts we have while awake may also occur while we sleep without any of them being at the that time true, I resolved to pretend that all the things that had ever entered my mind were no more true than the illusions of my dreams. But immediately I noticed that while I was trying thus to think everything false, it was necessary that I, who was thinking this, was something. And observing that this truth *'I am thinking, therefore I exist'* was so firm and sure that all the most extravagant suppositions of the sceptics were incapable of shaking it, I decided that I could accept it without scruple as the first principle of the philosophy I was seeking.

Next I examined attentively what I was. I saw that while I could pretend that I had no body and that there was no world and no place for me to be in, I could not for all that pretend that I did not exist. I saw on the contrary that from the mere fact that I thought of doubting the truth of other things, it followed quite evidently and certainly that I existed; whereas if I had merely ceased thinking, even if everything else I had ever 33 imagined had been true, I should have had no reason to believe that I existed. From this I knew I was a substance whose whole essence or nature is simply to think, and which does not require any place, or depend on any material thing, in order to exist. Accordingly this 'I' – that is, the soul by which I am what I am – is entirely distinct from the body, and indeed is easier to know than the body, and would not fail to be whatever it is, even if the body did not exist.

After this I considered in general what is required of a proposition in order for it to be true and certain; for since I had just found one that I knew to be such, I thought that I ought also to know what this certainty consists in. I observed that there is nothing at all in the proposition *'I am thinking, therefore I exist'* to assure me that I am speaking the truth, except that I see very clearly that in order to think it is necessary to exist. So I decided that I could take it as a general rule that the things we conceive very clearly and very distinctly are all true; only there is some difficulty in recognizing which are the things that we distinctly conceive.

Next, reflecting upon the fact that I was doubting and that consequently my being was not wholly perfect (for I saw clearly that it is a

greater perfection to know than to doubt), I decided to inquire into the source of my ability to think of something more perfect than I was; and I
34 recognized very clearly that this had to come from some nature that was in fact more perfect. Regarding the thoughts I had of many other things outside me, like the heavens, the earth, light, heat and numerous others, I had no such difficulty in knowing where they came from. For I observed nothing in them that seemed to make them superior to me; and so I could believe that, if they were true, they depended on my nature in so far as it had any perfection, and if they were not true, I got them from nothing – in other words, they were in me because I had some defect. But the same could not hold for the idea of a being more perfect than my own. For it was manifestly impossible to get this from nothing; and I could not have got it from myself since it is no less contradictory that the more perfect should result from the less perfect, and depend on it, than that something should proceed from nothing. So there remained only the possibility that the idea had been put into me by a nature truly more perfect than I was and even possessing in itself all the perfections of which I could have any idea, that is – to explain myself in one word – by God. To this I added that since I knew of some perfections that I did not possess, I was not the only being which existed (here, by your leave, I shall freely use some scholastic terminology), but there had of necessity to be some other, more perfect being on which I depended and from which I had acquired all that I possessed. For if I had existed alone and independently of every other
35 being, so that I had got from myself what little of the perfect being I participated in, then for the same reason I could have got from myself everything else I knew I lacked, and thus been myself infinite, eternal, immutable, omniscient, omnipotent; in short, I could have had all the perfections which I could observe to be in God. For, according to the arguments I have just advanced, in order to know the nature of God, as far as my own nature was capable of knowing it, I had only to consider, for each thing of which I found in myself some idea, whether or not it was a perfection to possess it; and I was sure that none of those which indicated any imperfection was in God, but that all the others were. Thus I saw that doubt, inconstancy, sadness and the like could not be in God, since I myself would have been very glad to be free from them. Besides this, I had ideas of many corporeal things capable of being perceived by the senses; for even if I were to suppose that I was dreaming and that whatever I saw or imagined was false, yet I could not deny that the ideas were truly in my mind. But since I had already recognized very clearly from my own case that the intellectual nature is distinct from the corporeal, and as I observed that all composition is evidence of dependence and that dependence is manifestly a defect, I concluded that it could

not be a perfection in God to be composed of these two natures, and consequently that he was not composed of them. But if there were any bodies in the world, or any intelligences or other natures that were not wholly perfect, their being must depend on God's power in such a 36 manner that they could not subsist for a single moment without him.

After that, wishing to seek other truths, I considered the object studied by geometers. I conceived of this as a continuous body, or a space indefinitely extended in length, breadth and height or depth, and divisible into different parts which may have various shapes and sizes, and may be moved or transposed in every way: for all this is assumed by geometers in their object of study. I went through some of their simpler demonstrations and noted that the great certainty which everyone ascribes to them is founded solely on their being conceived as evident (in accordance with the rule stated above). I noted also that there was nothing at all in these demonstrations which assured me of the existence of their object. For example, I saw clearly that the three angles of any given triangle must equal two right angles; yet for all that, I saw nothing which assured me that there existed any triangle in the world. Whereas when I looked again at the idea I had of a perfect being, I found that this included existence in the same way as – or even more evidently than – the idea of a triangle includes the equality of its three angles to two right angles, or the idea of a sphere includes the equidistance of all the points on the surface from the centre. Thus I concluded that it is at least as certain as any geometrical proof that God, who is this perfect being, is or exists.

But many are convinced that there is some difficulty in knowing God, 37 and even in knowing what their soul is. The reason for this is that they never raise their minds above things which can be perceived by the senses: they are so used to thinking of things only by imagining them (a way of thinking specially suited to material things) that whatever is unimaginable seems to them unintelligible. This is sufficiently obvious from the fact that even the scholastic philosophers take it as a maxim that there is nothing in the intellect which has not previously been in the senses; and yet it is certain that the ideas of God and of the soul have never been in the senses. It seems to me that trying to use one's imagination in order to understand these ideas is like trying to use one's eyes in order to hear sounds or smell odours – though there is this difference, that the sense of sight gives us no less assurance of the reality of its objects than do the senses of smell and hearing, while neither our imagination nor our senses could ever assure us of anything without the intervention of our intellect.

Finally, if there are still people who are not sufficiently convinced of the existence of God and of their soul by the arguments I have proposed,

I would have them know that everything else of which they may think themselves more sure – such as their having a body, there being stars and an earth, and the like – is less certain. For although we have a moral
38 certainty[1] about these things, so that it seems we cannot doubt them without being extravagant, nevertheless when it is a question of metaphysical certainty, we cannot reasonably deny that there are adequate grounds for not being entirely sure about them. We need only observe that in sleep we may imagine in the same way that we have a different body and see different stars and a different earth, without there being any of these things. For how do we know that the thoughts which come to us in dreams are any more false than the others, seeing that they are often no less lively and distinct? However much the best minds study this question, I do not believe they will be able to give any reason sufficient to remove this doubt unless they presuppose the existence of God. For in the first place, what I took just now as a rule, namely that everything we conceive very clearly and very distinctly is true, is assured only for the reasons that God is or exists, that he is a perfect being, and that everything in us comes from him. It follows that our ideas or notions, being real things and coming from God, cannot be anything but true, in every respect in which they are clear and distinct. Thus, if we frequently have ideas containing some falsity, this can happen only because there is something confused and obscure in them, for in that respect they participate in nothingness, that is, they are in us in this confused state only because we are not wholly perfect. And it is evident that it is no less
39 contradictory that falsity or imperfection as such should proceed from God than that truth or perfection should proceed from nothingness. But if we did not know that everything real and true within us comes from a perfect and infinite being then, however clear and distinct our ideas were, we would have no reason to be sure that they had the perfection of being true.

But once the knowledge of God and the soul has made us certain of this rule, it is easy to recognize that the things we imagine in dreams should in no way make us doubt the truth of the thoughts we have when awake. For if one happened even in sleep to have some very distinct idea (if, say, a geometer devised some new proof), one's being asleep would not prevent the idea from being true. And as to the most common error of our dreams, which consists in their representing various objects to us in the same way as our external senses do, it does not matter that this gives us occasion to doubt the truth of such ideas, for often they can also mislead us without our being asleep – as when those with jaundice see

1 See footnote 2, p. 289 below.

everything coloured yellow, or when stars or other very distant bodies appear to us much smaller than they are. For after all, whether we are awake or asleep, we ought never to let ourselves be convinced except by the evidence of our reason. It will be observed that I say 'our reason', not 'our imagination' or 'our senses'. Even though we see the sun very 40 clearly, we must not judge on that account that it is only as large as we see it; and we can distinctly imagine a lion's head on a goat's body without having to conclude from this that a chimera exists in the world. For reason does not insist that what we thus see or imagine is true. But it does insist that all our ideas or notions must have some foundation of truth; for otherwise it would not be possible that God, who is all-perfect and all-truthful, should have placed them in us. And our reasonings are never so evident or complete in sleep as in waking life, although sometimes our imaginings in sleep are as lively and distinct as in waking life, or more so. Hence reason also demands that, since our thoughts cannot all be true because we are not wholly perfect, what truth they do possess must inevitably be found in the thoughts we have when awake, rather than in our dreams.

Part Five

I would gladly go on and reveal the whole chain of other truths that I deduced from these first ones. But in order to do this I would have to discuss many questions that are being debated among the learned, and I do not wish to quarrel with them. So it will be better, I think, for me not to do this, and merely to say in general what these questions are, so as to let those who are wiser decide whether it would be useful for the public to be informed more specifically about them. I have always remained firm 41 in the resolution I had taken to assume no principle other than the one I have just used to demonstrate the existence of God and of the soul, and to accept nothing as true which did not seem to me clearer and more certain than the demonstrations of the geometers had hitherto seemed. And yet I venture to say that I have found a way to satisfy myself within a short time about all the principal difficulties usually discussed in philosophy. What is more, I have noticed certain laws which God has so established in nature, and of which he has implanted such notions in our minds, that after adequate reflection we cannot doubt that they are exactly observed in everything which exists or occurs in the world. Moreover, by considering what follows from these laws it seems to me that I have discovered many truths more useful and important than anything I had previously learned or even hoped to learn.

I endeavoured to explain the most important of these truths in a

treatise which certain considerations prevent me from publishing, and I know of no better way to make them known than by summarizing its contents.[1] My aim was to include in it everything I thought I knew about the nature of material things before I began to write it. Now a painter cannot represent all the different sides of a solid body equally well on his flat canvas, and so he chooses one of the principal ones, sets it facing the
42 light, and shades the others so as to make them stand out only when viewed from the perspective of the chosen side. In just the same way, fearing that I could not put everything I had in mind into my discourse, I undertook merely to expound quite fully what I understood about light. Then, as the occasion arose, I added something about the sun and fixed stars, because almost all light comes from them; about the heavens, because they transmit light; about planets, comets and the earth, because they reflect light; about terrestrial bodies in particular, because they are either coloured or transparent or luminous; and finally about man, because he observes these bodies. But I did not want to bring these matters too much into the open, for I wished to be free to say what I thought about them without having either to follow or to refute the accepted opinions of the learned. So I decided to leave our world wholly for them to argue about, and to speak solely of what would happen in a new world. I therefore supposed that God now created, somewhere in imaginary spaces, enough matter to compose such a world; that he variously and randomly agitated the different parts of this matter so as to form a chaos as confused as any the poets could invent; and that he then did nothing but lend his regular concurrence to nature, leaving it to act according to the laws he established. First of all, then, I described this matter, trying to represent it so that there is absolutely nothing, I think, which is clearer and more intelligible, with the exception of what has just
43 been said about God and the soul. In fact I expressly supposed that this matter lacked all those forms or qualities about which they dispute in the Schools, and in general that it had only those features the knowledge of which was so natural to our souls that we could not even pretend not to know them. Further, I showed what the laws of nature were, and without basing my arguments on any principle other than the infinite perfections of God, I tried to demonstrate all those laws about which we could have any doubt, and to show that they are such that, even if God created many worlds, there could not be any in which they failed to be observed. After this, I showed how, in consequence of these laws, the greater part of the matter of this chaos had to become disposed and arranged in a certain way, which made it resemble our heavens; and how, at the same time,

1 The treatise of which *The World* and the *Treatise on Man* are parts. See pp. 79–108 above.

some of its parts had to form an earth, some planets and comets, and others a sun and fixed stars. Here I dwelt upon the subject of light, explaining at some length the nature of the light that had to be present in the sun and the stars, how from there it travelled instantaneously across the immense distances of the heavens, and how it was reflected from the planets and comets to the earth. To this I added many points about the substance, position, motions and all the various qualities of these heavens and stars; and I thought I had thereby said enough to show that for anything observed in the heavens and stars of our world, something wholly similar had to appear, or at least could appear, in those of the world I was describing. From that I went on to speak of the earth in 44 particular: how, although I had expressly supposed that God had put no gravity into the matter of which it was formed, still all its parts tended exactly towards its centre; how, there being water and air on its surface, the disposition of the heavens and heavenly bodies (chiefly the moon), had to cause an ebb and flow similar in all respects to that observed in our seas, as well as a current of both water and air from east to west like the one we observe between the tropics; how mountains, seas, springs and rivers could be formed naturally there, and how metals could appear in mines, plants grow in fields, and generally how all the bodies we call 'mixed' or 'composite' could come into being there. Among other things, I took pains to make everything belonging to the nature of fire very clearly understandable, because I know nothing else in the world, apart from the heavenly bodies, that produces light. Thus I made clear how it is formed and fuelled, how sometimes it possesses only heat without light, and sometimes light without heat; how it can produce different colours and various other qualities in different bodies; how it melts some bodies and hardens others; how it can consume almost all bodies, or turn them into ashes and smoke; and finally how it can, by the mere force of its action, form glass from these ashes – something I took particular 45 pleasure in describing since it seems to me as wonderful a transmutation as any that takes place in nature.

Yet I did not wish to infer from all this that our world was created in the way I proposed, for it is much more likely that from the beginning God made it just as it had to be. But it is certain, and it is an opinion commonly accepted among theologians, that the act by which God now preserves it is just the same as that by which he created it. So, even if in the beginning God had given the world only the form of a chaos, provided that he established the laws of nature and then lent his concurrence to enable nature to operate as it normally does, we may believe without impugning the miracle of creation that by this means alone all purely material things could in the course of time have come to be just as we now see them. And their nature is much easier to conceive if we see them develop gradually in this way than if we consider them only in their completed form.

From the description of inanimate bodies and plants I went on to describe animals, and in particular men. But I did not yet have sufficient knowledge to speak of them in the same manner as I did of the other things – that is, by demonstrating effects from causes and showing from what seeds and in what manner nature must produce them. So I contented myself with supposing that God formed the body of a man
46 exactly like our own both in the outward shape of its limbs and in the internal arrangement of its organs, using for its composition nothing but the matter that I had described. I supposed, too, that in the beginning God did not place in this body any rational soul or any other thing to serve as a vegetative or sensitive soul, but rather that he kindled in its heart one of those fires without light which I had already explained, and whose nature I understood to be no different from that of the fire which heats hay when it has been stored before it is dry, or which causes new wine to seethe when it is left to ferment from the crushed grapes. And when I looked to see what functions would occur in such a body I found precisely those which may occur in us without our thinking of them, and hence without any contribution from our soul (that is, from that part of us, distinct from the body, whose nature, as I have said previously, is simply to think). These functions are just the ones in which animals without reason may be said to resemble us. But I could find none of the functions which, depending on thought, are the only ones that belong to us as men; though I found all these later on, once I had supposed that God created a rational soul and joined it to this body in a particular way which I described.

But so that you might see how I dealt with this subject, I shall give my explanation of the movement of the heart and the arteries. Being the first and most widespread movement that we observe in animals, it will
47 readily enable us to decide how we ought to think about all the others. But first, so there may be less difficulty in understanding what I shall say, I should like anyone unversed in anatomy to take the trouble, before reading this, to have the heart of some large animal with lungs dissected before him (for such a heart is in all respects sufficiently like that of a man), and to be shown the two chambers or cavities which are present in it. First, there is the cavity on the right, to which two very large tubes are connected: these are the vena cava, which is the principal receptacle of the blood and is like the trunk of a tree of which all the other veins of the body are the branches; and the arterial vein (ill-named because it is really an artery), which originates in the heart and after leaving it divides into

many branches that spread throughout the lungs. Then there is the cavity on the left, likewise connected to two tubes which are as large as the others or even larger: the venous artery (also ill-named because it is nothing but a vein), which comes from the lungs where it is divided into many branches intertwined with those of the arterial vein and with those of the windpipe (as it is called) through which the air we breathe enters; and the great artery which goes out from the heart and sends its branches throughout the body. I should also like the reader to be shown the eleven little membranes which, like so many little doors, open and close the four openings within these two cavities. Three are situated at the entrance to   48 the vena cava in such a way that they cannot prevent the blood contained in it from flowing into the right-hand cavity, and yet they effectively prevent it from flowing out. Three at the entrance to the arterial vein do just the opposite, readily permitting the blood in the right-hand cavity to pass into the lungs, but not permitting the blood in the lungs to return into it. Likewise two others at the entrance to the venous artery allow the blood in the lungs to flow into the left-hand cavity of the heart, but block its return; and three at the entrance to the great artery permit blood to leave the heart but prevent it from returning. There is no need to seek any reason for the number of these membranes beyond the fact that the opening to the venous artery, being oval because of its location, can easily be closed with two of them, whereas the other openings, being round, can be closed more effectively with three. I should like the reader also to observe that the great artery and the arterial vein have a much harder and firmer composition than the venous artery and the vena cava, and that the latter widen out before entering the heart to form two pouches, called the auricles, which are composed of flesh similar to that of the heart. He will observe that there is always more heat in the heart than in any other place in the body, and finally, that this heat is capable of causing a drop of blood to swell and expand as soon as it enters a   49 cavity of the heart, just as liquids generally do when they are poured drop by drop into some vessel which is very hot.

After that, I need say little in order to explain the movement of the heart. When its cavities are not full of blood, some blood necessarily flows from the vena cava into the right-hand cavity and from the venous artery into the left-hand cavity, for these two vessels are always full of blood and their entrances, which open into the heart, cannot be blocked. But as soon as two drops of blood have entered the heart in this way, one in each of its cavities, these drops, which must be very large because the openings through which they enter are very wide and the vessels from which they come are very full of blood, are rarefied and expand because of the heat they find there. In this way they make the whole heart swell,

and they push against and close the five little doors at the entrance to the two vessels from which they come, thus preventing any more blood from descending to the heart. Continuing to become more and more rarefied, they push open the six other little doors at the entrance to the other two vessels, going out through them and thereby causing all the branches of the arterial vein and of the great artery to swell almost at the same instant as the heart. Immediately afterwards, the heart contracts, as do these arteries as well, because the blood that entered them grows cold, and their six little doors close again while the five doors of the vena cava and
50 the venous artery reopen and allow the passage of two further drops of blood, which immediately makes the heart and the arteries swell, exactly as before. And it is because the blood thus entering the heart passes through the two pouches called the auricles that their movement is contrary to that of the heart, and they contract when it swells. Now those who are ignorant of the force of mathematical demonstrations and unaccustomed to distinguishing true reasons from probable may be tempted to reject this explanation without examining it. To prevent this, I would advise them that the movement I have just explained follows from the mere arrangement of the parts of the heart (which can be seen with the naked eye), from the heat in the heart (which can be felt with the fingers), and from the nature of the blood (which can be known through observation). This movement follows just as necessarily as the movement of a clock follows from the force, position, and shape of its counter-weights and wheels.

One may ask, however, why the blood in the veins is not used up as it flows continually into the heart, and why the arteries are never too full of blood, since all the blood that passes through the heart flows through them. To this I need give no reply other than that already published by an English physician, who must be praised for having broken the ice on this subject.[1] He is the first to teach that there are many small passages at the extremities of the arteries, through which the blood they receive from the heart enters the small branches of the veins, from there going immediately back to the heart, so that its course is nothing but a
51 perpetual circulation. He proves this very effectively by reference to the normal practice of surgeons, who bind an arm moderately tightly above a vein they have opened, so as to make the blood flow out more abundantly than if they had not bound the arm. But just the opposite happens if they bind the arm below, between the hand and the opening, or even if they bind it very tightly above the opening. For it is obvious that a moderately tight tourniquet can prevent the blood that is already

1 William Harvey (1578–1657), whose book on the circulation of the blood, *De Motu Cordis*, was published in 1628 and read by Descartes in 1632.

in the arm from returning to the heart through the veins, but does not prevent fresh blood from coming through the arteries. There are two reasons for this: first, the arteries are situated below the veins and their walls are harder and hence less easily compressed; and second, the blood which comes from the heart tends to flow through the arteries to the hand with more force than it does in returning to the heart through the veins. And since this blood comes out of the arm through an opening in one of the veins, there must necessarily be some passages below the tourniquet (that is, towards the extremity of the arm) through which it may flow from the arteries. Harvey also proves very soundly what he says about the circulation of the blood by pointing to certain small membranes which are arranged in various places along the veins in such a way that they do not permit the blood to pass from the middle of the body towards the extremities but only let it return from the extremities towards the heart. He proves his theory, moreover, by an experiment which shows that all the blood in the body can flow out of it in a very short time through a single artery, even if the artery is tightly bound close to the heart and cut between the heart and the tourniquet so that no one 52 could have any reason to imagine that the blood drained off comes from anywhere but the heart.

But there are many other facts which prove that the true cause of this movement of the blood is the one I have given.[1] First, there is the difference we see between the blood which flows from the veins and that which flows from the arteries. This can result only from the fact that the blood is rarefied and, as it were, distilled in passing through the heart, and is therefore thinner, livelier and warmer just after leaving it (that is, when in the arteries) than a little before entering it (that is, when in the veins). And if you look closely you will find this difference to be more evident near the heart than in places further from it. Then there is the hardness of the membranes of which the arterial vein and the great artery are composed: this shows well enough that the blood strikes against them with more force than against the veins. And why should the left-hand cavity of the heart and the great artery be larger and wider than the right-hand cavity and the arterial vein, if not because the blood in the venous artery, having been only in the lungs after passing through the heart, is thinner and more easily rarefied than that which comes immediately from the vena cava? And what could physicians learn by feeling the pulse if they did not know that, as the nature of the blood changes, it can be rarefied by the heat of the heart more or less strongly, and more or less quickly, than before? And if we examine how this heat is

---

1 See *Description of the Human Body* (below, pp. 316ff) for Descartes' criticism of Harvey's explanation of the movement of the blood.

communicated to the other parts of the body, must we not acknowledge
53 that this happens by means of the blood, which is reheated in passing
through the heart and spreads from there through the whole body? So it
is that if we remove the blood from some part of the body, we thereupon
remove the heat as well; and even if the heart were as hot as glowing iron,
it would not be able to reheat the feet and the hands as it does unless it
continually sent new blood to these parts. Then, too, we know from this
that the true function of respiration is to bring enough fresh air into the
lungs to cause the blood entering there from the right-hand cavity of the
heart, where it has been rarefied and almost changed into vapours, to
thicken immediately into blood again before returning to the left-hand
cavity. For if this did not happen the blood would not be fit to serve as
fuel for the fire in the heart. This is confirmed by seeing that animals
without lungs have only one cavity in their hearts, and that unborn
children, who cannot use their lungs while enclosed within their mother's
womb, have an opening through which blood flows from the vena cava
into the left-hand cavity of the heart, and a tube through which blood
comes from the arterial vein into the great artery without passing
through the lungs. Again, how would digestion take place in the stomach
if the heart did not send heat there through the arteries, together with
some of the most fluid parts of the blood which help to dissolve the food
we have put there? And is it not easy to understand the action that
converts the juice of this food into blood, if we consider that the blood
passing in and out of the heart is distilled perhaps more than one or two
54 hundred times each day? Again, what more do we need in order to
explain nutrition and the production of the various humours present in
the body? We need only say that as the blood is rarefied it flows with such
force from the heart towards the extremities of the arteries that some of
its parts come to rest in parts of the body where they drive out and
displace other parts of the blood; and certain parts of the blood flow to
some places rather than others according to the situation, shape, or
minuteness of the pores that they encounter, just as sieves with holes of
various sizes serve to separate different grains from each other. But the
most remarkable of all these facts is the generation of the animal spirits:
like a very fine[1] wind, or rather a very pure and lively flame, they rise
continuously in great abundance from the heart into the brain, passing
from there through the nerves to the muscles and imparting movement to
all the parts of the body. The parts of the blood which are the most
agitated and penetrating, and hence the best suited to compose these
spirits, make their way to the brain rather than elsewhere. For this we

---

1 See footnote 2, p. 100 above.

need suppose no cause other than the fact that they are carried there by the arteries which come most directly from the heart. For according to the laws of mechanics, which are identical with the laws of nature, when many things tend to move together towards a place where there is not enough room for all of them (as when the parts of blood coming from the left-hand cavity of the heart all tend towards the brain), the weakest and 55 least agitated must be pushed aside by the strongest, which thus arrive at that place on their own.

I explained all these matters in sufficient detail in the treatise I previously intended to publish.[1] And then I showed what structure the nerves and muscles of the human body must have in order to make the animal spirits inside them strong enough to move its limbs – as when we see severed heads continue to move about and bite the earth although they are no longer alive. I also indicated what changes must occur in the brain in order to cause waking, sleep and dreams; how light, sounds, smells, tastes, heat and the other qualities of external objects can imprint various ideas on the brain through the mediation of the senses; and how hunger, thirst, and the other internal passions can also send their ideas there. And I explained which part of the brain must be taken to be the 'common' sense,[2] where these ideas are received; the memory, which preserves them; and the corporeal imagination, which can change them in various ways, form them into new ideas, and, by distributing the animal spirits to the muscles, make the parts of this body move in as many different ways as the parts of our bodies can move without being guided by the will, and in a manner which is just as appropriate to the objects of the senses and the internal passions. This will not seem at all strange to those who know how many kinds of automatons, or moving machines, the skill of man can construct with the use of very few parts, in 56 comparison with the great multitude of bones, muscles, nerves, arteries, veins and all the other parts that are in the body of any animal. For they will regard this body as a machine which, having been made by the hands of God, is incomparably better ordered than any machine that can be devised by man, and contains in itself movements more wonderful than those in any such machine.

I made special efforts to show that if any such machines had the organs and outward shape of a monkey or of some other animal that lacks reason, we should have no means of knowing that they did not possess entirely the same nature as these animals; whereas if any such machines bore a resemblance to our bodies and imitated our actions as closely as possible for all practical purposes, we should still have two very certain

1 See footnote p. 132, above.
2 Cf. *Rules*, above p. 41, and *Treatise on Man*, above pp. 104ff.

means of recognizing that they were not real men. The first is that they could never use words, or put together other signs, as we do in order to declare our thoughts to others. For we can certainly conceive of a machine so constructed that it utters words, and even utters words which correspond to bodily actions causing a change in its organs (e.g. if you touch it in one spot it asks what you want of it, if you touch it in another it cries out that you are hurting it, and so on). But it is not conceivable that such a machine should produce different arrangements of words so
57   as to give an appropriately meaningful answer to whatever is said in its presence, as the dullest of men can do. Secondly, even though such machines might do some things as well as we do them, or perhaps even better, they would inevitably fail in others, which would reveal that they were acting not through understanding but only from the disposition of their organs. For whereas reason is a universal instrument which can be used in all kinds of situations, these organs need some particular disposition for each particular action; hence it is for all practical purposes impossible for a machine to have enough different organs to make it act in all the contingencies of life in the way in which our reason makes us act.

Now in just these two ways we can also know the difference between man and beast. For it is quite remarkable that there are no men so dull-witted or stupid – and this includes even madmen – that they are incapable of arranging various words together and forming an utterance from them in order to make their thoughts understood; whereas there is no other animal, however perfect and well-endowed it may be, that can do the like. This does not happen because they lack the necessary organs, for we see that magpies and parrots can utter words as we do, and yet they cannot speak as we do: that is, they cannot show that they are thinking what they are saying. On the other hand, men born deaf and
58   dumb, and thus deprived of speech-organs as much as the beasts or even more so, normally invent their own signs to make themselves understood by those who, being regularly in their company, have the time to learn their language. This shows not merely that the beasts have less reason than men, but that they have no reason at all. For it patently requires very little reason to be able to speak; and since as much inequality can be observed among the animals of a given species as among human beings, and some animals are more easily trained than others, it would be incredible that a superior specimen of the monkey or parrot species should not be able to speak as well as the stupidest child – or at least as well as a child with a defective brain – if their souls were not completely different in nature from ours. And we must not confuse speech with the natural movements which express passions and which can be imitated by

machines as well as by animals. Nor should we think, like some of the ancients, that the beasts speak, although we do not understand their language. For if that were true, then since they have many organs that correspond to ours, they could make themselves understood by us as well as by their fellows. It is also a very remarkable fact that although many animals show more skill than we do in some of their actions, yet the same animals show none at all in many others; so what they do better does not prove that they have any intelligence, for if it did then they would have more intelligence than any of us and would excel us in everything. It 59 proves rather that they have no intelligence at all, and that it is nature which acts in them according to the disposition of their organs. In the same way a clock, consisting only of wheels and springs, can count the hours and measure time more accurately than we can with all our wisdom.

After that, I described the rational soul, and showed that, unlike the other things of which I had spoken, it cannot be derived in any way from the potentiality of matter, but must be specially created.[1] And I showed how it is not sufficient for it to be lodged in the human body like a helmsman in his ship, except perhaps to move its limbs, but that it must be more closely joined and united with the body in order to have, besides this power of movement, feelings and appetites like ours and so constitute a real man. Here I dwelt a little upon the subject of the soul, because it is of the greatest importance. For after the error of those who deny God, which I believe I have already adequately refuted, there is none that leads weak minds further from the straight path of virtue than that of imagining that the souls of the beasts are of the same nature as ours, and hence that after this present life we have nothing to fear or to hope for, any more than flies and ants. But when we know how much the beasts differ from us, we understand much better the arguments which prove that our soul is of a nature entirely independent of the body, and consequently that it is not bound to die with it. And since we cannot see 60 any other causes which destroy the soul, we are naturally led to conclude that it is immortal.

Part Six

It is now three years since I reached the end of the treatise that contains all these things. I was beginning to revise it in order to put it in the hands of a publisher, when I learned that some persons to whom I defer and who have hardly less authority over my actions than my own reason has over my thoughts, had disapproved of a physical theory published a little

1 The section of the *Treatise on Man* referred to here has not survived.

while before by someone else.[1] I will not say that I accepted this theory, but only that before their condemnation I had noticed nothing in it that I could imagine to be prejudicial either to religion or to the state, and hence nothing that would have prevented me from publishing it myself, if reason had convinced me of it. This made me fear that there might be some mistake in one of my own theories, in spite of the great care I had always taken never to adopt any new opinion for which I had no certain demonstration, and never to write anything that might work to anyone's disadvantage. That was enough to make me change my previous decision to publish my views. For although I had had very strong reasons for this decision, my inclination, which has always made me dislike the business of writing books, prompted me to find excuses enough for deciding

61   otherwise. The reasons, on one side and the other, are such that not only do I have some interest in stating them here, but also the public may be interested to know what they are.

I have never made much of the products of my own mind; and so long as the only fruits I gathered from the method I use were my own satisfaction regarding certain difficulties in the speculative sciences, or else my attempts to govern my own conduct by the principles I learned from it, I did not think I was obliged to write anything about it. For as regards conduct, everyone is so full of his own wisdom that we might find as many reformers as heads if permission to institute change in these matters were granted to anyone other than those whom God has set up as sovereigns over his people or those on whom he has bestowed sufficient grace and zeal to be prophets. As regards my speculations, although they pleased me very much, I realized that other people had their own which perhaps pleased them more. But as soon as I had acquired some general notions in physics and had noticed, as I began to test them in various particular problems, where they could lead and how much they differ from the principles used up to now, I believed that I could not keep them secret without sinning gravely against the law which obliges us to do all in our power to secure the general welfare of mankind. For they opened my eyes to the possibility of gaining knowledge which would be very useful in life, and of discovering a practical philosophy which might

62   replace the speculative philosophy taught in the schools. Through this philosophy we could know the power and action of fire, water, air, the stars, the heavens and all the other bodies in our environment, as distinctly as we know the various crafts of our artisans; and we could use this knowledge – as the artisans use theirs – for all the purposes for which it is appropriate, and thus make ourselves, as it were, the lords and

---

1 Galileo, whose *Dialogue Concerning the Two Chief World Systems* was published in 1632 and condemned by the Congregation of the Holy Office in 1633.

masters of nature. This is desirable not only for the invention of innumerable devices which would facilitate our enjoyment of the fruits of the earth and all the goods we find there, but also, and most importantly, for the maintenance of health, which is undoubtedly the chief good and the foundation of all the other goods in this life. For even the mind depends so much on the temperament and disposition of the bodily organs that if it is possible to find some means of making men in general wiser and more skilful than they have been up till now, I believe we must look for it in medicine. It is true that medicine as currently practised does not contain much of any significant use; but without intending to disparage it, I am sure there is no one, even among its practitioners, who would not admit that all we know in medicine is almost nothing in comparison with what remains to be known, and that we might free ourselves from innumerable diseases, both of the body and of the mind, and perhaps even from the infirmity of old age, if we had sufficient knowledge of their causes and of all the remedies that nature has provided. Intending as I did to devote my life to the pursuit of such 63 indispensable knowledge, I discovered a path which would, I thought, inevitably lead one to it, unless prevented by the brevity of life or the lack of observations.[1] And I judged that the best remedy against these two obstacles was to communicate faithfully to the public what little I had discovered, and to urge the best minds to try and make further progress by helping with the necessary observations, each according to his inclination and ability, and by communicating to the public everything they learn. Thus, by building upon the work of our predecessors and combining the lives and labours of many, we might make much greater progress working together than anyone could make on his own.

I also noticed, regarding observations,[1] that the further we advance in our knowledge, the more necessary they become. At the beginning, rather than seeking those which are more unusual and highly contrived, it is better to resort only to those which, presenting themselves spontaneously to our senses, cannot be unknown to us if we reflect even a little. The reason for this is that the more unusual observations are apt to mislead us when we do not yet know the causes of the more common ones, and the factors on which they depend are almost always so special and so minute that it is very difficult to discern them. But the order I have adopted in this regard is the following. First I tried to discover in general the principles or first causes of everything that exists or can exist in the 64 world. To this end I considered nothing but God alone, who created the

---

1 Fr. *expériences*, a term which Descartes often uses when talking of scientific observations, and which sometimes comes close to meaning 'experiments' in the modern sense (its root being derived from Lat. *experior*, 'to test').

world; and I derived these principles only from certain seeds of truth which are naturally in our souls. Next I examined the first and most ordinary effects deducible from these causes. In this way, it seems to me, I discovered the heavens, the stars, and an earth; and, on the earth, water, air, fire, minerals, and other such things which, being the most common of all and the simplest, are consequently the easiest to know. Then, when I sought to descend to more particular things, I encountered such a variety that I did not think the human mind could possibly distinguish the forms or species of bodies that are on the earth from an infinity of others that might be there if it had been God's will to put them there. Consequently I thought the only way of making these bodies useful to us was to progress to the causes by way of the effects and to make use of many special observations. And now, reviewing in my mind all the objects that have ever been present to my senses, I venture to say that I have never noticed anything in them which I could not explain quite easily by the principles I had discovered. But I must also admit that the power of nature is so ample and so vast, and these principles so simple and so general, that I notice hardly any particular effect of which I do not

65 know at once that it can be deduced from the principles in many different ways; and my greatest difficulty is usually to discover in which of these ways it depends on them. I know no other means to discover this than by seeking further observations whose outcomes vary according to which of these ways provides the correct explanation. Moreover, I have now reached a point where I think I can see quite clearly what line we should follow in making most of the observations which serve this purpose; but I see also that they are of such a kind and so numerous that neither my dexterity nor my income (were it even a thousand times greater than it is) could suffice for all of them. And so the advances I make in the knowledge of nature will depend henceforth on the opportunities I get to make more or fewer of these observations. I resolved to make this known in the treatise I had written, and to show clearly how the public could benefit from such knowledge. This would oblige all who desire the general well-being of mankind – that is, all who are really virtuous, not virtuous only in appearance or merely in repute – both to communicate to me the observations they have already made and to assist me in seeking those which remain to be made.

Since then, however, other considerations have made me change my mind. I have come to think that I must continue writing down anything I consider at all important, when I discover its truth, and that I should take as much care over these writings as I would if I intended to have them

66 published. For this will give me all the more reason to examine them closely, as undoubtedly we always look more carefully at something we

think is to be seen by others than at something we do only for ourselves; and often what seemed true to me when I first conceived it has looked false when I tried to put it on paper. This plan will also ensure both that I lose no opportunity to benefit the public if I can, and that if my writings have any value, those who get them after my death can make the most appropriate use of them. But I was determined not to agree to their publication during my lifetime, so that neither the opposition and controversy they might arouse, nor the reputation they might gain for me, would make me lose any of the time I planned to devote to my self-instruction. Every man is indeed bound to do what he can to procure the good of others, and a man who is of no use to anyone else is strictly worthless. Nevertheless it is also true that our concern ought to extend beyond the present, and that it is good to neglect matters which may profit the living when we aim to do other things which will benefit posterity even more. In any case I am willing to acknowledge that the little I have learned so far is almost nothing in comparison with that which I do not know but which I hope to be able to learn. Those who gradually discover the truth in the sciences are like people who become 67 rich and find they have less trouble making large profits than they had in making much smaller ones when they were poorer. Or they may be compared with military commanders, whose forces tend to grow in proportion to their victories, but who need more skill to maintain their position after losing a battle than they do to take towns and provinces after winning one. For attempting to overcome all the difficulties and errors that prevent our arriving at knowledge of the truth is indeed a matter of fighting battles: we lose a battle whenever we accept some false opinion concerning an important question of general significance, and we need much more skill afterwards to regain our former position than we do to make good progress when we already have principles which are well-founded. For my part, if I have already discovered a few truths in the sciences (and I hope that the contents of this volume warrant the judgement that I have found some), I can say that these discoveries merely result from and depend upon my surmounting of five or six principal difficulties in battles where I reckon I had fortune on my side. I even venture to say that I think I need to win only two or three other such battles in order to achieve my aims completely, and that my age is not so far advanced that I may not in the normal course of nature still have the time to do this. But the more hopeful I am of being able to use my 68 remaining years effectively, the more I think I am obliged to plan my time carefully; and many occasions for wasting time would undoubtedly arise if I published the fundamental principles of my physics. For although these principles are almost all so evident that they need only to be understood to be believed, and although I think I can demonstrate all of them, yet since it is impossible that they should accord with all the diverse opinions of other men, I foresee that I should often be distracted by the controversies they would arouse.

It may be claimed that such controversies would be useful. Not only would they make me aware of my mistakes, but also they would enable others to have a better understanding of anything worthwhile that I may have discovered; and, as many people are able to see more than one alone, so these others might begin to make use of my discoveries and help me with theirs. But although I recognize that I am extremely prone to error, and I almost never trust the first thoughts that come to me, at the same time my acquaintance with the objections that may be raised prevents me from expecting any benefit from them. For I have already had frequent experience of the judgements both of those I held to be my friends and of some I thought indifferent towards me, and even of certain others whose malice and envy would, I knew, make them eager enough to reveal what affection would hide from my friends. But it has rarely happened that an objection has been raised which I had not wholly

69 foreseen, except when it was quite wide of the mark. Thus I have almost never encountered a critic of my views who did not seem to be either less rigorous or less impartial than myself. Nor have I ever observed that any previously unknown truth has been discovered by means of the disputations practised in the schools. For so long as each side strives for victory, more effort is put into establishing plausibility than in weighing reasons for and against; and those who have long been good advocates do not necessarily go on to make better judges.

As for the benefit that others might gain from the communication of my thoughts, this could not be so very great. For I have not yet taken them sufficiently far: I need to add many things to them before applying them in practice. And I think I can say without vanity that if anyone is capable of making these additions it must be myself rather than someone else – not that there may not be many minds in the world incomparably better than mine, but because no one can conceive something so well, and make it his own, when he learns it from someone else as when he discovers it himself. This is especially true in the case under consideration. I have often explained some of my opinions to highly intelligent persons who seemed to understand them quite distinctly when I told them about them; but, when they repeated them, I observed that they almost always changed them in such a way that I could no longer

70 acknowledge them as my own. For this reason I should like to beg future generations never to believe that I am the source of an opinion they hear unless I have published it myself. I do not wonder at the absurdities

attributed to all the ancient philosophers whose writings we do not possess; nor do I conclude from these attributions that their thoughts were highly unreasonable. As they were some of the best minds of their time, I conclude rather that their thoughts have been misreported. We see too that it has almost never happened that any of their followers has surpassed them; and I am sure that Aristotle's most passionate contemporary followers would count themselves fortunate if they had as much knowledge of nature as he had, even on the condition that they should never know any more. They are like ivy, which never seeks to climb higher than the trees which support it, and often even grows downward after reaching the tree-tops. For it seems to me that they too take downward steps, or become somehow less knowledgeable than if they refrained from study, when, not content with knowing everything which is intelligibly explained in their author's writings, they wish in addition to find there the solution to many problems about which he says nothing and about which perhaps he never thought. But this manner of philosophizing is very convenient for those with only mediocre minds, for the obscurity of the distinctions and principles they use makes it possible for them to speak about everything as confidently as if they knew it, and to defend all they say against the most subtle and clever thinkers without 71 anyone having the means to convince them that they are wrong. In this they seem to resemble a blind man who, in order to fight without disadvantage against someone who can see, lures him into the depths of a very dark cellar. These philosophers, I may say, have an interest in my refraining from publishing the principles of the philosophy I use. For my principles are so very simple and evident that in publishing them I should, as it were, be opening windows and admitting daylight into that cellar where they have gone down to fight. But even the best minds have no reason to wish to know my principles. For if they want to be able to speak about everything and acquire the reputation of being learned, they will achieve this more readily by resting content with plausibility, which can be found without difficulty in all kinds of subjects, than by seeking the truth; for the truth comes to light only gradually in certain subjects, and it obliges us frankly to confess our ignorance where other subjects are concerned. But if they prefer the knowledge of some few truths to the vanity of appearing ignorant of nothing (and undoubtedly the former is preferable), and if they wish to follow a plan similar to mine, then in that case I need tell them nothing more than I have already said in this discourse. For if they are capable of making further progress than I have made, they will be all the more capable of discovering for themselves everything I think I have discovered. Inasmuch as I have examined everything in an orderly manner, it is certain that what still remains for

72   me to discover is in itself more difficult and more hidden than anything I
      have thus far been able to discover; and they would have much less
      pleasure in learning it from me than in learning it for themselves. Besides,
      by investigating easy matters first and then moving on gradually to more
      difficult ones, they will acquire habits more useful to them than all my
      instructions could be. For my part, I am convinced that if from my youth
      I had been taught all the truths I have since sought to demonstrate, and so
      had learned them without any difficulty, I should perhaps never have
      known any others; or at least I should never have acquired the habit 'and
      facility, which I think I have, for always finding new truths whenever I
      apply myself in searching for them. In short, if there was ever a task
      which could not be accomplished so well by someone other than the
      person who began it, it is the one on which I am working.

      True, as regards observations which may help in this work, one man
      could not possibly make them all. But also he could not usefully employ
      other hands than his own, except those of artisans, or such persons as he
      could pay, who would be led by the hope of gain (a most effective motive)
      to do precisely what he ordered them to do. For voluntary helpers, who
      might offer to help him from curiosity or a desire to learn, usually
      promise more than they achieve and make fine proposals which never
73   come to anything. In addition, they would inevitably wish to be rewarded
      by having certain difficulties explained to them, or at any rate by
      compliments and useless conversation, which could not but waste a lot of
      his time. And as for the observations that others have already made, even
      if they were willing to communicate them to him (something which those
      who call them 'secrets' would never do), they are for the most part bound
      up with so many details or superfluous ingredients that it would be very
      hard for him to make out the truth in them. Besides, he would find almost
      all of these observations to be so badly explained or indeed so mistaken –
      because those who made them were eager to have them appear to
      conform with their principles – that it would simply not be worthwhile
      for him to spend the time required to pick out those which he might find
      useful. So if there were someone in the world whom we knew for sure to
      be capable of making discoveries of the greatest possible importance and
      public utility, and whom other men accordingly were eager to help in
      every way to achieve his ends, I do not see how they could do anything
      for him except to contribute towards the expenses of the observations
      that he would need and, further, prevent unwelcome visitors from
      wasting his free time. But I am not so presumptuous that I wish to
      promise anything extraordinary, nor do I entertain thoughts so vain as
      the supposition that the public ought to take a great interest in my
      projects. Apart from that, I am not so mean-spirited that I would

willingly accept from anyone a favour that I might be thought not to   74
deserve.

All these considerations taken together caused me to decide, three years ago, that I did not wish to publish the treatise I had ready then, and made me resolve not to publish any other work during my lifetime which was so general in scope or by which the foundations of my physics might be understood. Since then, however, two further reasons have compelled me to include here some essays on particular topics and to give to the public some account of my actions and plans. The first is that, if I failed to do so, then many who knew of my earlier intention to publish certain writings might suppose that my reasons for not doing so were more discreditable to me than they are. I am not excessively fond of glory – indeed if I dare to say so, I dislike it in so far as I regard it as opposed to that tranquillity which I value above everything else. At the same time I have never tried to conceal my actions as if they were crimes, or taken many precautions to remain unknown. For if I had done this I thought I would do myself an injustice, and moreover that would have given me a certain sort of disquiet, which again would have been opposed to the perfect peace of mind I am seeking. And since my indifference as to whether I was well-known or not made it unavoidable that I should gain some sort of reputation, I thought I ought to do my best at least to avoid getting a bad one. The other reason compelling me to write this is that   75 every day I am becoming more and more aware of the delay which my project of self-instruction is suffering because of the need for innumerable observations which I cannot possibly make without the help of others. Although I do not flatter myself with any expectation that the public will share my interests, yet at the same time I am unwilling to be so unfaithful to myself as to give those who come after me cause to reproach me some day on the grounds that I could have left them many far better things if I had not been so remiss in making them understand how they could contribute to my projects.

I thought it convenient for me to choose certain subjects which, without being highly controversial and without obliging me to reveal more of my principles than I wished, would nonetheless show quite clearly what I can, and what I cannot, achieve in the sciences. I cannot tell if I have succeeded in this, and I do not wish to anticipate anyone's judgements about my writings by speaking about them myself. But I shall be very glad if they are examined. In order to provide more opportunity for this, I beg all who have any objections to take the trouble to send them to my publisher, and when he informs me about them I shall attempt to append my reply at the same time, so that readers can see both sides together, and decide the truth all the more easily. I do not promise

76 to make very long replies, but only to acknowledge my errors very frankly if I recognize them; and where I cannot see them I shall simply say what I consider is required for defending what I have written, without introducing any new material, so as to avoid getting endlessly caught up in one topic after another.

Should anyone be shocked at first by some of the statements I make at the beginning of the *Optics* and the *Meteorology* because I call them 'suppositions' and do not seem to care about proving them, let him have the patience to read the whole book attentively, and I trust that he will be satisfied. For I take my reasonings to be so closely interconnected that just as the last are proved by the first, which are their causes, so the first are proved by the last, which are their effects. It must not be supposed that I am here committing the fallacy that the logicians call 'arguing in a circle'. For as experience makes most of these effects quite certain, the causes from which I deduce them serve not so much to prove them as to explain them; indeed, quite to the contrary, it is the causes which are proved by the effects. And I have called them 'suppositions' simply to make it known that I think I can deduce them from the primary truths I have expounded above; but I have deliberately avoided carrying out these deductions in order to prevent certain ingenious persons from taking the opportunity to construct, on what they believe to be my principles, some extravagant philosophy for which I shall be blamed. These persons imagine that they can learn in a single day what it has taken someone else twenty years to think out, as soon as he has told them only two or three words about it; whereas the more penetrating and

77 acute they are, the more prone to error they are and the less capable of truth. As to the opinions that are wholly mine, I do not apologize for their novelty. If the reasons for them are considered well, I am sure they will be found to be so simple and so much in agreement with common sense as to appear less extraordinary and strange than any other views that people may hold on the same subjects. I do not boast of being the first to discover any of them, but I do claim to have accepted them not because they have, or have not, been expressed by others, but solely because reason has convinced me of them.

If artisans are not immediately able to put into operation the invention explained in the *Optics*, I do not think it can on that account be said to be defective.[1] For much skill and practice are needed for making and adjusting the machines I have described, and although my description does not omit any details, I should be no less astonished if they succeeded at the first attempt than if someone could learn to play the lute excellently

---

1 Here Descartes refers to the method of cutting lenses described in Discourse 10 of the *Optics*.

in a single day simply by being given a good fingering chart. And if I am writing in French, my native language, rather than Latin, the language of my teachers, it is because I expect that those who use only their natural reason in all its purity will be better judges of my opinions than those who give credence only to the writings of the ancients. As to those who combine good sense with application – the only judges I wish to have – I am sure they will not be so partial to Latin that they will refuse to listen to my arguments because I expound them in the vernacular. 78

For the rest, I do not wish to speak here in detail about the further progress I hope to make in the sciences, or to commit myself in the eyes of the public by making any promise that I am not sure of fulfilling. I will say only that I have resolved to devote the rest of my life to nothing other than trying to acquire some knowledge of nature from which we may derive rules in medicine which are more reliable than those we have had up till now. Moreover, my inclination makes me so strongly opposed to all other projects, and especially to those which can be useful to some persons only by harming others, that if circumstances forced me to engage in any such pursuit, I do not think I would be capable of succeeding in it. Of this I make here a public declaration, fully recognizing that it cannot serve to make me eminent in the world; but then I have no desire to be such. And I shall always hold myself more obliged to those by whose favour I enjoy uninterrupted leisure than to any who might offer me the most honourable positions in the world.

OPTICS

DISCOURSE ONE: LIGHT

The conduct of our life depends entirely on our senses, and since sight is the noblest and most comprehensive of the senses, inventions which serve to increase its power are undoubtedly among the most useful there can be. And it is difficult to find any such inventions which do more to increase the power of sight than those wonderful telescopes which, though in use for only a short time, have already revealed a greater number of new stars and other new objects above the earth than we had seen there before. Carrying our vision much further than our forebears could normally extend their imagination, these telescopes seem to have opened the way for us to attain a knowledge of nature much greater and

(82) more perfect than they possessed . . . But inventions of any complexity do not reach their highest degree of perfection right away, and this one is still sufficiently problematical to give me cause to write about it. And since the construction of the things of which I shall speak must depend on the skill of craftsmen, who usually have little formal education, I shall try

83 to make myself intelligible to everyone; and I shall try not to omit anything, or to assume anything that requires knowledge of other sciences. This is why I shall begin by explaining light and light-rays; then, having briefly described the parts of the eye, I shall give a detailed account of how vision comes about; and, after noting all the things which are capable of making vision more perfect, I shall show how they can be aided by the inventions which I shall describe.

Now since my only reason for speaking of light here is to explain how its rays enter into the eye, and how they may be deflected by the various bodies they encounter, I need not attempt to say what is its true nature. It will, I think, suffice if I use two or three comparisons in order to facilitate that conception of light which seems most suitable for explaining all those of its properties that we know through experience and then for deducing all the others that we cannot observe so easily. In this I am imitating the astronomers, whose assumptions are almost all false or uncertain, but who nevertheless draw many very true and certain consequences from them because they are related to various observations they have made.

No doubt you have had the experience of walking at night over rough ground without a light, and finding it necessary to use a stick in order to guide yourself. You may then have been able to notice that by means of 84 this stick you could feel the various objects situated around you, and that you could even tell whether they were trees or stones or sand or water or grass or mud or any other such thing. It is true that this kind of sensation is somewhat confused and obscure in those who do not have long practice with it. But consider it in those born blind, who have made use of it all their lives: with them, you will find, it is so perfect and so exact that one might almost say that they see with their hands, or that their stick is the organ of some sixth sense given to them in place of sight. In order to draw a comparison from this, I would have you consider the light in bodies we call 'luminous' to be nothing other than a certain movement, or very rapid and lively action, which passes to our eyes through the medium of the air and other transparent bodies, just as the movement or resistance of the bodies encountered by a blind man passes to his hand by means of his stick. In the first place this will prevent you from finding it strange that this light can extend its rays instantaneously from the sun to us. For you know that the action by which we move one end of a stick must pass instantaneously to the other end, and that the action of light would have to pass from the heavens to the earth in the same way, even though the distance in this case is much greater than that between the ends of a stick. Nor will you find it strange that by means of this action we can see all sorts of colours. You may perhaps even be 85 prepared to believe that in the bodies we call 'coloured' the colours are nothing other than the various ways in which the bodies receive light and reflect it against our eyes. You have only to consider that the differences a blind man notes between trees, rocks, water and similar things by means of his stick do not seem any less to him than the differences between red, yellow, green and all the other colours seem to us. And yet in all those bodies the differences are nothing other than the various ways of moving the stick or of resisting its movements. Hence you will have reason to conclude that there is no need to suppose that something material passes from objects to our eyes to make us see colours and light, or even that there is something in the objects which resembles the ideas or sensations that we have of them. In just the same way, when a blind man feels bodies, nothing has to issue from the bodies and pass along his stick to his hand; and the resistance or movement of the bodies, which is the sole cause of the sensations he has of them, is nothing like the ideas he forms of them. By this means, your mind will be delivered from all those little

images flitting through the air, called 'intentional forms',[1] which so
exercise the imagination of the philosophers. You will even find it easy to
settle the current philosophical debate concerning the origin of the action
which causes visual perception. For, just as our blind man can feel the
86 bodies around him not only through the action of these bodies when they
move against his stick, but also through the action of his hand when they
do nothing but resist the stick, so we must acknowledge that the objects
of sight can be perceived not only by means of the action in them which is
directed towards our eyes, but also by the action in our eyes which is
directed towards them. Nevertheless, because the latter action is nothing
other than light, we must note that it is found only in the eyes of those
creatures which can see in the dark, such as cats, whereas a man normally
sees only through the action which comes from the objects. For experience shows us that these objects must be luminous or illuminated in order
to be seen, and not that our eyes must be luminous or illuminated in
order to see them. But because our blind man's stick differs greatly from
the air and the other transparent bodies through the medium of which we
see, I must make use of yet another comparison.

Consider a wine-vat at harvest time, full to the brim with half-pressed
grapes, in the bottom of which we have made one or two holes through
which the unfermented wine can flow.[2] Now observe that, since there is
no vacuum in nature (as nearly all philosophers acknowledge), and yet
87 there are many pores in all the bodies we perceive around us (as
experience can show quite clearly), it is necessary that these pores be
filled with some very subtle and very fluid matter, which extends without
interruption from the heavenly bodies to us. Now, if you compare this
subtle matter with the wine in the vat, and compare the less fluid or
coarser parts of the air and the other transparent bodies with the bunches
of grapes which are mixed in with the wine, you will readily understand
the following. The parts of wine at one place tend to go down in a
straight line through one hole at the very instant it is opened, and at the
same time through the other hole, while the parts at other places also
tend at the same time to go down through these two holes, without these
actions being impeded by each other or by the resistance of the bunches
of grapes in the vat. This happens even though the bunches support each
other and so do not tend in the least to go down through the holes, as
does the wine, and at the same time they can even be moved in many
other ways by the bunches which press upon them. In the same way, all
the parts of the subtle matter in contact with the side of the sun facing us

1 A reference to the scholastic doctrine that material objects transmit to the soul 'forms' or
'images' (Fr. *espèces*, Lat. *species*) resembling them.
2 A diagram of the wine-vat is omitted here.

tend in a straight line towards our eyes at the very instant they are opened, without these parts impeding each other, and even without their being impeded by the coarser parts of the transparent bodies which lie between them. This happens whether these bodies move in other ways – like the air which is almost always agitated by some wind – or are motionless – say, like glass or crystal. And note here that it is necessary to 88 distinguish between the movement and the action or the tendency to move. For we may very easily conceive that the parts of wine at one place should tend towards one hole and at the same time towards the other, even though they cannot actually move towards both holes at the same time, and that they should tend exactly in a straight line towards one and towards the other, even though they cannot move exactly in a straight line because of the bunches of grapes which are between them. In the same way, considering that the light of a luminous body must be regarded as being not so much its movement as its action, you must think of the rays of light as nothing other than the lines along which this action tends. Thus there is an infinity of such rays which come from all the points of a luminous body towards all the points of the bodies it illuminates, just as you can imagine an infinity of straight lines along which the 'actions' coming from all the points of the surface of the wine tend towards one hole, and an infinity of others along which the 'actions' coming from the same points tend also towards the other hole, without either impeding the other.

Moreover, these rays must always be imagined to be exactly straight when they pass through a single transparent body which is uniform throughout. But when they meet certain other bodies, they are liable to be deflected by them, or weakened, in the same way that the movement of a ball or stone thrown into the air is deflected by the bodies it 89 encounters. For it is very easy to believe that the action or tendency to move (which, I have said, should be taken for light) must in this respect obey the same laws as motion itself. In order that I may give a complete account of this third comparison, consider that a ball passing through the air may encounter bodies that are soft or hard or fluid. If these bodies are soft, they completely stop the ball and check its movement, as when it strikes linen sheets or sand or mud. But if they are hard, they send the ball in another direction without stopping it, and they do so in many different ways. For their surface may be quite even and smooth, or rough and uneven; if even, either flat or curved; if uneven, its unevenness may consist merely in its being composed of many variously curved parts, each quite smooth in itself, or also in its having many different angles or points, or some parts harder than others, or parts which are moving (their movements being varied in a thousand imaginable ways). And it must be noted that the ball, besides moving in the simple and ordinary way which takes it from one place to another, may move in yet a second way, turning on its axis, and that the speed of the latter movement may have many different relations with that of the former. Thus, when many balls coming from the same direction meet a body whose surface is completely 90 smooth and even, they are reflected uniformly and in the same order, so that if this surface is completely flat they keep the same distance between them after having met it as they had beforehand; and if it is curved inward or outward they come towards each other or go away from each (91) other in the same order, more or less, on account of this curvature ... It is necessary to consider, in the same manner, that there are bodies which break up the light-rays that meet them and take away all their force (*viz.*, bodies called 'black', which have no colour other than that of shadows); and there are others which cause the rays to be reflected, some in the same order as they receive them (*viz.* bodies with highly polished surfaces, which can serve as mirrors, both flat and curved), and others in 92 many directions in complete disarray. Among the latter, again, some bodies cause the rays to be reflected without bringing about any other change in their action (*viz.* bodies we call 'white'), and others bring about an additional change similar to that which the movement of a ball undergoes when we graze it (*viz.* bodies which are red, or yellow, or blue or some other such colour). For I believe I can determine the nature of each of these colours, and reveal it experimentally; but this goes beyond the limits of my subject.[1] All I need to do here is to point out that the light-rays falling on bodies which are coloured and not polished are usually reflected in every direction even if they come from only a single direction ... Finally, consider that the rays are also deflected, in the same 93 way as the ball just described, when they fall obliquely on the surface of a transparent body and penetrate this body more or less easily than the body from which they come. This mode of deflection is called 'refraction'.

DISCOURSE TWO: REFRACTION

Later on we shall need to know how to determine exactly the quantity of this refraction, and since the comparison I have just used enables this to be understood quite easily, I think it appropriate for me to try to explain it here without more ado. I shall speak first about reflection, in order to make it easier to understand refraction. Let us suppose that a ball impelled by a tennis racquet from A to B meets at point B the surface of the ground CBE, which stops its further passage and causes it to be deflected; and let us see in what direction it will go [Fig. 1]. To avoid

1 Cf. *Description of the Human Body*, p. 323 below.

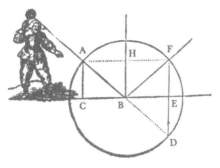

Fig. 1

getting involved in new difficulties, let us assume that the ground is perfectly flat and hard, and that the ball always travels at a constant speed, both in its downward passage and in rebounding, leaving aside entirely the question of the power which continues to move it when it is 94 no longer in contact with the racquet, and without considering any effect of its weight, size or shape. For there is no point in going into such details here, since none of these factors is involved in the action of light to which the present inquiry must be related. It is only necessary to note that the power, whatever it may be, which causes the ball to continue moving is different from that which determines it to move in one direction rather than another. It is very easy to recognize this from the fact that the movement of the ball depends upon the force with which it has been impelled by the racquet, and this same force could have made it move in any other direction as easily as towards B; whereas the ball's tending towards B is determined by the position of the racquet, which could have determined the ball in the same way even if a different force had moved it. This shows already that it is not impossible for the ball to be deflected by its encounter with the ground, and hence that there could be a change in its determination to tend towards B without any change in the force of its movement, since these are two different things. Consequently we must not imagine, as many of our philosophers do, that it is necessary for the ball to stop at point B for a moment before returning towards F. For if its motion were once interrupted by such a halt, no cause could be found which would make it start up again afterwards. Moreover, it must be noted that not only the determination to move in a certain direction but 95 also the motion itself, and in general any sort of quantity, can be divided into all the parts of which we can imagine that it is composed. And we can easily imagine that the determination of the ball to move from A towards B is composed of two others, one making it descend from line AF towards line CE and the other making it at the same time go from the left AC towards the right FE, so that these two determinations joined together direct it to B along the straight line AB. And then it is easy to understand that its encounter with the ground can prevent only one of these two determinations, leaving the other quite unaffected. For it must indeed prevent the one which made the ball descend from AF towards CE, because the ground occupies all the space below CE. But why should it prevent the other, which made the ball move to the right, seeing that it is not at all opposed to the determination in that direction? So, to discover in precisely what direction the ball must rebound, let us describe a circle, with its centre at B, which passes through point A; and let us say that in as much time as the ball will take to move from A to B, it must inevitably return from B to a certain point on the circumference of the circle. This holds in so far as the circumference contains all the points

96   which are as far from B as A is, and the ball is supposed to be moving always at a constant speed. Next, in order to determine precisely to which point on the circumference the ball must return, let us draw three straight lines AC, HB, and FE, perpendicular to CE, so that the distance between AC and HB is neither greater nor less than that between HB and FE. And let us say that in as much time as the ball took to move towards the right side from A (one of the points on the line AC) to B (one of those on the line HB), it must also advance from the line HB to some point on the line FE. For all the points on the line FE are equidistant from the corresponding points on HB, as are those on line AC; and also the ball is as much determined to advance towards that side as it was before. So it is that the ball cannot arrive simultaneously both at some point on the line FE and at some point on the circumference of the circle AFD, unless this point is either D or F, as these are the only two points where the circumference and the line intersect. Accordingly, since the ground prevents the ball from passing towards D, it is necessary to conclude that it must inevitably go towards F. And so you can easily see how reflection takes place, namely at an angle always equal to the one we call the angle of incidence. In the same way, if a light-ray coming from point A falls at point B on the surface of a flat mirror CBE, it is reflected towards F in such manner that the angle of reflection FBE is neither greater nor less than the angle of incidence ABC.

97   We come now to refraction. First let us suppose that a ball impelled from A towards B encounters at point B not the surface of the earth, but a linen sheet CBE which is so thin and finely woven that the ball has enough force to puncture it and pass right through, losing only some of its speed (say, a half) in doing so. Now given this, in order to know what path it must follow, let us consider again that its motion is entirely different from its determination to move in one direction rather than

another – from which it follows that the quantity of these two factors must be examined separately. And let us also consider that, of the two parts of which we can imagine this determination to be composed, only the one which was making the ball tend in a downward direction can be changed in any way through its colliding with the sheet, while the one which was making the ball tend to the right must always remain the same as it was, because the sheet offers no opposition at all to the determination in this direction. Then, having described the circle AFD with its centre at B [Fig. 2], and having drawn at right angles to CBE the three straight lines AC, HB, FE so that the distance between FE and HB is twice that between HB and AC, we shall see that the ball must tend towards the point I. For, since the ball loses half its speed in passing through the sheet CBE, it must take twice as much time to descend from B to some point on   98 the circumference of the circle AFD as it took to go from A to B above the sheet. And since it loses none of its former determination to advance to the right, in twice the time it took to pass from the line AC to HB it must cover twice the distance in the same direction, and consequently it must arrive at some point on the straight line FE simultaneously with its reaching some point on the circumference of the circle AFD. This would be impossible if it did not go towards I, as this is the only point below the sheet CBE where the circle AFD and the straight line FE intersect.

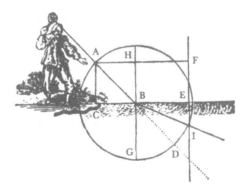

Fig. 2

Now let us suppose that the ball coming from A towards D does not strike a sheet at point B, but rather a body of water, the surface of which reduces its speed by exactly a half, as did the sheet. The other conditions being given as before, I say that this ball must pass from B in a straight line not towards D, but towards I. For, in the first place, it is certain that the surface of the water must deflect it towards that point in the same

way as the sheet, seeing that it reduces the force of the ball by the same
amount, and that it is opposed to the ball in the same direction. Then, as
for the rest of the body of water which fills all the space between B and I,
99   although it resists the ball more or less than did the air which we
supposed there before, we should not say for this reason that it must
deflect it more or less. For the water may open up to make way for the
ball just as easily in one direction as in another, at least if we always
assume, as we do, that the ball's course is not changed by its heaviness or
lightness, or by its size or shape or any other such extraneous cause. And
we may note here that the deflection of the ball by the surface of the
water or the sheet is greater, the more oblique the angle at which it
encounters it, so that if it encounters it at a right angle (as when it is
impelled from H towards B) it must pass beyond in a straight line
towards G without being deflected at all. But if it is impelled along a line
such as AB [Fig. 3], which is so sharply inclined to the surface of the
water or sheet CBE that the line FE (drawn as before) does not intersect
the circle AD, the ball ought not to penetrate it at all, but ought to
rebound from its surface B towards the air L, in the same way as if it had
struck the earth at that point. People have sometimes experienced this to
their regret when, firing artillery pieces towards the bottom of a river for
fun, they have wounded those on the shore at the other side.

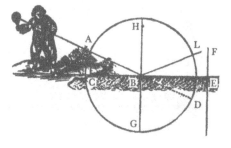

Fig. 3

But let us make yet another assumption here, and suppose that the ball,
100   having been first impelled from A to B, is again impelled at point B by the
racquet CBE which increases the force of its motion, say by a third, so
that it can then make as much headway in two seconds as it previously
made in three. This will have the same effect as if the ball were to meet at
point B a body of such nature that it could pass through its surface CBE
one-third again more easily than through the air [Fig. 4]. And it follows
manifestly from what has already been demonstrated that if you describe
the circle AD as before, and the lines AC, HB, FE so that there is a third

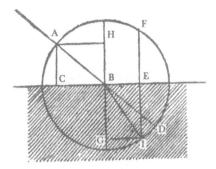

Fig. 4

less distance between FE and HB than between HB and AC, then point I, where the straight line FE and the circular line AD intersect, will indicate the position towards which the ball must be deflected when at point B.

Now we can also draw the converse of this conclusion and say that since the ball which comes in a straight line from A to B is deflected when at point B and moves on towards I, this means that the force or ease with which it penetrates the body CBEI is related to that with which it leaves the body ACBE as the distance between AC and HB is related to that between HB and FI – that is, as the line CB is to BE.

Finally, in so far as the action of light in this respect obeys the same laws as the movement of the ball, it must be said that when its rays pass obliquely from one transparent body into another, which they penetrate more or less easily than the first, they are deflected in such a way that their inclination to the surface between these bodies is always less sharp on the side of the more easily penetrated body, and the degree of this inclination varies exactly in proportion to the varying degrees of penetrability of the respective bodies.[1] Only it must be noted carefully that this inclination has to be measured by the quantity of the straight lines (CB or AH, EB or IG, and the like) compared to each other, not by that of angles such as ABH or GBI, and still less by that of angles like DBI which we call 'angles of refraction'. For the ratio or proportion between these angles varies with all the different inclinations of the rays, whereas that between the lines AH and IG, or the like, remains the same in all refractions caused by the same bodies. Thus, for example [Fig. 5], suppose a ray passes through the air from A towards B and, meeting the surface of a lens CBR at point B, is deflected towards I in this lens; and

1 Without stating it explicitly, Descartes here enunciates the law now known as Snell's Law, according to which *sin i = n sin r*, where *i* is the angle of incidence, *r* the angle of refraction, and *n* a constant specific to the refractive medium. Cf. letter to Mersenne, June 1632.

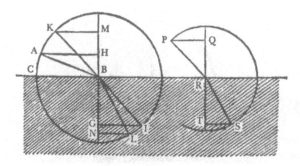

Fig. 5

suppose another ray coming from K towards B is deflected towards L, and another coming from P towards R is deflected towards S. In this case there must be the same proportion between the lines KM and LN, or PQ and ST, as between AH and IG, but not the same between the angles KBM and LBN, or PRQ and SRT, as between ABH and IBG.

102   So now you see the way in which refractions have to be measured. Although we need to refer to experience in order to determine their quantity, in so far as it depends on the particular nature of the bodies in which they occur, nonetheless we can do this easily enough and with sufficient certainty since all refractions are reduced in this way to a common measure. In fact, to discover all the refractions occurring at a given surface, it suffices to examine only those of a single ray, and we can avoid every error if in addition we examine the refractions in several other rays. So, if we wish to know the quantity of the refractions which occur at the surface CBR, separating the air AKP from the lens LIS, we need only determine the refraction of the ray ABI by examining the proportion between lines AH and IG. Then, if we suspect we have failed in this experiment, we must determine the refraction in several other rays, like KBL or PRS; and if we find the same proportion between KM and LN, and between PQ and ST, as between AH and IG, we shall have no further cause to doubt the truth of our observation.

When you make these observations, however, you will perhaps be amazed to find that light-rays are more sharply inclined in air than in water, at the surfaces where their refraction occurs, and still more in water than in glass; while just the opposite occurs in the case of a ball, 103 which is inclined more sharply in water than in air, and which cannot pass through glass at all. For example [Fig. 6], if a ball impelled through the air from A towards B meets a surface of water CBE at point B, it will be deflected from B towards V; and in the case of a ray, it will go in quite a different direction, from B towards I. You will no longer find this strange, however, if you recall the nature that I ascribed to light, when I

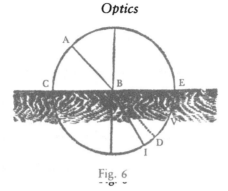

Fig. 6

said it is nothing but a certain movement or an action received in a very subtle matter which fills the pores of other bodies. And you should consider too that, just as a ball loses more of its motion in striking a soft body than a hard one and rolls less easily on a carpet than on a completely bare table, so the action of this subtle matter can be impeded much more by the parts of the air (which, being as it were soft and badly joined, do not offer it much resistance) than by those of water, which offer it more resistance; and still more by those of water than by those of glass, or of crystal. Thus, in so far as the minute parts of a transparent body are harder and firmer, the more easily they allow the light to pass; for the light does not have to drive any of them out of their places, as a ball must expel the parts of water in order to find a passage through them.

Moreover, knowing in this way the cause of the refractions which 104 occur in water and glass and generally in all the other transparent bodies around us, we can note that the refractions occurring when the rays emerge from these bodies must be wholly similar to those occurring when they enter them. So, if the ray coming from A towards B is deflected from B towards I in passing from the air into a lens, the one which returns from I towards B must also be deflected from B towards A. Nevertheless other bodies may well be found (chiefly in the sky) in which refractions result from other causes, and so are not reciprocal in this way. And certain cases may also be found in which the rays must be curved, though they merely pass through a single transparent body, just as the motion of a ball is often curved because it is deflected in one direction by its weight and in another by the action with which we have impelled it, or for various other reasons. For in the end, I venture to say, the three comparisons which I have just used are so appropriate that all the particular features which may be observed in them correspond to certain features which prove to be entirely similar in the case of light; but I have tried to explain only those which have the most bearing on my subject. And I do not wish to have you consider anything else here, except that

the surfaces of transparent bodies which are curved deflect the rays
105 passing through each of their points in the same way as would the flat
surfaces that we can imagine touching these bodies at the same points.
So, for example [Fig. 7], the refractions of the rays AB, AC, AD, which

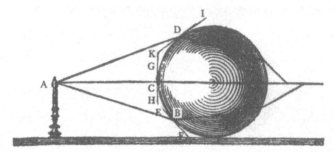

Fig. 7

come from the flame A and fall on the curved surface of the crystal ball
BCD, must be regarded in the same way as if AB fell on flat surface EBF,
AC on GHC, and AD on IDK, and likewise for the others. From this you
can see that these rays may be variously focussed or dispersed, according
as they fall on surfaces which are differently curved. But now it is time for
me to begin describing the structure of the eye, so as to enable you to
understand how the rays which enter it are so disposed there as to cause
visual perception ...[1]

109   DISCOURSE FOUR: THE SENSES IN GENERAL

Now I must tell you something about the nature of the senses in general,
the more easily to explain that of sight in particular. We know for certain
that it is the soul which has sensory perceptions, and not the body. For
when the soul is distracted by an ecstasy or deep contemplation, we see
that the whole body remains without sensation, even though it has
various objects touching it. And we know that it is not, properly
speaking, because of its presence in the parts of the body which function
as organs of the external senses that the soul has sensory perceptions, but
because of its presence in the brain, where it exercises the faculty called
the 'common' sense.[2] For we observe injuries and diseases which attack
the brain alone and impede all the senses generally, even though the rest
of the body continues to be animated. We know, lastly, that it is through

1 Discourse Three, on the eye, is omitted here. For an English version of this and material
   omitted below, see *Descartes: Discourse on Method, Optics, Geometry and Meteorology*, tr. P. J. Olscamp (Indianapolis: Bobbs-Merrill, 1965).
2 Cf. *Rules*, p. 41 above, and *Passions*, pp. 341ff below. ·

the nerves that the impressions formed by objects in the external parts of the body reach the soul in the brain. For we observe various accidents which cause injury only to a nerve, and destroy sensation in all the parts of the body to which this nerve sends its branches, without causing it to diminish elsewhere . . .[1] We must take care not to assume – as our (112) philosophers commonly do – that in order to have sensory perceptions the soul must contemplate certain images[2] transmitted by objects to the brain; or at any rate we must conceive the nature of these images in an entirely different manner from that of the philosophers. For since their conception of the images is confined to the requirement that they should resemble the objects they represent, the philosophers cannot possibly show us how the images can be formed by the objects, or how they can be received by the external sense organs and transmitted by the nerves to the brain. Their sole reason for positing such images was that they saw how easily a picture can stimulate our mind to conceive the objects depicted in it, and so it seemed to them that, in the same way, the mind must be stimulated, by little pictures formed in our head, to conceive the objects that affect our senses. We should, however, recall that our mind can be stimulated by many things other than images – by signs and words, for example, which in no way resemble the things they signify. And if, in order to depart as little as possible from accepted views, we prefer to maintain that the objects which we perceive by our senses really send images of themselves to the inside of our brain, we must at least 113 observe that in no case does an image have to resemble the object it represents in all respects, for otherwise there would be no distinction between the object and its image. It is enough that the image resembles its object in a few respects. Indeed the perfection of an image often depends on its not resembling its object as much as it might. You can see this in the case of engravings: consisting simply of a little ink placed here and there on a piece of paper, they represent to us forests, towns, people, and even battles and storms; and although they make us think of countless different qualities in these objects, it is only in respect of shape that there is any real resemblance. And even this resemblance is very imperfect, since engravings represent to us bodies of varying relief and depth on a surface which is entirely flat. Moreover, in accordance with the rules of perspective they often represent circles by ovals better than by other circles, squares by rhombuses better than by other squares, and similarly for other shapes. Thus it often happens that in order to be more perfect as

---

1 There follows an account of the function of the nerves and animal spirits in producing sensation and movement. Cf. *Treatise on Man*, AT XI 132ff and *Passions*, pp. 331–8 below.
2 See footnote 1, p. 154 above.

an image and to represent an object better, an engraving ought not to resemble it. Now we must think of the images formed in our brain in just the same way, and note that the problem is to know simply how they can enable the soul to have sensory perceptions of all the various qualities of the objects to which they correspond – not to know how they can
114 resemble these objects. For instance, when our blind man touches bodies with his stick, they certainly do not transmit anything to him except in so far as they cause his stick to move in different ways according to the different qualities in them, thus likewise setting in motion the nerves in his hand, and then the regions of his brain where these nerves originate. This is what occasions his soul to have sensory perception of just as many different qualities in these bodies as there are differences in the movements caused by them in his brain.

DISCOURSE FIVE: THE IMAGES WHICH ARE FORMED ON THE BACK OF THE EYE

You see, then, that in order to have sensory perceptions the soul does not need to contemplate any images resembling the things which it perceives. And yet, for all that, the objects we look at do imprint quite perfect images of themselves on the back of our eyes. This has been very ingeniously explained by the following comparison. Suppose a chamber is all shut up apart from a single hole, and a glass lens is placed in front of this hole with a white sheet stretched at a certain distance behind it so that the light coming from objects outside forms images on the sheet.
115 Now it is said that the room represents the eye; the hole, the pupil; the lens, the crystalline humour, or rather all the parts of the eye which cause some refraction; and the sheet, the internal membrane, which is composed of the optic nerve-endings.

But you may become more certain of this if, taking the eye of a newly dead person (or failing that, the eye of an ox or some other large animal), you carefully cut away the three surrounding membranes at the back so as to expose a large part of the humour without spilling any. Then cover the hole with some white body thin enough to let light pass through (e.g. a piece of paper or an egg-shell), and put this eye in the hole of a specially made shutter so that its front faces a place where there are various objects lit up by the sun, and its back faces the inside of the room where you are standing. (No light must enter the room except what comes through this eye, all of whose parts you know to be entirely transparent.) Having done this, if you look at the white body you will see there, not perhaps without wonder and pleasure, a picture representing in natural perspective all the
116 objects outside – at any rate you will if you ensure that the eye keeps its

natural shape, according to the distance of the objects (for if you squeeze   117
it just a little more or less than you ought, the picture becomes less
distinct) . . .[1]

Now, when you have seen this picture in the eye of a dead animal, and   (124)
considered its causes, you cannot doubt that a quite similar picture is
formed in the eye of a living person, on the internal membrane for which
we substituted the white body – indeed, a much better one is formed
there since the humours in this eye are full of animal spirits and so are
more transparent and more exactly of the shape necessary for this to
occur. (And also, perhaps in the eye of an ox the shape of the pupil,
which is not round, prevents the picture from being so perfect.) . . .

The images of objects are not only formed in this way at the back of   (128)
the eye but also pass beyond into the brain . . .[2]

DISCOURSE SIX: VISION   130

Now, when this picture thus passes to the inside of our head, it still bears
some resemblance to the objects from which it proceeds. As I have amply
shown already, however, we must not think that it is by means of this
resemblance that the picture causes our sensory perception of these
objects – as if there were yet other eyes within our brain with which we
could perceive it. Instead we must hold that it is the movements
composing this picture which, acting directly upon our soul in so far as it
is united to our body, are ordained by nature to make it have such
sensations. I will explain this in more detail. All the qualities which we
perceive in the objects of sight can be reduced to six principal ones: light,
colour, position, distance, size and shape. First, regarding light and
colour (the only qualities belonging properly to the sense of sight), we
must suppose our soul to be of such a nature that what makes it have the
sensation of light is the force of the movements taking place in the
regions of the brain where the optic nerve-fibres originate, and what
makes it have the sensation of colour is the manner of these movements.   131
Likewise, the movements in the nerves leading to the ears make the soul
hear sounds; those in the nerves of the tongue make it taste flavours; and,
in general, movements in the nerves anywhere in the body make the soul
have a tickling sensation if they are moderate, and a pain when they are
too violent. But in all this there need be no resemblance between the ideas
which the soul conceives and the movements which cause these ideas.
You will readily grant this if you note that people struck in the eye seem to
see countless sparks and flashes before them, even though they shut their

1 A diagram is omitted here and the text abridged.
2 Here Descartes repeats the account given in the *Treatise on Man*, pp. 105f above.

eyes or are in a very dark place; hence this sensation can be ascribed only to the force of the blow, which sets the optic nerve-fibres in motion as a bright light would do. The same force might make us hear a sound if it affected the ears, or feel pain if it affected some other part of the body. This is also confirmed by the fact that whenever you force your eyes to look at the sun, or at some other very bright light, they retain its impression for a short time afterwards, so that even with your eyes shut you seem to see various colours which change and pass from one to another as they fade away. This can only result from the fact that the optic nerve-fibres have been set in motion with extraordinary force, and cannot come to rest as soon as they usually can. But the agitation
132   remaining in them when the eyes are shut is not great enough to represent the bright light that caused it, and thus it represents the less vivid colours. That these colours change as they fade away shows that their nature consists simply in the diversity of the movement, exactly as I have already suggested. And finally this is evidenced by the frequent appearance of colours in transparent bodies, for it is certain that nothing can cause this except the various ways in which the light-rays are received there. One example is the appearance of a rainbow in the clouds, and a still clearer example is the likeness of a rainbow seen in a piece of glass cut on many sides.

But we must consider in detail what determines the quantity of the light which is seen, i.e. the quantity of the force with which each of the optic nerve-fibres is moved. For it is not always equal to the light which is in the objects, but varies in proportion to their distance and the size of the pupil, and also in proportion to the area at the back of the eye which may
(133)   be occupied by the rays coming from each point of the object ... We must also consider that we cannot discriminate the parts of the bodies we are looking at except in so far as they differ somehow in colour; and distinct vision of these colours depends not only on the fact that all the rays coming from each point of the object converge in almost as many different points at the back of the eye, and on the fact that no rays reach the same points from elsewhere ... but also on the great number of optic nerve-fibres in the area which the image occupies at the back of the eye.
134   For example, if an object is composed of ten thousand parts capable of sending rays to a certain area at the back of the eye in ten thousand different ways, and consequently of making ten thousand colours simultaneously visible, these parts nonetheless will enable the soul to discriminate only at most a thousand colours, if we suppose that in this area there are only a thousand fibres of the optic nerve. Thus ten parts of the object, acting together upon each of the fibres, can move it in just one single way made up of all the ways in which they act, so that the area

occupied by each fibre has to be regarded as if it were only a single point. This is why a field decked out in countless different colours often appears from a distance to be all white or all blue; why, in general, all bodies are seen less distinctly from a distance than close at hand; and finally why the greater the area which we can make the image of a single object occupy at the back of the eye, the more distinctly it can be seen. We shall need to take special note of this fact later on.

As regards position, i.e. the orientation of each part of an object relative to our body, we perceive it by means of our eyes exactly as we do by means of our hands. Our knowledge of it does not depend on any image, nor on any action coming from the object, but solely on the position of the tiny parts of the brain where the nerves originate. For this position changes ever so slightly each time there is a change in the position of the limbs in which the nerves are embedded. Thus it is ordained by nature to enable the soul not only to know the place 135 occupied by each part of the body it animates relative to all the others, but also to shift attention from these places to any of those lying on the straight lines which we can imagine to be drawn from the extremity of each part and extended to infinity. In the same way, when the blind man, of whom we have already spoken so much, turns his hand A towards E [Fig. 8], or again his hand C towards E, the nerves

Fig. 8

embedded in that hand cause a certain change in his brain, and through this change his soul can know not only the place A or C but also all the other places located on the straight line AE or CE; in this way his soul can turn its attention to the objects B and D, and determine the places they occupy without in any way knowing or thinking of those which his hands occupy. Similarly, when our eye or head is turned in some direction, our soul is informed of this by the change in the brain which is caused by the nerves embedded in the muscles used for these movements. ... You must not, therefore, find it strange that objects can be seen in their true position even though the picture they imprint upon the eye is 136 inverted. This is just like our blind man's being able to feel, at one and the same time, the object B (to his right) by means of his left hand, and the object D (to his left) by means of his right hand. And as the blind man does not judge a body to be double although he touches it with his two

137 hands, so too, when both our eyes are disposed in the manner required to direct our attention to one and the same place, they need only make us see a single object there, even though a picture of it is formed in each of our eyes.

The seeing of distance depends no more than does the seeing of position upon any images emitted from objects. Instead it depends in the first place on the shape of the body of the eye. For as we have said, for us to see things close to our eyes this shape must be slightly different from the shape which enables us to see things farther away; and as we adjust the shape of the eye according to the distance of objects, we change a certain part of our brain in a manner that is ordained by nature to make our soul perceive this distance. Ordinarily this happens without our reflecting upon it – just as, for example, when we clasp some body with our hand, we adjust our hand to its size and shape and thus feel it by means of our hand without needing to think of these movements. In the second place, we know distance by the relation of the eyes to one another. Our blind man holding the two sticks AE and CE (whose length I assume he does not know) and knowing only the distance between his two hands A and C and the size of the angles ACE and CAE, can tell from this knowledge, as if by a natural geometry, where the point E is. And similarly, when our two eyes A and B are turned towards point X, the length of the line AB and the size of the two angles XAB and XBA enable

138 us to know where the point X is. We can do the same thing also with the aid of only one eye, by changing its position.[1] Thus, if we keep it turned towards X and place it first at point A and immediately afterwards at point B, this will be enough to make our imagination contain the magnitude of the line AC together with that of the two angles XAB and XBA, and thus enable us to perceive the distance from point X. And this is done by a mental act which, though only a very simple act of the imagination, involves a kind of reasoning quite similar to that used by surveyors when they measure inaccessible places by means of two different vantage points. We have yet another way of perceiving distance, namely by the distinctness or indistinctness of the shape seen, together with the strength or weakness of the light. Thus, if we gaze fixedly towards X [Fig. 9], the rays coming from objects 10 and 12 do not converge so exactly upon R or T, at the back of our eye, as they would if

1 A diagram is omitted here.

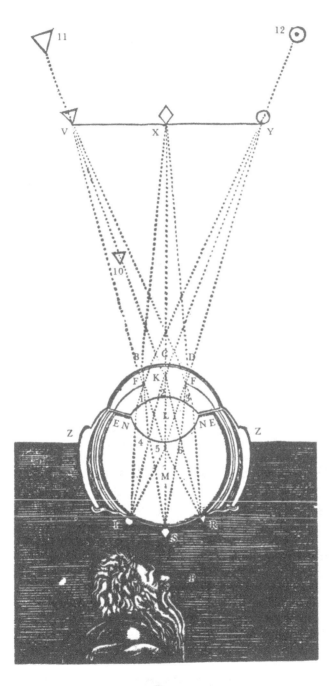

Fig. 9

these objects were at points V and Y. From this we see that they are farther from us, or nearer to us, than X. Then, the light coming from object 10 to our eye is stronger than it would be if that object were near V, and from this we judge it to be nearer; and the light coming from object 12 is weaker than it would be if it were near Y, and so we judge it to be farther away. Finally, we may already have from another source an image of an object's size, or its position, or the distinctness of its shape and its colours, or merely the strength of the light coming from it; and
139 this may enable us to imagine its distance, if not actually to see it. For
140 example, when we observe from afar some body we are used to seeing close at hand, we judge its distance much better than we would if its size were less well known to us. If we are looking at a mountain lit up by sunlight beyond a forest covered in shadow, it is solely the position of the forest that makes us judge it the nearer. And when we look at two ships out at sea, one smaller than the other but proportionately nearer so that they appear equal in size, we can use the difference in their shapes and colours, and in the light they send to us, to judge which is the more distant.

Concerning the manner in which we see the size and shape of objects, I need not say anything in particular since it is wholly included in the way we see the distance and the position of their parts. That is, we judge their size by the knowledge or opinion that we have of their distance, compared with the size of the images they imprint on the back of the eye – and not simply by the size of these images. This is sufficiently obvious from the fact that the images imprinted by objects very close to us are a hundred times bigger than those imprinted by objects ten times farther away, and yet they do not make us see the objects a hundred times larger; instead they make the objects look almost the same size, at least if their distance does not deceive us. It is obvious too that we judge shape by the knowledge or opinion that we have of the position of the various parts of an object, and not by the resemblance of the pictures in our eyes. For
141 these pictures usually contain only ovals and rhombuses when they make us see circles and squares.

But in order that you may have no doubts at all that vision works as I have explained it, I would again have you consider the reasons why it sometimes deceives us. First, it is the soul which sees, and not the eye; and it does not see directly, but only by means of the brain. That is why madmen and those who are asleep often see, or think they see, various objects which are nevertheless not before their eyes: namely, certain vapours disturb their brain and arrange those of its parts normally engaged in vision exactly as they would be if these objects were present. Then, because the impressions which come from outside pass to the 'common' sense by way of the nerves, if the position of these nerves is changed by any unusual cause, this may make us see objects in places other than where they are ... Again, because we normally judge that the (142) impressions which stimulate our sight come from places towards which we have to look in order to sense them, we may easily be deceived when they happen to come from elsewhere. Thus, those whose eyes are affected by jaundice, or who are looking through yellow glass or shut up in a room where no light enters except through such glass, attribute this colour to all the bodies they look at. And the person inside the dark room which I described earlier attributes to the white body the colours of the objects outside because he directs his sight solely upon that body. And if our eyes see objects through lenses and in mirrors, they judge them to be at points where they are not and to be smaller or larger than they are, or inverted as well as smaller (namely, when they are somewhat distant from the eyes). This occurs because the lenses and mirrors deflect the rays coming from the objects, so that our eyes cannot see the objects distinctly 143 except by making the adjustments necessary for looking towards the points in question.[1] This will readily be known by those who take the trouble to examine the matter. In the same way they will see how far the 144 ancients went wrong in their catoptrics when they tried to determine the location of the images in concave and convex mirrors. It must also be noted that all our methods for recognizing distance are highly unreliable. For the shape of the eye undergoes hardly any perceptible variation when the object is more than four or five feet away, and even when the object is nearer the shape varies so little that no very precise knowledge can be obtained from it. And if one is looking at an object at all far away, there is also hardly any variation in the angles between the line joining the two eyes (or two positions of the same eye) and the lines from the eyes to the object. As a consequence, even our 'common' sense seems incapable of receiving in itself the idea of a distance greater than approximately one or two hundred feet. This can be verified in the case of the moon and the sun. Although they are among the most distant bodies that we can see, and their diameters are to their distances roughly as one to a hundred, they normally appear to us as at most only one or two feet in diameter – although we know very well by reason that they are extremely large and extremely far away. This does not happen because we cannot conceive them as any larger, seeing that we easily conceive towers and mountains which are much larger. It happens, rather, because we cannot conceive them as more than one or two hundred feet away, and consequently their diameters cannot appear to us to be more than one or two feet. The

---

1 A diagram is omitted here, and the text is slightly condensed.

145 position of these bodies also helps to mislead us. For usually, when they are very high in the sky at midday, they seem smaller than they do when they are rising or setting, and we can notice their distance more easily because there are various objects between them and our eyes. And, by measuring them with their instruments, the astronomers prove clearly that they appear larger at one time than at another not because they are seen to subtend a greater angle, but because they are judged to be farther away. It follows that the axiom of the ancient optics – which says that the apparent size of objects is proportional to the size of the angle of vision – is not always true. We are also deceived because white or luminous bodies, and generally all those which have a great power to stimulate the sense of sight, always appear just a little nearer and larger than they would if they had less such power. The reason why such bodies appear nearer is that the movement with which the pupil contracts to avoid their strong light is so connected with the movement which disposes the whole eye to see near objects distinctly – a movement by which we judge the distance of such objects – that the one hardly ever takes place without the other occurring to some extent as well. (In the same way, we cannot fully close the first two fingers of our hand without the third bending a little too, as if to close with the others.) The reason why these white or

146 luminous bodies appear larger is not only that our estimation of their size depends on that of their distance, but also that they impress larger images on the back of the eye. For it must be noted that the back of the eye is covered by the ends of optic nerve-fibres which, though very small, still have some size. Thus each of them may be affected in one of its parts by one object and in other parts by other objects. But it is capable of being moved in only a single way at any given time; so when the smallest of its parts is affected by some very brilliant object, and the others by different objects that are less brilliant, the whole of it moves in accordance with the most brilliant object, presenting its image but not that of the others. Thus, suppose the ends of these little fibres are 1, 2, 3 [Fig. 10] and the rays which come, for example, from a star to trace an image on the back of the eye are spread over 1, and also slightly beyond over the six nerve-endings marked 2 (which I suppose are reached by no other rays

Fig. 10

except very weak ones from regions of the sky next to the star). In this case the image of the star will be spread over the whole area occupied by the six nerve-endings marked 2 and may even spread throughout that occupied by the twelve marked 3 if the disturbance is strong enough to be propagated to them as well. So you can see that the stars, while appearing rather small, nevertheless appear much larger than their extreme distance should cause them to appear. And even if they were not perfectly round, they could not fail to appear so – just as a square tower seen from afar 147 looks round, and all bodies that trace only very small images in the eye cannot trace there the shapes of their angles. Finally, as regards judgement of distance by size, shape, colour, or light, pictures drawn in perspective show how easy it is to make mistakes. For often the things depicted in such pictures appear to us to be farther off than they are because they are smaller, while their outlines are more blurred, and their colours darker or fainter, than we imagine they ought to be.[1]

1 The contents of the rest of the *Optics*, and of the *Meteorology* and the *Geometry*, are as follows:

Optics
Discourse Seven: The means of perfecting vision
Discourse Eight: The shapes that the transparent bodies must have in order to deflect rays through refraction in all the ways which are useful to vision
Discourse Nine: The description of telescopes
Discourse Ten: The method of cutting lenses

Meteorology
Discourse 1: The nature of terrestrial bodies
Discourse 2: Vapours and exhalations
Discourse 3: Salt
Discourse 4: Winds
Discourse 5: Clouds
Discourse 6: Snow, rain and hail
Discourse 7: Storms, lightning and all the other fires that blaze in the air
Discourse 8: The rainbow
Discourse 9: The colours of clouds and the circles or coronas that we sometimes see around the heavenly bodies
Discourse 10: The appearance of many suns

Geometry
Book 1: Problems that can be solved by constructions using only circles and straight lines
Book 2: The nature of curved lines
Book 3: Problems requiring the construction of solids and supersolids

Principles of Philosophy

Translator's preface

As early as 1640 Descartes had begun to work on a presentation of his philosophical system 'in an order which will make it easy to teach' (letter to Mersenne of 31 December). What he planned was a comprehensive university textbook which would rival and, he hoped, eventually replace the traditional texts based on Aristotle. He particularly wanted to include, though in a more circumspect form, material from his suppressed treatise, *The World*. 'My *World*', he wrote to Constantijn Huygens on 31 January 1642, 'would be out already were it not that first of all I want to teach it to speak Latin. I shall call it the *Summa Philosophiae*, to help it gain a better reception among the Schoolmen, who are now persecuting it and trying to smother it at birth.'

The title which Descartes eventually adopted was *Principia Philosophiae*, and the Latin text was first published by Elzevir of Amsterdam in 1644. The work runs to four parts, each divided into a large number of short sections or 'articles' (there are five hundred and four in all). Part One expounds Descartes' metaphysical doctrines (though they are presented in a very different fashion from that of the *Meditations*); Part Two gives a full account of the principles of Cartesian physics; Part Three gives a detailed explanation, in accordance with those principles, of the nature of the universe; and Part Four deals similarly with the origins of the earth and a wide variety of terrestrial phenomena. A further two parts were originally planned, to deal with plants and animals, and man, but these were never completed (see below, Part Four, article 188).

A French version of the *Principles*, by the Abbé Claude Picot (c. 1601–68), was published by Le Gras of Paris in 1647; Descartes gave the translation his enthusiastic approval (see his prefatory letter, below p. 179). The French text diverges considerably from the original Latin, and some (though certainly not all) of these departures were probably authorized by Descartes; the modern translator therefore has to decide what to do when the two versions differ. One strategy, adopted by Haldane and Ross,[1] is to provide a translation 'made from the Latin version collated with the French', but the result is an uneasy amalgam which often leaves it unclear whether a given passage represents

---

1 See General Introduction, above p. viii.

Descartes' original text of 1644. To avoid this drawback, the present version always provides, in the first instance, a direct rendering of Descartes' original Latin. A translation of the French version has, however, also been included in cases where the French illuminates, or provides a useful supplement to, the Latin; but such material from the French version is always placed within diamond brackets < >, or relegated to footnotes, to indicate that it is not to be found in Descartes' original text.

The decision about how often to append a rendering of the French is made easier by the fact that the departures from the Latin turn out, on careful scrutiny, to fall into two distinct categories. (1) Often Picot will loosely paraphrase the text, sometimes virtually rewriting the original in an attempt to illuminate Descartes' meaning. In most cases there seems no good reason to render these interpretative paraphrases, since they seldom improve on the splendid clarity and precision of Descartes' Latin, and sometimes introduce needless complications of their own (in Part One, article 24, for example, the French version inserts a gratuitous reference to innate notions which makes the subsequent train of thought incomprehensible). (2) Quite apart from paraphrases and reinterpretations of the original, we find, especially in Parts Two to Four, a good deal of completely new material, often of considerable interest, which has no counterpart at all in the Latin. This can vary from a brief supplementary comment illustrating some point (e.g. Part Three, article 29) to an extended discussion which can sometimes double the original length of an article (e.g. Part Four, article 203). Much of this new material seems too valuable to omit; moreover, there is evidence that some of the additions were authorized by Descartes or even directly added by him when he looked at Picot's version (thus, Frans Burman, who questioned Descartes about the laws of impact in Part Two, reports him as remarking that 'since many were complaining of the obscurity of these laws, he supplied a little clarification and further explanation in the French edition of the *Principles*'[1]).

The *Principles of Philosophy* is a very long work, and it has been necessary to abridge it for the present edition. The translation that follows, which is based on the texts in Volumes VIII A (Latin) and IX B (French) of Adam and Tannery,[2] includes all the material that is philosophical in the modern sense, as well as substantial portions of what would nowadays be called 'scientific' material, particularly where this throws light on Descartes' general conception of science. Part One is translated in its entirety; in Parts Two, Three and Four, selected articles are translated; the titles alone are supplied for the remaining articles.

J.C.

---

1 AT v 168; for further evidence see AT IX B, *Avertissement*.
2 See General Introduction, above, p. x.

[Preface to the French edition]

Author's letter to the translator of the book which may here serve as a preface[1]

Sir,[2]

The version of my *Principles* which you have taken the trouble to make is so polished and so thorough as to make me hope that the work will be more widely read in French than in Latin, and better understood. My only concern is that the title may put off those many people who have not had an education based on letters or who have a low opinion of philosophy because the philosophy they have been taught has not satisfied them. This makes me think that it would be a good idea to add a preface explaining the subject of the book, my purpose in writing it, and the benefit which may be derived from it. But although it would seem to be up to me to produce this preface because I ought to know these things better than anyone else, all I can persuade myself to do here is to summarize the principal points which I think such a preface should deal 2 with. I leave it to your discretion to pass on to the public as many of them as you consider to be pertinent.

First of all, I would have wished to explain what philosophy is, beginning with the most commonplace points. For example, the word 'philosophy' means the study of wisdom, and by 'wisdom' is meant not only prudence in our everyday affairs but also a perfect knowledge of all things that mankind is capable of knowing, both for the conduct of life and for the preservation of health and the discovery of all manner of skills. In order for this kind of knowledge to be perfect it must be deduced from first causes; thus, in order to set about acquiring it – and it is this activity to which the term 'to philosophize' strictly refers – we must start with the search for first causes or principles. These principles must satisfy two conditions. First, they must be so clear and so evident that the human mind cannot doubt their truth when it attentively concentrates on them; and, secondly, the knowledge of other things must depend on them, in the sense that the principles must be capable of being

---

1 This preface first appeared in the 1647 French edition. The original Latin text of 1644 contains no preface apart from the short dedicatory letter to Elizabeth translated below, pp. 190–2.
2 The addressee is the Abbé Picot; see Translator's preface, above p. 177.

known without knowledge of these other matters, but not *vice versa*.
Next, in deducing from these principles the knowledge of things which
depend on them, we must try to ensure that everything in the entire chain
of deductions which we draw is very manifest. In truth it is only God who
3 is perfectly wise, that is to say, who possesses complete knowledge of the
truth of all things; but men can be said to possess more or less wisdom
depending on how much knowledge they possess of the most important
truths. I think that everything I have just said would be accepted by all
people of learning.

   Next, I would have looked at the benefits of this philosophy and
shown that it encompasses everything which the human mind is capable
of knowing. Thus we should consider that it is this philosophy alone
which distinguishes us from the most savage and barbarous peoples, and
that a nation's civilization and refinement depends on the superiority of
the philosophy which is practised there. Hence the greatest good that a
state can enjoy is to possess true philosophers. As for the individual, it is
not only beneficial to live with those who apply themselves to this study;
it is incomparably better to undertake it oneself. For by the same token
it is undoubtedly much better to use one's own eyes to get about, and also
to enjoy the beauty of colours and light, than to close one's eyes and be
led around by someone else. Yet even the latter is much better than
keeping one's eyes closed and having no guide but oneself. Living
without philosophizing is exactly like having one's eyes closed without
ever trying to open them; and the pleasure of seeing everything which our
sight reveals is in no way comparable to the satisfaction accorded by
knowledge of the things which philosophy enables us to discover. Lastly,
the study of philosophy is more necessary for the regulation of our
4 morals and our conduct in this life than is the use of our eyes to guide our
steps. The brute beasts, who have only their bodies to preserve, are
continually occupied in looking for food to nourish them; but human
beings, whose most important part is the mind, should devote their main
efforts to the search for wisdom, which is the true food of the mind. And I
am sure that there are many people who would not fail to make the
search if they had some hope of success and knew how much they were
capable of. No soul, however base, is so strongly attached to the objects
of the senses that it does not sometimes turn aside and desire some other,
greater good, even though it may often not know what this good consists
in. Those who are most favoured by fortune and possess health, honour
and riches in abundance are no more exempt from this desire than
anyone else. On the contrary, I am convinced that it is just such people
who long most ardently for another good – a higher good than all those
that they already possess. Now this supreme good, considered by natural

reason without the light of faith, is nothing other than the knowledge of the truth through its first causes, that is to say wisdom, of which philosophy is the study. Since all these points are absolutely true, they would easily carry conviction if they were properly argued.

What prevents these points being accepted is the widespread experience that those who profess to be philosophers are often less wise and less reasonable than those who have never applied themselves to philosophy. And so at this point I would have explained briefly what all the 5 knowledge which we now possess consists in and the levels of wisdom that have so far been attained. The first level contains only notions which are so clear in themselves that they can be acquired without meditation. The second comprises everything we are acquainted with through sensory experience. The third comprises what we learn by conversing with other people. And one may add a fourth category, namely what is learned by reading books – not all books, but those which have been written by people who are capable of instructing us well; for in such cases we hold a kind of conversation with the authors. I think that all the wisdom which is generally possessed is acquired in these four ways. I am not including divine revelation in the list, because it does not lead us on by degrees but raises us at a stroke to infallible faith. Now in all ages there have been great men who have tried to find a fifth way of reaching wisdom – a way which is incomparably more elevated and more sure than the other four. This consists in the search for the first causes and the true principles which enable us to deduce the reasons for everything we are capable of knowing; and it is above all those who have laboured to this end who have been called philosophers. I am not sure, however, that there has been anyone up till now who has succeeded in this project. The first and most important of those whose writings have come down to us are Plato and Aristotle. The only difference between these two is that the former, following the footsteps of his master Socrates, ingenuously confessed that he had never yet been able to discover anything certain. 6 He was content instead to write what seemed to him to be probable, and accordingly he used his imagination to devise various principles by means of which he tried to account for other things. Aristotle, by contrast, was less candid. Although he had been Plato's disciple for twenty years, and possessed no principles apart from those of Plato, he completely changed the method of stating them and put them forward as true and certain, though it seems most unlikely that he in fact considered them to be so. Now these two men had a great deal of intelligence and much wisdom of the kind that is acquired in the four ways mentioned above, and this gave them such great authority that those who came after them were content to follow their opinions rather than look for something better. The main dispute among their disciples was about whether everything should be called into doubt or whether there were some things which were certain – a dispute which led both sides into extravagant errors. Some of those who were in favour of doubt extended it even to the actions of life, so that they neglected to employ common prudence in their behaviour; while those who took the side of certainty supposed that it had to depend on the senses and trusted them entirely, to the point where Epicurus, it is said, was rash enough to affirm, against all the arguments of the astronomers, that the sun is no larger than it appears. A fault which may be observed in the majority of disputes is that since the truth lies

7   midway between two positions which are being maintained, the disputants on each side move further and further away from it as their desire to contradict the opposing view increases. But the error of those who leaned too far towards the side of doubt was not followed for very long, while the opposing error has to some extent been corrected by the recognition that the senses deceive us in many cases. Nevertheless, I am not sure that anyone has yet expunged the second error completely by explaining the following point: on the one hand, certainty does not lie in the senses but solely in the understanding, when it possesses evident perceptions; on the other hand, so long as we possess only the kind of knowledge that is acquired by the first four degrees of wisdom we should not doubt the probable truths which concern the conduct of life, while at the same time we should not consider them to be so certain that we are incapable of changing our views when we are obliged to do so by some evident reason. Because of failure to recognize this truth, or to make use of it in the case of those few who have recognized it, the majority of those aspiring to be philosophers in the last few centuries have blindly followed Aristotle. Indeed they have often corrupted the sense of his writings and attributed to him various opinions which he would not recognize to be his, were he now to return to this world. Those who have not followed Aristotle (and this group includes many of the best minds) have nevertheless been saturated with his opinions in their youth (since these are the only opinions taught in the Schools) and this has so dominated their outlook that they have been unable to arrive at knowledge of true principles. Although I respect all these thinkers and would not wish to make myself disliked by criticizing them, I can give a proof of what I say

8   which I do not think any of them will reject, namely that they have all put forward as principles things of which they did not possess perfect knowledge. For example, there is not one of them, so far as I know, who has not supposed there to be weight in terrestrial bodies. Yet although experience shows us very clearly that the bodies we call 'heavy' descend towards the centre of the earth, we do not for all that have any

knowledge of the nature of what is called 'gravity', that is to say, the cause or principle which makes bodies descend in this way,[1] and we must derive such knowledge from some other source. The same can be said of the void and of atoms and of heat and cold, dryness and humidity, salt, sulphur, mercury and all other similar things which some people have proposed as their first principles. Now none of the conclusions deduced from a principle which is not evident can themselves be evident, even though they may be deduced from the principle in an evident manner. It follows that none of the arguments based on such principles have been able to provide their proponents with certain knowledge of anything, and accordingly such arguments have not been able to bring them one step further in their search for wisdom. If they have discovered anything true, it has been solely by means of one of the four methods set out above. Nevertheless, I do not wish to detract in any way from the reputation which any of these philosophers may claim. I am simply obliged to point out, for the consolation of those who have never studied, the following similarity with what happens when we travel: so long as we turn our back on the place we wish to get to, then the longer and faster we walk the further we get from our destination, so that even if we are 9 subsequently set on the right road we cannot reach our goal as quickly as we would have done had we never walked in the wrong direction. The same thing happens if we have bad principles. The more we develop them and the more carefully we work at deducing various consequences from them in our belief that we are philosophizing well, the further we move from knowledge of the truth and from wisdom. The conclusion that must be drawn from this is that among those who have studied whatever has been called philosophy up till now, those who have learnt the least are the most capable of learning true philosophy.

After fully explaining these matters, I would have wanted next to put down the reasons which serve to prove that the true principles, enabling one to reach the highest degree of wisdom which constitutes the supreme good of human life, are the principles which I have set down in this book. Just two reasons are enough to prove the point: the first is that the principles are very clear, and the second is that they enable all other things to be deduced from them. These are the only two conditions that such principles must meet. Now I can easily prove that the principles are very clear. This is shown by the way in which I discovered them, namely by rejecting everything in which I could discover the least occasion for doubt; for it is certain that principles which it was impossible to reject in this way, when one attentively considered them, are the clearest and most evident that the human mind can know. Thus I considered that someone

1 See footnote 1, p. 234 below.

who wishes to doubt everything cannot, for all that, doubt that he exists
10 while he is doubting; and that what reasons in this way, being unable to
doubt itself while doubting everything else, is not what we call our body
but what we call our soul or our thought. Accordingly I took the being or
existence of this thought as my first principle, and from it I deduced very
clearly the following principles. There is a God who is the author of
everything there is in the world; further, since he is the source of all
truth, he certainly did not create in us an understanding of the kind
which would be capable of making a mistake in its judgements concerning the things of which it possesses a very clear and very distinct
perception. These are all the principles that I make use of with regard to
immaterial or metaphysical things, and from them I deduce very clearly
the principles of corporeal or physical things, namely that there are
bodies which are extended in length, breadth and depth, and which have
various shapes and move in various ways. Here, in total, are all the
principles which I use to deduce the truth of other things. The other
reason which proves the clarity of these principles is that they have been
known for all time and indeed accepted as true and indubitable by
everyone, with the sole exception of the existence of God, which some
people have called into doubt because they have attributed too much to
sensory perceptions, and God cannot be seen or touched. Yet although
all the truths which I include among my principles have been known for
all time by everyone, there has, so far as I know, been no one up till now
who has recognized them as the principles of philosophy, that is to say, as
11 the principles which enable us to deduce the knowledge of all the other
things to be found in the world. This is why it remains for me here to
prove that they do indeed qualify as principles of this sort; and I think
that the best way of doing this is to get people to see by experience that
this is so, that is to say, to invite my readers to read this book. Admittedly,
I have not dealt with all things, for this would be impossible. But I think I
have explained all the things I have had occasion to deal with in such a
way that those who read the book attentively will be convinced that in
order to arrive at the highest knowledge of which the human mind is
capable there is no need to look for any principles other than those I
have provided. This will be especially clear if, after reading what I have
written and also perusing the writings of others, the reader takes the
trouble to consider the number and the diversity of the topics explained
in my book, and sees by comparison how few plausible arguments others
have been able to produce in attempting to explain these same topics by
means of principles which differ from mine. To enable my readers to
undertake this survey with greater ease, I could have told them that those
who have absorbed my opinions find it much easier to understand and

recognize the true value of other people's writings than those who have not absorbed my views. This is the exact opposite of what I said above about those who have started with traditional philosophy, namely that the more they have studied it the less fitted they generally are to acquire a sound grasp of true philosophy.

I would also have added a word of advice about the way to read this book. I should like the reader first of all to go quickly through the whole book like a novel, without straining his attention too much or stopping at the difficulties which may be encountered. The aim should be merely to ascertain in a general way which matters I have dealt with. After this, if he finds that these matters deserve to be examined and he has the curiosity to ascertain their causes, he may read the book a second time in order to observe how my arguments follow. But if he is not always able to see this fully, or if he does not understand all the arguments, he should not give up at once. He should merely mark with a pen the places where he finds the difficulties and continue to read on to the end without a break. If he then takes up the book for the third time, I venture to think he will now find the solutions to most of the difficulties he marked before; and if any still remain, he will discover their solution on a final re-reading.

An examination of the nature of many different minds has led me to observe that there are almost none that are so dull and slow as to be incapable of forming sound opinions or indeed of grasping all the most advanced sciences, provided they receive proper guidance. And this may also be proved by reason. For since the principles in question are clear, and nothing is permitted to be deduced from them except by very evident reasoning, everyone has enough intelligence to understand the things which depend on them. If we leave aside the problems caused by preconceived opinions, from which no one is entirely free (although those who have studied bad science the most are the greatest victims), then it almost always happens that people of moderate intelligence neglect to study because they do not think they are capable of it, while the others, who are keenest, press on too quickly, with the result that they often accept principles which are not evident, and draw uncertain inferences from them. This is why I should like to assure those who are over-diffident about their powers that there is nothing in my writings which they are not capable of completely understanding provided they take the trouble to examine them. I would, however, also like to warn the others that even the most excellent minds will need a great deal of time and attention in order to look at all the things which I set myself to include.

Following on from this, in order to get people to see the purpose I had in publishing my work, I would wish to explain here the order which I think we should follow when we aim to instruct ourselves. First of all, a

man who still possesses only the ordinary and imperfect knowledge that can be acquired in the four ways explained above should try before anything else to devise for himself a code of morals which is sufficient to regulate the actions of his life. For this is something which permits no delay, since we should endeavour above all else to live well. After that, he should study logic. I do not mean the logic of the Schools, for this is strictly speaking nothing but a dialectic which teaches ways of expounding to others what one already knows or even of holding forth without judgement about things one does not know. Such logic corrupts good sense rather than increasing it. I mean instead the kind of logic which
14 teaches us to direct our reason with a view to discovering the truths of which we are ignorant. Since this depends to a great extent on practice, it is good for the student to work for a long time at practising the rules on very easy and simple questions like those of mathematics. Then, when he has acquired some skill in finding the truth on these questions, he should begin to tackle true philosophy in earnest. The first part of philosophy is metaphysics, which contains the principles of knowledge, including the explanation of the principal attributes of God, the non-material nature of our souls and all the clear and distinct notions which are in us. The second part is physics, where, after discovering the true principles of material things, we examine the general composition of the entire universe and then, in particular, the nature of this earth and all the bodies which are most commonly found upon it, such as air, water, fire, magnetic ore and other minerals. Next we need to examine individually the nature of plants, of animals and, above all, of man, so that we may be capable later on of discovering the other sciences which are beneficial to man. Thus the whole of philosophy is like a tree. The roots are metaphysics, the trunk is physics, and the branches emerging from the trunk are all the other sciences, which may be reduced to three principal ones, namely medicine, mechanics and morals. By 'morals' I understand the highest and most perfect moral system, which presupposes a complete knowledge of the other sciences and is the ultimate level of wisdom.
15   Now just as it is not the roots or the trunk of a tree from which one gathers the fruit, but only the ends of the branches, so the principal benefit of philosophy depends on those parts of it which can only be learnt last of all. I am ignorant of almost all of these; but the earnest desire I have always had to render service to the public led me, twelve years ago, to publish a number of essays on subjects where it seemed to me that I had learnt something. The first part of these essays was a *Discourse on the Method of rightly conducting one's reason and seeking the truth in the sciences*, where I summarized the principal rules of logic and of an imperfect moral code which we may follow provisionally while we do

not yet know a better one. The remaining parts were three treatises: the *Optics*, the *Meteorology* and the *Geometry*. In the *Optics* my purpose was to show that one could make sufficient progress in philosophy to enable one to achieve knowledge of the arts which are beneficial for life; for the designing of telescopes, which I explained there, is one of the most difficult projects ever attempted.[1] In the *Meteorology* I wanted people to recognize the difference that exists between the philosophy I practise and that which is taught in the Schools, where the same subject-matter is normally dealt with.[2] Finally, in the *Geometry*, I aimed to demonstrate that I had discovered several things which had hitherto been unknown, and thus to promote the belief that many more things may yet be discovered, in order to stimulate everyone to undertake the search for truth. Later on, foreseeing the difficulty which many would have in grasping the foundations of metaphysics, I tried to explain the principal points in a book of *Meditations*. Although this work is not very large, the size of the volume was increased, and the contents greatly clarified, by the addition of the objections that several very learned persons sent me on the subject, and by the replies I made to them. And finally, when I thought that these earlier works had sufficiently prepared the minds of my readers to accept the *Principles of Philosophy*, I published these too. I divided the book into four parts. The first contains the principles of knowledge, i.e. what may be called 'first philosophy' or 'metaphysics'; so in order to gain a sound understanding of this part it is appropriate to read first of all the *Meditations* which I wrote on the same subject. The other three parts contain all that is most general in physics, namely an explanation of the first laws or principles of nature and the manner of composition of the heavens, the fixed stars, the planets, the comets and, in general, the entire universe. Next comes a particular account of the nature of this earth and of air, water, fire and magnetic ore, which are the bodies that are most commonly found upon it, and also an account of all the qualities which we observe in these bodies, such as light, heat, weight and so on. In this way I consider myself to have embarked on an explanation of the whole of philosophy in an orderly way, without having omitted any of the

16

---

1 Discourses 8 and 9 of the *Optics* provide detailed discussion of the optimum shape and configuration of telescopic lenses.

2 'I regard the minute parts of terrestrial bodies as being all composed of one single kind of matter, and believe that each of them could be divided repeatedly in infinitely many ways, and that there is no more difference between them than there is between stones of various different shapes cut from the same rock ... But to keep the peace with the [scholastic] philosophers, I have no wish to deny any further items which they may imagine in bodies over and above what I have described, such as their "substantial forms", their "real qualities", and so on. It simply seems to me that my arguments will be all the more acceptable in so far as I can make them depend on fewer things.' *Meteorology*, Discourse 1 (AT VI 239).

17 things which ought to precede the topics I wrote about last. But in order to bring the plan to its conclusion I should have to go on to explain in the same manner the nature of all the particular bodies which exist on the earth, namely minerals, plants, animals and, most importantly, man. And then to conclude, I should have to give an exact account of medicine, morals and mechanics. This is what I should have to do in order to give to mankind a body of philosophy that is quite complete; and I do not yet feel so old, or so diffident about my powers, or so far away from knowledge of these remaining topics, that I would not now boldly try to bring the plan to its conclusion, provided I had the resources to make all the observations[1] I should need in order to back up and justify my arguments. But this, I can see, would require great expense – too great for an individual like myself unless he were assisted by the public. And since I do not see that I can expect such assistance, I think that in future I should be content to study for my own private instruction and that future generations will forgive me if from now on I give up working on their behalf.

Meanwhile, to show how I think I have already served posterity, I will here point out the fruits which I am sure can be derived from my principles. The first is the satisfaction which will be felt in using them to discover many truths which have been unknown up till now. For although the truth often does not touch our imagination as much as falsehood and pretence, because it seems less striking and more plain,
18 nevertheless the satisfaction it produces is always more durable and more solid. The second benefit is that the study of these principles will accustom people little by little to form better judgements about all the things they come across, and hence will make them wiser. The effect so produced will be the opposite of that produced by ordinary philosophy. For it is easy to observe in those we call 'pedants' that philosophy makes them less capable of reasoning than they would be if they had never learnt it. The third benefit is that the truths contained in these principles, because they are very clear and very certain, will eliminate all ground for dispute, and so will dispose people's minds to gentleness and harmony. This is the opposite result to that produced by the debates in the Schools, which – slowly and without their noticing it – make the participants more argumentative and opinionated, and hence are perhaps the major cause of the heresies and disagreements which now plague the world. The last and greatest fruit of these principles is that they will enable those who develop them to discover many truths which I have not explained at all. Thus, moving little by little from one truth to the next, they may in time acquire a perfect knowledge of all philosophy, and reach the highest

1 Fr. *expériences*; Cf. *Discourse*, part 6, pp. 143ff, and footnote p. 143 above.

level of wisdom. One sees in all the arts that although they are at first rough and imperfect, nevertheless, because they contain some element of truth, the effect of which is revealed by experience, they are gradually perfected by practice. So it is in philosophy: when one has true principles and follows them, one cannot fail to come upon other truths from time to time. Indeed the best way of proving the falsity of Aristotle's principles is to point out that they have not enabled any progress to be made in all the many centuries in which they have been followed.   19

I am well aware that there are some people who are so hasty and use so little circumspection in what they do that even with very solid foundations they cannot construct anything certain. Since such people are normally quicker than anyone else at producing books, they may in a short time wreck everything I have done. For although I have carefully tried to banish doubt and uncertainty from my style of philosophizing, they may introduce these elements into it if their writings are accepted as mine, or as containing my opinions. I recently had some experience of this from one of those who were reckoned to be particularly anxious to follow me; indeed, I had written of him somewhere that I was 'so confident of his intelligence' that I did not think he held any views that I would not 'gladly have acknowledged as my own'.[1] Last year he published a book entitled *The Foundations of Physics* in which, as far as physics and medicine are concerned, it appears that everything he wrote was taken from my writings – both from those I have published and also from a still imperfect work on the nature of animals which fell into his hands. But because he copied down the material inaccurately and changed the order and denied certain truths of metaphysics on which the whole of physics must be based, I am obliged to disavow his work entirely. And I must also beg my readers never to attribute to me any   20 opinion they do not find explicitly stated in my writings. Furthermore, they should not accept any opinion as true – whether in my writings or elsewhere – unless they see it to be very clearly deduced from true principles.

I am also very well aware that many centuries may pass before all the truths that can be deduced from these principles are actually so deduced. For the majority of truths remaining to be discovered depend on various particular observations[2] which we never happen on by chance but which must be sought out with care and expense by very intelligent people. It

---

1 These enthusiastic comments appeared in Descartes' open letter to Voetius (*Epistola ad G. Voetium*) published in 1643 (AT VIII B 163). The reference is to Henricus Regius (1598–1679), Professor of Medicine at Utrecht, whose *Fundamenta physices* appeared in 1646. For details of Descartes' relationship with Regius see Translator's preface to *Comments on a Certain Broadsheet*, below p. 293.

2 Fr. *expériences*; see footnote above p. 143.

will not easily come about that the same people who have the capacity to make good use of these observations will have the means to make them. What is more, the majority of the best minds have formed such a bad opinion of the whole of philosophy, because of the faults they have noticed in the philosophy that has been current up till now, that they certainly will not apply themselves to look for a better one. But perhaps the difference which they see between these principles of mine and all those of other philosophers, as well as the long chain of truths that can be deduced from them, will finally make them realize how important it is to continue in the search for these truths, and to what a high level of wisdom, and to what perfection and felicity of life, these truths can bring us. If they realize this, I venture to believe that there will not be one of them who does not try to apply himself to such a beneficial study, or at least favours and willingly assists with all his resources those who devote themselves to it with success. My earnest wish is that our descendants may see the happy outcome of this project.

[Dedicatory Letter to Elizabeth]

AT VIIIA
1

To Her Serene Highness the Princess Elizabeth
eldest daughter of Frederick, King of Bohemia,
Count Palatine and Elector of the Holy Roman Empire

Your Serene Highness,
   The greatest reward which I have received from the writings I have previously published is that you have deigned to read them; for as a result they have provided the occasion for my being admitted into the circle of your acquaintance. And my subsequent experience of your great talents leads me to think that it would be a service to mankind to set them down as an example to posterity. It would ill become me to use flattery or to put forward any assertion which has not been thoroughly scrutinized, especially in a work in which I shall be trying to lay down the foundations of the truth. And I know that your generous and modest nature will welcome the simple and unadorned judgement of a philosopher more than the polished compliments of those with smoother

2 tongues. I shall therefore write only what I know to be true either from reason or by experience, and in this introduction I propose to philosophize just as I do throughout the rest of the book.
   There is a great difference between apparent virtues and true ones; and even in the case of true virtues, there is a great difference between those which are derived from an exact knowledge of things and those which are accompanied by some measure of ignorance. What I understand by

'apparent virtues' are certain vices which are not very common and are the opposites of other better known ones; because they are farther removed from such vices than the virtues which occupy an intermediate position, they are usually more admired. Thus it is more common to find people who timidly flee from danger than to find people who rashly throw themselves into it; and so rashness is contrasted with the vice of timidity, as if it were a virtue, and is commonly valued more highly than true courage. Similarly, someone who is over-generous is often more highly praised than one who gives liberally; and again, no one acquires a great reputation for piety more easily than the superstitious or hypocritical person.

As for the true virtues, many of them arise not solely from the knowledge of what is right but from some error. Thus goodness is often the result of simplicity, piety the result of fear, and courage the result of desperation. Because such virtues differ from each other, they go by different names. But the pure and genuine virtues, which proceed solely from knowledge of what is right, all have one and the same nature and are included under the single term 'wisdom'. For whoever possesses the firm and powerful resolve always to use his reasoning powers correctly, as far as he can, and to carry out whatever he knows to be best, is truly wise, so far as his nature permits. And simply because of this, he will possess justice, courage, temperance, and all the other virtues; but they will be interlinked in such a way that no one virtue stands out among the others. Such virtues are far superior to those which owe their distinguishing marks to some admixture of vice, but because they are less well known to the majority they do not normally receive such lavish praise.

Now there are two prerequisites for the kind of wisdom just described, namely the perception of the intellect and the disposition of the will. But whereas what depends on the will is within the capacity of everyone, there are some people who possess far sharper intellectual vision than others. Those who are by nature somewhat backward intellectually should make a firm and faithful resolution to do their utmost to acquire knowledge of what is right, and always to pursue what they judge to be right; this should suffice to enable them, despite their ignorance on many points, to achieve wisdom according to their lights and thus to find great favour with God. Nevertheless they will be left far behind by those who possess not merely a very firm resolve to act rightly but also the sharpest intelligence combined with the utmost zeal for acquiring knowledge of the truth.

That such zeal is abundantly present in Your Highness is clear from the fact that neither the diversions of the Court nor the customary education that so often condemns young ladies to ignorance has been able to prevent you from studying all the worthwhile arts and sciences. And the outstanding and incomparable sharpness of your intelligence is obvious from the penetrating examination you have made of all the secrets of these sciences, and from the fact that you have acquired an exact knowledge of them in so short a time. I have even greater evidence of your powers – and this is special to myself – in the fact that you are the only person I have so far found who has completely understood all my previously published works. Many other people, even those of the utmost acumen and learning, find them very obscure; and it generally happens with almost everyone else that if they are accomplished in Metaphysics they hate Geometry, while if they have mastered Geometry they do not grasp what I have written on First Philosophy. Your intellect is, to my knowledge, unique in finding everything equally clear; and this is why my use of the term 'incomparable' is quite deserved. And when I consider that such a varied and complete knowledge of all things is to be found not in some aged pedant who has spent many years in contemplation but in a young princess whose beauty and youth call to mind one of the Graces rather than gray-eyed Minerva or any of the Muses, then I cannot but be lost in admiration.

Finally, I see that all the necessary conditions for perfect and sublime wisdom, both on the side of knowledge and on the side of the will, shine forth in your character. For, together with your royal dignity, you show an extraordinary kindness and gentleness which, though continually buffeted by the blows of fortune, has never become embittered or broken. I am so overwhelmed by this that I consider that this statement of my philosophy should be offered and dedicated to the wisdom which I so admire in you – for philosophy is nothing else but the study of wisdom. And indeed my desire to be known as a philosopher is no greater than my desire to be known as

Your Serene Highness's most devoted servant,
     Descartes

PART ONE

The Principles of Human Knowledge

1. *The seeker after truth must, once in the course of his life, doubt everything, as far as is possible.*

Since we began life as infants, and made various judgements concerning the things that can be perceived by the senses before we had the full use of our reason, there are many preconceived opinions that keep us from knowledge of the truth.[1] It seems that the only way of freeing ourselves from these opinions is to make the effort, once in the course of our life, to doubt everything which we find to contain even the smallest suspicion of uncertainty.

2. *What is doubtful should even be considered as false.*

Indeed, it will even prove useful, once we have doubted these things, to consider them as false, so that our discovery of what is most certain and easy to know may be all the clearer.

3. *This doubt should not meanwhile be applied to ordinary life.*

This doubt, while it continues, should be kept in check and employed solely in connection with the contemplation of the truth. As far as ordinary life is concerned, the chance for action would frequently pass us by if we waited until we could free ourselves from our doubts, and so we are often compelled to accept what is merely probable. From time to time we may even have to make a choice between two alternatives, even though it is not apparent that one of the two is more probable than the other.

4. *The reasons for doubt concerning the things that can be perceived by the senses.*

Given, then, that our efforts are directed solely to the search for truth, our initial doubts will be about the existence of the objects of sense-

---

1 Some examples of such preconceived opinions are given in art. 71, pp. 218f below.

6 perception and imagination. The first reason for such doubts is that from time to time we have caught out the senses when they were in error, and it is prudent never to place too much trust in those who have deceived us even once. The second reason is that in our sleep we regularly seem to have sensory perception of, or to imagine, countless things which do not exist anywhere; and if our doubts are on the scale just outlined, there seem to be no marks by means of which we can with certainty distinguish being asleep from being awake.

5. *The reasons for doubting even mathematical demonstrations.*
Our doubt will also apply to other matters which we previously regarded as most certain – even the demonstrations of mathematics and even the principles which we hitherto considered to be self-evident. One reason for this is that we have sometimes seen people make mistakes in such matters and accept as most certain and self-evident things which seemed false to us. Secondly, and most importantly, we have been told that there is an omnipotent God who created us. Now we do not know whether he may have wished to make us beings of the sort who are always deceived even in those matters which seem to us supremely evident; for such constant deception seems no less a possibility than the occasional deception which, as we have noticed on previous occasions, does occur. We may of course suppose that our existence derives not from a supremely powerful God but either from ourselves or from some other source; but in that case, the less powerful we make the author of our coming into being, the more likely it will be that we are so imperfect as to be deceived all the time.

6. *We have free will, enabling us to withhold our assent in doubtful matters and hence avoid error.*
But whoever turns out to have created us, and however powerful and however deceitful he may be, in the meantime we nonetheless experience within us the kind of freedom which enables us always to refrain from believing things which are not completely certain and thoroughly examined. Hence we are able to take precautions against going wrong on any occasion.

7. *It is not possible for us to doubt that we exist while we are doubting; and this is the first thing we come to know when we philosophize in an orderly way.*
7 In rejecting – and even imagining to be false – everything which we can in any way doubt, it is easy for us to suppose that there is no God and no heaven, and that there are no bodies, and even that we ourselves have no hands or feet, or indeed any body at all. But we cannot for all that

suppose that we, who are having such thoughts, are nothing. For it is a contradiction to suppose that what thinks does not, at the very time when it is thinking, exist. Accordingly, this piece of knowledge[1] – *I am thinking, therefore I exist* – is the first and most certain of all to occur to anyone who philosophizes in an orderly way.

8. *In this way we discover the distinction between soul and body, or between a thinking thing and a corporeal thing.*

This is the best way to discover the nature of the mind and the distinction between the mind and the body. For if we, who are supposing that everything which is distinct from us is false,[2] examine what we are, we see very clearly that neither extension nor shape nor local motion, nor anything of this kind which is attributable to a body, belongs to our nature, but that thought alone belongs to it. So our knowledge of our thought is prior to, and more certain than, our knowledge of any corporeal thing; for we have already perceived it, although we are still in doubt about other things.

9. *What is meant by 'thought'.*

By the term 'thought', I understand everything which we are aware of as happening within us, in so far as we have awareness of it. Hence, *thinking* is to be identified here not merely with understanding, willing and imagining, but also with sensory awareness. For if I say 'I am seeing, or I am walking, therefore I exist', and take this as applying to vision or walking as bodily activities, then the conclusion is not absolutely certain. This is because, as often happens during sleep, it is possible for me to think I am seeing or walking, though my eyes are closed and I am not moving about; such thoughts might even be possible if I had no body at all. But if I take 'seeing' or 'walking' to apply to the actual sense or awareness of seeing or walking, then the conclusion is quite certain, since it relates to the mind, which alone has the sensation or thought that it is seeing or walking.

10. *Matters which are very simple and self-evident are only rendered more obscure by logical definitions, and should not be counted as items of knowledge which it takes effort to acquire.*

I shall not here explain many of the other terms which I have already used or will use in what follows, because they seem to me to be sufficiently self-evident. I have often noticed that philosophers make the

---

1 '. . . this inference' (French version).

2 Lat. *falsum*. Descartes uses this term to refer not only to propositions which are false, but also to objects which are unreal, spurious or non-existent. The French version here reads: 'we who are now thinking that there is nothing outside of our thought which truly is or exists . . .'

mistake of employing logical definitions in an attempt to explain what was already very simple and self-evident; the result is that they only make matters more obscure. And when I said that the proposition *I am thinking, therefore I exist* is the first and most certain of all to occur to anyone who philosophizes in an orderly way, I did not in saying that deny that one must first know what thought, existence and certainty are, and that it is impossible that that which thinks should not exist, and so forth. But because these are very simple notions, and ones which on their own provide us with no knowledge of anything that exists, I did not think they needed to be listed.

11. *How our mind is better known than our body.*
In order to realize that the knowledge of our mind is not simply prior to and more certain than the knowledge of our body, but also more evident, we should notice something very well known by the natural light: nothingness possesses no attributes or qualities. It follows that, wherever we find some attributes or qualities, there is necessarily some thing or substance to be found for them to belong to; and the more attributes we discover in the same thing or substance, the clearer is our knowledge of that substance. Now we find more attributes in our mind than in anything else, as is manifest from the fact that whatever enables us to know anything else cannot but lead us to a much surer knowledge of our own mind. For example, if I judge that the earth exists from the fact that I touch it or see it, this very fact undoubtedly gives even greater
9   support for the judgement that my mind exists. For it may perhaps be the case that I judge that I am touching the earth even though the earth does not exist at all; but it cannot be that, when I make this judgement, my mind which is making the judgement does not exist. And the same applies in other cases <regarding all the things that come into our mind, namely that we who think of them exist, even if they are false or have no existence>.

12. *Why this fact does not come to be known to all alike.*
Disagreement on this point has come from those who have not done their philosophizing in an orderly way; and the reason for it is simply that they have never taken sufficient care to distinguish the mind from the body. Although they may have put the certainty of their own existence before that of anything else, they failed to realize that they should have taken 'themselves' in this context to mean their minds alone. They were inclined instead to take 'themselves' to mean only their bodies – the bodies which they saw with their eyes and touched with their hands, and

to which they incorrectly attributed the power of sense-perception; and this is what prevented them from perceiving the nature of the mind.

13. *The sense in which knowledge of all other things depends on the knowledge of God.*

The mind, then, knowing itself, but still in doubt about all other things, looks around in all directions in order to extend its knowledge further. First of all, it finds within itself ideas of many things; and so long as it merely contemplates these ideas and does not affirm or deny the existence outside itself of anything resembling them, it cannot be mistaken. Next, it finds certain common notions from which it constructs various proofs; and, for as long as it attends to them, it is completely convinced of their truth. For example, the mind has within itself ideas of numbers and shapes, and it also has such common notions as: *If you add equals to equals the results will be equal*; from these it is easy to demonstrate that the three angles of a triangle equal two right angles, and so on. And so the mind will be convinced of the truth of this and similar conclusions, so long as it attends to the premises from which it deduced them. But it cannot attend to them all the time; and subsequently,[1] recalling that it is still ignorant as to whether it may have been created with the kind of nature that makes it go wrong even in matters which appear most   10 evident, the mind sees that it has just cause to doubt such conclusions, and that the possession of certain knowledge will not be possible until it has come to know the author of its being.

14. *The existence of God is validly inferred from the fact that necessary existence is included in our concept of God.*

The mind next considers the various ideas which it has within itself, and finds that there is one idea – the idea of a supremely intelligent, supremely powerful and supremely perfect being – which stands out from all the others. <And it readily judges from what it perceives in this idea, that God, who is the supremely perfect being, is, or exists. For although it has distinct ideas of many other things it does not observe anything in them to guarantee the existence of their object.> In this one idea the mind recognizes existence – not merely the possible and contingent existence which belongs to the ideas of all the other things which it distinctly perceives, but utterly necessary and eternal existence. Now on the basis of its perception that, for example, it is necessarily contained in the idea of a triangle that its three angles should equal two

---

1 '... when it happens that it remembers a conclusion without attending to the sequence which enables it to be demonstrated' (added in French version).

right angles, the mind is quite convinced that a triangle does have three angles equalling two right angles. In the same way, simply on the basis of its perception that necessary and eternal existence is contained in the idea of a supremely perfect being, the mind must clearly conclude that the supreme being does exist.

15. *Our concepts of other things do not similarly contain necessary*
    existence, but merely contingent existence.
The mind will be even more inclined to accept this if it considers that it cannot find within itself an idea of any other thing such that necessary existence is seen to be contained in the idea in this way. And from this it understands that the idea of a supremely perfect being is not an idea which was invented by the mind, or which represents some chimera, but that it represents a true and immutable nature which cannot but exist, since necessary existence is contained within it.

16. *Preconceived opinions prevent the necessity of the existence of God*
    from being clearly recognized by everyone.
Our mind will, as I say, easily accept this, provided that it has first of all completely freed itself from preconceived opinions. But we have got into the habit of distinguishing essence from existence in the case of all other things; and we are also in the habit of making up at will various ideas of things which do not exist anywhere and have never done so. Hence, at times when we are not intent on the contemplation of the supremely perfect being, a doubt may easily arise as to whether the idea of God is not one of those which we made up at will, or at least one of those which do not include existence in their essence.

17. *The greater the objective perfection in any of our ideas, the greater*
    its cause must be.
When we reflect further on the ideas that we have within us, we see that some of them, in so far as they are merely modes of thinking, do not differ much one from another; but in so far as one idea represents one thing and another represents another, they differ widely; and the greater the amount of objective[1] perfection they contain within themselves, the more perfect their cause must be. For example, if someone has within himself the idea of a highly intricate machine, it would be fair to ask what was the cause of his possession of the idea: did he somewhere see such a machine made by someone else; or did he make such a close study of mechanics, or is his own ingenuity so great, that he was able to think it up on his own, although he never saw it anywhere? All the intricacy

1 If an idea represents some object which is F, the idea is said to possess 'objective' F-ness, or to contain F-ness 'objectively'. Cf. Med. III: vol. II, p. 28.

which is contained in the idea merely objectively – as in a picture – must be contained in its cause, whatever kind of cause it turns out to be; and it must be contained not merely objectively or representatively, but in actual reality, either formally or eminently,[1] at least in the case of the first and principal cause.

18. *This gives us a second reason for concluding that God exists.*
Since, then, we have within us the idea of God, or a supreme being, we may rightly inquire into the cause of our possession of this idea. Now we find in the idea such immeasurable greatness that we are quite certain that it could have been placed in us only by something which truly possesses the sum of all perfections, that is, by a God who really exists. For it is very evident by the natural light not only that nothing comes from nothing but also that what is more perfect cannot be produced by – that is, cannot have as its efficient and total cause – what is 12 less perfect. Furthermore, we cannot have within us the idea or image of anything without there being somewhere, either within us or outside us, an original which contains in reality all the perfections belonging to the idea. And since the supreme perfections of which we have an idea are in no way to be found in us, we rightly conclude that they reside in something distinct from ourselves, namely God – or certainly that they once did so, from which it most evidently follows that they are still there.

19. *Even if we do not grasp the nature of God, his perfections are known to us more clearly than any other thing.*
This is sufficiently certain and manifest to those who are used to contemplating the idea of God and to considering his supreme perfections. Although we do not fully grasp these perfections, since it is in the nature of an infinite being not to be fully grasped by us, who are finite, nonetheless we are able to understand them more clearly and distinctly than any corporeal things. This is because they permeate our thought to a greater extent, being simpler and unobscured by any limitations. <Furthermore, there is no reflection which can better serve to perfect our understanding, or which is more important than this, in so far as the consideration of an object which has no limits to its perfections fills us with satisfaction and assurance.>

20. *We did not make ourselves, but were made by God; and consequently he exists.*
However, this is something that not everyone takes note of. When people have an idea of some intricate machine, they generally know

1 To possess a property *formally* is to possess it strictly as defined; to possess it *eminently* is to possess it in some higher or more perfect form.

where they got the idea from; but we do not in the same way have a recollection of the idea of God being sent to us from God, since we have always possessed it. Accordingly, we should now go on to inquire into the source of our being, given that we have within us an idea of the supreme perfections of God. Now it is certainly very evident by the natural light that a thing which recognizes something more perfect than itself is not the source of its own being; for if so, it would have given itself all the perfections of which it has an idea. Hence, the source of its being can only be something which possesses within itself all these perfections – that is, God.

13   21. *The fact that our existence has duration is sufficient to demonstrate the existence of God.*

It will be impossible for anything to obscure the clarity of this proof, if we attend to the nature of time or of the duration of things. For the nature of time is such that its parts are not mutually dependent, and never coexist. Thus, from the fact that we now exist, it does not follow that we shall exist a moment from now, unless there is some cause – the same cause which originally produced us – which continually reproduces us, as it were, that is to say, which keeps us in existence. For we easily understand that there is no power in us enabling us to keep ourselves in existence. We also understand that he who has so great a power that he can keep us in existence, although we are distinct from him, must be all the more able to keep himself in existence; or rather, he requires no other being to keep him in existence, and hence, in short, is God.

22. *Our method of recognizing the existence of God leads to the simultaneous recognition of all the other attributes of God, in so far as they can be known by the natural power of the mind.*

There is a great advantage in proving the existence of God by this method, that is to say, by means of the idea of God. For the method enables us at the same time to come to know the nature of God, in so far as the feebleness of our nature allows. For when we reflect on the idea of God which we were born with, we see that he is eternal, omniscient, omnipotent, the source of all goodness and truth, the creator of all things, and finally, that he possesses within him everything in which we can clearly recognize some perfection that is infinite or unlimited by any imperfection.

23. *God is not corporeal, and does not perceive through the senses as we do; and he does not will the evil of sin.*

There are many things such that, although we recognize some perfection in them, we also find in them some imperfection or limitation, and these therefore cannot belong to God. For example, the nature of body includes divisibility along with extension in space, and since being divisible is an imperfection, it is certain that God is not a body. Again, the fact that we perceive through the senses is for us a perfection of a kind; but all sense-perception involves being acted upon, and to be acted upon is to be dependent on something else. Hence it cannot in any way be supposed that God perceives by means of the senses, but only that he understands and wills. And even his understanding and willing does not happen, as in our case, by means of operations that are in a certain sense distinct one from another; we must rather suppose that there is always a single identical and perfectly simple act by means of which he simultaneously understands, wills and accomplishes everything. When I say 'everything' I mean all *things*: for God does not will the evil of sin, which is not a thing.

14

24. *We pass from knowledge of God to knowledge of his creatures by remembering that he is infinite and we are finite.*

Now since God alone is the true cause of everything which is or can be, it is very clear that the best path to follow when we philosophize will be to start from the knowledge of God himself and try to deduce an explanation of the things created by him. This is the way to acquire the most perfect scientific knowledge, that is, knowledge of effects through their causes. In order to tackle this task with a reasonable degree of safety and without risk of going wrong we must take the precaution of always bearing in mind as carefully as possible both that God, the creator of all things, is infinite, and that we are altogether finite.

25. *We must believe everything which God has revealed, even though it may be beyond our grasp.*

Hence, if God happens to reveal to us something about himself or others which is beyond the natural reach of our mind – such as the mystery of the Incarnation or of the Trinity – we will not refuse to believe it, despite the fact that we do not clearly understand it. And we will not be at all surprised that there is much, both in the immeasurable nature of God and in the things created by him, which is beyond our mental capacity.

26. *We should never enter into arguments about the infinite. Things in which we observe no limits – such as the extension of the world, the division of the parts of matter, the number of the stars, and so on – should instead be regarded as indefinite.*

Thus we will never be involved in tiresome arguments about the infinite. For since we are finite, it would be absurd for us to determine anything concerning the infinite; for this would be to attempt to limit it and grasp

15   it. So we shall not bother to reply to those who ask if half an infinite line would itself be infinite, or whether an infinite number is odd or even, and so on. It seems that nobody has any business to think about such matters unless he regards his own mind as infinite. For our part, in the case of anything in which, from some point of view, we are unable to discover a limit, we shall avoid asserting that it is infinite, and instead regard it as indefinite. There is, for example, no imaginable extension which is so great that we cannot understand the possibility of an even greater one; and so we shall describe the size of possible things as indefinite. Again, however many parts a body is divided into, each of the parts can still be understood to be divisible and so we shall hold that quantity is indefinitely divisible. Or again, no matter how great we imagine the number of stars to be, we still think that God could have created even more; and so we will suppose the number of stars to be indefinite. And the same will apply in other cases.

27. *The difference between the indefinite and the infinite.*
Our reason for using the term 'indefinite' rather than 'infinite' in these cases is, in the first place, so as to reserve the term 'infinite' for God alone. For in the case of God alone, not only do we fail to recognize any limits in any respect, but our understanding positively tells us that there are none. Secondly, in the case of other things, our understanding does not in the same way positively tell us that they lack limits in some respect; we merely acknowledge in a negative way that any limits which they may have cannot be discovered by us.

28. *It is not the final but the efficient causes of created things that we must inquire into.*
When dealing with natural things we will, then, never derive any explanations from the purposes which God or nature may have had in view when creating them <and we shall entirely banish from our philosophy the search for final causes>. For we should not be so arrogant as to suppose that we can share in God's plans. We should, instead,

16   consider him as the efficient cause of all things; and starting from the divine attributes which by God's will we have some knowledge of, we shall see, with the aid of our God-given natural light, what conclusions should be drawn concerning those effects which are apparent to our senses.[1] At the same time we should remember, as noted earlier, that the

---

1 '. . . and we shall be assured that what we have once clearly and distinctly perceived to belong to the nature of these things has the perfection of being true' (added in French version, which also omits the last sentence of this article).

natural light is to be trusted only to the extent that it is compatible with divine revelation.

29. *God is not the cause of our errors.*

The first attribute of God that comes under consideration here is that he is supremely truthful and the giver of all light. So it is a complete contradiction to suppose that he might deceive us or be, in the strict and positive sense, the cause of the errors to which we know by experience that we are prone. For although the ability to deceive may perhaps be regarded among us men as a sign of intelligence, the will to deceive must undoubtedly always come from malice, or from fear and weakness, and so cannot belong to God.

30. *It follows that everything that we clearly perceive is true; and this removes the doubts mentioned earlier.*

It follows from this that the light of nature or faculty of knowledge which God gave us can never encompass any object which is not true in so far as it is indeed encompassed by this faculty, that is, in so far as it is clearly and distinctly perceived. For God would deserve to be called a deceiver if the faculty which he gave us was so distorted that it mistook the false for the true <even when we were using it properly>. This disposes of the most serious doubt which arose from our ignorance about whether our nature might not be such as to make us go wrong even in matters which seemed to us utterly evident. Indeed, this argument easily demolishes all the other reasons for doubt which were mentioned earlier. Mathematical 17 truths should no longer be suspect, since they are utterly clear to us. And as for our senses, if we notice anything here that is clear and distinct, no matter whether we are awake or asleep, then provided we separate it from what is confused and obscure we will easily recognize – whatever the thing in question – which are the aspects that may be regarded as true. There is no need for me to expand on this point here, since I have already dealt with it in the *Meditations on Metaphysics*;[1] and a more precise explanation of the point requires knowledge of what I shall be saying later on.

31. *Our errors, if considered in relation to God, are merely negations; if considered in relation to ourselves they are privations.*

Yet although God is no deceiver, it often happens that we fall into error. In order to investigate the origin and cause of our errors and learn to guard against them, we should realize that they do not depend on our

---

1 Cf. Med. VI: vol. II, pp. 54ff.

intellect so much as on our will. Moreover, errors are not things, requiring the real concurrence of God for their production. Considered in relation to God they are merely negations,[1] and considered in relation to ourselves they are privations.

32. *We possess only two modes of thinking: the perception of the intellect and the operation of the will.*

All the modes of thinking that we experience within ourselves can be brought under two general headings: perception, or the operation of the intellect, and volition, or the operation of the will. Sensory perception, imagination and pure understanding are simply various modes of perception; desire, aversion, assertion, denial and doubt are various modes of willing.

33. *We fall into error only when we make judgements about things which we have not sufficiently perceived.*

Now when we perceive something, so long as we do not make any assertion or denial about it, we clearly avoid error. And we equally avoid error when we confine our assertions or denials to what we clearly and distinctly perceive should be asserted or denied. Error arises only when, as often happens, we make a judgement about something even though we do not have an accurate perception of it.

34. *Making a judgement requires not only the intellect but also the will.*

In order to make a judgement, the intellect is of course required since, in the case of something which we do not in any way perceive, there is no judgement we can make. But the will is also required so that, once something is perceived in some manner, our assent may then be given. Now a judgement — some kind of judgement at least — can be made without the need for a complete and exhaustive perception of the thing in question; for we can assent to many things which we know only in a very obscure and confused manner.

35. *The scope of the will is wider than that of the intellect, and this is the cause of error.*

Moreover, the perception of the intellect extends only to the few objects presented to it, and is always extremely limited. The will, on the other hand, can in a certain sense be called infinite, since we observe without exception that its scope extends to anything that can possibly be an object of any other will — even the immeasurable will of God. So it is easy

1 '... that is, he did not bestow on us everything which he was able to bestow, but which equally we can see he was not obliged to give us' (added in French version).

for us to extend our will beyond what we clearly perceive; and when we do this it is no wonder that we may happen to go wrong.

36. *Our errors cannot be imputed to God.*

But it must not in any way be imagined that, because God did not give us an omniscient intellect, this makes him the author of our errors. For it is of the nature of a created intellect to be finite; and it is of the nature of a finite intellect that its scope should not extend to everything.

37. *The supreme perfection of man is that he acts freely or voluntarily, and it is this which makes him deserve praise or blame.*

The extremely broad scope of the will is part of its very nature. And it is a supreme perfection in man that he acts voluntarily, that is, freely; this makes him in a special way the author of his actions and deserving of praise for what he does. We do not praise automatons for accurately producing all the movements they were designed to perform, because the production of these movements occurs necessarily. It is the designer who is praised for constructing such carefully-made devices; for in constructing them he acted not out of necessity but freely. By the same principle, when we embrace the truth, our doing so voluntarily is much more to our credit than would be the case if we could not do otherwise.

19

38. *The fact that we fall into error is a defect in the way we act, not a defect in our nature. The faults of subordinates may often be attributed to their masters, but never to God.*

The fact that we fall into error is a defect in the way we act or in the use we make of our freedom, but not a defect in our nature. For our nature remains the same whether we judge correctly or incorrectly. And although God could have endowed our intellect with a discernment so acute as to prevent our ever going wrong, we have no right to demand this of him. Admittedly, when one of us men has the power to prevent some evil, but does not prevent it, we say that he is the cause of the evil; but we must not similarly suppose that because God could have brought it about that we never went wrong, this makes him the cause of our errors. The power which men have over each other was given them so that they might employ it in discouraging others from evil; but the power which God has over all men is both absolute and totally free. So we should give him the utmost thanks for the goods which he has so lavishly bestowed upon us, instead of unjustly complaining that he did not bestow on us all the gifts which it was in his power to bestow.

39. *The freedom of the will is self-evident.*

That there is freedom in our will, and that we have power in many cases to give or withhold our assent at will, is so evident that it must be

counted among the first and most common notions that are innate in us.
This was obvious earlier on when, in our attempt to doubt everything, we
20 went so far as to make the supposition of some supremely powerful
author of our being who was attempting to deceive us in every possible
way. For in spite of that supposition, the freedom which we experienced
within us was nonetheless so great as to enable us to abstain from
believing whatever was not quite certain or fully examined. And what we
saw to be beyond doubt even during the period of that supposition is as
self-evident and as transparently clear as anything can be.

40. *It is also certain that everything was preordained by God.*
But now that we have come to know God, we perceive in him a power so
immeasurable that we regard it as impious to suppose that we could ever
do anything which was not already preordained by him. And we can
easily get ourselves into great difficulties if we attempt to reconcile this
divine preordination with the freedom of our will, or attempt to grasp
both these things at once.

41. *How to reconcile the freedom of our will with divine preordination.*
But we shall get out of these difficulties if we remember that our mind is
finite, while the power of God is infinite – the power by which he not
only knew from eternity whatever is or can be, but also willed it and
preordained it. We may attain sufficient knowledge of this power to
perceive clearly and distinctly that God possesses it; but we cannot get a
sufficient grasp of it to see how it leaves the free actions of men
undetermined. Nonetheless, we have such close awareness of the freedom
and indifference which is in us, that there is nothing we can grasp more
evidently or more perfectly. And it would be absurd, simply because we
do not grasp one thing, which we know must by its very nature be
beyond our comprehension, to doubt something else of which we have an
intimate grasp and which we experience within ourselves.

42. *Although we do not want to go wrong, nevertheless we go wrong by
     our own will.*
Now that we know that all our errors depend on the will, it may seem
21 surprising that we should ever go wrong, since there is no one who wants
to go wrong. But there is a great difference between choosing to go wrong
and choosing to give one's assent in matters where, as it happens, error is
to be found. And although there is in fact no one who expressly wishes to
go wrong, there is scarcely anyone who does not often wish to give his
assent to something which, though he does not know it, contains some
error. Indeed, precisely because of their eagerness to find the truth,

people who do not know the right method of finding it often pass judgement on things of which they lack perception, and this is why they fall into error.

43. *We never go wrong when we assent only to what we clearly and distinctly perceive.*

It is certain, however, that we will never mistake the false for the true provided we give our assent only to what we clearly and distinctly perceive. I say that this is certain, because God is not a deceiver, and so the faculty of perception which he has given us cannot incline to falsehood; and the same goes for the faculty of assent, provided its scope is limited to what is clearly perceived. And even if there were no way of proving this, the minds of all of us have been so moulded by nature that whenever we perceive something clearly, we spontaneously give our assent to it and are quite unable to doubt its truth.

44. *When we give our assent to something which is not clearly perceived, this is always a misuse of our judgement, even if by chance we stumble on the truth. The giving of our assent to something unclear happens because we imagine that we clearly perceived it on some previous occasion.*

It is also certain that when we assent to some piece of reasoning when our perception of it is lacking, then either we go wrong, or, if we do stumble on the truth, it is merely by accident, so that we cannot be sure that we are not in error. Of course it seldom happens that we assent to something when we are aware of not perceiving it, since the light of nature tells us that we should never make a judgement except about things we know. What does very often give rise to error is that there are many things which we think we perceived in the past; once these things are committed to memory, we give our assent to them just as we would if we had fully perceived them, whereas in reality we never perceived them at all.

45. *What is meant by a clear perception, and by a distinct perception.*

Indeed there are very many people who in their entire lives never perceive anything with sufficient accuracy to enable them to make a judgement about it with certainty. A perception which can serve as the basis for a 22 certain and indubitable judgement needs to be not merely clear but also distinct. I call a perception 'clear' when it is present and accessible to the attentive mind – just as we say that we see something clearly when it is present to the eye's gaze and stimulates it with a sufficient degree of strength and accessibility. I call a perception 'distinct' if, as well as being clear, it is so sharply separated from all other perceptions that it contains within itself only what is clear.

46. *The example of pain shows that a perception can be clear without being distinct, but cannot be distinct without being clear.*

For example, when someone feels an intense pain, the perception he has of it is indeed very clear, but is not always distinct. For people commonly confuse this perception with an obscure judgement they make concerning the nature of something which they think exists in the painful spot and which they suppose to resemble the sensation of pain; but in fact it is the sensation alone which they perceive clearly. Hence a perception can be clear without being distinct, but not distinct without being clear.

47. *In order to correct the preconceived opinions of our early childhood we must consider the simple notions and what elements in each of them are clear.*

In our childhood the mind was so immersed in the body that although there was much that it perceived clearly, it never perceived anything distinctly. But in spite of this the mind made judgements about many things, and this is the origin of the many preconceived opinions which most of us never subsequently abandon. To enable us to get rid of these preconceived opinions, I shall here briefly list all the simple notions which are the basic components of our thoughts; and in each case I shall distinguish the clear elements from those which are obscure or liable to lead us into error.

48. *All the objects of our perception may be regarded either as things or affections of things, or as eternal truths. The former are listed here.*

All the objects of our perception we regard either as things, or affections of things, or else as eternal truths which have no existence outside our thought.[1] The most general items which we regard as things are 23 *substance, duration, order, number* and any other items of this kind which extend to all classes of things. But I recognize only two ultimate classes of things: first, intellectual or thinking things, i.e. those which pertain to mind or thinking substance; and secondly, material things, i.e. those which pertain to extended substance or body. Perception, volition and all the modes both of perceiving and of willing are referred to thinking substance; while to extended substance belong size

---

1 An 'affection' of a thing is one of its qualities or modes; see art. 56, below. The French version omits this technical term and simply distinguishes between, on the one hand, 'things which have some existence', and, on the other hand, 'truths which are nothing outside our thought'.

(that is, extension in length, breadth and depth), shape, motion, position, divisibility of component parts and the like. But we also experience within ourselves certain other things which must not be referred either to the mind alone or to the body alone. These arise, as will be made clear later on, in the appropriate place,[1] from the close and intimate union of our mind with the body. This list includes, first, appetites like hunger and thirst; secondly, the emotions or passions of the mind which do not consist of thought alone, such as the emotions of anger, joy, sadness and love; and finally, all the sensations, such as those of pain, pleasure, light, colours, sounds, smells, tastes, heat, hardness and the other tactile qualities.

49. *It is not possible – or indeed necessary – to give a similar list of eternal truths.*

Everything in the preceding list we regard either as a thing or as a quality or mode of a thing. But when we recognize that it is impossible for anything to come from nothing, the proposition *Nothing comes from nothing* is regarded not as a really existing thing, or even as a mode of a thing, but as an eternal truth which resides within our mind. Such truths are termed common notions or axioms. The following are examples of this class: *It is impossible for the same thing to be and not to be at the same time; What is done cannot be undone; He who thinks cannot but exist while he thinks*; and countless others. It would not be easy to draw up a list of all of them; but nonetheless we cannot fail to know them when the occasion for thinking about them arises, provided that we are not blinded by preconceived opinions.

50. *Eternal truths are clearly perceived; but, because of preconceived opinions, not all of them are clearly perceived by everyone.*

In the case of these common notions, there is no doubt that they are capable of being clearly and distinctly perceived; for otherwise they would not properly be called common notions. But some of them do not really have an equal claim to be called 'common' among all people, since they are not equally well perceived by everyone. This is not, I think, because one man's faculty of knowledge extends more widely than another's, but because the common notions are in conflict with the preconceived opinions of some people who, as a result, cannot easily grasp them. But the selfsame notions are perceived with the utmost clarity by other people who are free from such preconceived opinions.

---

1 See Part 4, art. 189–91, pp. 279ff below.

51. *What is meant by 'substance' – a term which does not apply*
    univocally to God and his creatures.

In the case of those items which we regard as things or modes of things, it
is worthwhile examining each of them separately. By *substance* we can
understand nothing other than a thing which exists in such a way as to
depend on no other thing for its existence. And there is only one
substance which can be understood to depend on no other thing whatsoever, namely God. In the case of all other substances, we perceive that
they can exist only with the help of God's concurrence. Hence the term
'substance' does not apply *univocally*, as they say in the Schools, to God
and to other things; that is, there is no distinctly intelligible meaning of
the term which is common to God and his creatures. <In the case of
created things, some are of such a nature that they cannot exist without
other things, while some need only the ordinary concurrence of God in
order to exist. We make this distinction by calling the latter 'substances'
and the former 'qualities' or 'attributes' of those substances.>

52. *The term 'substance' applies univocally to mind and to body. How a*
    substance itself is known.

25 But as for corporeal substance and mind (or created thinking substance), these can be understood to fall under this common concept:
things that need only the concurrence of God in order to exist. However,
we cannot initially become aware of a substance merely through its being
an existing thing, since this alone does not of itself have any effect on us.
We can, however, easily come to know a substance by one of its
attributes, in virtue of the common notion that nothingness possesses no
attributes, that is to say, no properties or qualities. Thus, if we perceive
the presence of some attribute, we can infer that there must also be
present an existing thing or substance to which it may be attributed.

53. *To each substance there belongs one principal attribute; in the case*
    of mind, this is thought, and in the case of body it is extension.

A substance may indeed be known through any attribute at all; but each
substance has one principal property which constitutes its nature and
essence, and to which all its other properties are referred. Thus extension
in length, breadth and depth constitutes the nature of corporeal substance; and thought constitutes the nature of thinking substance. Everything else which can be attributed to body presupposes extension, and is
merely a mode of an extended thing; and similarly, whatever we find in
the mind is simply one of the various modes of thinking. For example,
shape is unintelligible except in an extended thing; and motion is

unintelligible except as motion in an extended space; while imagination, sensation and will are intelligible only in a thinking thing. By contrast, it is possible to understand extension without shape or movement, and thought without imagination or sensation, and so on; and this is quite clear to anyone who gives the matter his attention.

54. *How we can have clear and distinct notions of thinking substance and of corporeal substance, and also of God.*

Thus we can easily have two clear and distinct notions or ideas, one of created thinking substance, and the other of corporeal substance, provided we are careful to distinguish all the attributes of thought from the attributes of extension. We can also have a clear and distinct idea of uncreated and independent thinking substance, that is of God. Here we must simply avoid supposing that the idea adequately represents everything which is to be found in God; and we must not invent any additional features, but concentrate only on what is really contained in the idea and on what we clearly perceive to belong to the nature of a supremely perfect being. And certainly no one can deny that we possess such an idea of God, unless he reckons that there is absolutely no knowledge of God to be found in the minds of men.

55. *How we can also have a distinct understanding of duration, order and number.*

We shall also have a very distinct understanding of *duration*, *order* and *number*, provided we do not mistakenly tack on to them any concept of substance. Instead, we should regard the duration of a thing simply as a mode under which we conceive the thing in so far as it continues to exist. And similarly we should not regard order or number as anything separate from the things which are ordered and numbered, but should think of them simply as modes under which we consider the things in question.

56. *What modes, qualities and attributes are.*

By *mode*, as used above, we understand exactly the same as what is elsewhere meant by an *attribute* or *quality*. But we employ the term *mode* when we are thinking of a substance as being affected or modified; when the modification enables the substance to be designated as a substance of such and such a kind, we use the term *quality*; and finally, when we are simply thinking in a more general way of what is in a substance, we use the term *attribute*. Hence we do not, strictly speaking, say that there are modes or qualities in God, but simply attributes, since in the case of God, any variation is unintelligible. And even in the case of created things, that which always remains unmodified – for example existence or duration in a thing which exists and endures – should be called not a quality or a mode but an attribute.

57. Some attributes are in things and others in thought. What duration and time are.

27 Now some attributes or modes are in the very things of which they are said to be attributes or modes, while others are only in our thought. For example, when time is distinguished from duration taken in the general sense and called the measure of movement, it is simply a mode of thought. For the duration which we understand to be involved in movement is certainly no different from the duration involved in things which do not move. This is clear from the fact that if there are two bodies moving for an hour, one slowly and the other quickly, we do not reckon the amount of time to be greater in the latter case than the former, even though the amount of movement may be much greater. But in order to measure the duration of all things, we compare their duration with the duration of the greatest and most regular motions which give rise to years and days, and we call this duration 'time'. Yet nothing is thereby added to duration, taken in its general sense, except for a mode of thought.

58. Number and all universals are simply modes of thinking.
In the same way, number, when it is considered simply in the abstract or in general, and not in any created things, is merely a mode of thinking; and the same applies to all the other *universals*, as we call them.

59. How universals arise. The five common universals: genus, species, differentia, property, accident.
These universals arise solely from the fact that we make use of one and the same idea for thinking of all individual items which resemble each other: we apply one and the same term to all the things which are represented by the idea in question, and this is the universal term. When we see two stones, for example, and direct our attention not to their nature but merely to the fact that there are two of them, we form the idea of the number which we call 'two'; and when we later see two birds or two trees, and consider not their nature but merely the fact that there are two of them, we go back to the same idea as before. This, then, is the universal idea; and we always designate the number in question by the same
28 universal term 'two'. In the same way, when we see a figure made up of three lines, we form an idea of it which we call the idea of a triangle; and we later make use of it as a universal idea, so as to represent to our mind all the other figures made up of three lines. Moreover, when we notice that some triangles have one right angle, and others do not, we form the

universal idea of a right-angled triangle; since this idea is related to the preceding idea as a special case, it is termed a *species*. And the rectangularity is the universal *differentia* which distinguishes all right-angled triangles from other triangles. And the fact that the square on the hypotenuse is equal to the sum of the squares on the other two sides is a *property* belonging to all and only right-angled triangles. Finally, if we suppose that some right-angled triangles are in motion while others are not, this will be a universal *accident* of such triangles. Hence five universals are commonly listed: *genus, species, differentia, property* and *accident*.

60. *Three sorts of distinction: firstly, what is meant by a 'real distinction'.*

Now number, in things themselves, arises from the distinction between them. But *distinction* can be taken in three ways: as a *real* distinction, a *modal* distinction, or a *conceptual* distinction. Strictly speaking, a *real* distinction exists only between two or more substances; and we can perceive that two substances are really distinct simply from the fact that we can clearly and distinctly understand one apart from the other. For when we come to know God, we are certain that he can bring about anything of which we have a distinct understanding. For example, even though we may not yet know for certain that any extended or corporeal substance exists in reality, the mere fact that we have an idea of such a substance enables us to be certain that it is capable of existing. And we can also be certain that, if it exists, each and every part of it, as delimited by us in our thought, is really distinct from the other parts of the same substance. Similarly, from the mere fact that each of us understands himself to be a thinking thing and is capable, in thought, of excluding from himself every other substance, whether thinking or extended, it is certain that each of us, regarded in this way, is really distinct from every other thinking substance and from every corporeal substance. And even if we suppose that God has joined some corporeal substance to such a thinking substance so closely that they cannot be more closely conjoined, thus compounding them into a unity, they nonetheless remain really distinct. For no matter how closely God may have united them, the power which he previously had of separating them, or keeping one in being without the other, is something he could not lay aside; and things which God has the power to separate, or to keep in being separately, are really distinct.

61. *What is meant by a 'modal distinction'.*

A *modal* distinction can be taken in two ways: firstly, as a distinction between a mode, properly so called, and the substance of which it is a mode; and secondly, as a distinction between two modes of the same substance. The first kind of modal distinction can be recognized from the fact that we can clearly perceive a substance apart from the mode which we say differs from it, whereas we cannot, conversely, understand the mode apart from the substance. Thus there is a modal distinction between shape or motion and the corporeal substance in which they inhere; and similarly, there is a modal distinction between affirmation or recollection and the mind. The second kind of modal distinction is recognized from the fact that we are able to arrive at knowledge of one mode apart from another, and *vice versa*, whereas we cannot know either mode apart from the substance in which they both inhere. For example, if a stone is in motion and is square-shaped, I can understand the square shape without the motion and, conversely, the motion without the square shape; but I can understand neither the motion nor the shape apart from 30 the substance of the stone. A different case, however, is the distinction by which the mode of one substance is distinct from another substance or from the mode of another substance. An example of this is the way in which the motion of one body is distinct from another body, or from the mind; or the way in which motion differs from doubt.[1] It seems more appropriate to call this kind of distinction a real distinction, rather than a modal distinction, since the modes in question cannot be clearly understood apart from the really distinct substances of which they are modes.

62. *What is meant by a 'conceptual distinction'.*

Finally, a *conceptual distinction* is a distinction between a substance and some attribute of that substance without which the substance is unintelligible; alternatively, it is a distinction between two such attributes of a single substance. Such a distinction is recognized by our inability to form a clear and distinct idea of the substance if we exclude from it the attribute in question, or, alternatively, by our inability to perceive clearly the idea of one of the two attributes if we separate it from the other. For example, since a substance cannot cease to endure without also ceasing to be, the distinction between the substance and its duration is merely a conceptual one. And in the case of all the modes of thought[2] which we consider as being in objects, there is merely a conceptual distinction between the modes and the object which they are thought of as applying to; and the same is true of the distinction between the modes

---

1 In place of *dubitatione* ('doubt') AT read *duratione* ('duration'); the former reading is undoubtedly correct, and is followed in the French version.
2 See above, art. 57 and 58.

themselves when these are in one and the same object.[1] I am aware that elsewhere I did lump this type of distinction with the modal distinction, namely at the end of my Replies to the First Set of Objections to the *Meditations on First Philosophy*[2]; but that was not a suitable place for making a careful distinction between the two types; it was enough for my purposes to distinguish both from the real distinction.

63. How thought and extension may be distinctly recognized as constituting the nature of mind and of body.

Thought and extension can be regarded as constituting the natures of intelligent substance and corporeal substance; they must then be considered as nothing else but thinking substance itself and extended substance itself – that is, as mind and body. In this way we will have a very clear and distinct understanding of them. Indeed, it is much easier for us to have an understanding of extended substance or thinking substance than it is for us to understand substance on its own, leaving out the fact that it thinks or is extended. For we have some difficulty in abstracting the notion of substance from the notions of thought and extension, since the distinction between these notions and the notion of substance itself is merely a conceptual distinction. A concept is not any more distinct because we include less in it; its distinctness simply depends on our carefully distinguishing what we do include in it from everything else.

64. How thought and extension may also be distinctly recognized as modes of a substance.

Thought and extension may also be taken as modes of a substance, in so far as one and the same mind is capable of having many different thoughts; and one and the same body, with its quantity unchanged, may be extended in many different ways (for example, at one moment it may be greater in length and smaller in breadth or depth, and a little later, by contrast, it may be greater in breadth and smaller in length).[3] The distinction between thought or extension and the substance will then be a modal one; and our understanding of them will be capable of being just as clear and distinct as our understanding of the substance itself, provided they are regarded not as substances (that is, things which are separate from other things) but simply as modes of things. By regarding

---

1 For this sentence the French version substitutes: 'And in general all the attributes which cause us to have different thoughts concerning a single thing, such as the extension of a body and its property of being divided into several parts, do not differ from the body ... or from each other, except in so far as we sometimes think confusedly of one without thinking of the other.'   2 See vol. II, pp. 85f.
3 Cf. the example of the wax in Med. II: vol. II, p. 20.

them as being in the substances of which they are modes, we distinguish
them from the substances in question and see them for what they really
are. If, on the other hand, we attempted to consider them apart from the
substances in which they inhere, we would be regarding them as things
which subsisted in their own right, and would thus be confusing the ideas
of a mode and a substance.

32 **65. *How the modes of thought and extension are to be known.***
There are various modes of thought such as understanding, imagination,
memory, volition, and so on; and there are various modes of extension,
or modes which belong to extension, such as all shapes, the positions of
parts and the motions of the parts. And, just as before, we shall arrive at
the best perception of all these items if we regard them simply as modes
of the things in which they are located. As far as motion is concerned, it
will be best if we think simply of local motion, without inquiring into the
force which produces it (though I shall attempt to explain this later in the
appropriate place[1]).

66. *How sensations, emotions and appetites may be clearly known,*
despite the fact that we are frequently wrong in our judgements
concerning them.
There remains sensations, emotions and appetites.[2] These may be clearly
perceived provided we take great care in our judgements concerning
them to include no more than what is strictly contained in our perception
– no more than that of which we have inner awareness. But this is a very
difficult rule to observe, at least with regard to sensations. For all of us
have, from our early childhood, judged that all the objects of our
sense-perception are things existing outside our minds and closely
resembling our sensations, i.e. the perceptions that we had of them. Thus,
on seeing a colour, for example, we supposed we were seeing a thing
located outside us which closely resembled the idea of colour that we
experienced within us at the time. And this was something that, because
of our habit of making such judgements, we thought we saw clearly and
distinctly – so much so that we took it for something certain and
indubitable.

67. *We frequently make mistakes, even in our judgements concerning*
pain.
The same thing happens with regard to everything else of which we have
sensory awareness, even to pleasure and pain. For, although we do not

1 In Part 2; see especially art. 43 and 44.
2 These are the items remaining from the objects of perception listed above, art. 48.

suppose that these exist outside us, we generally regard them not as being in the mind alone, or in our perception, but as being in the hand or foot or in some other part of our body. But the fact that we feel a pain as it were in our foot does not make it certain that the pain exists outside our mind, in the foot, any more than the fact that we see light as it were in the sun, makes it certain the light exists outside us, in the sun. Both these beliefs are preconceived opinions of our early childhood, as will become clear below. 33

68. *How to distinguish what we clearly know in such matters from what can lead us astray.*

In order to distinguish what is clear in this connection from what is obscure, we must be very careful to note that pain and colour and so on are clearly and distinctly perceived when they are regarded merely as sensations or thoughts. But when they are judged to be real things existing outside our mind, there is no way of understanding what sort of things they are. If someone says he sees colour in a body or feels pain in a limb, this amounts to saying that he sees or feels something there of which he is wholly ignorant, or, in other words, that he does not know what he is seeing or feeling. Admittedly, if he fails to pay sufficient attention, he may easily convince himself that he has some knowledge of what he sees or feels, because he may suppose that it is something similar to the sensation of colour or pain which he experiences within himself. But if he examines the nature of what is represented by the sensation of colour or pain – what is represented as existing in the coloured body or the painful part – he will realize that he is wholly ignorant of it.

69. *We know size, shape and so forth in quite a different way from the way in which we know colours, pains and the like.*

This will be especially clear if we consider the wide gap between our knowledge of those features of bodies which we clearly perceive, as stated earlier,[1] and our knowledge of those features which must be referred to the senses, as I have just pointed out. To the former class belong the size of the bodies we see, their shape, motion, position, duration, number and so on (by 'motion' I mean local motion: philosophers have imagined that there are other kinds of motion distinct from local motion, thereby only making the nature of motion less intelligible to themselves).[2] To the latter class belong the colour in a body, as well as 34

1 See above, art. 48.
2 By 'local motion' is meant, roughly, movement from place to place (see further Part 2, art. 24 and 25, below pp. 233f). Scholastic philosophers, following Aristotle, sometimes classified any alteration (e.g. a quantitative or a qualitative change) as a type of motion; various other distinctions, e.g. that between 'natural' and 'violent' motion, were also commonplace. See also *The World*, p. 94 above.

pain, smell, taste and so on. It is true that when we see a body we are just as certain of its existence in virtue of its having a visible colour as we are in virtue of its having a visible shape; but our knowledge of what it is for the body to have a shape is much clearer than our knowledge of what it is for it to be coloured.

70. *There are two ways of making judgements concerning the things that can be perceived by the senses: the first enables us to avoid error, while the second allows us to fall into error.*

It is clear, then, that when we say that we perceive colours in objects, this is really just the same as saying that we perceive something in the objects whose nature we do not know, but which produces in us a certain very clear and vivid sensation which we call the sensation of colour. But the way in which we make our judgement can vary very widely. As long as we merely judge that there is in the objects (that is, in the things, whatever they may turn out to be, which are the source of our sensations) something whose nature we do not know, then we avoid error; indeed, we are actually guarding against error, since the recognition that we are ignorant of something makes us less liable to make any rash judgement about it. But it is quite different when we suppose that we perceive colours in objects. Of course, we do not really know what it is that we are calling a colour; and we cannot find any intelligible resemblance between the colour which we suppose to be in objects and that which we experience in our sensation. But this is something we do not take account of; and, what is more, there are many other features, such as size, shape and number which we clearly perceive to be actually or at least possibly present in objects in a way exactly corresponding to our sensory perception or understanding. And so we easily fall into the error of judging that what is called colour in objects is something exactly like the colour of which we have sensory awareness; and we make the mistake of thinking that we clearly perceive what we do not perceive at all.

35

71. *The chief cause of error arises from the preconceived opinions of childhood.*

It is here that the first and main cause of all our errors may be recognized. In our early childhood the mind was so closely tied to the body that it had no leisure for any thoughts except those by means of which it had sensory awareness of what was happening to the body. It did not refer these thoughts to anything outside itself, but merely felt pain when something harmful was happening to the body and felt pleasure when something beneficial occurred. And when nothing very beneficial or harmful was happening to the body, the mind had various sensations corresponding to the different areas where, and ways in which, the body was being stimulated, namely what we call the sensations of tastes, smells, sounds, heat, cold, light, colours and so on – sensations which do not represent anything located outside our thought.[1] At the same time the mind perceived sizes, shapes, motions and so on, which were presented to it not as sensations but as things, or modes of things, existing (or at least capable of existing) outside thought, although it was not yet aware of the difference between things and sensations. The next stage arose when the mechanism of the body, which is so constructed by nature that it has the ability to move in various ways by its own power, twisted around aimlessly in all directions in its random attempts to pursue the beneficial and avoid the harmful; at this point the mind that was attached to the body began to notice that the objects of this pursuit or avoidance had an existence outside itself. And it attributed to them not only sizes, shapes, motions and the like, which it perceived as things or modes of things, but also tastes, smells and so on, the sensations of which were, it realized, produced by the objects in question. Moreover, since the mind judged everything in terms of its utility to the body in which it was immersed, it assessed the amount of reality in each object by the extent to which it was affected by it. As a result, it supposed that there was more substance or corporeality in rocks and metals than in water or air, since it felt more hardness and heaviness in them. Indeed, it regarded the air as a mere nothing, so long as it felt no wind or cold or heat in it. And because the light coming from the stars appeared no brighter than that produced by the meagre glow of an oil lamp, it did not imagine any star as being any bigger than this. And because it did not observe that the earth turns on its axis or that its surface is curved to form a globe, it was rather inclined to suppose that the earth was immobile and its surface flat. Right from infancy our mind was swamped with a thousand such preconceived opinions; and in later childhood, forgetting that they were adopted without sufficient examination, it regarded them as known by the senses or implanted by nature, and accepted them as utterly true and evident.

36

72. *The second cause of error is that we cannot forget our preconceived opinions.*

In later years the mind is no longer a total slave to the body, and does not refer everything to it. Indeed, it inquires into the truth of things considered in themselves, and discovers very many of its previous judgements to be false. But despite this, it is not easy for the mind to erase

1 '... but which vary according to the different movements which pass from all parts of our body to the part of the brain to which our mind is closely joined and united' (added in French version).

these false judgements from its memory; and as long as they stick there, they can cause a variety of errors. For example, in our early childhood we
37 imagined the stars as being very small; and although astronomical arguments now clearly show us that they are very large indeed, our preconceived opinion is still strong enough to make it very hard for us to imagine them differently from the way we did before.

73. *The third cause of error is that we become tired if we have to attend*
    to things which are not present to the senses; as a result, our
    judgements on these things are habitually based not on present
    perception but on preconceived opinion.

What is more, our mind is unable to keep its attention on things without some degree of difficulty and fatigue; and it is hardest of all for it to attend to what is not present to the senses or even to the imagination. This may be due to the very nature that the mind has as a result of being joined to the body; or it may be because it was exclusively occupied with the objects of sense and imagination in its earliest years, and has thus acquired more practice and a greater aptitude for thinking about them than it has for thinking about other things. The result of this is that many people's understanding of substance is still limited to that which is imaginable and corporeal, or even to that which is capable of being perceived by the senses. Such people do not know that the objects of the imagination are restricted to those which have extension, motion and shape, whereas there are many other things that are objects of the understanding. Also, they suppose that nothing can subsist unless it is a body, and that no body can subsist unless it can be perceived by the senses. Now since, as will be clearly shown below, there is nothing whose true nature we perceive by the senses alone, it turns out that most people have nothing but confused perceptions throughout their entire lives.

74. *The fourth cause of error is that we attach our concepts to words*
    which do not precisely correspond to real things.

Finally, because of the use of language, we tie all our concepts to the words used to express them; and when we store the concepts in our memory we always simultaneously store the corresponding words. Later on we find the words easier to recall than the things; and because of this it is very seldom that our concept of a thing is so distinct that we can separate it totally from our concept of the words involved. The thoughts of almost all people are more concerned with words than with things; and as a result people very often give their assent to words they do not
38 understand, thinking they once understood them, or that they got them

from others who did understand them correctly. This is not the place to give a precise account of all these matters, since the nature of the human body has not yet been dealt with – indeed the existence of any body has not yet been proved. Nonetheless, what has been said appears to be sufficiently intelligible to help us distinguish those of our concepts which are clear and distinct from those which are obscure and confused.

75. *Summary of the rules to be observed in order to philosophize correctly.*

In order to philosophize seriously and search out the truth about all the things that are capable of being known, we must first of all lay aside all our preconceived opinions, or at least we must take the greatest care not to put our trust in any of the opinions accepted by us in the past until we have first scrutinized them afresh and confirmed their truth. Next, we must give our attention in an orderly way to the notions that we have within us, and we must judge to be true all and only those whose truth we clearly and distinctly recognize when we attend to them in this way. When we do this we shall realize, first of all, that we exist in so far as our nature consists in thinking; and we shall simultaneously realize both that there is a God, and that we depend on him, and also that a consideration of his attributes enables us to investigate the truth of other things, since he is their cause. Finally, we will see that besides the notions of God and of our mind, we have within us knowledge of many propositions which are eternally true, such as 'Nothing comes from nothing'. We shall also find that we have knowledge both of a corporeal or extended nature which is divisible, moveable, and so on, and also of certain sensations which affect us, such as the sensations of pain, colours, tastes and so on (though we do not yet know the cause of our being affected in this way). When we contrast all this knowledge with the confused thoughts we had before, we will acquire the habit of forming clear and distinct concepts of all the things that can be known. These few instructions seem to me to 39 contain the most important principles of human knowledge.

76. *Divine authority must be put before our own perception; but, that aside, the philosopher should give his assent only to what he has perceived.*

But above all else we must impress on our memory the overriding rule that whatever God has revealed to us must be accepted as more certain than anything else. And although the light of reason may, with the utmost clarity and evidence, appear to suggest something different, we must still put our entire faith in divine authority rather than in our own judgement. But on matters where we are not instructed by divine faith, it is quite unworthy of a philosopher to accept anything as true if he has never established its truth by thorough scrutiny; and he should never rely on the senses, that is, on the ill-considered judgements of his childhood, in preference to his mature powers of reason.

PART TWO

The Principles of Material Things

1. The arguments that lead to the certain knowledge of the existence of material things.

Everyone is quite convinced of the existence of material things. But earlier on we cast doubt on this belief and counted it as one of the preconceived opinions of our childhood.[1] So it is necessary for us to investigate next the arguments by which the existence of material things may be known with certainty. Now, all our sensations undoubtedly come to us from something that is distinct from our mind. For it is not in our power to make ourselves have one sensation rather than another; this is obviously dependent on the thing that is acting on our senses. Admittedly one can raise the question of whether this thing is God or something different from God. But we have sensory awareness of, or rather as a result of sensory stimulation we have a clear and distinct perception of, some kind of matter, which is extended in length, breadth and depth, and has various differently shaped and variously moving parts which give rise to our various sensations of colours, smells, pain and so on. And if God were himself immediately producing in our mind the idea of such extended matter, or even if he were causing the idea to be produced by something which lacked extension, shape and motion, there would be no way of avoiding the conclusion that he should be regarded as a deceiver. For we have a clear understanding of this matter as something that is quite different from God and from ourselves or our mind; and we appear to see clearly that the idea of it comes to us from things located outside ourselves, which it wholly resembles. And we have already noted that it is quite inconsistent with the nature of God that he should be a deceiver.[2] The unavoidable conclusion, then, is that there exists something extended in length, breadth and depth and possessing all the properties which we clearly perceive to belong to an extended thing. And it is this extended thing that we call 'body' or 'matter'.

1 See Part I, art. 4. 2 Above, Part I, art. 29.

2. *The basis for our knowledge that the human body is closely conjoined with the mind.*

By the same token, the conclusion that there is a particular body that is more closely conjoined with our mind than any other body follows from our clear awareness that pain and other sensations come to us quite unexpectedly. The mind is aware that these sensations do not come from itself alone, and that they cannot belong to it simply in virtue of its being a thinking thing; instead, they can belong to it only in virtue of its being joined to something other than itself which is extended and moveable – namely what we call the human body. But this is not the place for a detailed explanation of its nature.

3. *Sensory perception does not show us what really exists in things, but merely shows us what is beneficial or harmful to man's composite nature.*

It will be enough, for the present, to note that sensory perceptions are related exclusively to this combination of the human body and mind. They normally tell us of the benefit or harm that external bodies may do to this combination, and do not, except occasionally and accidentally, show us what external bodies are like in themselves. If we bear this in mind we will easily lay aside the preconceived opinions acquired from the senses, and in this connection make use of the intellect alone, carefully attending to the ideas implanted in it by nature.

4. *The nature of body consists not in weight, hardness, colour, or the like, but simply in extension.*

If we do this, we shall perceive that the nature of matter, or body considered in general, consists not in its being something which is hard or heavy or coloured, or which affects the senses in any way, but simply in its being something which is extended in length, breadth and depth. For as regards hardness, our sensation tells us no more than that the parts of a hard body resist the motion of our hands when they come into contact with them. If, whenever our hands moved in a given direction, all the bodies in that area were to move away at the same speed as that of our approaching hands, we should never have any sensation of hardness. And since it is quite unintelligible to suppose that, if bodies did move away in this fashion, they would thereby lose their bodily nature, it follows that this nature cannot consist in hardness. By the same reasoning it can be shown that weight, colour, and all other such qualities that are perceived by the senses as being in corporeal matter, can be removed from it, while the matter itself remains intact; it thus follows that its nature does not depend on any of these qualities.

5. This truth about the nature of body is obscured by preconceived opinions concerning rarefaction and empty space.

But there are still two possible reasons for doubting that the true nature of body consists solely in extension. The first is the widespread belief that many bodies can be rarefied and condensed in such a way that when rarefied they possess more extension than when condensed. Indeed, the subtlety of some people goes so far that they distinguish the substance of a body from its quantity, and even its quantity from its extension.[1] The second reason is that if we understand there to be nothing in a given place   43 but extension in length, breadth and depth, we generally say not that there is a body there, but simply that there is a space, or even an empty space; and almost everyone is convinced that this amounts to nothing at all.

6. How rarefaction occurs.

But with regard to rarefaction and condensation, anyone who attends to his own thoughts, and is willing to admit only what he clearly perceives, will not suppose that anything happens in these processes beyond a change of shape. Rarefied bodies, that is to say, are those which have many gaps between their parts – gaps which are occupied by other bodies; and they become denser simply in virtue of the parts coming together and reducing or completely closing the gaps. In this last eventuality a body becomes so dense that it would be a contradiction to suppose that it could be made any denser. Now in this condition, the extension of a body is no less than when it occupies more space in virtue of the mutual separation of its parts; for whatever extension is comprised in the pores or gaps left between the parts must be attributed not to the body itself but to the various other bodies which fill the gaps. In just the same way, when we see a sponge filled with water or some other liquid, we do not suppose that in terms of its own individual parts it has a greater extension than when it is squeezed dry; we simply suppose that its pores are open wider, so that it spreads over a greater space.

7. This is the only intelligible way of explaining rarefaction.

I really do not see what has prompted others to say that rarefaction occurs through an increase of quantity, in preference to explaining it by means of this example of the sponge.[2] It is true that when air or water is rarefied, we do not see any pores being made larger, or any new body   44

---

1 Cf. *The World*, above p. 92.
2 Scholastic philosophers explained rarefaction in terms of a given amount of matter occupying a larger quantity or volume of space: for Descartes, however, this is unintelligible, since there is no real distinction between the notions of 'quantity', 'matter' and 'space'. See below, art. 8–12.

coming to fill them up. But to invent something unintelligible so as to provide a purely verbal explanation of rarefaction is surely less rational than inferring the existence of pores or gaps which are made larger, and supposing that some new body comes and fills them. Admittedly, we do not perceive this new body with any of our senses; but there is no compelling reason to believe that all the bodies which exist must affect our senses. Moreover, it is very easy for us to see how rarefaction can occur in this way, but we cannot see how it could occur in any other way. Finally, it is a complete contradiction to suppose that something should be augmented by new quantity or new extension without new extended substance, i.e. a new body, being added to it at the same time. For any addition of extension or quantity is unintelligible without the addition of substance which has quantity and extension. This will become clearer from what follows.

8. *The distinction between quantity or number and the thing that has*
   quantity or number is merely a conceptual distinction.
There is no real difference between quantity and the extended substance; the difference is merely a conceptual one, like that between number and the thing which is numbered. We can, for example, consider the entire nature of the corporeal substance which occupies a space of ten feet without attending to the specific measurement; for we understand this nature to be exactly the same in any part of the space as in the whole space. And, conversely, we can think of the number ten, or the continuous quantity *ten feet*, without attending to this determinate substance. For the concept of the number ten is exactly the same irrespective of whether it is referred to this measurement of ten feet or to anything else; and as for the continuous quantity *ten feet*, although this is
45 unintelligible without some extended substance of which it is the quantity, it can be understood apart from this determinate substance. In reality, however, it is impossible to take even the smallest fraction from the quantity or extension without also removing just as much from the substance; and conversely, it is impossible to remove the smallest amount from the substance without taking away just as much from the quantity or extension.

9. *If corporeal substance is distinguished from its quantity, it is*
   conceived in a confused manner as something incorporeal.
Others may disagree, but I do not think they have any alternative perception of the matter. When they make a distinction between substance and extension or quantity, either they do not understand anything by the term 'substance', or else they simply have a confused idea

of incorporeal substance, which they falsely attach to corporeal substance; and they relegate the true idea of corporeal substance to the category of extension, which, however, they term an accident. There is thus no correspondence between their verbal expressions and what they grasp in their minds.

10. *What is meant by 'space', or 'internal place'.*
There is no real distinction between space, or internal place,[1] and the corporeal substance contained in it; the only difference lies in the way in which we are accustomed to conceive of them. For in reality the extension in length, breadth and depth which constitutes a space is exactly the same as that which constitutes a body. The difference arises as follows: in the case of a body, we regard the extension as something particular, and thus think of it as changing whenever there is a new body; but in the case of a space, we attribute to the extension only a generic unity, so that when a new body comes to occupy the space, the extension of the space is reckoned not to change but to remain one and the same, so long as it retains the same size and shape and keeps the same position relative to certain external bodies which we use to determine the space in question.

11. *There is no real difference between space and corporeal substance.* 46
It is easy for us to recognize that the extension constituting the nature of a body is exactly the same as that constituting the nature of a space. There is no more difference between them than there is between the nature of a genus or species and the nature of an individual. Suppose we attend to the idea we have of some body, for example a stone, and leave out everything we know to be non-essential to the nature of body: we will first of all exclude hardness, since if the stone is melted or pulverized it will lose its hardness without thereby ceasing to be a body; next we will exclude colour, since we have often seen stones so transparent as to lack colour; next we will exclude heaviness, since although fire is extremely light it is still thought of as being corporeal; and finally we will exclude cold and heat and all other such qualities, either because they are not thought of as being in the stone, or because if they change, the stone is not on that account reckoned to have lost its bodily nature. After all this, we will see that nothing remains in the idea of the stone except that it is something extended in length, breadth and depth. Yet this is just what is

1 The scholastics distinguished between *locus internus*, or 'internal place' (the space occupied by a body), and *locus externus*, or 'external space' (the external surface containing a body). Descartes employs the traditional terminology here and at art. 13 below, but puts it to his own use.

comprised in the idea of a space – not merely a space which is full of bodies, but even a space which is called 'empty'.[1]

12. *The difference between space and corporeal substance lies in our way of conceiving them.*

There is, however, a difference in the way in which we conceive of space and corporeal substance. For if a stone is removed from the space or place where it is, we think that its extension has also been removed from that place, since we regard the extension as something particular and inseparable from the stone. But at the same time we think that the extension of the place where the stone used to be remains, and is the same as before, although the place is now occupied by wood or water or air or some other body, or is even supposed to be empty. For we are now considering extension as something general, which is thought of as being the same, whether it is the extension of a stone or of wood, or of water or of air or of any other body – or even of a vacuum, if there is such a thing – provided only that it has the same size and shape, and keeps the same position relative to the external bodies that determine the space in question.

13. *What is meant by 'external place'.*

The terms 'place' and 'space', then, do not signify anything different from the body which is said to be in a place; they merely refer to its size, shape and position relative to other bodies. To determine the position, we have to look at various other bodies which we regard as immobile; and in relation to different bodies we may say that the same thing is both changing and not changing its place at the same time. For example, when a ship is under way, a man sitting on the stern remains in one place relative to the other parts of the ship with respect to which his position is unchanged; but he is constantly changing his place relative to the neighbouring shores, since he is constantly receding from one shore and approaching another. Then again, if we believe the earth moves,[2] and suppose that it advances the same distance from west to east as the ship travels from east to west in the corresponding period of time, we shall again say that the man sitting on the stern is not changing his place; for we are now determining the place by means of certain fixed points in the heavens. Finally, if we suppose that there are no such genuinely fixed points to be found in the universe (a supposition which will be shown below to be probable[3]) we shall conclude that nothing has a permanent place, except as determined by our thought.

1 Lat. *vacuum.* See below, art. 16.   2 '... turns on its axis' (French version).
3 The French version has 'demonstrable' instead of 'probable'. Cf. Part 3, art. 29, p. 252 below.

14. *The difference between place and space.*

The difference between the terms 'place' and 'space' is that the former designates more explicitly the position, as opposed to the size or shape, 48 while it is the size and shape that we are concentrating on when we talk of space. For we often say that one thing leaves a given place and another thing arrives there, even though the second thing is not strictly of the same size and shape; but in this case we do not say it occupies the same space. By contrast, when something alters its position, we always say the place is changed, despite the fact that the size and shape remain unaltered. When we say that a thing is in a given place, all we mean is that it occupies such and such a position relative to other things; but when we go on to say that it fills up a given space or place, we mean in addition that it has precisely the size and shape of the space in question.

15. *How external place is rightly taken to be the surface of the surrounding body.*

Thus we always take a space to be an extension in length, breadth and depth. But with regard to place, we sometimes consider it as internal to the thing which is in the place in question, and sometimes as external to it. Now internal place is exactly the same as space; but external place may be taken as being the surface immediately surrounding what is in the place. It should be noted that 'surface' here does not mean any part of the surrounding body but merely the boundary between the surrounding and surrounded bodies, which is no more than a mode. Or rather what is meant is simply the common surface, which is not a part of one body rather than the other but is always reckoned to be the same, provided it keeps the same size and shape. For if there are two bodies, one surrounding the other, and the entire surrounding body changes, surface and all, the surrounded body is not therefore thought of as changing its place, provided that during this time it keeps the same position relative to the external bodies which are regarded as immobile. If, for example, we suppose that a ship on a river is being pulled equally in one direction by the current and in the opposite direction by the wind, so that it does not 49 change its position relative to the banks, we will all readily admit that it stays in the same place, despite the complete change in the surrounding surface.

16. *It is a contradiction to suppose there is such a thing as a vacuum, i.e. that in which there is nothing whatsoever.*

The impossibility of a vacuum, in the philosophical sense of that in which there is no substance whatsoever, is clear from the fact that there is no difference between the extension of a space, or internal place, and the extension of a body. For a body's being extended in length, breadth and depth in itself warrants the conclusion that it is a substance, since it is a complete contradiction that a particular extension should belong to nothing; and the same conclusion must be drawn with respect to a space that is supposed to be a vacuum, namely that since there is extension in it, there must necessarily be substance in it as well.

17. *The ordinary use of the term 'empty' does not imply the total absence of bodies.*

In its ordinary use the term 'empty'[1] usually refers not to a place or space in which there is absolutely nothing at all, but simply to a place in which there is none of the things that we think ought to be there. Thus a pitcher made to hold water is called 'empty' when it is simply full of air; a fishpond is called 'empty', despite all the water in it, if it contains no fish; and a merchant ship is called 'empty' if it is loaded only with sand ballast. And similarly a space is called 'empty' if it contains nothing perceivable by the senses, despite the fact that it is full of created, self-subsistent matter; for normally the only things we give any thought to are those which are detected by our senses. But if we subsequently fail to keep in mind what ought to be understood by the terms 'empty' and 'nothing', we may suppose that a space we call empty contains not just nothing perceivable by the senses but nothing whatsoever; that would be just as mistaken as thinking that the air in a jug is not a subsistent thing on the grounds that a jug is usually said to be empty when it contains nothing but air.

18. *How to correct our preconceived opinion regarding an absolute vacuum.*

Almost all of us fell into this error in our early childhood. Seeing no necessary connection between a vessel and the body contained in it, we reckoned there was nothing to stop God, at least, removing the body which filled the vessel, and preventing any other body from taking its place. But to correct this error we should consider that, although there is no connection between a vessel and this or that particular body contained in it, there is a very strong and wholly necessary connection between the concave shape of the vessel and the extension, taken in its general sense, which must be contained in the concave shape. Indeed, it is no less contradictory for us to conceive of a mountain without a valley than it is for us to think of the concavity apart from the extension contained within it, or the extension apart from the substance which is

---

1 Lat. *vacuum*, from *vacuus*, 'void', 'unoccupied'; cf. art. 18.

extended; for, as I have often said, nothingness cannot possess any extension. Hence, if someone asks what would happen if God were to take away every single body contained in a vessel, without allowing any other body to take the place of what had been removed, the answer must be that the sides of the vessel would, in that case, have to be in contact. For when there is nothing between two bodies they must necessarily touch each other. And it is a manifest contradiction for them to be apart, or to have a distance between them, when the distance in question is nothing; for every distance is a mode of extension, and therefore cannot exist without an extended substance.

19. *The preceding conclusion confirms what we said regarding rarefaction.*

We have thus seen that the nature of corporeal substance consists simply   51
in its being something extended; and its extension is no different from what is normally attributed to space, however 'empty'. From this we readily see that no one part of it can possibly occupy more space at one time than at another, and hence that rarefaction cannot occur except in the way explained earlier on.[1] Similarly, there cannot be more matter or corporeal substance in a vessel filled with lead or gold or any other body, no matter how heavy and hard, than there is when it contains only air and is thought of as empty. This is because the quantity of the parts of matter does not depend on their heaviness or hardness, but solely on their extension, which is always the same for a given vessel.

20. *The foregoing results also demonstrate the impossibility of atoms.*

We also know that it is impossible that there should exist atoms, that is, pieces of matter that are by their very nature indivisible <as some philosophers have imagined>. For if there were any atoms, then no matter how small we imagined them to be, they would necessarily have to be extended; and hence we could in our thought divide each of them into two or more smaller parts, and hence recognize their divisibility. For anything we can divide in our thought must, for that very reason, be known to be divisible; so if we were to judge it to be indivisible, our judgement would conflict with our knowledge. Even if we imagine that God has chosen to bring it about that some particle of matter is incapable of being divided into smaller particles, it will still not be correct, strictly speaking, to call this particle indivisible. For, by making it indivisible by any of his creatures, God certainly could not thereby take away his own power of dividing it, since it is quite impossible for him to diminish his

---

1 See above, art. 6, p. 225.

52   own power, as has been noted above.[1] Hence, strictly speaking, the
     particle will remain divisible, since it is divisible by its very nature.

     21. *Similarly, the extension of the world is indefinite.*
     What is more we recognize that this world, that is, the whole universe of
     corporeal substance, has no limits to its extension. For no matter where
     we imagine the boundaries to be, there are always some indefinitely
     extended spaces beyond them, which we not only imagine but also
     perceive to be imaginable in a true fashion, that is, real. And it follows
     that these spaces contain corporeal substance which is indefinitely
     extended. For, as has already been shown very fully, the idea of the
     extension which we conceive to be in a given space is exactly the same as
     the idea of corporeal substance.

     22. *Similarly, the earth and the heavens are composed of one and the
          same matter; and there cannot be a plurality of worlds.*
     It can also easily be gathered from this that celestial matter is no different
     from terrestrial matter.[2] And even if there were an infinite number of
     worlds, the matter of which they were composed would have to be
     identical; hence, there cannot in fact be a plurality of worlds, but only
     one. For we very clearly understand that the matter whose nature
     consists simply in its being an extended substance already occupies
     absolutely all the imaginable space in which the alleged additional worlds
     would have to be located; and we cannot find within us an idea of any
     other sort of matter.

     23. *All the variety in matter, all the diversity of its forms, depends on
          motion.*
     The matter existing in the entire universe is thus one and the same, and it
     is always recognized as matter simply in virtue of its being extended. All
     the properties which we clearly perceive in it are reducible to its
     divisibility and consequent mobility in respect of its parts, and its
     resulting capacity to be affected in all the ways which we perceive as
     being derivable from the movement of the parts. If the division into parts
     occurs simply in our thought, there is no resulting change; any variation
53   in matter or diversity in its many forms depends on motion. This seems to
     have been widely recognized by the philosophers, since they have stated
     that nature is the principle of motion and rest. And what they meant by

     ---

     1 Cf. Part 1, art. 60, above p. 213.
     2 Descartes here rejects the scholastic doctrine of a radical difference in kind between
       'sublunary' or terrestrial phenomena and the incorruptible world of the heavens.

'nature' in this context is what causes all corporeal things to take on the characteristics of which we are aware in experience.

24. What is meant by 'motion' in the ordinary sense of the term.

Motion, in the ordinary sense of the term, is simply *the action by which a body travels from one place to another.* By 'motion', I mean local motion; for my thought encompasses no other kind, and hence I do not think that any other kind should be imagined to exist in nature.[1] Now I pointed out above that the same thing can be said to be changing and not changing its place at the same time;[2] and similarly the same thing can be said to be moving and not moving. For example, a man sitting on board a ship which is leaving port considers himself to be moving relative to the shore which he regards as fixed; but he does not think of himself as moving relative to the ship, since his position is unchanged relative to its parts. Indeed, since we commonly think all motion involves action, while rest consists in the cessation of action, the man sitting on deck is more properly said to be at rest than in motion, since he does not have any sensory awareness of action in himself.

25. What is meant by 'motion' in the strict sense of the term.

If, on the other hand, we consider what should be understood by *motion,* not in common usage but in accordance with the truth of the matter, and if our aim is to assign a determinate nature to it, we may say that *motion is the transfer of one piece of matter, or one body, from the vicinity of the other bodies which are in immediate contact with it, and which are regarded as being at rest, to the vicinity of other bodies.* By 'one body' or 'one piece of matter' I mean whatever is transferred at a given time, even 54 though this may in fact consist of many parts which have different motions relative to each other. And I say 'the transfer' as opposed to the force or action which brings about the transfer, to show that motion is always in the moving body as opposed to the body which brings about the movement. The two are not normally distinguished with sufficient care; and I want to make it clear that the motion of something that moves is, like the lack of motion in a thing which is at rest, a mere mode of that thing and not itself a subsistent thing, just as shape is a mere mode of the thing which has shape.

26. No more action is required for motion than for rest.

It should be noted that in this connection we are in the grip of a strong preconceived opinion, namely the belief that more action is needed for

---

1 See note to Part I, art. 69, p. 217. 2 Above, art. 13, p. 228.

motion than for rest. We have been convinced of this since early childhood owing to the fact that our bodies move by our will, of which we have inner awareness, but remain at rest simply in virtue of sticking to the earth by gravity,[1] the force of which we do not perceive through the senses. And because gravity and many other causes of which we are unaware produce resistance when we try to move our limbs, and make us tired, we think that a greater action or force is needed to initiate a motion than to stop it; for we take *action* to be the effort we expend in moving our limbs and moving other bodies by the use of our limbs. We will easily get rid of this preconceived opinion if we consider that it takes an effort on our part not only to move external bodies, but also, quite often, to stop them, when gravity and other causes are insufficient to arrest their movement. For example, the action needed to move a boat which is at rest in still water is no greater than that needed to stop it suddenly when 55   it is moving – or rather it is not much greater, for one must subtract the weight of the water displaced by the ship and the viscosity of the water, both of which could gradually bring it to a halt.

27. *Motion and rest are merely various modes of a body in motion.*
We are dealing here not with the action which is understood to exist in the body which produces or arrests the motion, but simply with the transfer of a body, and with the absence of a transfer, i.e. rest. So it is clear that this transfer cannot exist outside the body which is in motion, and that when there is a transfer of motion, the body is in a different state from when there is no transfer, i.e. when it is at rest. Thus motion and rest are nothing else but two different modes of a body.

28. *Motion in the strict sense is to be referred solely to the bodies which are contiguous with the body in motion.*
In my definition I specified that the transfer occurs from the vicinity of contiguous bodies to the vicinity of other bodies; I did not say that there was a transfer from one place to another. This is because, as explained above,[2] the term 'place' has various meanings, depending on how we think of it; but when we understand motion as a transfer occurring from the vicinity of contiguous bodies, then, given that only one set of bodies

---

1 Lat. *gravitas*, literally 'heaviness'. In scholastic physics this term was used to refer to the supposed inherent tendency of terrestrial bodies to downward motion. For Descartes' own use of the term, and his purely mechanistic explanation of heaviness, see below Part 4, art. 20–3. It should be remembered that neither for the scholastics nor for Descartes did the term 'gravity' have its modern (post-Newtonian) connotation of a universal attractive force.
2 See above, Part 2, art. 10, p. 227.

can be contiguous with the same moving body at any one time, we
cannot assign several simultaneous motions to this body, but only one.

29. *And it is to be referred only to those contiguous bodies which are*
    regarded as being at rest.

I further specified that the transfer occurs from the vicinity not of *any*
contiguous bodies but from the vicinity of those which 'are regarded as
being at rest'. For transfer is in itself a reciprocal process: we cannot
understand that a body AB is transferred from the vicinity of a body CD
without simultaneously understanding that CD is transferred from the
vicinity of AB. Exactly the same force and action is needed on both sides. 56
So if we wished to characterize motion strictly in terms of its own nature,
without reference to anything else, then in the case of two contiguous
bodies being transferred in opposite directions, and thus separated, we
should say that there was just as much motion in the one body as in the
other. But this would clash too much with our ordinary way of speaking.
For we are used to standing on the earth and regarding it as at rest; so
although we may see some of its parts, which are contiguous with other
smaller bodies, being transferred out of their vicinity, we do not for that
reason think of the earth itself as in motion.

30. *Why, if there are two contiguous bodies which are separated from*
    each other, motion is attributed to one of them rather than the other.

The principal reason for this is that motion is understood to belong to the
whole body in motion. Now it cannot be understood to belong to the
whole earth, in virtue of the transfer of some of its parts from the vicinity
of smaller contiguous bodies; for often we may observe several such
transfers occurring on the earth in opposite directions. Let the body
EFGH be the earth [see Fig. 1], and suppose that on its surface the body
AB is transferred from E towards F, and simultaneously the body CD is
transferred from H to G. Now this very fact means that the parts of the
earth contiguous with AB are transferred from B towards A; and to

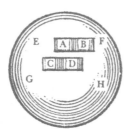

Fig. 1

produce this transfer, the action in these parts must be just as great as that in the body AB, and must be of an identical nature. But for all that, we do not understand the earth to be in motion from B towards A, or from east to west;[1] for, if so, the fact that those of its parts which are contiguous with the body CD are being transferred from C to D would, by the same reasoning, require us to understand the earth to be moving in the other direction, from west to east – which contradicts the former supposition. Hence, to avoid too great a departure from the ordinary way of speaking, we shall say in this case not that the earth moves, but merely that the bodies AB and CD move; and similarly in other cases. But meanwhile we will remember that whatever is real and positive in moving bodies – that in virtue of which they are said to move – is also to be found in the other bodies which are contiguous with them, even though these are regarded merely as being at rest.

31. *How there may be countless different motions in the same body.*
Each body has only one proper motion, since it is understood to be moving away from only one set of bodies, which are contiguous with it and at rest. But it can also share in countless other motions, namely in cases where it is a part of other bodies which have other motions. For example, if someone walking on board ship has a watch in his pocket, the wheels of the watch have only one proper motion, but they also share in another motion because they are in contact with the man who is taking his walk, and they and he form a single piece of matter. They also share in an additional motion through being in contact with the ship tossing on the waves; they share in a further motion through contact with the sea itself; and lastly, they share in yet another motion through contact with the whole earth, if indeed the whole earth is in motion. Now all the motions will really exist in the wheels of the watch, but it is not easy to have an understanding of so many motions all at once, nor can we have knowledge of all of them. So it is enough to confine our attention to that single motion which is the proper motion of each body.

32. *How even the proper motion unique to each body may be*
    considered as a plurality of motions.
The single motion that is the proper motion of each body may also be considered as if it were made up of several motions. For example, we may distinguish two different motions in a carriage wheel – a circular motion about the axle and a rectilinear motion along the line of the road. But

---

1 The original texts (both Latin and French) have the terms 'east' and 'west' transposed throughout this article. The corrections adopted here and three lines lower down seem necessary to make sense of the diagram.

that these are not really distinct is clear from the fact that every single point on the moving object describes only one line. It does not matter that the line is often very twisted so that it seems to have been produced by many different motions; for we can imagine any line at all – even a straight line, which is the simplest of all – as arising from an infinite number of different motions. Thus if the line AB travels towards CD [see Fig. 2], and at the same time the point A travels towards B, the straight

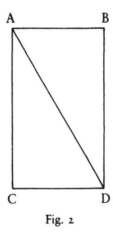

Fig. 2

line AD described by the point A will depend on two rectilinear motions, from A to B and from AB to CD, in just the same way as the curve described by any point of the wheel depends on a rectilinear motion and a circular motion. Although it is often useful to separate a single motion into several components in this way in order to facilitate our perception of it, nevertheless, absolutely speaking, there is only one motion that should be counted for any given body.

33. *How in every case of motion there is a complete circle of bodies moving together.*
I noted above[1] that every place is full of bodies, and that the same portion of matter always takes up the same amount of space, <so that it is impossible for it to fill a greater or lesser space, or for any other body to occupy its place while it remains there>. It follows from this that each body can move only in a <complete> circle <of matter, or ring of bodies which all move together at the same time>: a body entering a given place expels another, and the expelled body moves on and expels another, and so on, until the body at the end of the sequence enters the place left by the

1 Art. 18 and 19, pp. 230f.

first body at the precise moment when the first body is leaving it. We can easily understand this in the case of a perfect circle, since we see that no

59 vacuum and no rarefaction or condensation is needed to enable part A of the circle [see Fig. 3] to move towards B, provided that B simultaneously moves towards C, C towards D and D towards A. But the same thing is intelligible even in the case of an imperfect circle however irregular it may be, provided we notice how all the variations in the spaces can be compensated for by variations in speed. Thus all the matter contained in the space EFGH [see Fig. 4] can move in a circle without the need for

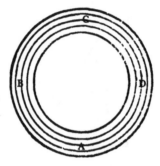

Fig. 3

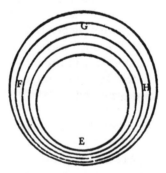

Fig. 4

any condensation or vacuum, and the part that is around E can move towards G while the part that is around G simultaneously moves towards E, with this sole proviso: if the space in G is supposed to be four times as wide as the space at E and twice as wide as the space at F and H, then the speed of the motion at E must be four times greater than that at G and twice as great as that at F or H; and at every other location an increase in speed must similarly compensate for a narrower space. In this way, the amount of matter passing through any given part of the circle in any given time will always be equal.

34. *From this it follows that the number of particles into which matter is divided is in fact indefinite, although it is beyond our power to grasp them all.*
It must, however, be admitted that in the case of this motion we come upon something the truth of which our mind perceives, while at the same time being unable to grasp exactly how it occurs. For what happens is an infinite, or indefinite,[1] division of the various particles of matter; and the resulting subdivisions are so numerous that however small we make a 60 particle in our thought, we always understand that it is in fact divided into other still smaller particles. For it is impossible for the matter which now fills space G successively to fill all the spaces between G and E, which get gradually smaller by countless stages, unless some part of that matter adjusts its shape to the innumerable different volumes of those spaces. And for this to come about, it is necessary that all its imaginable particles, which are in fact innumerable, should shift their relative positions to some tiny extent. This minute shifting of position is a true case of division.

35. *How this division comes about; and the fact that it undoubtedly takes place, even though it is beyond our grasp.*
It should be noted, however, that I am not here speaking of the whole of this matter, but merely of some part of it. We may suppose that two or three of its parts at G are as wide as the space at E, and that there are also several smaller parts which remain undivided; but nevertheless we can still understand them to move in a circle towards E, provided they have mixed up with them various other particles which somehow bend and change shape in such a way as to join onto them. Now the former group do not change their own shape, but merely adapt their speed depending on the place they are to occupy, while the latter group exactly fill all the crevices which the former do not occupy. We cannot grasp in our thought how this indefinite division comes about, but we should not therefore doubt that it occurs. For we clearly perceive that it necessarily follows from what we <already> know most evidently of the nature of matter, and we perceive that it belongs to the class of things which are beyond the grasp of our finite minds.

---

1 See above, Part I, art. 26, pp. 201f.

61   36. *God is the primary cause of motion; and he always preserves the*
        same quantity of motion in the universe.

After this consideration of the nature of motion, we must look at its
cause. This is in fact twofold: first, there is the universal and primary
cause – the general cause of all the motions in the world; and second
there is the particular cause which produces in an individual piece of
matter some motion which it previously lacked. Now as far as the
general cause is concerned, it seems clear to me that this is no other than
God himself. In the beginning <in his omnipotence> he created matter,
along with its motion and rest; and now, merely by his regular
concurrence, he preserves the same amount of motion and rest in the
material universe as he put there in the beginning. Admittedly motion is
simply a mode of the matter which is moved. But nevertheless it has a
certain determinate quantity; and this, we easily understand, may be
constant in the universe as a whole while varying in any given part. Thus
if one part of matter moves twice as fast as another which is twice as
large, we must consider that there is the same quantity of motion in each
part; and if one part slows down, we must suppose that some other part
of equal size speeds up by the same amount. For we understand that
God's perfection involves not only his being immutable in himself, but
also his operating in a manner that is always utterly constant and
immutable. Now there are some changes whose occurrence is guaranteed
either by our own plain experience or by divine revelation, and either our
perception or our faith shows us that these take place without any change
in the creator; but apart from these we should not suppose that any other
changes occur in God's works, in case this suggests some inconstancy in
62   God. Thus, God imparted various motions to the parts of matter when he
first created them, and he now preserves all this matter in the same way,
and by the same process by which he originally created it;[1] and it follows
from what we have said that this fact alone makes it most reasonable to
think that God likewise always preserves the same quantity of motion in
matter.

   37. *The first law of nature: each and every thing, in so far as it can,*
       always continues in the same state; and thus what is once in motion
       always continues to move.

From God's immutability we can also know certain rules or laws of
nature, which are the secondary and particular causes of the various
motions we see in particular bodies. The first of these laws is that each

---

1 There is for Descartes no real distinction between God's action in creating the universe
   and his action in preserving it or maintaining it in existence. See below, art. 42, p. 243,
   and Med. III: vol. II, p. 33.

thing, in so far as it is simple and undivided, always remains in the same state, as far as it can, and never changes except as a result of external causes. Thus, if a particular piece of matter is square, we can be sure without more ado that it will remain square for ever, unless something coming from outside changes its shape. If it is at rest, we hold that it will never begin to move unless it is pushed into motion by some cause. And if it moves, there is equally no reason for thinking it will ever lose this motion of its own accord and without being checked by something else. Hence we must conclude that what is in motion always, so far as it can, continues to move. But we live on the Earth, whose composition is such that all motions occurring near it are soon halted, often by causes undetectable by our senses. Hence from our earliest years we have often judged that such motions, which are in fact stopped by causes unknown to us, come to an end of their own accord. And we tend to believe that what we have apparently experienced in many cases holds good in all cases – namely that it is in the very nature of motion to come to an end, or to tend towards a state of rest. This, of course, <is a false preconceived opinion which> is utterly at variance with the laws of nature; for rest is the opposite of motion, and nothing can by its own nature tend towards its opposite, or towards its own destruction.

63

38. *The motion of projectiles.*
Indeed, our everyday experience of projectiles completely confirms this first rule of ours. For there is no other reason why a projectile should persist in motion for some time after it leaves the hand that throws it, except that what is once in motion continues to move until it is slowed down by bodies that are in the way.[1] And it is clear that projectiles are normally slowed down, little by little, by the air or other fluid bodies in which they are moving, and that this is why their motion cannot persist for long. The fact that air offers resistance to other moving bodies may be confirmed either by our own experience, through the sense of touch if we beat the air with a fan, or by the flight of birds. And in the case of any other fluid, the resistance offered to the motion of a projectile is even more obvious than in the case of air.

39. *The second law of nature: all motion is in itself rectilinear; and hence any body moving in a circle always tends to move away from the centre of the circle which it describes.*
The second law is that every piece of matter, considered in itself, always tends to continue moving, not in any oblique path but only in a straight

---

1 Cf. *The World*, ch. 7: above p. 95.

line. This is true despite the fact that many particles are often forcibly deflected by the impact of other bodies; and, as I have said above,[1] in any motion the result of all the matter moving simultaneously is a kind of circle. The reason for this second rule is the same as the reason for the first rule, namely the immutability and simplicity of the operation by which God preserves motion in matter. For he always preserves the

64   motion in the precise form in which it is occurring at the very moment when he preserves it, without taking any account of the motion which v as occurring a little while earlier. It is true that no motion takes place in a single instant of time; but clearly whatever is in motion is determined, at the individual instants which can be specified as long as the motion lasts, to continue moving in a given direction along a straight line, and never in a curve . . .[2]

(65)   40. *The third law: if a body collides with another body that is stronger than itself, it loses none of its motion; but if it collides with a weaker body, it loses a quantity of motion equal to that which it imparts to the other body.*

The third law of nature is this: when a moving body collides with another, if its power of continuing in a straight line is less than the resistance of the other body, it is deflected so that, while the quantity of motion is retained, the direction is altered; but if its power of continuing is greater than the resistance of the other body, it carries that body along with it, and loses a quantity of motion equal to that which it imparts to the other body. Thus we find that when hard projectiles strike some other hard body, they do not stop, but rebound in the opposite direction; when, by contrast, they encounter a soft body, they are immediately halted because they readily transfer all their motion to it. All the particular causes of the changes which bodies undergo are covered by this third law – or at least the law covers all changes which are themselves corporeal. I am not here inquiring into the existence or nature of any power to move bodies which may be possessed by human minds, or the minds of angels, since I am reserving this topic for a treatise *On Man* <which I hope to produce>.[3]

41. *The proof of the first part of this rule.*
The first part of this law is proved by the fact that there is a difference between motion considered in itself <the motion of a thing> and its

1 Art. 33, p. 237.
2 Descartes proceeds to illustrate the point by the example of a stone shot from a sling. Cf. Part 3, art. 57, p. 259.
3 This treatise, originally planned to form Part 6 of the *Principles* (see below Part 4, art. 188, p. 279, was never written. It is not to be confused with the earlier *Treatise on Man* (pp. 99–108 above).

determination in a certain direction; for the determination of the direction can be altered, while the motion remains constant. As I have said above, everything that is not composite but simple, as motion is, always persists in being <as it is in itself and not in relation to other things>, so long as it is not destroyed by an external cause <by meeting another object>. Now if one body collides with a second, hard body <in its path which it is quite incapable of pushing>, there is an obvious reason why its motion should not remain fixed in the same direction, <namely the resistance of the body which deflects its path>; but there is no reason why its motion should be stopped or diminished, <since it is not removed by the other body or by any other cause, and> since one motion is not the opposite of another motion. Hence it follows that the motion in question ought not to diminish at all.

42. *The proof of the second part of this rule.*

The second part of the law is proved from the immutability of the workings of God, by means of which the world is continually preserved through an action identical with its original act of creation. For the whole of space is filled with bodies, and the motion of every single body is rectilinear in tendency; hence it is clear that when he created the world in the beginning God did not only impart various motions to different parts of the world, but also produced all the reciprocal impulses and transfers of motion between the parts. Thus, since God preserves the world by the selfsame action and in accordance with the selfsame laws as when he created it, the motion which he preserves is not something permanently fixed in given pieces of matter, but something which is mutually transferred when collisions occur. The very fact that creation is in a continual state of change is thus evidence of the immutability of God.[1]

43. *The nature of the power which all bodies have to act on, or resist, other bodies.*

In this connection we must be careful to note what it is that constitutes the power of any given body to act on, or resist the action of, another body. This power consists simply in the fact that everything tends, so far as it can, to persist in the same state, as laid down in our first law. Thus what is joined to another thing has some power of resisting separation from it; and what is separated has some power of remaining separate. Again, what is at rest has some power of remaining at rest and consequently of resisting anything that may alter the state of rest; and

---

1 '... is no way incompatible with the immutability of God, and may even serve as evidence to establish it' (French version).

what is in motion has some power of persisting in its motion, i.e. of
67 continuing to move with the same speed and in the same direction. An
estimate of this last power must depend firstly on the size of the body
in question and the size of the surface which separates it from other
bodies, and secondly on the speed of the mction, and on the various ways
in which different bodies collide, and the degree of opposition involved.

44. *The opposite of motion is not some other motion but a state of rest;*
and the opposite of the determination of a motion in a given
direction is its determination in the opposite direction.

It should be noted that one motion is in no way contrary to another of
equal speed. Strictly speaking there are only two sorts of opposition to be
found here. One is the opposition between motion and rest, together with
the opposition between swiftness and slowness of motion (in so far, that
is, as such slowness shares something of the nature of rest). And the
second sort is the opposition between the determination of motion in a
given direction and an encounter somewhere in that direction with
another body which is at rest or moving in another direction. The degree
of this opposition varies in accordance with the direction in which a body
is moving when it collides with another.

45. *How to determine how much the motion of a given body is altered*
by collision with other bodies. This is calculated by means of the
following rules.

To enable us to determine, in the light of this, how individual bodies
increase or diminish their motions or change direction as a result of
collision with other bodies, all that is necessary is to calculate the power
of any given body to produce or resist motion; we also need to lay it
down as a firm principle that the stronger power always produces its
effects. Our calculation would be easy if there were only two bodies
colliding, and these were perfectly hard, and so isolated from all other
bodies that no surrounding bodies impeded or augmented their motions.
In this case they would obey the rules that follow.[1]

---

1 Descartes' seven rules for calculating the speed and direction of bodies after impact cover
seven ideal cases, which are, respectively: (1) where two bodies of equal size and speed
collide head on; (2) as in case (1), but where one body is larger; (3) as in (1) but where
one body is travelling faster; (4) where one body is at rest and larger; (5) where one body
is at rest and smaller; (6) where one body is at rest and the bodies are equal in size; and
(7) where two bodies collide when travelling in the same direction. The calculations in all
seven rules presuppose that 'quantity of motion', measured as the product of size
(extension) and speed, is preserved. For an English version of these articles, and other
material omitted below, see V. R. and R. P. Miller, *Descartes, Principles of philosophy*
(Dordrecht: Reidel, 1983), pp. 64f.

46. *The first rule.* (68)

47. *The second rule.*

48. *The third rule.*

49. *The fourth rule.*

50. *The fifth rule.* (69)

51. *The sixth rule.*

52. *The seventh rule.*
... These matters do not need proof since they are self-evident <the (70) demonstrations are so certain that even if our experience seemed to show us the opposite, we should still be obliged to have more faith in our reason than in our senses>.

53. *The application of these rules is difficult because each body is simultaneously in contact with many others.*
<In fact it often happens that experience may appear to conflict with the rules I have just explained, but the reason for this is evident.> Since no bodies in the universe can be so isolated from all others, and no bodies in our vicinity are normally perfectly hard, the calculation for determining how much the motion of a given body is altered by collision with another body is much more difficult than those given above. <So in order to judge whether the above rules are observed here or not, it is not sufficient to know how two bodies can act against one another on impact.> We have to take into account all the other bodies which are touching them on every side, and these have very different effects depending on whether they are hard or fluid. So we must now inquire what this difference consists in.

54. *What hard bodies are, and what fluid bodies are.*
... If we go on to inquire how it comes about that some bodies readily abandon their place to other bodies, while others do not, we can easily see that a body already in motion does not prevent another body 71 occupying the place which it is spontaneously leaving; a body at rest, on the other hand, cannot be expelled from its place except by some force <coming from outside, which produces a change>. Hence we may infer that fluids are bodies made up of numerous tiny particles which are agitated by a variety of mutually distinct motions; while hard bodies are those whose particles are all at rest relative to each other.

55. *There is no glue binding together the parts of hard bodies apart from the simple fact that they are at rest <relative to each other>.*

We certainly cannot think up any kind of glue which could fix together the particles of two bodies any more firmly than is achieved simply by their being at rest. For what could such a glue be? It could not be a substance, for since the particles are themselves substances, there is no reason why another substance should join them more effectively than they join themselves together. Nor could the 'glue' be any mode distinct from their being at rest. For what mode could be more contrary to the motion that separates them than their being at rest? And we recognize no other categories of things apart from substances and their modes.

56. *The particles of fluid bodies move with equal force in all directions. And if a hard body is present in a fluid, the smallest force is able to set it in motion.*

As far as fluids are concerned, even though we cannot observe through our senses any motion of their particles, because they are too small, such motion is easily inferred from their effects, especially in the case of air and water. For air and water corrupt many other bodies; and no corporeal action – and corruption is such an action – can occur without local motion . . .

(73) 57. *The proof of the above.*

(75) 58. *If any particles of a fluid move more slowly than a hard body which is present inside it, the fluid in that area does not behave as a fluid.*

59. *If a hard body is pushed by another hard body, it does not get all its motion from it; it also gets some of its motion from the surrounding fluid.*

(76) 60. *However, it cannot acquire a greater speed from the fluid than it acquires from the hard body that strikes it.*

61. *When an entire fluid body moves in a given direction at one time it necessarily carries with it any hard body which may be contained inside it.*

(77) 62. *The fact that a hard body is carried along by a fluid in this way does not mean that it is itself in motion.*

63. *Why some bodies are so hard that, despite their small size, they cannot easily be divided by our hands.*

64. *The only principles which I accept, or require, in physics are those of* (78)
    geometry and pure mathematics; these principles explain all natural
    phenomena, and enable us to provide quite certain demonstrations
    regarding them.

I will not here add anything about shapes or about the countless different
kinds of motions that can be derived from the infinite variety of different
shapes. These matters will be quite clear in themselves when the time
comes for me to deal with them. I am assuming that my readers know the
basic elements of geometry already, or have sufficient mental aptitude to
understand mathematical demonstrations. For I freely acknowledge that
I recognize no matter in corporeal things apart from that which the
geometers call quantity, and take as the object of their demonstrations, 79
i.e. that to which every kind of division, shape and motion is applicable.
Moreoever, my consideration of such matter involves absolutely nothing
apart from these divisions, shapes and motions; and even with regard to
these, I will admit as true only what has been deduced from indubitable
common notions so evidently that it is fit to be considered as a
mathematical demonstration. And since all natural phenomena can be
explained in this way, as will become clear in what follows, I do not think
that any other principles are either admissible or desirable in physics.

PART THREE

The Visible Universe

1. *We cannot over-estimate the vastness of the works of God.*
The various principles of material things that we have so far discovered
have been derived not from the preconceived opinions of the senses, but
from the light of reason, so that we cannot doubt their truth. Our next
task is to examine whether these principles alone enable us to explain all
natural phenomena <i.e. the effects which we perceive by means of our
senses>. Let us begin with the phenomena which are most universal –
those on which all the others depend; that is to say, let us start with the
general structure of the entire visible world. In order to philosophize
correctly about this, two points must be noted to begin with. The first is
that we must bear in mind the infinite power and goodness of God, and
not be afraid that our imagination may over-estimate the vastness,
beauty and perfection of his works. On the contrary, we must beware of
positing limits here, when we have no certain knowledge of any, on pain
of appearing to have an insufficient appreciation of the magnificence of
God's creative power.

2. *We must beware of being so presumptuous as to think we understand
the ends which God set before himself in creating the world.*
The second point is that <we must always remember that our mental
capacity is very mediocre, and> we must beware of having too high an
opinion of ourselves. We should be doing this if we chose to assign limits
to the world in the absence of knowledge based on reason or divine
revelation – as if our powers of thought could stretch beyond what God
81 has actually made. And it would be the height of presumption if we were
to imagine that all things were created by God for our benefit alone, or
even to suppose that the power of our minds can grasp the ends which he
set before himself in creating the universe.

3. *The sense in which it may be said that all things were created for man.*
In ethics it may admittedly be an act of piety to assert that God made
everything for our benefit, since this may impel us all the more to give
him thanks and burn with love for him. Indeed the assertion is in a sense

true, since we can make some use of all things, if only by exercising our minds in contemplating them, and thus adoring God for his marvellous works. But nevertheless it is wholly improbable that all things were in fact made for our benefit, in the sense that they have no other use. And in the study of physics such a supposition would be utterly ridiculous and inept, since there is no doubt that many things exist, or once existed, though they are now here no longer, which have never been seen or thought of by any man, and have never been of any use to anyone.

4. *Experiential phenomena and their use in philosophy.*
The principles which we have so far discovered are so vast and so fertile, that their consequences are far more numerous than the entire observed contents of the visible world; indeed, they are so numerous that we could never <in a lifetime> make a complete survey of them even in our thought. But I shall now put forward for scrutiny a brief account of the principal phenomena of nature whose causes we must now examine. Our purpose is not to use these phenomena as the basis for proving anything, for we aim to deduce an account of effects from their causes, not to deduce an account of causes from their effects. The intention is simply to direct our 82 mind to a consideration of some effects rather than others from among the countless effects which we take to be producible from the selfsame causes.

5. *The ratio between the distances and sizes of the sun, earth and moon.*

6. *The distances of the remaining planets from the sun.*

7. *It is impossible to over-estimate the remoteness of the fixed stars.*

8. *If the earth were viewed from the heavens it would appear simply as a planet, smaller than Jupiter or Saturn.*

9. *The sun and the fixed stars shine by their own light.* (83)

10. *The light of the moon and the other planets is borrowed from the sun.*

11. *There is no difference, with respect to light, between the earth and the planets.* (84)

12. *The moon, when it is new, is illuminated by the earth.*

13. *The sun can be counted as one of the fixed stars, and the earth as one of the planets.*

14. *The fixed stars always keep the same distance between each other; but this is not true of the planets.*

15. *The observed motions of the planets may be explained by various hypotheses.*

85 When a sailor on the high seas in calm weather looks out from his own ship and sees other ships a long way off changing their mutual positions, he can often be in doubt whether the motion responsible for this change of position should be attributed to this or that ship, or even to his own. In the same way, the paths of the planets, when seen from the earth, are of a kind which makes it impossible for us to know, simply on the basis of the observed motions, what proper motions should be attributed to any given body. And since their paths are very uneven and are very complicated, it is not easy to explain them except by selecting one pattern, among all those which can make their movements intelligible, and supposing the movements to occur in accordance with it. To this end, astronomers have produced three different hypotheses, i.e. suppositions, which are regarded not as being true, but merely as being suitable for explaining the appearances.

16. *Ptolemy's hypothesis does not account for the appearances.*
The first of these hypotheses is that of Ptolemy. Since this is in conflict with many observations <made recently> (especially the waxing and waning phases of light which are observed on Venus just as they are on the moon),[1] it is now commonly rejected by all philosophers, and hence I will here pass over it.

17. *There is no difference between the hypotheses of Copernicus and Tycho, if they are considered simply as hypotheses.*
The second hypothesis is that of Copernicus and the third that of Tycho Brahe. These two, considered simply as hypotheses, account for the appearances in the same manner and do not differ greatly, except that the Copernican version is a little simpler and clearer.[2] Indeed, Tycho would

---

1 The discovery, by telescopic observation, of the phases of Venus was first announced by Galileo in 1610; it was an insuperable problem for the traditional Ptolemaic model of the solar system, which placed the earth at the centre.
2 Nicolas Copernicus (1478–1543) proposed that the planets, including the earth, moved in circular orbits around the sun; Tycho Brahe (1546–1601) had the sun revolving around a central earth, but the other planets revolving around the sun.

have had no occasion to change it, had he not been attempting to unfold the actual truth of things, as opposed to a mere hypothesis.

18. *Tycho attributes less motion to the earth than Copernicus, if we go by what he actually says, but in reality he attributes more motion to it.*

Copernicus had no hesitation in attributing motion to the earth, but Tycho wished to correct him on this point, regarding it as absurd from the point of view of physics, and in conflict with the common opinion of mankind. But he did not pay sufficient attention to the true nature of motion, and hence, despite his verbal insistence that the earth is at rest, in actual fact he attributed more motion to it than did Copernicus.[1]   86

19. *My denial of the earth's motion is more careful than the Copernican view and more correct than Tycho's view.*

The only difference between my position and those of Copernicus and Tycho is that I propose to avoid attributing any motion to the earth, thus keeping closer to the truth than Tycho while at the same time being more careful than Copernicus. I will put forward the hypothesis that seems to be the simplest of all both for understanding the appearances and for investigating their natural causes. And I wish this to be considered simply as a hypothesis <or supposition that may be false> and not as the real truth.

20. *The fixed stars must be supposed to be extremely far distant from Saturn.*

21. *The sun, like a flame, is composed of matter which is extremely mobile, but it does not on that account move from one place to another.*

22. *The sun differs from a flame in not requiring fuel in the same way.*   (87)

23. *The fixed stars do not all turn on the same sphere; but each star has a vast space around it which is not occupied by any other star.*

24. *The heavens are fluid.*   (89)

25. *The heavens carry along with them all the bodies which they contain.*

---

1 Descartes' complaint seems to be that Tycho failed to recognize the essentially relative nature of motion; see below, art. 28, and above, Part 2, art. 25–30.

26. *The earth is at rest in its own heaven, but nonetheless it is carried along by it.*

(90) 27. *The same view should be taken of all the planets.*

28. *Strictly speaking, the earth does not move, any more than the planets, although they are all carried along by the heaven.*

Here we must bear in mind what I said above about the nature of motion,[1] namely that if we use the term 'motion' in the strict sense and in accordance with the truth of things, then motion is simply the transfer of one body from the vicinity of the other bodies which are in immediate contact with it, and which are regarded as being at rest, to the vicinity of other bodies. But it often happens that, in accordance with ordinary usage, any action whereby a body travels from one place to another is called 'motion'; and in this sense it can be said that the same thing moves and does not move at the same time, depending on how we determine its location. It follows from this that in the strict sense there is no motion occurring in the case of the earth or even the other planets, since they are not transferred from the vicinity of those parts of the heaven with which they are in immediate contact, in so far as these parts are considered as being at rest. Such a transfer would require them to move away from all these parts at the same time, which does not occur. But since the celestial material is fluid, at any given time different groups of particles move away from the planet with which they are in contact, by a motion which

91 should be attributed solely to the particles, not to the planet. In the same way, the partial transfers of water and air which occur on the surface of the earth are not normally attributed to the earth itself, but to the parts of water and air which are transferred.

29. *No motion should be attributed to the earth even if 'motion' is taken in the loose sense, in accordance with ordinary usage; but in this sense it is correct to say that the other planets move.*

But if we construe 'motion' in accordance with ordinary usage, then all the other planets, and even the sun and fixed stars should be said to move; but the same cannot without great awkwardness be said of the earth. For the common practice is to determine the position of the stars from certain sites on the earth that are regarded as being immobile: the stars are deemed to move in so far as they pass these fixed spots. This is convenient for practical purposes, and so is quite reasonable. Indeed all of us from earliest years have reckoned the earth to be not a globe but a

1 See Part 2, art. 25, p. 233.

flat surface, such that 'up' and 'down' are everywhere the same, and the four directions, east, west, south and north, are the same for any point on the surface; and we have all used these directions for specifying the location of any other body. But what of a philosopher who realizes that the earth is a globe contained in a fluid and mobile heaven, and that the sun and the fixed stars always preserve the same positions relative to each other? If he takes these bodies as immobile for the purpose of determining the earth's location, and thus asserts that the earth itself moves, his way of talking is quite unreasonable. First of all, location in the philosophical sense must be determined not by means of very remote bodies like the stars, but with reference to bodies which are contiguous with the body which is said to move. Secondly, if we follow ordinary usage, there is no reason for considering that it is the stars which are at rest rather than the earth, unless we believe that there are no other bodies beyond them from which they are receding, and with reference to which it can be said that they move but the earth is at rest (in the same sense as the earth is said to move with reference to the stars). Yet to believe this is 92 irrational. For since our mind is of such a nature as to recognize no limits in the universe, whoever considers the immensity of God and the weakness of our senses will conclude that it is much more reasonable to suspect that there may be other bodies beyond all the visible fixed stars; and that, with reference to these bodies, the earth may be said to be at rest, but all the stars may be said to be in simultaneous motion. This is surely more reasonable than supposing that there cannot possibly be any such bodies <because the creator's power is so imperfect; for this must be the supposition of those who maintain in this way that the earth moves. And if, later on, to conform to ordinary usage, we appear to attribute motion to the earth, it should be remembered that this is an improper way of speaking – rather like the way in which we may sometimes say that passengers asleep on a ferry 'move' from Calais to Dover, because the ship takes them there>.

30. *All the planets are carried round the sun by the heaven.*
Let us thus put aside all worries regarding the earth's motion, and suppose that the whole of the celestial matter in which the planets are located turns continuously like a vortex with the sun at its centre. Further, let us suppose that the parts of the vortex which are nearer the sun move more swiftly than the more distant parts, and that all the planets (including the earth) always stay surrounded by the same parts of celestial matter. This single supposition enables us to understand all the observed movements of the planets with great ease, without

invoking any machinery.[1] In a river there are various places where the
water twists around on itself and forms a whirlpool. If there is flotsam on
the water we see it carried around with the whirlpool, and in some cases
we see it also rotating about its own centre; further, the bits which are
nearer the centre of the whirlpool complete a revolution more quickly;
and finally, although such flotsam always has a circular motion, it
scarcely ever describes a perfect circle but undergoes some longitudinal
and latitudinal deviations. We can without any difficulty imagine all this
happening in the same way in the case of the planets, and this single
account explains all the planetary movements that we observe.

    31. *How the individual planets are carried along.*

(93) 32. *The movement of sun spots.*

    33. *How the earth rotates about its own centre, and the moon revolves
around the earth.*

(94) 34. *The motions of the heavens are not perfectly circular.*

    35. *The latitudinal inclinations of the planets [from the plane of the
ecliptic].*

(95) 36. *Their longitudinal motion [around the sun].*

    37. *All the phenomena [of the solar system] can be very easily
understood by means of this hypothesis.*

(96) 38. *According to Tycho's hypothesis the earth should be said to move
about its own centre.*

(97) 39. *It should also be said to move annually around the sun.*

    40. *The [annual] movement of the earth does not produce any apparent
change in the position of the fixed stars, on account of their immense
distance.*

(98) 41. *The supposition that the fixed stars are very distant is also required
to explain the motion of comets, which are now agreed to be celestial
bodies.*

  1 Earlier theories had suggested that the planets were carried along by complicated systems
of rotating spheres.

42. *The relevant phenomena include all the things we see here on earth; but initially there is no need to consider them all.*

In addition to these rather general phenomena, there are also many particular matters not only regarding the sun, the planets, the comets and the fixed stars, but also concerning the earth (namely everything that we see on its surface), which may be included among the relevant phenomena here. For, in order to come to know the true nature of this visible world, it is not enough to find causes which provide an explanation of what we see far off in the heavens; the selfsame causes must also allow everything which we see right here on earth to be deduced from them. There is, however, no need for us to consider all these terrestrial phenomena in order to determine the causes of more general things. But we shall know that we have determined such causes correctly afterwards, when we notice that they serve to explain not only the effects which we were originally looking at, but all these other phenomena, which we were not thinking of beforehand.

43. *If a cause allows all the phenomena to be clearly deduced from it, then it is virtually impossible that it should not be true.*

Suppose, then, that we use only principles which we see to be utterly evident, and that all our subsequent deductions follow by mathematical reasoning: if it turns out that the results of such deductions agree accurately with all natural phenomena, we would seem to be doing God an injustice if we suspected that the causal explanations discovered in this way were false. For this would imply that God had endowed us with such an imperfect nature that even the proper use of our powers of reasoning allowed us to go wrong.

44. *Nevertheless, I want the causes that I shall set out here to be regarded simply as hypotheses.*

When philosophizing about such important matters, however, it would seem to be excessively arrogant for us to assert that we have discovered the exact truth <where others have failed>; and so I should prefer to leave this claim on one side, and put forward everything that I am about to write simply as a hypothesis <which is perhaps far from the truth, so as to leave everyone free to make up his own mind>. And if it is thought that the hypothesis is false, I shall think I have achieved something sufficiently worthwhile if everything deduced from it agrees with our observations; for if this is so, we shall see that our hypothesis yields just as much practical benefit for our lives as we would have derived from knowledge of the actual truth <because we shall be able to use it just as effectively to manipulate natural causes so as to produce the effects we desire>.

45. *I shall even make some assumptions which are agreed to be false.*
Indeed, in order to provide a better explanation for the things found in nature, I shall take my investigation of their causes right back to a time before the period when I believe that the causes actually came into existence.[1] For there is no doubt that the world was created right from the start with all the perfection which it now has. The sun and earth and moon and stars thus existed in the beginning, and, what is more, the earth contained not just the seeds of plants but the plants themselves; and Adam and Eve were not born as babies but were created as fully grown people. This is the doctrine of the Christian faith, and our natural reason convinces us that it was so. For if we consider the infinite power of God, we cannot think that he ever created anything that was not wholly perfect of its kind. Nevertheless, if we want to understand the nature of plants or of men, it is much better to consider how they can gradually grow from seeds than to consider how they were created by God at the very beginning of the world. Thus we may be able to think up certain very simple and easily known principles which can serve, as it were, as the seeds from which we can demonstrate that the stars, the earth and indeed everything we observe in this visible world could have sprung. For although we know for sure that they never did arise in this way, we shall be able to provide a much better explanation of their nature by this method than if we merely described them as they now are <or as we believe them to have been created>. And since I believe I have in fact found such principles, I shall give a brief account of them here.

46. *The assumptions that I am making here in order to give an explanation of all phenomena.*
From what has already been said we have established that all the bodies in the universe are composed of one and the same matter, which is divisible into indefinitely many parts, and is in fact divided into a large number of parts which move in different directions and have a sort of circular motion; moreover, the same quantity of motion is always preserved in the universe.[2] However, we cannot determine by reason alone how big these pieces of matter are, or how fast they move, or what kinds of circle they describe. Since there are countless different configurations which God might have instituted here, experience alone must teach us which configurations he actually selected in preference to the rest. We are thus free to make any assumption on these matters with the sole

---

1 The French version reads: 'Indeed, so far from wishing my readers to believe everything I write, I propose to put forward certain propositions which I believe are absolutely false.'
2 See Part 2, esp. art. 20, 22, 33, 34, 39 and 40.

proviso that all the consequences of our assumption must agree with our experience. So, if we may, we will suppose that the matter of which the visible world is composed was originally divided by God into particles which were approximately equal, and of a size which was moderate, or intermediate when compared with those that now make up the heavens and stars. We will also suppose that the total amount of motion they possessed was equal to that now found in the universe; and that their motions were of two kinds, each of equal force. First, they moved individually and separately about their own centres, so as to form a fluid body such as we take the heavens to be; and secondly, they moved together in groups around certain other equidistant points corresponding to the present centres of the fixed stars, and also around other rather more numerous points equalling the number of the planets <and the comets>, ... so as to make up as many different vortices[1] as there are now heavenly bodies in the universe.

47. *The falsity of these suppositions does not prevent the consequences deduced from them being true and certain.*

These few assumptions seem to me to be sufficient to serve as the causes <or principles> from which all the effects observed in our universe would arise in accordance with the laws of nature set out above.[2] And I do not   102
think it is possible to think up any alternative principles for explaining the real world that are simpler, or easier to understand, or even more probable. It may be possible to start from primeval chaos <as described by the poets, i.e. a total confusion in all parts of the universe> and deduce from it, in accordance with the laws of nature, the precise organization now to be found in things; and I once undertook to provide such an explanation.[3] But confusion seems less in accordance with the supreme   103
perfection of God the creator of all things than proportion or order; and it is not possible for us to have such a distinct perception of it. What is more, no proportion or order is simpler or easier to know than that characterized by complete equality in every respect. This is why I am supposing at this point that all the particles of matter were initially equal in respect both of their size and their motion; and I am allowing no inequality in the universe beyond that which exists in the position of the fixed stars, which is so clearly apparent to anyone looking at the night sky that it is quite impossible to deny it. In fact it makes very little difference what initial suppositions are made, since all subsequent change

1 'From now on I shall use this word to refer to all the matter which revolves in this way around each of the centres' (added in French version).
2 Part 2, art. 37–40, pp. 240ff.
3 Cf. *The World*, ch. 6 (above, p. 90); *Discourse*, part 5 (above, p. 132).

must occur in accordance with the laws of nature. And there is scarcely any supposition that does not allow the same effects (albeit more laboriously) to be deduced in accordance with the same laws of nature. For by the operation of these laws matter must successively assume all the forms of which it is capable; and, if we consider these forms in order, we will eventually be able to arrive at the form which characterizes the universe in its present state. Hence in this connection we need not fear that any error can arise from a false supposition.

48. *How all the particles of celestial matter become spherical.*

(104) 49. *There must be other more subtle matter <more tiny particles> around these spherical particles <to fill all the space in that area>.*

50. *The particles of this more subtle matter can be very easily divided.*

51. *And they move very quickly.*

(105) 52. *There are three elements of this visible world.*
  We have ... two very different kinds of matter which can be said to be the first two elements of this visible universe. The first element is made up of matter which is so violently agitated that when it meets other bodies it is divided into particles of indefinite smallness ... The second is composed of matter divided into spherical particles which are still very minute when compared with those that we can see with our eyes, but which have a definite fixed quantity and can be divided into other much smaller particles. The third element, which we shall discover a little later on, consists of particles which are much bulkier or have shapes less suited for motion. From these elements, as we shall show, all the bodies of this visible universe are composed. The sun and fixed stars are composed of the first element, the heavens from the second, and the earth with the planets and comets from the third ...

(106) 53. *Three heavens can also be distinguished in it.*

(107) 54. *How the sun and fixed stars were formed.*

(108) 55. *What light is.*
  It is a law of nature that all bodies moving in a circle move away from the

centre of their motion in so far as they can.[1] I shall now explain as carefully as I can the force by means of which the globules of the second element . . . strive to move away from their centres of motion; for the nature of light consists in this alone, as will be shown below, and there are many other matters which depend on knowledge of this point.

56. *The striving after motion in inanimate things, and how it should be understood.*

When I say that the globules of the second element 'strive' to move away from the centres around which they revolve, it should not be thought that I am implying that they have some thought from which this striving proceeds. I mean merely that they are positioned and pushed into motion in such a way that they will in fact travel in that direction, unless they are prevented by some other cause.

57. *How the same body can be said to strive to move in different directions at the same time.*

Often many different causes act simultaneously on the same body, and one may hinder the effect of another. So, depending on the causes we are considering, we may say that the body is tending or striving to move in different directions at the same time. For example, the stone A [see Fig. 5]

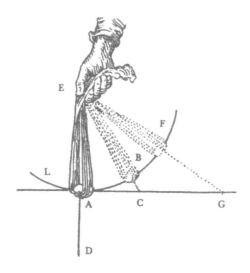

Fig. 5

1 See Part 2, art. 39, above p. 241.

in the sling EA which is swung about the centre E tends to go from A to B, if we consider all the causes which go to determine its motion, since it does in fact go in this direction. But if we concentrate simply on the power of moving which is in the stone itself, we shall say that when it is at point A it tends towards C, in accordance with the law stated above (supposing, of course, that the line AC is a straight line which touches the circle at point A). For if the stone were to leave the sling at the exact moment when it arrived from L at point A, it would in fact go from A towards C, not towards B; and although the sling may prevent this outcome, it does not prevent the 'striving'. Finally, if we concentrate not on the stone's total power of moving but only on that part which is checked by the sling, and we distinguish this from the remaining part which produces the actual result, we shall say that when the stone is at point A, it tends to move simply towards D, or that it 'strives' to move away from the centre E along the straight line EAD.

(110) 58. *How bodies moving in a circle strive to move away from their centre of motion.*

(111) 59. *The extent of the force of this striving.*

(112) 60. *This striving is found in celestial matter.*

61. *This is the cause of the sun and the fixed stars being round.*

(113) 62. *It is also the reason why celestial matter strives to move away from all the points of the circumference of each star or of the sun.*

(114) 63. *The globules of celestial matter do not hinder each other in this striving.*

(115) 64. *This striving explains all the properties of light. And as a result of it, light could be seen to emanate from the stars, despite the lack of any light-producing force in the stars themselves.*

(116) 65. *The poles of each celestial vortex touch the parts of other vortices which are remote from their poles.*

(117) 66. *There must be some deflection in the motion of the vortices so that they can move in harmony.*

(118) 67. *The poles of any two vortices cannot be in contact.*

(199)   153. *Why the moon moves faster and diverges less from its mean motion*
         in conjunction than in quadrature; and why its heaven is not round.

(200)   154. *Why the secondary planets which are around Jupiter move so fast,*
         while those around Saturn move so slowly, or not at all.

(201)   155. *Why the distance between the poles of the equator and the ecliptic*
         is so great.

(202)   156. *Why the distance is gradually lessening.*

         157. *The ultimate and most general cause of all the inequalities to be*
             found in the motions of the bodies in the universe.
         Lastly, we shall not be surprised at the fact that all the planets, despite
         their constant tendency to move in a circular fashion, never describe
         perfect circles but are always subject to slight deviations of all kinds,
         both longitudinal and latitudinal. For all the bodies that are in the
         universe are contiguous and interact with each other <a vacuum being
         quite impossible>, so that the motion of any one body depends on the
         motion of all the others, and hence is subject to countless variations. I
         think I have here given a satisfactory explanation of absolutely every
         phenomenon that we observe in the heavens above us. It remains for us
         to deal next with the phenomena we see here on earth.

PART FOUR

The Earth

1. *The false hypothesis which I have already used must be retained to provide an explanation of the true natures of things.*

Although, as I have already pointed out,[1] I am unwilling to believe that the bodies in this visible universe were ever produced in the manner described above, I must still retain the same hypothesis for explaining what we observe here on earth. For if, as I hope, I can show clearly that this method, and no other, enables us to supply causes for all natural objects, it will be fair to conclude that <although the world was not made in this fashion in the beginning, but was created ready-made by God> the nature of these objects is exactly the same as it would be if they had in fact been produced in the manner described.

2. *How, according to this hypothesis, the earth was produced.*

3. *The division of the earth into three regions. The description of the first.* (204)

4. *The description of the second.* (205)

5. *The description of the third.*

6. *The particles of the third element which are in this third region must be fairly large.*

7. *These particles can be changed by the action of the first and second elements.* (206)

8. *They are bigger than the globules of the second element but less solid and less agitated.*

9. *From the beginning they have formed successive layers around the earth.*

---

1 Part 3, art. 45, p. 256 above.

(207)   10. *Various gaps have been left around them, which are filled with matter of the first and second elements.*

      11. *The globules of the second element were originally smaller, the nearer they were to the centre of the earth.*

      12. *And they had narrower passages to pass through.*

(208)   13. *The thicker particles were not always below the thinner.*

      14. *The original formation of various bodies in the third region of the earth.*

      15. *The forces which caused these bodies to be produced. First, the general motion of the celestial globules.*

(209)   16. *The first effect of this first force is to make bodies transparent.*

(210)   17. *How a solid and hard body can have enough passages to transmit rays of light.*

      18. *The second effect of this first force is to separate one body from another and to purify liquids.*

(211)   19. *The third effect is to make drops of liquid round.*

(212)   20. *Explanation of the second force, which is called 'gravity'.*[1]
The force of gravity does not differ greatly from the third action of the celestial globules. These globules, merely in virtue of their indiscriminate motion in all directions exert an equal pressure on all the particles of each drop of liquid, thus pressing them towards the centre of the drop and making the drop itself round. And in virtue of the selfsame motion, when the globules are prevented from moving in a straight line by encountering the entire mass of the earth, they propel all the earth's particles towards the centre, and this is what the 'gravity' of terrestrial bodies consists in.

      21. *All the parts of the earth, considered in themselves, are not heavy but light.*
To achieve a perfect understanding of the nature of gravity, we must first of all note the following point. Imagine that all the spaces around the earth unoccupied by terrestrial matter were empty, i.e. contained nothing

           1 See footnote 1, p. 234 above.

except bodies which in no way hindered or assisted the motion of other bodies (which is the only intelligible way of understanding the term 'empty'); and suppose further that the earth revolved about its axis by its own motion in the space of twenty-four hours. In this case all the terrestrial particles which were not very firmly joined together would leap off in all directions towards the heavens. In just the same way, if you throw sand on a spinning top you will see it immediately fly off and disperse in all directions. Thus the earth would have to be called light rather than heavy.

22. What the lightness of the celestial matter consists in. 213
Since, however, there is no such vacuum, and the earth is not driven[1] by its own motion but by the celestial matter which surrounds it and pervades all its pores, it behaves like a body at rest. Yet in so far as the whole of the celestial matter moves uniformly with the earth as it drives it, it has no force of heaviness or lightness. But in so far as its parts have a greater degree of agitation than they use up in driving the earth, and are prevented, by encountering the earth, from continuing their rectilinear motion, they always move away from the earth as far as they can, and this is what their lightness consists in.

23. How all the parts of the earth are driven downwards by the celestial matter, and so become heavy.
Next we should note that the power which the individual particles of celestial matter have to move away from <the centre of> the earth cannot achieve its effect unless, in moving upwards, the particles displace various terrestrial particles, thus pushing them and driving them downwards. Now all the space around the earth is occupied either by particles of terrestrial bodies or by celestial matter. All the globules of the celestial matter have an equal tendency to move away from the earth and thus no individual one has the force to displace any other. But the particles of terrestrial bodies do not have this tendency to so great an extent. So whenever any celestial globules have any terrestrial particles above them they must exert all their force to displace them. Thus the gravity of any terrestrial body is not strictly produced by all the celestial matter surrounding it, but only and exactly by the part of it which rises into the space left by the body as it descends, and hence which equals it in size . . .

24. How much heaviness there is in each body. (214)

---

1 The Latin is ambiguous as to whether the motion referred to is the earth's diurnal rotation or its annual revolution. The French version specifies the former.

... Consider how amazing are the properties of magnets and of fire, and how different they are from the properties we commonly observe in other bodies: how a huge flame can be kindled from a tiny spark in a moment <when it falls on a large quantity of powder>, and how great its power is; or how the fixed stars radiate their light <instantly> in every direction over such an enormous distance. In this book I have deduced the causes – which I believe to be quite evident – of these and many other phenomena from principles which are known to all and admitted by all, namely the shape, size, position and motion of particles of matter. And anyone who considers all this will readily be convinced that there are no powers in stones and plants that are so mysterious, and no marvels attributed to sympathetic and antipathetic influences that are so asto- 315 nishing, that they cannot be explained in this way. In short, there is nothing in the whole of nature (nothing, that is, which should be referred to purely corporeal causes, i.e. those devoid of thought and mind) which is incapable of being deductively explained on the basis of these selfsame principles; and hence it is quite unnecessary to add any further principles to the list.

188. *What must be borrowed from [my proposed] treatises on animals*
    and on man in order to complete our knowledge of material things.
I would not add anything further to this fourth part of the *Principles of Philosophy* if, as I originally planned, I was going on to write two further parts – a fifth part on living things, i.e. animals and plants, and a sixth part on man. But I am not yet completely clear about all the matters which I would like to deal with there, and I do not know whether I shall ever have enough free time to complete these sections. So, to avoid delaying the publication of the first four parts any longer, and to make sure there are no gaps caused by my keeping material back for the two final parts, I shall here add a few observations concerning the objects of the senses. Up till now I have described this earth and indeed the whole visible universe as if it were a machine: I have considered only the various shapes and movements of its parts. But our senses show us much else besides – namely colours, smells, sounds and such-like; and if I were to say nothing about these it might be thought that I had left out the most important part of the explanation of the things in nature.

189. *What sensation is and how it operates.*
It must be realized that the human soul, while informing[1] the entire body, nevertheless has its principal seat in the brain; it is here alone that the

---

1 Lat. *informare*. Descartes occasionally employs this standard scholastic term, though of course he rejects the Aristotelian account of the soul as the 'form' of the body. The French version has simply 'while being united to the entire body'.

soul not only understands and imagines but also has sensory awareness. Sensory awareness comes about by means of nerves, which stretch like threads from the brain to all the limbs, and are joined together in such a way that hardly any part of the human body can be touched without producing movement in several of the nerve-ends that are scattered around in that area. This movement is then transmitted to the other ends of the nerves which are all grouped together in the brain around the seat of the soul, as I explained very fully in Chapter Four of the *Optics*.[1] The result of these movements being set up in the brain by the nerves is that the soul or mind that is closely joined to the brain is affected in various ways, corresponding to the various different sorts of movements. And the various different states of mind, or thoughts, which are the immediate result of these movements are called sensory perceptions, or in ordinary speech, sensations.

190. *Various kinds of sensation. First, internal sensations, i.e. emotional states of the mind and natural appetites.*

The wide variety in sensations is a result, firstly, of differences in the nerves themselves, and secondly of differences in the sorts of motion which occur in particular nerves. It is not that each individual nerve produces a particular kind of sensation; indeed, there are only seven principal groups of nerves, of which two have to do with internal sensations and five with external sensations. The nerves which go to the stomach, oesophagus, throat, and other internal parts whose function is to keep our natural wants supplied, produce one kind of internal sensation, which is called 'natural appetite' <e.g. hunger and thirst>. The nerves which go to the heart and the surrounding area <including the diaphragm>, despite their very small size, produce another kind of internal sensation which comprises all the disturbances or passions and emotions of the mind such as joy, sorrow, love, hate and so on. For example, when the blood has the right consistency so that it expands in the heart more readily than usual, it relaxes the nerves scattered around the openings, and sets up a movement which leads to a subsequent movement in the brain producing a natural feeling of joy in the mind; and other causes produce the same sort of movement in these tiny nerves, thereby giving the same feeling of joy. Thus, if we imagine ourselves enjoying some good, the act of imagination does not itself contain the feeling of joy, but it causes the spirits[2] to travel from the brain to the muscles in which these nerves are embedded. This causes the openings of

---

1 *Optics*, above pp. 164ff; Cf. *Treatise on Man*, above pp. 100ff; *Passions*, below pp. 340ff.
2 I.e. the so-called 'animal spirits'; Cf. *Passions*, below, pp. 330ff.

the heart to expand, and this in turn produces the movement in the tiny nerves of the heart which must result in the feeling of joy. In the same way, when we hear good news, it is first of all the mind which makes a judgement about it and rejoices with that intellectual joy which occurs without any bodily disturbance and which, for that reason, the Stoics allowed that the man of wisdom could experience <although they required him to be free of all passion>. But later on, when the good news is pictured in the imagination, the spirits flow from the brain to the muscles around the heart and move the tiny nerves there, thereby causing a movement in the brain which produces in the mind a feeling of animal joy. Or again, if the blood is too thick and flows sluggishly into the ventricles of the heart and does not expand enough inside it, it produces a different movement in the same small nerves around the heart; when this movement is transmitted to the brain it produces a feeling of sadness in the mind, although the mind itself may perhaps not know of any reason why it should be sad. And there are several other causes capable of producing the same feeling <by setting up the same kind of movement in these nerves.> Other movements in these tiny nerves produce different emotions such as love, hatred, fear, anger and so on; I am here thinking of these simply as emotions or passions of the soul, that is, as confused thoughts, which the mind does not derive from itself alone but experiences as a result of something happening to the body with which it is closely conjoined. These emotions are quite different in kind from the distinct thoughts which we have concerning what is to be embraced or desired or shunned. The same applies to the natural appetites such as hunger and thirst which depend on the nerves of the stomach, throat and 318 so forth: they are completely different from the volition to eat, drink and so on. But, because they are frequently accompanied by such volition or appetition, they are called appetites.

191. *The external senses. First, the sense of touch.*
As far as the external senses are concerned, five are commonly listed corresponding to the five kinds of objects stimulating the sensory nerves, and the five kinds of confused thoughts which the resulting motions produce in the soul. First of all there are the nerves terminating in the skin all over the body.[1] These nerves may be touched, via the skin, by various external bodies; and these bodies, though remaining intact, stimulate the nerves in various different ways – in one way by their hardness, in another way by their heaviness, in another way by their heat,

---

1 'First there is the sense of touch, which has as its object all the bodies which can move some part of the flesh or skin of our body, and has as its organ all the nerves which are found in this part of the body and move with it' (French version).

in another way by their humidity, and so on. Corresponding to the different ways in which the nerves are moved, or have their normal motion checked, various different sensations are produced in the mind; and this is how the various tactile qualities get their names. <We call these qualities hardness, heaviness, heat, humidity and so on, but all that is meant by these terms is that the external bodies possess what is required to bring it about that our nerves excite in the soul the sensations of hardness, heaviness, heat etc.>. Moreover, when the nerves are stimulated with unusual force, but without any damage being occasioned to the body, a pleasurable sensation arises <which is a confused thought in the soul and> which is naturally agreeable to the mind because it is a sign of robust health in the body with which it is closely conjoined <in so far as it can undergo the action causing the pleasure without being damaged>. But if there is some bodily damage, there is a sensation of pain <in the soul, even though the action causing the pain may be only marginally more forceful>. This explains why bodily pleasure and pain arise from such very similar objects, although the sensations are completely opposite.

192. *Taste.*
Then there <is the least subtle sense after that of touch, namely taste. Its organs> are other nerves scattered through the tongue and neighbouring areas. The same external bodies, this time split up into particles and floating in the saliva from the mouth, stimulate these nerves in various ways corresponding to their many different shapes <sizes or movements>, and thus produce the sensations of various tastes.

193. *Smell.*
Thirdly, there <is the sense of smell. Its organs> are two other nerves (or appendages to the brain, since they do not go outside the skull) which are 319   stimulated by separate particles of the same bodies that float in the air. The particles in question cannot be of any kind whatsoever: they must be sufficiently light and energetic to be drawn into the nostrils and through the pores of the so-called spongy bone, thus reaching the two nerves. The various movements of the nerves produce the sensations of various smells.

194. *Hearing.*
Fourthly, there <is hearing, whose object is simply various vibrations in the ear. For there> are two other nerves, found in the inmost chambers of the ears, which receive tremors and vibrations from the whole body of surrounding air. When the air strikes the tympanic membrane it produces a disturbance in the little chain of three small bones attached to it; and

the sensations of different sounds arise from the various different movements in these bones.

195. *Sight*
Finally, there are the optic nerves <which are the organs of the most subtle of all the senses, that of sight>. The extremities of these nerves, which make up the coating inside the eye called the retina, are moved not by air or any external bodies entering the eye, but simply by globules of the second element <which pass through the pores and all the fluids and transparent membranes of the eye>. This is the origin of the sensations of light and colours, as I have already explained adequately in the *Optics* and *Meteorology*.[1]

196. *The soul has sensory awareness only in so far as it is in the brain.*
There is clear proof that the soul's sensory awareness, via the nerves, of what happens to the individual limbs of the body does not come about in virtue of the soul's presence in the individual limbs, but simply in virtue of its presence in the brain <or because the nerves by their motions transmit to it the actions of external objects which touch the parts of the body where the nerves are embedded>. Firstly, there are various diseases which affect only the brain but remove or interfere with all sensation. Again, sleep occurs only in the brain, yet every day it deprives us of a great part of our sensory faculties, though these are afterwards restored on waking. Next, when the brain is undamaged, if there is an obstruction in the paths by which the nerves reach the brain from the external limbs, 320 this alone is enough to destroy sensation in those limbs. Lastly, we sometimes feel pain in certain limbs even though there is nothing to cause pain in the limbs themselves; the cause of the pain lies in the other areas through which the nerves travel in their journey from the limbs to the brain. This last point can be proved by countless observations, but it will suffice to mention one here. A girl with a seriously infected hand used to have her eyes bandaged whenever the surgeon visited her, to prevent her being upset by the surgical instruments. After a few days her arm was amputated at the elbow because of a creeping gangrene, and wads of bandages were put in its place so that she was quite unaware that she had lost her arm. However she continued to complain of pains, now in one then in another finger of the amputated hand. The only possible reason for this is that the nerves which used to go from the brain down to the hand now terminated in the arm near the elbow, and were being agitated

---

1 Cf. *Optics*, above pp. 167ff.

by the same sorts of motion as must previously have been set up in the hand, so as to produce in the soul, residing in the brain, the sensation of pain in this or that finger. <And this shows clearly that pain in the hand is felt by the soul not because it is present in the hand but because it is present in the brain.>

197. *The nature of the mind is such that various sensations can be produced in it simply by motions in the body.*

It can also be proved that the nature of our mind is such that the mere occurrence of certain motions in the body can stimulate it to have all manner of thoughts which have no likeness to the movements in question. This is especially true of the confused thoughts we call sensations or feelings. For we see that spoken or written words excite all sorts of thoughts and emotions in our minds. With the same paper, pen and ink, if the tip of the pen is pushed across the paper in a certain way it will form letters which excite in the mind of the reader thoughts of battles, storms and violence, and emotions of indignation and sorrow; but if the movements of the pen are just slightly different they will produce quite different thoughts of tranquillity, peace and pleasure, and quite opposite emotions of love and joy. It may be objected that speech or writing does not immediately excite in the mind any emotions, or images of things apart from the words themselves; it merely occasions various acts of understanding which afterwards result in the soul's constructing within itself the images of various things. But what then will be said of the sensations of pain and pleasure? A sword strikes our body and cuts it; but the ensuing pain is completely different from the local motion of the sword or of the body that is cut – as different as colour or sound or smell or taste. We clearly see, then, that the sensation of pain is excited in us merely by the local motion of some parts of our body in contact with another body; so we may conclude that the nature of our mind is such that it can be subject to all the other sensations merely as a result of other local motions.

198. *By means of our senses we apprehend nothing in external objects beyond their shapes, sizes and motions.*

Moreover, we observe no differences between the various nerves which would support the view that different nerves allow different things to be transmitted to the brain from the external sense organs; indeed, we are not entitled to say that anything reaches the brain except for the local motion of the nerves themselves. And we see that this local motion produces not only sensations of pain and pleasure but also those of light and sound. If someone is struck in the eye, so that the vibration of the blow reaches the retina, this will cause him to see many sparks of flashing light, yet the light is not outside his eye. And if someone puts a finger in his ear he will hear a throbbing hum which comes simply from the movement of air trapped in the ear. Finally, let us consider heat and other qualities perceived by the senses, in so far as those qualities are in objects, as well as the forms of purely material things, for example the form of fire: we often see these arising from the local motion of certain bodies and producing in turn other local motions in other bodies. Now we understand very well how the different size, shape and motion of the particles of one body can produce various local motions in another body. But there is no way of understanding how these same attributes (size, shape and motion) can produce something else whose nature is quite different from their own – like the substantial forms and real qualities which many <philosophers> suppose to inhere in things; and we cannot understand how these qualities or forms could have the power subsequently to produce local motions in other bodies. Not only is all this unintelligible, but we know that the nature of our soul is such that different local motions are quite sufficient to produce all the sensations in the soul. What is more, we actually experience the various sensations as they are produced in the soul, and we do not find that anything reaches the brain from the external sense organs except for motions of this kind. In view of all this we have every reason to conclude that the properties in external objects to which we apply the terms light, colour, smell, taste, sound, heat and cold – as well as the other tactile qualities and even what are called 'substantial forms' – are, so far as we can see, simply various 323 dispositions in those objects[1] which make them able to set up various kinds of motions in our nerves <which are required to produce all the various sensations in our soul>.

199. *There is no phenomenon of nature which has been overlooked in this treatise.*

A simple enumeration will make it clear that there is no phenomenon of nature which I have omitted to consider in this treatise. For a list of natural phenomena cannot include anything which is not apprehended by the senses. Now I have given an account of the various sizes, shapes and motions which are to be found in all bodies; and apart from these the only things which we perceive by our senses as being located outside us are light, colour, smell, taste, sound and tactile qualities. And I have just demonstrated that these are nothing else in the objects – or at least we cannot apprehend them as being anything else – but certain dispositions depending on size, shape and motion. <So the entire visible world, in so

1 '... in the shapes, sizes, positions and movements of their parts' (French version).

far as it is simply visible or perceivable by the senses, contains nothing apart from the things I have given an account of here.>

200. *I have used no principles in this treatise which are not accepted by everyone; this philosophy is nothing new but is extremely old and very common.*

I should also like it to be noted that in attempting to explain the general nature of material things I have not employed any principle which was not accepted by Aristotle and all other philosophers of every age. So this philosophy is not new, but the oldest and most common of all. I have considered the shapes, motions and sizes of bodies and examined the necessary results of their mutual interaction in accordance with the laws of mechanics, which are confirmed by reliable everyday experience. And who has ever doubted that bodies move and have various sizes and shapes, and that their various different motions correspond to these differences in size and shape; or who doubts that when bodies collide bigger bodies are divided into many smaller ones and change their shapes? We detect these facts not just with one sense but several – sight, touch and hearing; and they can also be distinctly imagined and understood by us. But the same cannot be said of the other characteristics like colour, sound and the rest, each of which is perceived not by several senses but by one alone; for the images of them which we have in our thought are always confused, and we do not know what they really are.

201. *There are corporeal particles which cannot be perceived by the senses.*

I do consider, however, that there are many particles in each body which are <so small that they are> not perceived with any of our senses; and this may not meet with the approval of those who take their own senses as the measure of what can be known. <But to desire that our human reasoning should go no further than what we can see is, I think, to do it a great injustice.> Yet who can doubt that there are many bodies so minute that we do not detect them by any of our senses? One simply has to consider something which is slowly growing or shrinking and ask what it is that is being added or taken away hour by hour. A tree grows day by day; and it is unintelligible to suppose that it gets bigger than it was before unless we understand there to be some body which is added to it. But who has ever detected with the senses the minute bodies that are added to a growing tree in one day? It must be admitted, at least by those <philosophers> who accept that quantity is indefinitely divisible, that its parts could be made so tiny as to be imperceptible by any of the senses. And it certainly should not be surprising that we are unable to perceive very minute bodies through our senses. For our nerves, which must be set in motion by objects in order to produce a sensation, are not themselves very minute, but are like small cords made up of many smaller particles; hence they cannot be set in motion by very minute bodies. No one who uses his reason will, I think, deny the advantage of using what happens in large bodies, as perceived by our senses, as a model for our ideas about what happens in tiny bodies which elude our senses merely because of their small size. This is much better than explaining matters by inventing all sorts of strange objects which have no resemblance to what is perceived   325 by the senses <such as 'prime matter', 'substantial forms' and the whole range of qualities that people habitually introduce, all of which are harder to understand than the things they are supposed to explain>.

202. *The philosophy of Democritus differs from my own just as much as*
    it does from the standard view <of Aristotle and others>.

It is true that Democritus also imagined certain small bodies having various sizes, shapes and motions, and supposed that all bodies that can be perceived by the senses arose from the conglomeration and mutual interaction of these corpuscles; and yet his method of philosophizing generally meets with total rejection. This rejection, however, has never been based on the fact that his philosophy deals with certain particles so minute as to elude the senses, and assigns various sizes, shapes and motions to them; for no one can doubt that there are in fact many such particles, as I have just shown. The reasons for the rejection are the following. First, Democritus supposed his corpuscles to be indivisible – a notion which leads me to join those who reject his philosophy. Secondly, he imagined there to be a vacuum around the corpuscles, whereas I demonstrate the impossibility of a vacuum. Thirdly, he attributed gravity to these corpuscles, whereas my understanding is that there is no such thing as gravity in any body taken on its own, but that it exists only as a function of, and in relation to, the position and motion of other bodies.[1] And lastly, Democritus did not show how particular things arose merely from the interaction of corpuscles; or, if he did show this in some cases, his explanations were not entirely consistent, if we may judge from those of his opinions which have survived. I leave others to judge whether my own writings on philosophy have up to now been reasonably consistent <and sufficiently fertile in the results that can be deduced from them. As for the consideration of shapes, sizes and motions, this is something that has been adopted not only by Democritus but also by Aristotle and all the other philosophers. Now I reject all of Democritus' suppositions, with

1 See above, Part 2, art. 20; Part 4, art. 20–3.

this one exception, and I also reject practically all the suppositions of the other philosophers. Hence it is clear that my method of philosophizing has no more affinity with the Democritean method than with any of the other particular sects>.

203. *How we may arrive at knowledge of the shapes <sizes> and motions of particles that cannot be perceived by the senses.*

In view of the fact that I assign determinate shapes, sizes, and motions to the imperceptible particles of bodies just as if I had seen them, but nonetheless maintain that they cannot be perceived, some people may be led to ask how I know what these particles are like. My reply is this. First of all <I considered in general all the clear and distinct notions which our understanding can contain with regard to material things. And I found no others except for the notions we have of shapes, sizes and motions, and the rules in accordance with which these three things can be modified by each other – rules which are the principles of geometry and mechanics. And I judged as a result that all the knowledge which men have of the natural world must necessarily be derived from these notions; for all the other notions we have of things that can be perceived by the senses are confused and obscure, and so cannot serve to give us knowledge of anything outside ourselves, but may even stand in the way of such knowledge. Next> I took the simplest and best known principles, knowledge of which is naturally implanted in our minds; and working from these I considered, in general terms, firstly, what are the principal differences which can exist between the sizes, shapes and positions of bodies which are imperceptible by the senses merely because of their small size, and, secondly, what observable effects would result from their various interactions. Later on, when I observed just such effects in objects that can be perceived by the senses, I judged that they in fact arose from just such an interaction of bodies that cannot be perceived – especially since it seemed impossible to think up any other explanation for them. In this matter I was greatly helped by considering artefacts. For I do not recognize any difference between artefacts and natural bodies except that the operations of artefacts are for the most part performed by mechanisms which are large enough to be easily perceivable by the senses – as indeed must be the case if they are to be capable of being manufactured by human beings. The effects produced in nature, by contrast, almost always depend on structures which are so minute that they completely elude our senses. Moreover, mechanics is a division or special case of physics, and all the explanations belonging to the former also belong to the latter; so it is no less natural for a clock constructed with this or that set of wheels to tell the time than it is for a tree which grew from this or that seed to produce the appropriate fruit. Men who are experienced in dealing with machinery can take a particular machine whose function they know and, by looking at some of its parts, easily form a conjecture about the design of the other parts, which they cannot see. In the same way I have attempted to consider the observable effects and parts of natural bodies and track down the imperceptible causes and particles which produce them.

204. *With regard to the things which cannot be perceived by the senses, it*   327
is enough to explain their possible nature, even though their actual
nature may be different <and this is all that Aristotle tried to do>.
However, although this method may enable us to understand how all the things in nature could have arisen, it should not therefore be inferred that they were in fact made in this way. Just as the same craftsman could make two clocks which tell the time equally well and look completely alike from the outside but have completely different assemblies of wheels inside, so the supreme craftsman of the real world could have produced all that we see in several different ways. I am very happy to admit this; and I shall think I have achieved enough provided only that what I have written is such as to correspond accurately with all the phenomena of nature. This will indeed be sufficient for application in ordinary life, since medicine and mechanics, and all the other arts which can be fully developed with the help of physics, are directed only towards items that can be perceived by the senses and are therefore to be counted among the phenomena of nature.[1] And in case anyone happens to be convinced that Aristotle achieved – or wanted to achieve – any more than this, he himself expressly asserts in the first book of the *Meteorologica*, at the beginning of Chapter Seven, that when dealing with things not manifest to the senses, he reckons he has provided adequate reasons and demonstrations if he can simply show that such things are capable of occurring in accordance with his explanations.

205. *Nevertheless my explanations appear to be at least morally certain*[2].
It would be disingenuous, however, not to point out that some things are considered as morally certain, that is, as having sufficient certainty for

---

1 '... are directed simply towards applying certain observable bodies to each other in such a way that certain observable effects are produced as a result of natural causes. And by imagining what the various causes are, and considering their results, we shall achieve our aim irrespective of whether these imagined causes are true or false, since the result is taken to be no different, as far as the observable effects are concerned' (French version).
2 By 'moral certainty' is meant certainty sufficient for ordinary practical purposes. See first sentence of this article, where the French version runs: '... moral certainty is certainty which is sufficient to regulate our behaviour, or which measures up to the certainty we have on matters relating to the conduct of life which we never normally doubt, though we know that it is possible, absolutely speaking, that they may be false'.

application to ordinary life, even though they may be uncertain in relation to the absolute power of God. <Thus those who have never been in Rome have no doubt that it is a town in Italy, even though it could be the case that everyone who has told them this has been deceiving them.> Suppose for example that someone wants to read a letter written in Latin but encoded so that the letters of the alphabet do not have their proper

328 value, and he guesses that the letter B should be read whenever A appears, and C when B appears, i.e. that each letter should be replaced by the one immediately following it. If, by using this key, he can make up Latin words from the letters, he will be in no doubt that the true meaning of the letter is contained in these words. It is true that his knowledge is based merely on a conjecture, and it is conceivable that the writer did not replace the original letters with their immediate successors in the alphabet, but with others, thus encoding quite a different message; but this possibility is so unlikely <especially if the message contains many words> that it does not seem credible. Now if people look at all the many properties relating to magnetism, fire and the fabric of the entire world, which I have deduced in this book from just a few principles, then, even if they think that my assumption of these principles was arbitrary and groundless, they will still perhaps acknowledge that it would hardly have been possible for so many items to fit into a coherent pattern if the original principles had been false.

206. *Indeed, my explanations possess more than moral certainty.*
Besides, there are some matters, even in relation to the things in nature, which we regard as absolutely, and more than just morally, certain. <Absolute certainty arises when we believe that it is wholly impossible that something should be otherwise than we judge it to be.> This certainty is based on a metaphysical foundation, namely that God is supremely good and in no way a deceiver, and hence that the faculty which he gave us for distinguishing truth from falsehood cannot lead us into error, so long as we are using it properly and are thereby perceiving something distinctly. Mathematical demonstrations have this kind of certainty,[1] as does the knowledge that material things exist; and the same goes for all evident reasoning about material things. And perhaps even these results of mine will be allowed into the class of absolute certainties, if people consider how they have been deduced in an unbroken chain from the first and simplest principles of human knowledge. Their certainty will be

329 especially appreciated if it is properly understood that we can have no

1 '... for we see clearly that it is impossible that two and three added together should make more or less than five; or that a square should have only three sides, and so on' (added in French version).

sensory awareness of external objects unless these objects produce some local motion in our nerves; and that the fixed stars, owing to their enormous distance from us, cannot produce such motion unless there is also some motion occurring both in them and also throughout the entire intervening part of the heavens.[1] Once this is accepted, then it seems that all the other phenomena, or at least the general features of the universe and the earth which I have described, can hardly be intelligibly explained except in the way I have suggested.

207. *I submit all my views to the authority of the Church.*

Nevertheless, mindful of my own weakness, I make no firm pronouncements, but submit all these opinions to the authority of the Catholic Church and the judgement of those wiser than myself. And I would not wish anyone to believe anything except what he is convinced of by evident and irrefutable reasoning.

THE END

1 '. . . from which it follows very evidently that the heavens must be fluid, i.e. composed of small particles which move separately from each other, or at least that they must contain such particles. For whatever I can be said to have assumed in Part 3, art. 46 can be reduced to the sole assertion that the heavens are fluid' (added in French version).

Comments on a Certain Broadsheet

Translator's preface

Descartes' *Comments on a Certain Broadsheet (Notae in Programma quoddam)* was written in Latin and published by the house of Elzevir at Amsterdam early in 1648. The work was Descartes' response to a broadsheet published anonymously by Henri de Roy (Henricus Regius, 1598–1679) towards the end of 1647. Regius was Professor of Medicine at the University of Utrecht, and an enthusiastic supporter of Descartes' physics. His teaching of Descartes' doctrines was vigorously opposed by the Rector of the University, Gisbert Voet (Voetius), who attempted to have Regius removed from his Chair.

For several years Regius enjoyed an amicable pupil-master relationship with Descartes, who apparently had a high regard for his intellect. The friendship between the two men, however, deteriorated after the publication of Regius' *Foundations of Physics* in 1646. The first half of Regius' work deals with physics, along lines very similar to those of Descartes' *Principles of Philosophy* (1644); the second half, which deals with physiology, among other biological subjects, anticipates many of Descartes' as yet unpublished ideas, to which Regius had access through personal notes. Descartes complained that Regius had not only borrowed many of his ideas, but had also seriously distorted them. Regius, moreover, disagreed not only with much of Descartes' metaphysics, but also with Descartes' thesis that physics requires rationally grounded metaphysical foundations. Descartes dissociated himself from Regius in his prefatory letter to the translator of the French edition of the *Principles of Philosophy* (1647).[1] Regius responded to Descartes' repudiation of his views by publishing a broadsheet, which lists, in the form of numbered theses, the points of disagreement between them.

The first edition of the *Comments*, which was published without Descartes' knowledge, contains an anonymous preface and a verse encomium to Descartes; since Descartes disapproved of these, they have not been included in the present translation, which follows the text in volume VIII B of Adam and Tannery.[2]   D.M.

1 See above, p. 189.
2 Cf. General Introduction, p. x above.

341 *published in Belgium towards the end of 1647, entitled 'An account of the human mind, or rational soul, which explains what it is and what it can be'*

A few days ago I received two pamphlets attacking me, the one openly and directly, the other covertly and indirectly. I am quite unconcerned about the former;[1] I am even grateful to the author, for the result of his grotesque efforts is simply a heap of worthless quibbles and slanders which no one could believe – a result which bears witness to the fact that he was unable to find in my writings anything which he could justly censure. Thus, in criticizing my writings he has confirmed their truth more effectively than he would have done by praising them – and all at the expense of his own reputation. The other work contains nothing that

342 openly refers to me; it is published anonymously, and without the name of the printer.[2] Nevertheless, it troubles me more, for it expresses opinions which I judge to be positively harmful and mistaken. It is issued in the form of a broadsheet which can be fixed to church doors, and may thus strike the eye of any chance reader. It is said, moreover, that in an earlier printing of the sheet, in a slightly different format, a certain individual was named as the author – one who is regarded by many as propounding doctrines identical to my own. I am forced, therefore, to expose his errors, so that they will not be attributed to me by those who come across these papers without having read my own writings.

The following is the broadsheet in its latest form.

AN ACCOUNT OF THE HUMAN MIND, OR RATIONAL SOUL, WHICH EXPLAINS WHAT IT IS AND WHAT IT CAN BE

(1) The human mind is that by means of which man immediately performs acts of thinking. It consists solely in the faculty, or inner principle, of thinking.

(2) So far as the nature of things is concerned, the possibility seems to be open that the mind can be either a substance or a mode of a corporeal substance. Or, if we are to follow some philosophers, who hold that extension and thought are

343 attributes which are present in certain substances, as in subjects, then since these attributes are not opposites but merely different, there is no reason why the mind

1 *Consideratio Theologica*, Jacques de Rives (Jacobus Revius), 1648.
2 The broadsheet published anonymously by Henri de Roy (Regius). See Translator's preface.

should not be a sort of attribute co-existing with extension in the same subject, though the one attribute is not included in the concept of the other. For whatever we can conceive of can exist. Now, it is conceivable that the mind is some such item; for none of these implies a contradiction. Therefore it is possible that the mind is some such item.

(3) Thus, those who assert that we clearly and distinctly conceive the human mind as necessarily (or actually)[1] and really distinct from the body are mistaken.

(4) In many passages in Holy Scripture, however, it is revealed that the mind is nothing but a substance or entity which is really distinct from the body, is actually separable from it, and is capable of existing on its own apart from the body. So this fact, which some people may find doubtful by nature (if we are seeking exact, as distinct from merely probable, truth and knowledge)[2] is for us, through its divine revelation in Scripture, now beyond doubt.

(5) The fact that we can have doubts about the existence of the body, but never about the existence of the mind, is no objection. For this just goes to show that, so long as we have doubts about the existence of the body, we cannot say that the mind is a mode of the body.

(6) The human mind is a substance really distinct from the body; nevertheless, so 344 long as it is in the body, it is organic in all its actions. Thus, as the disposition of the body varies, so the mind has different thoughts.

(7) Since the mind is by nature different from the body and from the disposition of the body, and cannot arise from this disposition, it is incorruptible.

(8) Since, in our conception of it, the mind has no parts or any extension, it is pointless asking whether it exists as a whole in the whole body, or as a whole in the individual parts of the body.

(9) The mind can be affected by imaginary things just as much as by real things; hence, if we are seeking not merely probable, but precise and exact knowledge of reality,[3] it is by nature doubtful whether any bodies are really perceived by us. Nevertheless, the divine revelation of Scripture removes even this doubt, and shows it to be indubitable that God created heaven and earth and everything in them, and keeps them in existence even now.

(10) The bond which keeps the soul conjoined with the body is the law of the immutability of nature, according to which everything remains in its present state so long as it is not disturbed by anything else.

(11) Since the mind is a substance which is newly created in the process of generation, the correct view seems to be that the rational soul is brought into 345 existence by God during this process, through an immediate act of creation.

(12) The mind has no need of ideas, or notions, or axioms which are innate: its faculty of thinking is all it needs for performing its own acts.

(13) Thus all common notions which are engraved in the mind have their origin in observation of things or in verbal instruction.

---

1 The phrase in brackets is contained as a footnote to the first edition of the *Comments* (1648).
2 The clause in brackets is contained as a footnote to the first edition of the *Comments*.
3 The clause, 'if we are ... reality', is contained in a footnote to the first edition.

(14) Even the idea of God which is implanted in the mind has its origin either in divine revelation, or in verbal instruction, or in observation of things.

(15) Our concept of God, or the idea of God which is present in our mind, does not in itself constitute a very strong argument for proving the existence of God, for it is not the case that everything of which we have an explicit conception exists; and the idea of God, in so far as we have such a conception (and an imperfect one at that), no more transcends our characteristic powers of thinking than the concept of any other thing whatever.

(16) The mind has two different sorts of thought: intellect and volition.

(17) Intellect comprises perception and judgement.

346 (18) Perception comprises sense-perception, memory, and imagination.

(19) Sense-perception consists entirely in the perception of some corporeal motion, which requires no intentional forms;[1] it takes place not in the external sense organs, but in the brain alone.

(20) The will is free and, in the case of natural things, is indifferent as between opposites – as we know from our own inner awareness.

(21) The will is self-determining, and should no more be said to be blind than vision should be said to be deaf.

'No one acquires a great reputation for piety more easily than the superstitious or hypocritical person.'[2]

AN EXAMINATION OF THE BROADSHEET

Comments on the title

I notice that in the *title* we are promised not just bald assertions about the
347 rational soul, but an explanation of it. We must suppose, then, that the broadsheet contains all the arguments – or at any rate the main ones – which the author had, not only for proving, but also for explicating, his assertions, and that no other arguments are to be expected from him. I approve of his calling the rational soul the 'human mind', for by using this expression he avoids the ambiguity in the term 'soul', and he is following me in this respect.

Comments on the individual articles

In the *first* article his intention seems to be to provide a *definition* of the rational soul; but his definition is imperfect, for he fails to specify its genus, i.e. to say whether it is a substance, or a mode, or something else. He gives only the differentia, which he has taken from me, for as far as I know, no one before me has stated that the rational soul consists solely in thought, that is, in the faculty of thinking or the internal principle by means of which we think.

---

1 See footnote 1, p. 154 above.
2 Quoted from Descartes' dedicatory letter to Princess Elizabeth in the *Principles*. See above, p. 191.

In the *second* article he begins by asking what the genus of the rational soul is, and says 'The nature of things seems to leave open the possibility that the human mind is either a substance or a mode of a corporeal substance.'

This assertion involves a contradiction, just as much as if he had said 'The nature of things leaves open the possibility that a mountain exists either with or without a valley.' We must of course distinguish between on the one hand things which by their very nature are susceptible of change – such as the fact that at present I am writing or not writing as the case may be, or the fact that one person is prudent, another imprudent – and on the other hand things which never change, such as everything which belongs to the essence of something (as philosophers generally acknowledge). It can undoubtedly be said of contingent items that the nature of things leaves open the possibility that they may be either in one state or in a different state. For example, at present I may be either writing or not writing. But when it is a question of the essence of something, it would be quite foolish and self-contradictory to say that the nature of things leaves open the possibility that the essence of something may have a different character from the one it actually has. The impossibility of existing without a valley is part of the nature of a mountain; and it belongs just as much to the nature of the human mind that it is what it is, *viz.* that it is a substance (if it is a substance), or a mode of a corporeal thing (if such it is). Our author tries to convince us on this score, and to prove his point he adds the words, 'or if we are to follow some philosophers'. In the expression 'some philosophers' he is obviously referring to me, for I am the first to have regarded thought as the principal attribute of an incorporeal substance, and extension as the principal attribute of a corporeal substance.[1] But I did not say that these attributes are present in the substances as in subjects distinct from them. We must take care here not to understand the word 'attribute' to mean simply 'mode', for we term an 'attribute' whatever we recognize as being naturally ascribable to something, whether it be a mode which is susceptible of change, or the absolutely immutable essence of the thing in question. Thus God has many attributes, but no modes. Again, one of the attributes of any substance is its subsisting on its own. The extension of a body, moreover, may take on various different modes: a body's being spherical constitutes one mode, being square a different mode. But considered in itself, the extension itself – the subject of these modes – is not a mode of the corporeal substance, but an attribute which constitutes its natural essence. Lastly there are various modes of thought, for

348

349

---

1 Cf. *Principles*, Part 1, art. 53: p. 210 above.

affirmation is a different mode of thinking from denial, and so on. But thought itself, as the internal principle from which these modes spring and in which they are present, is not conceived as a mode, but as an attribute which constitutes the nature of a substance. Whether this substance is corporeal or incorporeal is the question at issue here.

He adds 'these attributes are not opposites, but merely different'. Again there is a contradiction in this statement. For, when the question concerns attributes which constitute the essence of some substances, there can be no greater opposition between them than the fact that they are different; and when he acknowledges that the one attribute is different from the other, this is tantamount to saying that the one attribute is not the other; but 'is' and 'is not' are contraries. He says 'since they are not opposites but merely different, there is no reason why the mind should not be a sort of attribute co-existing with extension in the same subject, though the one attribute is not included in the concept of the other'.[1] There is a manifest contradiction in this statement, for the author is taking something which can hold strictly speaking only for modes and inferring that it holds for any attribute whatsoever; but he nowhere proves that the mind, or the internal principle of thought, is such a mode. On the contrary, I shall presently show that it is not, on the basis of what he actually says in article five. As for the attributes which constitute the natures of things, it cannot be said that those which are different, and such that the concept of the one is not contained in the concept of the other, are present together in one and the same subject; for that would be equivalent to saying that one and the same subject has two different natures – a statement that implies a contradiction, at least when it is a question of a simple subject (as in the present case) rather than a composite one.

Three points should be borne in mind here. If the author had properly understood them, he would never have fallen into such manifest errors.

First, it is part of the nature of a mode that, although we can readily understand a substance apart from a mode, we cannot *vice versa* clearly understand a mode unless at the same time we have a conception of the substance of which it is a mode (as I explained in the *Principles*, Part 1, article 61).[2] All philosophers are agreed on this point. But it is clear from his fifth article that our author has paid no attention to this rule, for he admits there that we can have doubts about the existence of the body, whereas we have no doubts about the existence of the mind. It follows from this that we can understand the mind apart from the body; hence it is not a mode of the body.

1 Art. 2, p. 294 above.   2 See p. 214 above.

Second, I wish at this point to stress the difference between simple entities and composite entities. A composite entity is one which is found to have two or more attributes, each one of which can be distinctly understood apart from the other. For, in virtue of the fact that one of these attributes can be distinctly understood apart from the other, we know that the one is not a mode of the other, but is a thing, or attribute of a thing, which can subsist without the other. A simple entity, on the other hand, is one in which no such attributes are to be found. It is clear 351 from this that a subject which we understand to possess solely extension and the various modes of extension is a simple entity; so too is a subject which we recognize as having thought and the various modes of thought as its sole attribute. But that which we regard as having at the same time both extension and thought is a composite entity, namely a man – an entity consisting of a soul and a body. Our author seems here to have taken a man to be simply a body, of which the man's mind is a mode.

Lastly, we should note that in subjects which are composed of several substances, one such substance often stands out; and we view this substance in such a way that any of the other substances which we associate with it are nothing but modes of it. Thus a man who is dressed can be regarded as a compound of a man and clothes. But with respect to the man, his being dressed is merely a mode, although clothes are substances. In the same way, in the case of a man, who is composed of a soul and a body, our author might be regarding the body as the principal element, in relation to which having a soul or the possession of thought is nothing but a mode. But it is absurd to infer from this that the soul itself, or that in virtue of which the body thinks, is not a substance distinct from the body.

He endeavours to support his contention by means of the following syllogism: 'Whatever we can conceive of can exist. Now it is conceivable that the mind is some such item (*viz.* a substance or a mode of a corporeal substance); for none of these implies a contradiction. Therefore ...'.[1] We should note that even though the rule, 'Whatever we can conceive of can exist',[2] is my own, it is true only so long as we are dealing 352 with a conception which is clear and distinct, a conception which embraces the possibility of the thing in question, since God can bring about whatever we clearly perceive to be possible. But we ought not to use this rule heedlessly, because it is easy for someone to imagine that he properly understands something when in fact he is blinded by some preconception and does not understand it at all. This is just what happens when the author maintains that there is no contradiction

1 Art. 2, p. 294 above.   2 Cf. Med. vi: vol. ii, p. 50.

involved in saying that one and the same thing possesses one or the other of two totally different natures, i.e. that it is a substance or a mode. If he had merely said that he could see no reason for regarding the human mind as an incorporeal substance, rather than a mode of a corporeal substance, we could have excused his ignorance. Moreover, if he had said that human intelligence could find no reasons which might decisively settle the question one way or the other, his arrogance would indeed be blameworthy, but his statement would involve no obvious contradiction. But when he says that the nature of things leaves open the possibility that the same thing is either a substance or a mode,[1] what he says is quite self-contradictory, and shows how irrational his mind is.

In the *third* article he pronounces judgement upon *me*. For it was *I* who wrote that the human mind can be perceived clearly and distinctly as a substance which is distinct from a corporeal substance.[2] Our author, however, proclaims that I am mistaken, though the only arguments he has to support him are the ones expounded in the preceding article, and these involve a contradiction. But I shall not spend further time on this. Nor do I propose to examine the somewhat ambiguous phrase, 'necessarily (or actually)', for it is of no great importance.

353   I decline also to examine the views about Holy Scripture expressed in the *fourth* article, as I do not wish to appear to be assuming the right to question someone else's religion. I shall simply say that in this context three different sorts of questions should be distinguished. First, some things are believed through faith alone – such as the mystery of the Incarnation, the Trinity, and the like. Secondly, other questions, while having to do with faith, can also be investigated by natural reason: among the latter, orthodox theologians usually count the questions of the existence of God, and the distinction between the human soul and the body. Thirdly, there are questions which have nothing whatever to do with faith, and which are the concern solely of human reasoning, such as the problem of squaring the circle, or of making gold by the techniques of alchemy, and the like. Just as it is an abuse of Scripture to presume to solve problems of the third sort on the basis of some mistaken interpretation of the Bible, so it diminishes the authority of Scripture to undertake to demonstrate questions of the first kind by means of arguments derived solely from philosophy. Theologians, however, all contend that it needs to be shown that such questions are not incompatible with the natural light, and it is principally to this task that they devote their studies. As to questions of the second sort, not only do they not regard them as being resistant to the natural light, but they even encourage philosophers to

---

1 Cf. art. 2, p. 294 above.   2 Cf. *Second Replies*, prop. 4: vol. II, p. 119.

demonstrate them to the best of their ability by arguments which are grounded in human reason.[1] But I have never seen anyone who maintained that the nature of things does not exclude the possibility of something's being in a different state from the one described in Holy Scripture, unless his intention was to show indirectly that he had no faith in Scripture. For, since we were born men before we became Christians we cannot believe that anyone would seriously embrace opinions which he thinks contrary to that right reason which constitutes being a man, simply in order to cling to the faith which makes him a Christian. But perhaps this is not what our author is saying, for his words are: 'this fact, which some people may find doubtful by nature, is for us, through its divine revelation in scripture, now beyond doubt'.[2] In this statement I find a double contradiction. The first one lies in his supposition that the essence of one and the same thing is, by nature, doubtful, and hence is subject to change, for it is self-contradictory that the essence of something does not always remain the same – the supposition that it changes entails that the thing in question will be a different thing, and will require a different name. The second contradiction lies in the words 'some people', for, owing to the fact that nature is the same for everyone, what can be doubtful only for some is not by nature doubtful.

The *fifth* article should be related to the second rather than the fourth, for in it the author is not concerned with divine revelation, but with the nature of the mind – with the question whether it is a substance or a mode. In order to show that it is possible to defend the thesis that the mind is nothing but a mode, he tries to get round an objection taken from my writings. I wrote that we cannot doubt that our mind exists, because from the very fact that we are doubting, it follows that our mind exists, but for all that, we can doubt whether any bodies exist[3]. From this I concluded and demonstrated that we clearly perceive the mind as an existing thing, or substance, even though we have no conception of any body whatever and even deny that any bodies exist, and hence that the concept of the mind does not in itself involve any concept of body. He thinks that he can explode this argument by saying that 'this just goes to show that, so long as we have doubts about the existence of the body, we cannot say that the mind is a mode of the body'. He shows here that he is utterly ignorant of what it is that philosophers term a 'mode'. As I explained above, the nature of a mode is such that it cannot be understood at all unless the concept of the thing of which it is a mode is implied in its own concept. Our author admits that the mind can

354

355

---

1 Cf. Dedicatory Letter to the *Meditations*: vol. II, p. 4.
2 Art. 4, p. 295 above.   3 Cf. Med. VI: vol. II, p. 54.

sometimes be understood apart from the body, *viz.* when there are doubts about the existence of the body. It follows from this that, at least when such doubts are entertained, the mind cannot be said to be a mode of the body. Now what is sometimes true of the essence or nature of something is always true of it. Nevertheless the author asserts that 'the nature of things leaves open the possibility that the mind is merely a mode of the body'.[1] These two statements manifestly contradict each other.

In the *sixth* article I fail to grasp his meaning. I do remember hearing in the Schools that 'the soul is an actuality of the organic body',[2] but till this day I have never heard the soul itself termed 'organic'. So I beg our author's pardon if I set forth my conjectures, not as true fact, but simply as mere conjectures, for I have nothing to say here that is certain. There are, I think, two mutually incompatible statements which come to mind: one is that the human mind is a substance which is really distinct from the body. The author does make this statement quite explicitly, but so far as he can, he provides reasons for not accepting it, and contends that it can be proved only by the authority of Holy Scripture. The other statement is that the same human mind is 'organic' or is instrumental in all its acts, i.e. it does not perform any actions on its own, but is something of which the body makes use, just as it makes use of the 356 arrangement[3] of its limbs and other corporeal modes. So in fact he asserts, though not quite in so many words, that 'the mind is nothing but a mode of the body', as though he had set the sights of all his arguments on this one target. These two statements are so manifestly contradictory that I do not think the author intended the reader to accept both at the same time; I think he deliberately muddled them together, with the aim of satisfying in some way his more simple-minded readers and fellow theologians by citing the authority of Scripture, while the more sharp-witted of his readers would recognize that he is speaking ironically when he says that 'the mind is distinct from the body', and that he is entirely of the opinion that the mind is nothing but a mode.

Again, in the *seventh* and *eighth* articles, he seems to be speaking merely ironically. He employs the same Socratic style in the latter part of the *ninth* article. But in the first part he gives a reason for his assertion, and so it seems that we must take him seriously when he says that it is by nature doubtful whether any bodies are really perceived by us. His reason for this assertion is that 'the mind can be affected by imaginary things just

---

1 Art. 2, p. 294 above.
2 A scholastic formulation of Aristotle's definition of the soul as 'first actuality' of the body. See Aristotle, *De Anima*, II, I, 412a27.
3 Reading *conformatio* instead of *confirmatio*, ('strengthening'), AT.

as much as by real things'. If this reason is sound, it has to be supposed that strictly speaking we cannot make any use of the intellect, but only of the faculty which is usually called the 'common' sense, the faculty which receives the forms[1] of things, be they real or imaginary, and by way of which they affect the mind – a faculty which, philosophers commonly admit, animals also possess.[2] Of course, we may be affected not only by images of real things but also by those which occur in our brain from other causes (as happens in sleep); even so, since we possess understanding and are not made in the same way as a horse or a mule, we distinguish by the light of reason between one sort of image and the other with the utmost clarity. I have explained in my writings the method of distinguishing correctly and reliably between these two sorts of images, and my account is so exact that I am confident that no one who has read it, and is capable of understanding it, can possibly be sceptical about it.

It is possible to suspect that the author is again being ironical in the *tenth* and *eleventh* articles. If the soul is believed to be a substance, it is ridiculous and absurd to say 'The bond which keeps it conjoined with the body is the law of the immutability of nature, according to which everything remains in its present state so long as it is not disturbed by anything else.' For, whether things are conjoined or separated, it is equally true that they persist in the same state so long as nothing changes it. Yet this is not the point at issue here, but rather, how it comes about that the mind is conjoined with the body rather than separated from it. If, however, the supposition is that the soul is a mode of the body, it is correct to say that we need seek no other bond to account for the soul's being joined to the body beyond the fact that it remains in the state in which it is, since the 'state' of a mode is nothing other than its inhering in the thing of which it is a mode.

In article *twelve* the author's disagreement with me seems to be merely verbal. When he says that the mind has no need of ideas, or notions, or axioms which are innate, while admitting that the mind has the power of thinking (presumably natural or innate), he is plainly saying the same thing as I, though verbally denying it. I have never written or taken the view that the mind requires innate ideas which are something distinct from its own faculty of thinking. I did, however, observe that there were certain thoughts within me which neither came to me from external objects nor were determined by my will, but which came solely from the power of thinking within me; so I applied the term 'innate' to the ideas or notions which are the forms of these thoughts in order to distinguish them from others, which I called 'adventitious' or 'made up'.[3] This is the

1 See footnote 1, p. 154 above.
2 Cf. Med. VI: vol. II, p. 59, and *Rules*, p. 41 above.   3 Cf. Med. III: vol. II, p. 26.

same sense as that in which we say that generosity is 'innate' in certain families, or that certain diseases such as gout or stones are innate in others: it is not so much that the babies of such families suffer from these diseases in their mother's womb, but simply that they are born with a certain 'faculty' or tendency to contract them.

In article *thirteen* he draws an extraordinary conclusion from the preceding article. Because the mind has no need of innate ideas, its power of thinking being sufficient, he says, 'all common notions which are engraved in the mind have their origin in observation of things or in verbal instruction' – as if the power of thinking could achieve nothing on its own, could never perceive or think anything except what it receives through observation of things or through verbal instruction, i.e. from the senses. But this is so far from being true that, on the contrary, if we bear well in mind the scope of our senses and what it is exactly that reaches our faculty of thinking by way of them, we must admit that in no case are the ideas of things presented to us by the senses just as we form them in our thinking. So much so that there is nothing in our ideas which is not innate to the mind or the faculty of thinking, with the sole exception of those circumstances which relate to experience, such as the fact that we judge that this or that idea which we now have immediately before our mind refers to a certain thing situated outside us. We make such a judgement not because these things transmit the ideas to our mind through the sense organs, but because they transmit something which, at exactly that moment, gives the mind occasion to form these ideas by means of the faculty innate to it. Nothing reaches our mind from external objects through the sense organs except certain corporeal motions, as our author himself asserts in article nineteen, in accordance with my own principles. But neither the motions themselves nor the figures arising from them are conceived by us exactly as they occur in the sense organs, as I have explained at length in my *Optics*.[1] Hence it follows that the very ideas of the motions themselves and of the figures are innate in us. The ideas of pain, colours, sounds and the like must be all the more innate if, on the occasion of certain corporeal motions, our mind is to be capable of representing them to itself, for there is no similarity between these ideas and the corporeal motions. Is it possible to imagine anything more absurd than that all the common notions within our mind arise from such motions and cannot exist without them? I would like our author to tell me what the corporeal motion is that is capable of forming some common notion to the effect that 'things which are equal to a third thing are equal to each other', or any other he cares to take. For all such

___

1 *Optics*, pp. 153 and 167 above; cf. also *Treatise on Man*, pp. 101ff above.

motions are particular, whereas the common notions are universal and bear no affinity with, or relation to, the motions.

In article *fourteen* he goes on to assert that even the idea of God which is within us derives its being not from our faculty of thinking, in which the idea is innate, 'but from divine revelation, or verbal instruction, or observation of things'. It is easier to recognize the error in this assertion if we consider that something can be said to derive its being from something else for two different reasons: either the other thing is its proximate and primary cause, without which it cannot exist, or it is a remote and merely accidental cause, which gives the primary cause occasion to produce its effect at one moment rather than another. Thus workers are the primary and proximate causes of their work, whereas those who give them orders to do the work, or promise to pay for it, are accidental and remote causes, for the workers might not do the work without instructions. There is, however, no doubt that verbal instruction or observation of things is often a remote cause which induces us to give some attention to the idea which we can have of God, and to bring it directly before our mind. But no one can say that this is the proximate and efficient cause of the idea, except someone who thinks that all we can ever understand about God is what he is called, namely 'God', or what corporeal form painters use to represent him. If the observation is visual, all it can, by its own unaided power, present to the mind are pictures, and indeed pictures which are composed of nothing more than a variety of corporeal motions, as the author himself tells us. If the observation is auditory, all it presents are words and utterances. If the observation is by means of the other senses, it cannot have any reference to God. It is surely obvious to everyone that, strictly speaking, sight in itself presents nothing but pictures, and hearing nothing but utterances and sounds. So everything over and above these utterances and pictures which we think of as being signified by them is represented to us by means of ideas which come to us from no other source than our own faculty of thinking. Consequently these ideas, along with that faculty, are innate in us, i.e. they always exist within us potentially, for to exist in some faculty is not to exist actually, but merely potentially, since the term 'faculty' denotes nothing but a potentiality. But no one can assert that we can know nothing of God other than his name or the corporeal image which artists give him, unless he is prepared openly to admit that he is an atheist and indeed totally lacking in intellect.

In article *fifteen*, after giving us his opinion concerning God, our author controverts all the arguments which I used to demonstrate the existence of God. At this point we can only marvel at the impudence of the man, in his supposing that he can so easily and so briefly overturn all the arguments which I composed only after prolonged and careful meditation, and which I took an entire book to expound. But all the arguments which I adduced for this purpose reduce to two. The first is that, as I have shown,[1] we have a conception or idea of God which is such that if we attend to the idea closely and thoroughly examine the issue in the way I have explained, we shall recognize, simply from this scrutiny, that it is not possible that God does not exist, since existence is contained in the concept of God – and not just possible or contingent existence, as in the ideas of all other things, but absolutely necessary and actual existence. Besides I am not alone in regarding this argument as a certain and evident demonstration; many others do so as well, including those pre-eminently learned and intelligent men who have examined the argu-

362 ment with care. Here is how the author of the broadsheet controverts my argument: 'Our concept of God, or the idea of God which is present in our mind, does not in itself constitute a very strong argument for proving the existence of God, for it is not the case that everything of which we have an explicit conception exists.' This statement shows that while he has read my writings, he has by no means been able, or willing, to understand them. For the force of my argument does not derive from the idea of God understood in a general sense, but from a particular characteristic of the idea, a characteristic which is most evident in our idea of God and which is not to be found in the concept of any other thing, namely the necessity of existence, which is required for the consummation of the perfections without which God cannot be understood. The second argument which I used to demonstrate the existence of God was based on the fact (which I clearly proved) that we would not have had the ability to understand all the perfections which we recognize in God, if it were not true that God exists and that we were created by him.[2] Our author thinks that he has thoroughly demolished this argument with his assertion that 'the idea we have of God no more transcends our characteristic powers of thinking than the concept of any other thing whatever'.[3] If he means by this simply that the concept which we have of God without the aid of supernatural grace is no less natural than any of our concepts of other things, then his view agrees with mine; but on that basis he has no case against me. If, however, he thinks that in the concept of God no more objective perfections are implied than in all other

363 concepts taken together, then he is clearly mistaken. It is just this superabundance of perfections, in which our concept of God surpasses all others, that I have used as the basis of my argument.

---

1 See Med. v: vol. II, pp. 45ff.   2 See Med. III: vol. II, pp. 28ff.
3 Art. 18, p. 296 above.

In the remaining six articles there is nothing worth commenting on except that when the author wishes to distinguish the properties of the soul, he speaks of them in a quite confused and inappropriate manner. I have stated that all these properties reduce to two principal ones, of which one is the perception of the intellect and the other the determination of the will,[1] these our author calls 'intellect' and 'volition' respectively.[2] He then goes on to divide what he calls 'intellect' into 'perception' and 'judgement'.[3] But he differs from me on this point. For I saw that over and above perception, which is a prerequisite of judgement, we need affirmation and negation to determine the form of the judgement, and also that we are often free to withhold our assent, even if we perceive the matter in question. Hence I assigned the act of judging itself, which consists simply in assenting (i.e. in affirmation or denial) to the determination of the will rather than to the perception of the intellect. Later on, in enumerating the forms of perception, he lists only sense-perception, memory, and imagination.[4] We may gather from this that he does not admit any pure understanding, i.e. understanding which is not concerned with any corporeal images, and hence that his view is that we have no knowledge of God, or of the human mind, or of other incorporeal things. The only explanation for this that I can think of is that what thoughts he has on these matters are so confused that he is never aware of having a pure thought, a thought which is quite distinct from any corporeal image. 364

At the end, he adds the following sentence taken from one of my writings: 'No one acquires a great reputation for piety more easily than the superstitious or hypocritical person.' What he means by this I cannot see, unless his reference to hypocrisy has to do with his frequently resorting to irony, though I hardly think that he can acquire a great reputation for piety that way.

To sum up, I am forced to admit that I blush with shame to think that in the past I have praised this author as a man of the most penetrating intelligence, and have written somewhere or other that 'I do not think he teaches any doctrines which I would be unwilling to acknowledge as my own.'[5] But when I wrote that sentence, the only examples of his work that I had seen were ones in which he was faithfully copying me, with the exception of just one expression,[6] which had such unfortunate results for

1 Cf. *Principles*, Part I, art. 32, p. 204 above.   2 Art. 16, p. 296 above.
3 Art. 17, *ibid.*   4 Art. 18, *ibid.*
5 Cf. *Letter to Voetius* (published 1643) where Descartes says 'Nevertheless I credit Regius with an exceedingly sharp and penetrating intellect, so that there is hardly anything in his writings which I would not be happy to acknowledge as my own' (AT VIIIB 163).
6 *Viz.* the sentence, 'Man is an entity only accidentally'. See Descartes' letters to Regius of mid-December 1641 and January 1642 (AT III 460 and 508).

him that I hoped he would make no further attempt of this sort. In other matters, I could see, he made a great show of embracing opinions which I considered to be absolutely true; so I put this down to his intelligence and insight. But now my wider experience compels me to think that it is not so much the love of truth which grips him as the love of novelty. He regards everything he has learnt from others as old-fashioned and obsolete, and nothing seems novel enough for him if he has not wrung it

365 from his own brain. Yet so unfortunate are his own inventions that I have never noticed any word in his writings (save what he had copied from others) which in my view did not contain some error. I must therefore warn all those who are convinced that he is a champion of my opinions that there is not one of them of which he does not give a wrong and distorted account; and I have in mind here not just my views on metaphysics, on which he openly contradicts me, but also on physics, which he deals with somewhere in his writings. So I find this learned doctor's treatment of my writings and his efforts at interpreting (or rather, falsifying) them much more annoying than the most bitter attacks which others have made upon them.

Indeed I have never yet seen one of these harsh critics who did not foist upon me views which were utterly different from my own, and so preposterous and silly that I had no fear that any man of intelligence could be persuaded that they were mine. Thus as I write these words, I have just received two new pamphlets put together by an opponent of just this sort.[1] In the first of these it is stated that there are 'some innovators who deny that we can have any firm trust in the senses, and who contend that philosophers can deny that there is a God and doubt his existence, while at the same time they admit that actual conceptions of God, forms,[2] and ideas of him are naturally implanted in the human mind'. In the second pamphlet we are told that these innovators 'have the audacity to proclaim that God should be called the efficient cause of himself not just in a negative sense but also in a positive sense'. In each of these pamphlets the sole concern is to pile up arguments to prove: first, that we have no *actual* knowledge of God in our mother's womb, and hence that 'no actual form or idea of God is innate in our mind'; second,

366 that 'we must not say that there is no God' and that 'those who do are atheists and should be punished by law'; and third, that God is not the 'efficient' cause of himself.

I might well suppose that all these assertions were not directed against me, for my name is not mentioned in these pamphlets, and not one of the views attacked strikes me as being anything but utterly absurd and false.

---

1 *Gemina Disputatio Metaphysica de Deo*, Jacques de Rives (1647).
2 Lat. *species*: see footnote 1, p. 154 above.

Nevertheless, they are not unlike those views which have often been slanderously imputed to me in the past by men of that stamp; secondly, no one else is known to whom these views could be attributed; and lastly, many people are in no doubt that I am the object of attack in these pamphlets. For these reasons I shall take this opportunity to instruct their author on the following points.

First, by 'innate ideas' I have never meant anything other than what the author himself, on page six of the second pamphlet, explicitly asserts to be true, *viz.* that 'there is present in us a natural power which enables us to know God'. But I have never written or even thought that such ideas are *actual*, or that they are some sort of 'forms' which are distinct from our faculty of thinking. Indeed, there is no one more opposed than I to the useless lumber of scholastic entities; so much so that I could hardly keep from laughing when I saw the enormous battalion of arguments which the gentleman had painstakingly mustered – quite without malice, no doubt – to prove that 'babies have no actual conception of God while they are in their mother's womb' – as if he were thereby mounting a devastating assault upon me.

Secondly, I have never even taught that 'God is to be denied, or that he can deceive us, or that everything should be doubted, or that we should 367 entirely withdraw our confidence in the senses, or that we should not distinguish between being asleep and being awake', and other things of that sort – doctrines of which I am sometimes accused by ignorant detractors. I have explicitly disavowed all such views, and refuted them with very strong arguments – stronger, I venture to add, than any that anyone before me has employed in refuting them. In order to achieve an easier and more effective refutation of them, I proposed at the beginning of my *Meditations* to treat all such matters as doubtful. I was not the first to discover such doubts: the sceptics have long been harping on this theme. What could be more perverse than to ascribe to a writer views which he reports simply in order to refute? What could be more foolish than to pretend that during the interval in which such views are being stated, pending their refutation, they are the doctrines of the writer, and hence that someone who mentions the arguments of the atheists is temporarily an atheist? What more childish than to object that if he were to die before he discovered or wrote down his 'hoped for refutation' he would die an atheist, and that in the meantime he has been conveying a pernicious doctrine, and moreover that 'evil should not be done for the sake of beneficial ends', and so forth? Someone perhaps will say that I conveyed these false views, not as the opinions of others, but as my own. But so what? In the same book in which I related them I refuted all of them, and one could even see from the very title of the book that I was utterly opposed to believing them, since it promises 'demonstrations of the existence of God'. Is there anyone so dull as to imagine that the author of a book with such a title did not know, when writing the first pages, what he had undertaken to demonstrate in the rest of the book? I conveyed the objections as my own simply because the meditative style, which in my judgement was the most appropriate for expounding my arguments, demanded this approach. If this explanation does not satisfy our hostile critics, I should like to know what they would say about Holy Scripture (which should not be compared with the writings of mere men), when they see that there are some things in it which can be properly understood only if they are viewed as the utterances of impious people, or at any rate of people other than the Holy Ghost or the Prophets. For example, these sentences from Chapter 2 of Ecclesiastes: 'There is nothing better for a man than that he should eat and drink, and that he should make his soul enjoy good in his labour. This also I saw, that it was from the hand of God. For who can eat or who else can hasten thereunto, more than I?' And in the following chapter: 'I said in mine heart concerning the estate of the sons of men, that God might manifest them, and that they might see that they themselves are beasts; for that which befalleth the sons of men befalleth beasts; even one thing befalleth them: as the one dieth, so dieth the other; yea, they have all one breath: so that a man hath no pre-eminence above a beast.' Do they believe that the Holy Ghost here is instructing us that we should fill our bellies and wallow in pleasures, or that our souls are no more immortal than the souls of beasts? I do not think they are quite so mad as to believe that. So they ought not to slander me just because in my writings I have not availed myself of precautions which have never been observed by any other writer (nor, even, by the Holy Ghost).

Thirdly and lastly, I must advise the author of these pamphlets that I have never written that God should be called 'the efficient cause of himself not just in a negative sense but also in a positive sense', as he is rash enough to allege on page eight of the second booklet. However carefully he sifts, scans and pores over my writings, he will not find in them anything like this – quite the reverse in fact.[1] Anyone who has read my writings, or has any knowledge of me, or at least does not think me utterly silly, knows that I am totally opposed to such extravagant views. Hence I can only wonder what these slanderers are aiming at. For if they want to convince people that I wrote things the very opposite of which are to be found in my writings, they should first have taken the precaution of suppressing all my publications, and should even have

---

1 Cf. Fourth Replies: vol. 11, pp. 164ff.

erased all recollection of them from the memory of those who have already read them. While these things remain undone, they are doing more harm to themselves than to me. It is a wonder also that they should so bitterly and zealously attack me, despite the fact that I have never provoked or harmed them (though no doubt if roused I could have hurt them), while they take no action against many others who devote entire books to the refutation of their doctrines, and ridicule them as hood-winked simpletons. But I do not want to add anything here which might make them give up their established practice of attacking me in their books, since I am very pleased to see that they think me so important. But in the meantime I pray that they recover their good sense.

Written at Egmont, Holland, towards the end of December, 1647.

Description of the Human Body

Translator's preface

The extracts that follow, which are based on the text in Volume XI of Adam and Tannery,[1] are from an unfinished treatise, *La Description du corps humain*, first published by Clerselier in 1664 with his edition of the *Treatise on Man*. (The alternative title 'On the formation of the foetus', which Clerselier placed at the head of each page, properly relates only to Part Four of the treatise.) The work dates from the winter of 1647/8, as we know from a letter to Princess Elizabeth of January 1648, where Descartes talks of working on a 'description of the functions of the animal and of man'. Frans Burman, who interviewed Descartes in April 1648, provides the following additional information:

In the treatise on the animal which he [Descartes] worked on this winter he noticed the following: although his aim was merely to explain the functions of the animal, he saw that he could hardly do this without having to explain the formation of the animal right from the beginning. And this was something that he found to be derivable from his principles to the extent that he was able to give a reason for the existence of the eye, nose, brain and so on. He saw, moreover, that the nature of these things was so constituted in accordance with his principles that it could not be otherwise. But these were all matters which he did not wish to go into at such length, and so he gave up writing the treatise.[2]

J.C.

1 See General Introduction, p. x above.
2 AT v 170.

DESCRIPTION OF THE HUMAN BODY
AND OF ALL ITS FUNCTIONS
*both those which do not in any way depend on the soul, and
those which do, and including the chief cause of the
formation of the parts of the body*

Part One

PREFACE

There is no more fruitful exercise than attempting to know ourselves. The benefits we may expect from such knowledge not only relate to ethics, as many would initially suppose, but also have a special importance for medicine. I believe that we would have been able to find many very reliable rules, both for curing illness and for preventing it, and even 224 for slowing down the ageing process, if only we had spent enough effort on getting to know the nature of our body, instead of attributing to the soul functions which depend solely on the body and on the disposition of its organs.

Since childhood, however, we have all found by experience that many bodily movements occur in obedience to the will, which is one of the faculties of the soul, and this has led us to believe that the soul is the principle responsible for all bodily movement. Our ignorance of anatomy and mechanics has also played a major role here. For in restricting our consideration to the outside of the human body, we have never imagined that it has within it enough organs or mechanisms to move of its own accord in all the different ways which we observe. Our error was reinforced by our belief that no movement occurs inside a corpse, though it possesses the same organs as a living body, and lacks only a soul.

But when we try to get to know our nature more distinctly we can see that our soul, in so far as it is a substance which is distinct from the body, is known to us merely through the fact that it thinks, that is to say, understands, wills, imagines, remembers and has sensory perceptions; for all these functions are kinds of thought. The other functions which some people attribute to the soul, such as moving the heart and the arteries, 225 digesting food in the stomach and so on, do not involve any thought, and

314

are simply bodily movements; further, it is more common for a body to be moved by another body than for it to be moved by a soul. Hence, we have less reason to attribute such functions to the soul than to the body.

We can also observe that when some part of our body is harmed, for example when a nerve is irritated, the result is that the part in question ceases to obey our will as it normally does, and sometimes is subject to convulsive movements despite our wishes. This shows that the soul cannot produce any movement in the body without the appropriate disposition of the bodily organs which are required for making the movement. On the contrary, when all the bodily organs are appropriately disposed for some movement, the body has no need of the soul in order to produce that movement; and, as a result, all the movements which we in no way experience as depending on our thought must be attributed not to the soul, but simply to the disposition of the organs. Even the movements which we call 'voluntary' occur principally as a result of this disposition of the organs, since, although it is the soul that determines the movements, they cannot be produced without the requisite disposition of the organs, no matter how much we may will this to happen.

Furthermore, although all these movements cease in a corpse, once the soul has quit the body, we must not infer that it is the soul which produces them; the only inference we may make is that it is one and the same cause which both makes the body unfitted to produce these movements and makes the soul leave the body.

It is true that we may find it hard to believe that the mere disposition of the bodily organs is sufficient to produce in us all the movements which are in no way determined by our thought. So I will now try to prove the point, and to give such a full account of the entire bodily machine that we will have no more reason to think that it is our soul which produces in it the movements which we know by experience are not controlled by our will than we have reason to think that there is a soul in a clock which makes it tell the time. 226

Everyone already has some knowledge of the different parts of the human body. That is to say, we all know that it is composed of a very large number of bones, muscles, nerves, veins and arteries, together with a heart, a brain, a liver, lungs and a stomach. Indeed, we have all at some time or other seen various animals cut open, and been able to look at the shape and arrangement of their insides, which very much resemble our own. This is all the anatomy that the reader will need to have studied in order to understand this book; for I will take care to explain any further details that need to be known as and when I have occasion to speak of them.

First of all, I want the reader to have a general notion of the entire machine which it is my task to describe. So I will say here that the heat in the heart is like the great spring or principle responsible for all the movements occurring in the machine. The veins are pipes which conduct the blood from all the parts of the body towards the heart, where it serves to

227 fuel the heat there. The stomach and the intestines are another much larger pipe perforated with many little holes through which the juices from the food ingested run into the veins; these then carry the juices straight to the heart. The arteries are yet another set of pipes through which the blood, which is heated and rarefied in the heart, passes from there into all the other parts of the body, bringing them heat and material to nourish them. Finally, the parts of the blood that are most agitated and lively are carried to the brain by the arteries coming directly from the heart in the straightest line of all; these parts of the blood make up a kind of air or very fine[1] wind which is called the 'animal spirits'. These dilate the brain and make it ready to receive impressions both from external objects and from the soul; and in receiving these impressions the brain acts as the organ or seat of the 'common' sense,[2] the imagination and the memory. Next, this same air or these same spirits flow from the brain through the nerves into all the muscles, thus making the nerves ready to function as organs for the external senses; they also inflate the muscles in various ways and thus impart movement to all the parts of the body.

These, in brief, are all the things which it is my task to describe in this book. The purpose is to enable us to know distinctly what there is in each of our actions which depends only on the body, and what there is which depends on the soul. This will enable us to make better use both of body and of soul and to cure or prevent the maladies of both.

Part Two

THE MOVEMENT OF THE HEART AND THE BLOOD[3]

(239) . . . This circular movement of the blood was first noticed by an English physician called Harvey, who deserves the highest possible praise for making such a valuable discovery . . .

(241) But Harvey was not so successful, in my view, on the question of the heart's movement. He imagined, against the general opinion of medical

---

1 Fr. *subtil*, by which Descartes means 'composed of very small, fast-moving particles'.
2 See footnote 1, above p. 41.
3 The first part of this section closely follows the exposition given in the *Treatise on Man* and the *Discourse*, Part 5 (pp. 100ff. and 134–7 above). For Harvey, see footnote p. 136 above.

men, and against the ordinary evidence of what we see, that when the heart lengthens, its cavities increase in size, and that when it shortens, they become narrower. I claim, instead, to demonstrate that they become even larger when the heart shortens.

The reasons which led Harvey to his view are the following. He observed that the heart becomes harder when it shortens; and that in the case of frogs and other animals which have little blood, it becomes whiter, or less red, when it lengthens; and finally, that if we make an incision down to the cavities, blood flows out through the incision at the moment when the heart shortens, but not when it lengthens. He believed that it was perfectly sound to infer from this that when the heart becomes hard it is contracting; he further inferred that the heart's becoming less red in certain animals is evidence that the blood is leaving it; and finally he thought that since blood is observed to come out via the incision, this obliges us to believe that the cause is a narrowing of the space containing the blood.

He could have supported this last point by a very striking experiment. If you slice off the pointed end of the heart in a live dog, and insert a finger into one of the cavities, you will feel unmistakably that every time the heart gets shorter it presses the finger, and every time it gets longer it stops pressing it. This seems to make it quite certain that the cavities are 242 narrower when there is more pressure on the finger than when there is less. Nevertheless, all that this proves is that observations may often lead us astray when we do not examine their possible causes with sufficient care. Admittedly, if the interior of the heart contracted, as Harvey imagines, this could cause it to become harder and less red in animals which have little blood; it could also cause the blood in the cavities to come out via the incision we have made; and finally, it could cause pressure on a finger inserted through the incision. But all this does not alter the fact that the same effects could also proceed from a different cause, namely the expansion of the blood which I have described.

In order to be in a position to tell which of these two causes is the true one, we will have to consider other observations which are not compatible with both explanations. The first such observation I can provide is this. If the heart becomes hard because of the contraction of the fibres inside it, this must reduce its size; if, instead, the cause of the hardening is the expansion of the blood within the heart, this must increase its size. Now we see when we make our observations that the heart does not diminish in size, but on the contrary, grows larger – which has led other medical men to conclude that it swells up during this phase. It is true, however, that the increase in size is not great; but the reason for this is

evident: the heart has several fibres stretched like cords from one side of
its cavities to the other, and these stop them opening a great deal.

243   There is another observation which shows that when the heart
shortens and gets hard its cavities do not thereby become narrower, but
on the contrary become wider. If you cut off the pointed end of the heart
in a young rabbit which is still alive, you will be able to see by inspection
that the cavities become slightly wider, and emit blood, when the heart
hardens; and even when they emit only very small drops of blood,
because very little blood remains in the animal's body, they still continue
to retain the same width. What stops them opening even wider are the
tiny fibres stretched from one side to the other, which hold them back.
What makes this less obviously apparent in the heart of a dog, or other
more vigorous animal, than it is in that of a young rabbit, is that the
fibres occupy a greater part of the cavities; they stiffen when the heart
becomes hard and can exert pressure on a finger placed in the cavities.
But for all that, the cavities do not become narrower; on the contrary,
they become wider.

I will add a third observation, which is as follows. When the blood
leaves the heart, it does not have the same qualities which it had when
entering: it is much hotter, more rarefied and more agitated. Now if we
suppose that the heart moves in the way Harvey describes, we must
imagine some faculty which causes this movement; yet the nature of this
faculty is much harder to conceive of than whatever Harvey purports to
244 explain by invoking it. What is more, we shall also have to suppose that
there are additional faculties which change the qualities of the blood
while it is in the heart. If, instead, we restrict our consideration to the expansion of the blood which must follow necessarily from the heat (which,
as everyone recognizes, is greater in the heart than in all the other parts of
the body), it will be plain to see that this expansion alone is sufficient to
move the heart in the way I have described, and also to change the nature
of the blood in the way which observation shows to be the case. Indeed, it
is sufficient to produce all the changes which one can imagine must be
required in order to prepare the blood, and make it more suited for
nourishing all the limbs and for employment in all the functions which it
facilitates in the body. Thus we do not have to suppose, in order to
explain all this, any unknown or strange faculties.

For surely the best and swiftest way of preparing the blood that we can
possibly imagine is that which is effected through fire or heat – the
strongest agent that we know of in nature. The heat rarefies the blood in
the heart, separates the tiny parts of the blood one from the other, and
divides them up and changes their shapes in all the ways we can imagine.

So I am very surprised that although it has always been known that there is more heat in the blood than in the whole of the rest of the body, and that blood can be rarefied by heat, no one has so far noticed that it is the rarefaction of the blood, and this alone, that is the cause of the heart's movement. It may seem that Aristotle thought of this when he remarked, in Chapter Twenty of his book *On Respiration*, 'this movement is similar   245 to the action of a liquid boiled by heat'. He also said that the pulse is caused by the 'juices from ingested food continually entering the heart and raising its inmost skin'.[1] But since he makes no mention in this passage either of the blood or of the way in which the heart is made, it is clearly only by chance that he happened to say something approaching the truth; he possessed no certain knowledge on the matter. What is more, Aristotle's view on this question was not adopted by anyone, even though on many other questions where his views are much less plausible he had the good fortune to gain a large number of followers.

Nevertheless, it is so important to know the true cause of the heart's movement that without such knowledge it is impossible to know anything which relates to the theory of medicine. For all the other functions of the animal are dependent on this, as will be clearly seen in what follows.

Part Three

NUTRITION[2]

... But in order to achieve a distinct understanding of this point, we   (247) should bear in mind that the parts of all living bodies which require nutrition to sustain them (i.e. animals and plants) are continually undergoing change. So there is no difference between those parts we call *fluid*, such as the blood, the humours and the spirits, and those we call *solid*, such as bones, flesh, nerves and skin, beyond the fact that each particle of these latter parts moves much more slowly than the particles of the former.

To conceive how these particles move we must suppose that all the solid parts are composed simply of small fibres stretching out and folding back and sometimes intertwining in various ways. Each fibre emerges from a place on one of the branches of an artery; and the fluid parts, i.e. the humours and the spirits, flow alongside these little fibres, through the

---

1 Aristotle, *Parva Naturalia* 480a4.
2 Descartes begins this section of the work by arguing that it is the arterial blood (rather than that returning to the heart through the veins) which serves to nourish all the regions of the body; its particles, being small and fast-moving, can easily enter among the strands composing the various solid parts of the body.

spaces around them, thus making up an infinite number of small channels, all originating in the arteries and normally emerging from the pores of the arteries which are nearest to the roots of the fibres alongside which they run. After following the fibres through various twists and turns in the body they finally come to the surface of the skin; and the humours and spirits then evaporate into the outer air through its pores.

In addition to these pores through which the humours and spirits run, there are many other much narrower pores through which there continually passes material of the first two elements which I described in my *Principles*.[1] The agitated material of the first two elements encounters the agitated material of the humours and the spirits; they in turn, as they run alongside the little fibres making up the solid parts of the body, continually make the fibres move forward slightly, albeit very slowly. Thus each part of every fibre travels from the place where the fibre has its roots to the surface of the limb where it terminates; and on arrival it encounters the air, or the other bodies touching the surface of the skin, which makes it separate from the rest of the fibre. Thus some part is always being detached from the end of each fibre, and at the same time another part is being attached to the root, in the way I have already described. If the detached part emerges at the skin, it evaporates in the air; but if it emerges at the surface of some muscle or some other interior part, it mixes with the fluid parts and flows with them to wherever they are going, i.e. sometimes outside the body and sometimes through the veins towards the heart, where the fluid parts often return.

Thus we may see that all the parts of the little fibres which make up the solid parts of the body have a movement which is no different from that of the humours and the spirits, except that it is much slower; similarly, the movement of the humours and the spirits is slower than that of the more subtle material.[2]

249   These different speeds are the cause of the various solid or fluid parts becoming larger or smaller as they rub against one another; they behave in different ways depending on the different constitution of each body. When one is young, for example, the little fibres which make up the solid parts are not yet very tightly joined together, and the channels along which the fluid parts flow are fairly large; hence the movement of the fibres is slower than when one is old. Also, more matter is being attached to their roots than is being detached from their extremities, which causes them to grow longer and get stronger; their increase in size is the means whereby the body grows.

1 See Part III, art. 52, above p. 258.
2 See footnote 1, above p. 316.

When the humours which flow between the little fibres are not copious, they all pass fairly rapidly along the channels containing them, causing the body to grow taller and the solid parts to grow without getting any thicker. But when the humours are very copious, they cannot flow so easily between the little fibres of the solid particles; and in the case of those parts which have very irregular branch-like shapes and thus have the hardest passage of all between the fibres, the result is that little by little they become lodged there and form fat. Fat does not grow in the body by means of nourishment in the strict sense, as flesh does; it accumulates simply because many of its parts join together and stick one to the other, as do the parts of dead things.

When the humours become less copious they flow more easily and 250 more quickly, because the subtle matter and the accompanying spirits have more force to agitate them. This causes them gradually to pick up the particles of fat and carry them off, which is how people become thin.

As we get older, the little fibres which make up the solid parts of the body contract and stick together more and more, and in the end they attain such a degree of hardness that the body stops growing entirely, and even loses the ability to be nourished. This leads to such a disproportion between the solid parts and the fluid parts that life is extinguished by old age alone . . .[1]

Part Four (252)

THE PARTS OF THE BODY WHICH ARE FORMED IN THE SEMINAL MATERIAL

We may acquire an even more perfect knowledge of the way in which all the parts of the body are nourished if we consider how they were originally formed from the seminal material. Hitherto I have been unwilling to put my views on this topic in writing because I have not yet been able to make enough observations[2] to verify all the ideas I have had 253 on the subject. Nevertheless, I cannot forbear, in passing, to give some indication of the most general points; I hope I shall run the least risk of having to retract these later, in the light of fresh observations.

I leave the shape and arrangement of the particles of the seminal material quite unspecified; it is enough for me to state that the seed of plants, being hard and solid, may have its parts arranged and situated in a precise way that cannot be altered without destroying their efficacy. But

---

1 There follow further details of the role of the blood in nutrition.
2 Fr. *expériences*; see footnote, p. 143 above.

it is quite different in the case of the seminal material of animals, which is very fluid and is ordinarily produced by the copulation of the two sexes. This material is apparently just a disorganized mixture of two fluids which act on each other as a kind of yeast, generating mutual heat. Some of the particles thus acquire as much agitation as fire has, and expand and press on other particles, thereby putting them little by little into the state required for the formation of the parts of the body.

To achieve this result the two fluids in question do not need to be very different. We may observe how old dough makes new dough swell, or how the scum formed on beer is able to serve as yeast for another brew; and in the same way it is easy enough to accept that the seminal material of each sex functions as a yeast to that of the other, when the two fluids are mixed together.

254   Now I think that the first thing to happen in this mixture of seminal material is that heat is generated; and this bring it about that all the drops of the fluid no longer resemble each other. The heat acts in the same way as it does in new wine when it ferments, or in hay which is stored before it is dry: it causes a number of particles to gather together in some part of the space containing them, and then makes them expand and press upon other surrounding particles. This is how the heart begins to form.

Next, since the small parts which are expanded in this way tend to continue their movement in a straight line, and the heart which has begun to form resists them, they slowly move away and make their way to the area where the brain-stem forms later on; in so doing they displace other particles which move round in a circle so as to occupy their original place in the heart. These latter particles, after the short time needed for them to assemble in the heart, in turn expand and move away, following the same path as the earlier group. The result is that some particles from the earlier group which are still in position, together with others which have moved in from elsewhere to take the place of those which have meanwhile left, now move into the heart; here they expand and move away once more. This expansion, which occurs in various repeated phases in this way, is what the beating of the heart, or the pulse, consists in.

Concerning the material which passes into the heart, it should be noted that the violent agitation of the heat which makes it expand not only causes some of the particles to move away and become separated, but also causes others to gather; these press and bump against one another

255   and divide into many extremely small strands which stay so close to one another that only the very subtle matter (which I called the 'first element' in my *Principles*[1]) can occupy the spaces left around them. The particles

1 See *Principles*, Part III, art. 52, p. 258 above.

which join together in this way as they move out of the heart never leave the route by which they can go back into it – unlike the many other particles which penetrate the mass of seminal material more easily on every side; this material is the source from which new particles continue to move towards the heart, until it is all used up.

As a result of this, those who know the explanation of the nature of light which I gave both in my *Optics* and my *Principles*, and the explanation of the nature of colours which I gave in my *Meteorology*,[1] will easily be able to understand why the blood of all animals is red. For, as I explained in the works just cited, what makes us see light is simply the pressure of the material of the second element. The material, as I said, is composed of many small balls which are in mutual contact; and we have sensory awareness of two kinds of motion which these balls have. One is the motion by which they approach our eyes in a straight line, which 256 gives us the sensation of light; and the other is the motion whereby they turn about their own centres as they approach us. If the speed at which they turn is much smaller than that of their rectilinear motion, the body from which they come appears *blue* to us; while if the turning speed is much greater than that of their rectilinear motion, the body appears *red* to us. But the only type of body which could possibly make their turning motion faster is one whose tiny parts have such slender strands, and ones which are so close together (as I have shown those of the blood to be), that the only material revolving round them is that of the first element. The little balls of the second element encounter this material of the first element on the surface of the blood; this material of the first element then passes with a continuous, very rapid, oblique motion from one gap between the balls to another, thus moving in an opposite direction to the balls, so that they are forced by it to turn about their centres. Indeed, their speed of rotation is perforce more rapid than any other cause could produce, since the first element surpasses all other bodies in speed.

It is for virtually the same reason that iron appears red when it is hot or that coals appear red when they are burning: at such times their pores are filled only with material of the first element. But since these pores are not so constricted as those of blood, and the first element is present in large enough quantities to produce light, the shade of red is different from that of blood.

As soon as the heart begins to form in this way, the rarefied blood leaving it makes its way in a straight line in the direction of least resistance, *viz.* towards the region of the body where the brain forms later on; and the path taken by the blood begins to form the upper part of 257

1 *Optics*, pp. 152ff above; *Principles*, Part 3, art. 55–64; *Meteorology*, Disc. 8.

the great artery. Now, because of the resistance produced by the parts of seminal material which it encounters, the blood does not travel very far in a straight line without being pushed back towards the heart along the same path by which it came. But it cannot return down this path, because the way is blocked by the new blood which the heart is producing. This causes it to be deflected a little on its downward path, towards the side opposite to that from which new material is entering the heart. This is the side where we shall afterwards find the spine. The blood makes its way by this route towards the area where the genital organs will be formed, and that path which it takes on its descent is the lower part of the great artery. But because the parts of the seminal material also exert pressure from this side, they resist the movement of the blood; furthermore, the heart continually sends new blood towards the top and the bottom of this artery. So the blood is forced to make its way in a circular direction back towards the heart via the side farthest from the spine, where the chest is formed later on. The route which the blood takes in its return towards the heart is what we afterwards call the vena cava.[1]

---

1 There follow details of the further development of the heart and of the formation of the lungs and brain. Part 5 deals principally with the formation of the veins and arteries.

The Passions of the Soul

Translator's preface

Descartes' last philosophical work was written in French, printed in Holland, and published in Amsterdam and Paris in 1649 under the title *Les Passions de l'Ame*.[1] The book's publication in Paris seems to have been arranged by a 'friend' whose anonymous letters, with Descartes' replies, forms its preface.

Descartes composed the work largely at the urging of Princess Elizabeth of Bohemia (1618–80), and its origin can be traced in their correspondence. Elizabeth first mentions the passions when, wondering how the soul can be governed by the body given that they have nothing in common, she asks Descartes to explain 'the manner of [the soul's] actions and passions in the body' (20 June 1643). Descartes' reply – that the body causes the soul to have feelings and passions, and the soul causes the body to move, through an inexplicable 'union' between the soul and body – did not satisfy the princess. Nor was she satisfied when Descartes sought to answer her question with vague moralizing and practical advice for the control of the passions. Eventually she insisted that he give 'a definition of the passions, in order to make them well known' (13 September 1645). Descartes obliged by producing a little 'treatise on the passions' which he gave to Elizabeth in 1646. In the following year he entered into correspondence with Queen Christina of Sweden (1626–89), to whom he also sent a copy of the 'little treatise', which reportedly she read while hunting. This treatise, possibly a draft of the first two parts of the published work, seems also to have been seen by Clerselier, to whom Descartes says, in a letter of 23 April 1649, that he has been 'indolent in revising it and in adding the things you thought lacking, which will increase its length by a third'.

Invited to Sweden by Queen Christina, Descartes arrived in Stockholm in October 1649, a month before publication of *The Passions of the Soul*. Suffering from the rigours of the Swedish winter and the tedium of his courtly duties (which included giving lessons to the Queen at five o'clock in the morning), he contracted pneumonia and died in Stockholm on 11 February 1650.

R.S.

1 The translation below follows the text in volume XI of Adam and Tannery; see General Introduction, p. x above.

[The preface comprises a 'Notice from a friend of the author', two letters from the friend to Descartes, and Descartes' replies to these letters. The identity of the friend is unknown: several suggestions have been made (e.g. Clerselier, Picot, and Descartes himself), but none has been conclusively established. In the 'Notice' the friend asserts that Descartes sent him the work and gave him permission to add a preface and get it published, and that he proposes to make the preface consist simply of his correspondence with Descartes since this contains 'many points of which I believe the public would wish to be informed'. In his first letter, dated Paris, 6 November 1648, the friend complains about Descartes' failure to show him the treatise on the passions when they met in Paris the previous summer. Reproaching Descartes for the 'negligence and other faults' which keep him from pursuing his scientific research as actively as he ought, the friend threatens to publish the letter, so as to shame Descartes into greater activity and encourage public support for his research. Here is Descartes' reply.]

AT XI Sir,

323   Among the insults and reproaches which I find in the long letter you have taken the trouble to write me, I observe many things to my advantage – so many, indeed, that if you had this letter published, as you said you would, I fear it might be imagined that we were more closely associated than in fact we are, and that I had asked you to include things in the letter which decency forbade me to utter in public myself. That is why I shall not pause here to reply point by point. I shall merely give you two reasons which, I think, should prevent you from publishing this letter. First, I do not believe you can possibly achieve the aim which I assume you had in writing it. Second, my attitude is not at all what you imagine it to be. It is not indignation or disgust which prevents me from wishing to do everything in my power to serve the public. For I consider myself indebted to it for the favourable reception which many people have given to the works I have already published. I have not previously shown you my writings on the passions simply because I did not wish to be obliged

326

to show it to certain other persons who would not have made good use of it. In fact I had composed it only to be read by a princess whose mental 324 powers are so extraordinary that she can easily understand matters which seem very difficult to our learned doctors. So the only points I explained at length in it are those I thought to be novel. Lest you should doubt what I say, I promise to revise this work on the passions and add whatever I think necessary in order to make it more intelligible; then I shall send it to you, and you may do with it whatever you please. For I am, etc.

Egmont, 4 December 1648.

[In the second letter, dated 23 July 1649, the friend complains that he has not yet received the treatise, and says that he is beginning to think that Descartes promised to send it only to prevent publication of his previous letter. Here is Descartes' reply.]

Sir,   (325)
You are determined to think that I have used an artifice in order to prevent you from publishing the long letter which you wrote to me last year. I am quite innocent of this artifice; nor did I have any need to use it. For apart from the fact that I do not believe your letter could produce the effect you claim, I am not so lazy that my desire to gain self-instruction 326 and to write something useful for other men could be overpowered by fear of the work to which I would be committed if I received from the public the means of putting many observations[1] to the test. I cannot make excuses so easily for the negligence for which you blame me. For I confess that I have spent more time in revising the little treatise I am sending you than I had previously spent in composing it. And yet I have added only a few things to it, and I have changed nothing in the style, whose simplicity and brevity will reveal that my intention was to explain the passions only as a natural philosopher, and not as a rhetorician or even as a moral philosopher. Thus, I foresee that this treatise will fare less well than my other writings. Though more people may perhaps be drawn by its title to read it, yet only those who take the trouble to study it with care can possibly be satisfied with it. Such as it is, then, I put it into your hands, etc.

Egmont, 14 August 1649.

1 Fr. *expériences*; see footnote, p. 143 above.

PART ONE

327

The Passions in General

and incidentally the whole nature of man

1. *What is a passion with regard to one subject is always an action in some other regard*

The defects of the sciences we have from the ancients are nowhere more apparent than in their writings on the passions. This topic, about which knowledge has always been keenly sought, does not seem to be one of the more difficult to investigate since everyone feels passions in himself and so has no need to look elsewhere for observations to establish their nature. And yet the teachings of the ancients about the passions are so

328 meagre and for the most part so implausible that I cannot hope to approach the truth except by departing from the paths they have followed. That is why I shall be obliged to write just as if I were considering a topic that no one had dealt with before me. In the first place, I note that whatever takes place or occurs is generally called by philosophers a 'passion' with regard to the subject to which it happens and an 'action' with regard to that which makes it happen. Thus, although an agent and patient are often quite different, an action and passion must always be a single thing which has these two names on account of the two different subjects to which it may be related.

2. *To understand the passions of the soul we must distinguish its functions from those of the body*

Next I note that we are not aware of any subject which acts more directly upon our soul than the body to which it is joined. Consequently we should recognize that what is a passion in the soul is usually an action in the body. Hence there is no better way of coming to know about our passions than by examining the difference between the soul and the body, in order to learn to which of the two we should attribute each of the functions present in us.

328

3. *The rule we must follow in order to do this*

We shall not find this very difficult if we bear in mind that anything we experience as being in us, and which we see can also exist in wholly inanimate bodies, must be attributed only to our body. On the other hand, anything in us which we cannot conceive in any way as capable of belonging to a body must be attributed to our soul.

4. *The heat and the movement of the limbs proceed from the body, and thoughts from the soul*

Thus, because we have no conception of the body as thinking in any way at all, we have reason to believe that every kind of thought present in us belongs to the soul. And since we do not doubt that there are inanimate bodies which can move in as many different ways as our bodies, if not more, and which have as much heat or more (as experience shows in the case of a flame, which has in itself much more heat and movement than any of our limbs), we must believe that all the heat and all the movements present in us, in so far as they do not depend on thought, belong solely to the body.

5. *It is an error to believe that the soul gives movement and heat to the body*

In this way we shall avoid a very serious error which many have fallen into, and which I regard as the primary cause of our failure up to now to give a satisfactory explanation of the passions and of everything else belonging to the soul. The error consists in supposing that since dead bodies are devoid of heat and movement, it is the absence of the soul which causes this cessation of movement and heat. Thus it has been believed, without justification, that our natural heat and all the movements of our bodies depend on the soul; whereas we ought to hold, on the contrary, that the soul takes its leave when we die only because this heat ceases and the organs which bring about bodily movement decay.

6. *The difference between a living body and a dead body*

So as to avoid this error, let us note that death never occurs through the absence of the soul, but only because one of the principal parts of the body decays. And let us recognize that the difference between the body of a living man and that of a dead man is just like the difference between, on the one hand, a watch or other automaton (that is, a self-moving machine) when it is wound up and contains in itself the corporeal principle of the movements for which it is designed, together with everything else required for its operation; and, on the other hand, the same watch or machine when it is broken and the principle of its movement ceases to be active.

7. *A brief account of the parts of the body and of some of their functions*

To make this more intelligible I shall explain in a few words the way in which the mechanism of our body is composed. Everyone knows that within us there is a heart, brain, stomach, muscles, nerves, arteries, veins, and similar things. We know too that the food we eat goes down to the stomach and bowels, and that its juice then flows into the liver and all the veins, where it mixes with the blood they contain, thus increasing its quantity. Those who have heard anything at all about medicine know in addition how the heart is constructed and how the blood in the veins can flow easily from the vena cava into its right-hand side, pass from there into the lungs through the vessel called the arterial vein, then return from the lungs into the left-hand side of the heart through the vessel called the venous artery, and finally pass from there into the great artery, whose branches spread through the whole body. Likewise all those not completely blinded by the authority of the ancients, and willing to open their eyes to examine the opinion of Harvey regarding the circulation of the blood, do not doubt that the veins and arteries of the body are like streams through which the blood flows constantly and with great rapidity. It makes its way from the right-hand cavity of the heart through the arterial vein, whose branches are spread throughout the lungs and connected with those of the venous artery; and via this artery it passes from the lungs into the left-hand side of the heart. From there it goes into the great artery, whose branches are spread through the rest of the body and connected with the branches of the vena cava, which carries the same blood once again into the right-hand cavity of the heart. These two cavities are thus like sluices through which all the blood passes upon each complete circuit it makes through the body. It is known, moreover, that every movement of the limbs depends on the muscles, which are opposed to each other in such a way that when one of them becomes shorter it draws towards itself the part of the body to which it is attached, which simultaneously causes the muscle opposed to it to lengthen. Then, if the latter happens to shorten at some other time, it makes the former lengthen again, and draws towards itself the part to which they are attached. Finally, it is known that all these movements of the muscles, and likewise all sensations, depend on the nerves, which are like little threads or tubes coming from the brain and containing, like the brain itself, a certain very fine[1] air or wind which is called the 'animal spirits'.

---

1 Fr. *subtil*; see note 1, p. 316 above.

8. *The principle underlying all these functions* 333

But it is not commonly known how these animal spirits and nerves help to produce movements and sensations, or what corporeal principle makes them act. That is why, although I have already touched upon this question in other writings, I intend to speak briefly about it here.[1] While we are alive there is a continual heat in our hearts, which is a kind of fire that the blood of the veins maintains there. This fire is the corporeal principle underlying all the movements of our limbs.

9. *How the movement of the heart takes place*

Its first effect is that it makes the blood which fills the cavities of the heart expand. This causes the blood, now needing to occupy a larger space, to rush from the right-hand cavity into the arterial vein and from the left-hand cavity into the great artery. Then, when this expansion ceases, fresh blood immediately enters the right-hand cavity of the heart from the vena cava, and the left-hand cavity from the venous artery. For there are tiny membranes at the entrances to these four vessels which are so arranged that the blood can enter the heart only through the latter two 334 and leave it only through the former two. When the new blood has entered the heart it is immediately rarefied in the same way as before. This and this alone is what the pulse or beating of the heart and arteries consists in, and it explains why the beating is repeated each time new blood enters the heart. It is also the sole cause of the movement of the blood, making it flow constantly and very rapidly in all the arteries and veins, so that it carries the heat it acquires in the heart to all the other parts of the body, and provides them with nourishment.

10. *How the animal spirits are produced in the brain*

What is, however, more worthy of consideration here is that all the most lively and finest parts of the blood, which have been rarefied by the heat in the heart, constantly enter the cavities of the brain in large numbers. What makes them go there rather than elsewhere is that all the blood leaving the heart through the great artery follows a direct route towards this place, and since not all this blood can enter there because the passages are too narrow, only the most active and finest parts pass into it while the rest spread out into the other regions of the body. Now these very fine parts of the blood make up the animal spirits. For them to 335 do this the only change they need to undergo in the brain is to be separated from the other less fine parts of the blood. For what I am calling 'spirits' here are merely bodies: they have no property other than

---

1 See *Discourse*, part 5, pp. 135–9 above.

that of being extremely small bodies which move very quickly, like the jets of flame that come from a torch. They never stop in any place, and as some of them enter the brain's cavities, others leave it through the pores in its substance. These pores conduct them into the nerves, and then to the muscles. In this way the animal spirits move the body in all the various ways it can be moved.

11. *How the movements of the muscles take place*
For, as already mentioned, the sole cause of all the movements of the limbs is the shortening of certain muscles and the lengthening of the opposed muscles. What causes one muscle to become shorter rather than its opposite is simply that fractionally more spirits from the brain come to it than to the other. Not that the spirits which come directly from the brain are sufficient by themselves to move the muscles; but they cause the other spirits already in the two muscles to leave one of them very suddenly and pass into the other. In this way the one they leave becomes

336   longer and more relaxed, and the one they enter, being suddenly swollen by them, becomes shorter and pulls the limb to which it is attached. This is easy to understand, provided one knows that very few animal spirits come continually from the brain to each muscle, and that any muscle always contains a quantity of its own spirits. These move very quickly, sometimes merely eddying in the place where they are located (that is, when they find no passages open for them to leave from), and sometimes flowing into the opposed muscle. In each of the muscles there are small openings through which the spirits may flow from one into the other, and which are so arranged that when the spirits coming from the brain to one of the muscles are slightly more forceful than those going to the other, they open all the passages through which the spirits in the latter can pass into the former, and at the same time they close all the passages through which the spirits in the former can pass into the latter. In this way all the spirits previously contained in the two muscles are gathered very rapidly in one of them, thus making it swell and become shorter, while the other lengthens and relaxes.

12. *How external objects act upon the sense organs*
We still have to know what causes the spirits not to flow always in the
337   same way from the brain to the muscles, but to come sometimes more to some muscles than to others. In our case, indeed, one of these causes is the activity of the soul (as I shall explain further on). But in addition we must note two other causes, which depend solely on the body. The first consists in differences in the movements produced in the sense organs by

their objects. I have already explained this quite fully in the *Optics*.[1] But in order that readers of this work should not need to consult any other, I shall say once again that there are three things to consider in the nerves. First, there is the marrow, or internal substance, which extends in the form of tiny fibres from the brain, where they originate, to the extremities of the parts of the body to which they are attached. Next, there are the membranes surrounding the fibres, which are continuous with those surrounding the brain and form little tubes in which the fibres are enclosed. Finally, there are the animal spirits which, being carried by these tubes from the brain to the muscles, cause the fibres to remain so completely free and extended that if anything causes the slightest motion in the part of the body where one of the fibres terminates, it thereby causes a movement in the part of the brain where the fibre originates, just as we make one end of a cord move by pulling the other end.

13. *This action of external objects may direct the spirits into the muscles*   338
    in various different ways

I explained in the *Optics* how the objects of sight make themselves known to us simply by producing, through the medium of the intervening transparent bodies, local motions in the optic nerve-fibres at the back of our eyes, and then in the regions of the brain where these nerves originate.[2] I explained too that the objects produce as much variety in these motions as they cause us to see in the things, and that it is not the motions occurring in the eye, but those occurring in the brain, which directly represent these objects to the soul. By this example, it is easy to conceive how sounds, smells, tastes, heat, pain, hunger, thirst and, in general, all the objects both of our external senses and of our internal appetites, also produce some movement in our nerves, which passes through them into the brain. Besides causing our soul to have various different sensations, these various movements in the brain can also act without the soul, causing the spirits to make their way to certain muscles rather than others, and so causing them to move our limbs. I shall prove this here by one example only. If someone suddenly thrusts his hand in front of our eyes as if to strike us, then even if we know that he is our   339 friend, that he is doing this only in fun, and that he will take care not to harm us, we still find it difficult to prevent ourselves from closing our eyes. This shows that it is not through the mediation of our soul that they close, since this action is contrary to our volition, which is the only, or at least the principal, activity of the soul. They close rather because the mechanism of our body is so composed that the movement of the hand

1 See *Optics*, p. 165 above, and also *Treatise on Man*, pp. 101ff above.
2 See *Optics*, p. 167 above.

towards our eyes produces another movement in our brain, which directs the animal spirits into the muscles that make our eyelids drop.

14. *Differences among the spirits may also cause them to take various different courses*

The other cause which serves to direct the animal spirits to the muscles in various different ways is the unequal agitation of the spirits and differences in their parts. For when some of their parts are coarser and more agitated than others, they penetrate more deeply in a straight line into the cavities and pores of the brain, and in this way they are directed to muscles other than those to which they would go if they had less force.

340 15. *The causes of these differences*

And this inequality may arise from the different materials of which the spirits are composed. One sees this in the case of those who have drunk a lot of wine: the vapours of the wine enter the blood rapidly and rise from the heart to the brain, where they turn into spirits which, being stronger and more abundant than those normally present there, are capable of moving the body in many strange ways. Such an inequality of the spirits may also arise from various conditions of the heart, liver, stomach, spleen and all the other organs that help to produce them. In this connection we must first note certain small nerves embedded in the base of the heart, which serve to enlarge and contract the openings to its cavities, thus causing the blood, according to the strength of its expansion, to produce spirits having various different dispositions. It must also be observed that even though the blood entering the heart comes there from every other place in the body, it often happens nevertheless that it is driven there more from some parts than from others, because the nerves and muscles responsible for these parts exert more pressure on it or make it more agitated. And differences in these parts are matched by corresponding differences in the expansion of the blood in the heart, which results in the production of spirits having different qualities. Thus, for 341 example, the blood coming from the lower part of the liver, where the gall is located, expands in the heart in a different manner from the blood coming from the spleen; the latter expands differently from the blood coming from the veins of the arms or legs; and this expands differently again from the alimentary juices when, just after leaving the stomach and bowels, they pass rapidly to the heart through the liver.

16. *How all the limbs can be moved by the objects of the senses and by the spirits without the help of the soul*

Finally it must be observed that the mechanism of our body is so composed that all the changes occurring in the movement of the spirits may cause them to open some pores in the brain more than others. Conversely, when one of the pores is opened somewhat more or less than usual by an action of the sensory nerves, this brings about a change in the movement of the spirits and directs them to the muscles which serve to move the body in the way it is usually moved on the occasion of such an action. Thus every movement we make without any contribution from our will – as often happens when we breathe, walk, eat and, indeed, when we perform any action which is common to us and the beasts – depends solely on the arrangement of our limbs and on the route which 342 the spirits, produced by the heat of the heart, follow naturally in the brain, nerves and muscles. This occurs in the same way as the movement of a watch is produced merely by the strength of its spring and the configuration of its wheels.

17. The functions of the soul
Having thus considered all the functions belonging solely to the body, it is easy to recognize that there is nothing in us which we must attribute to our soul except our thoughts. These are of two principal kinds, some being actions of the soul and others its passions. Those I call its actions are all our volitions, for we experience them as proceeding directly from our soul and as seeming to depend on it alone. On the other hand, the various perceptions or modes of knowledge present in us may be called its passions, in a general sense, for it is often not our soul which makes them such as they are, and the soul always receives them from the things that are represented by them.

18. The will
Our volitions, in turn, are of two sorts. One consists of the actions of the 343 soul which terminate in the soul itself, as when we will to love God or, generally speaking, to apply our mind to some object which is not material. The other consists of actions which terminate in our body, as when our merely willing to walk has the consequence that our legs move and we walk.

19. Perception
Our perceptions are likewise of two sorts: some have the soul as their cause, others the body. Those having the soul as their cause are the perceptions of our volitions and of all the imaginings or other thoughts which depend on them. For it is certain that we cannot will anything without thereby perceiving that we are willing it. And although willing

something is an action with respect to our soul, the perception of such willing may be said to be a passion in the soul. But because this perception is really one and the same thing as the volition, and names are always determined by whatever is most noble, we do not normally call it a 'passion', but solely an 'action'.

344   20. *Imaginings and other thoughts formed by the soul*
When our soul applies itself to imagine something non-existent – as in thinking about an enchanted palace or a chimera – and also when it applies itself to consider something that is purely intelligible and not imaginable – for example, in considering its own nature – the perceptions it has of these things depend chiefly on the volition which makes it aware of them. That is why we usually regard these perceptions as actions rather than passions.

21. *Imaginings which are caused solely by the body*
Among the perceptions caused by the body, most of them depend on the nerves. But there are some which do not and which, like those I have just described, are called 'imaginings'. These differ from the others, however, in that our will is not used in forming them. Accordingly they cannot be numbered among the actions of the soul, for they arise simply from the fact that the spirits, being agitated in various different ways and coming upon the traces of various impressions which have preceded them in the brain,

345   make their way by chance through certain pores rather than others. Such are the illusions of our dreams and also the day-dreams we often have when we are awake and our mind wanders idly without applying itself to anything of its own accord. Now some of these imaginings are passions of the soul, taking the word 'passion' in its proper and more exact sense, and all may be regarded as such if the word is understood in a more general sense. Nonetheless, their cause is not so conspicuous and determinate as that of the perceptions which the soul receives by means of the nerves, and they seem to be mere shadows and pictures of these perceptions. So before we can characterize them satisfactorily we must consider how these other perceptions differ from one another.

22. *How these other perceptions differ from one another*
All the perceptions which I have not explained come to the soul by means of the nerves. They differ from one another in so far as we refer

some to external objects which strike our senses, others to our body or to certain of its parts, and still others to our soul.

23. *The perceptions we refer to objects outside us* 346

The perceptions we refer to things outside us, namely to the objects of our senses, are caused by these objects, at least when our judgements are not false. For in that case the objects produce certain movements in the organs of the external senses and, by means of the nerves, produce other movements in the brain, which cause the soul to have sensory perception of the objects. Thus, when we see the light of a torch and hear the sound of a bell, the sound and the light are two different actions which, simply by producing two different movements in some of our nerves, and through them in our brain, give to the soul two different sensations. And we refer these sensations to the subjects we suppose to be their causes in such a way that we think that we see the torch itself and hear the bell, and not that we have sensory perception merely of movements coming from these objects.

24. *The perceptions we refer to our body*

The perceptions we refer to our body or to certain of its parts are those of hunger, thirst and other natural appetites. To these we may add pain, heat and the other states we feel as being in our limbs, and not as being in 347 objects outside us. Thus, at the same time and by means of the same nerves we can feel the cold of our hand and the heat of a nearby flame or, on the other hand, the heat of our hand and the cold of the air to which it is exposed. This happens without there being any difference between the actions which make us feel the heat or cold in our hand and those which make us feel the heat or cold outside us, except that since one of these actions succeeds the other, we judge that the first is already in us, and that its successor is not yet there but in the object which causes it.

25. *The perceptions we refer to our soul*

The perceptions we refer only to the soul are those whose effects we feel as being in the soul itself, and for which we do not normally know any proximate cause to which we can refer them. Such are the feelings of joy, anger and the like, which are aroused in us sometimes by the objects which stimulate our nerves and sometimes also by other causes. Now all our perceptions, both those we refer to objects outside us and those we refer to the various states of our body, are indeed passions with respect to our soul, so long as we use the term 'passion' in its most general sense; 348 nevertheless we usually restrict the term to signify only perceptions which refer to the soul itself. And it is only the latter that I have undertaken to explain here under the title 'passions of the soul'.[1]

26. The imaginings which depend solely on the fortuitous movement of the spirits may be passions just as truly as the perceptions which depend on the nerves

It remains to be noted that everything the soul perceives by means of the nerves may also be represented to it through the fortuitous course of the spirits. The sole difference is that the impressions which come into the brain through the nerves are normally more lively and more definite than those produced there by the spirits – a fact that led me to say in article 21 that the latter are, as it were, a shadow or picture of the former. We must also note that this picture is sometimes so similar to the thing it represents that it may mislead us regarding the perceptions which refer to objects outside us, or even regarding those which refer to certain parts of our body. But we cannot be misled in the same way regarding the passions, in that they are so close and so internal to our soul that it cannot possibly feel them unless they are truly as it feels them to be. Thus 349 often when we sleep, and sometimes even when we are awake, we imagine certain things so vividly that we think we see them before us, or feel them in our body, although they are not there at all. But even if we are asleep and dreaming, we cannot feel sad, or moved by any other passion, unless the soul truly has this passion within it.

27. Definition of the passions of the soul

After having considered in what respects the passions of the soul differ from all its other thoughts, it seems to me that we may define them generally as those perceptions, sensations or emotions of the soul which

1 The classification given in articles 17–25 may be represented schematically as follows:

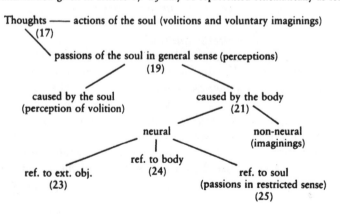

we refer particularly to it, and which are caused, maintained and strengthened by some movement of the spirits.

28. *Explanation of the first part of this definition*
We may call them 'perceptions' if we use this term generally to signify all the thoughts which are not actions of the soul or volitions, but not if we use it to signify only evident knowledge. For experience shows that those who are the most strongly agitated by their passions are not those who know them best, and that the passions are to be numbered among the 350 perceptions which the close alliance between the soul and the body renders confused and obscure. We may also call them 'sensations', because they are received into the soul in the same way as the objects of the external senses, and they are not known by the soul any differently. But it is even better to call them 'emotions' of the soul, not only because this term may be applied to all the changes which occur in the soul – that is, to all the various thoughts which come to it – but more particularly because, of all the kinds of thought which the soul may have, there are none that agitate and disturb it so strongly as the passions.

29. *Explanation of the other part of the definition*
I add that they refer particularly to the soul, in order to distinguish them from other sensations, some referred to external objects (e.g. smells, sounds and colours) and others to our body (e.g. hunger, thirst and pain). I also add that they are caused, maintained and strengthened by some movement of the spirits, both in order to distinguish them from our volitions (for these too may be called 'emotions of the soul which refer to it', but they are caused by the soul itself), and also in order to explain their ultimate and most proximate cause, which distinguishes them once again from other sensations.

30. *The soul is united to all the parts of the body conjointly* 351
But in order to understand all these things more perfectly, we need to recognize that the soul is really joined to the whole body, and that we cannot properly say that it exists in any one part of the body to the exclusion of the others. For the body is a unity which is in a sense indivisible because of the arrangement of its organs, these being so related to one another that the removal of any one of them renders the whole body defective. And the soul is of such a nature that it has no relation to extension, or to the dimensions or other properties of the matter of which the body is composed: it is related solely to the whole assemblage of the body's organs. This is obvious from our inability to conceive of a half or a third of a soul, or of the extension which a soul

occupies. Nor does the soul become any smaller if we cut off some part of the body, but it becomes completely separate from the body when we break up the assemblage of the body's organs.

31. *There is a little gland[1] in the brain where the soul exercises its functions more particularly than in the other parts of the body*

We need to recognize also that although the soul is joined to the whole body, nevertheless there is a certain part of the body where it exercises its functions more particularly than in all the others. It is commonly held that this part is the brain, or perhaps the heart – the brain because the sense organs are related to it, and the heart because we feel the passions as if they were in it. But on carefully examining the matter I think I have clearly established that the part of the body in which the soul directly exercises its functions is not the heart at all, or the whole of the brain. It is rather the innermost part of the brain, which is a certain very small gland situated in the middle of the brain's substance and suspended above the passage through which the spirits in the brain's anterior cavities communicate with those in its posterior cavities. The slightest movements on the part of this gland may alter very greatly the course of these spirits, and conversely any change, however slight, taking place in the course of the spirits may do much to change the movements of the gland.

32. *How we know that this gland is the principal seat of the soul*

Apart from this gland, there cannot be any other place in the whole body where the soul directly exercises its functions. I am convinced of this by the observation that all the other parts of our brain are double, as also are all the organs of our external senses – eyes, hands, ears and so on. But in so far as we have only one simple thought about a given object at any one time, there must necessarily be some place where the two images coming through the two eyes, or the two impressions coming from a single object through the double organs of any other sense, can come together in a single image or impression before reaching the soul, so that they do not present to it two objects instead of one. We can easily understand that these images or other impressions are unified in this gland by means of the spirits which fill the cavities of the brain. But they cannot exist united in this way in any other place in the body except as a result of their being united in this gland.

33. *The seat of the passions is not in the heart*

As for the opinion of those who think that the soul receives its passions in the heart, this is not worth serious consideration, since it is based solely on the fact that the passions make us feel some change in the heart. It is

1 The pineal gland; see *Treatise on Man*, p. 100 above.

easy to see that the only reason why this change is felt as occurring in the heart is that there is a small nerve which descends to it from the brain – just as pain is felt as in the foot by means of the nerves in the foot, and the stars are perceived as in the sky by means of their light and the optic nerves. Thus it is no more necessary that our soul should exercise its 354 functions directly in the heart in order to feel its passions there, than that it should be in the sky in order to see the stars there.

34. *How the soul and the body act on each other*
Let us therefore take it that the soul has its principal seat in the small gland located in the middle of the brain. From there it radiates through the rest of the body by means of the animal spirits, the nerves, and even the blood, which can take on the impressions of the spirits and carry them through the arteries to all the limbs. Let us recall what we said previously about the mechanism of our body. The nerve-fibres are so distributed in all the parts of the body that when the objects of the senses produce various different movements in these parts, the fibres are occasioned to open the pores of the brain in various different ways. This, in turn, causes the animal spirits contained in these cavities to enter the muscles in various different ways. In this manner the spirits can move the limbs in all the different ways they are capable of being moved. And all the other causes that can move the spirits in different ways are sufficient to direct them into different muscles. To this we may now add that the small gland which is the principal seat of the soul is suspended within the cavities containing these spirits, so that it can be moved by them in as 355 many different ways as there are perceptible differences in the objects. But it can also be moved in various different ways by the soul, whose nature is such that it receives as many different impressions – that is, it has as many different perceptions as there occur different movements in this gland. And conversely, the mechanism of our body is so constructed that simply by this gland's being moved in any way by the soul or by any other cause, it drives the surrounding spirits towards the pores of the brain, which direct them through the nerves to the muscles; and in this way the gland makes the spirits move the limbs.

35. *Example of the way in which the impressions of objects are united in the gland in the middle of the brain*
Thus, for example, if we see some animal approaching us, the light reflected from its body forms two images, one in each of our eyes; and these images form two others, by means of the optic nerves, on the internal surface of the brain facing its cavities. Then, by means of the spirits that fill these cavities, the images radiate towards the little gland which the spirits surround: the movement forming each point of one of

356   the images tends towards the same point on the gland as the movement forming the corresponding point of the other image, which represents the same part of the animal. In this way, the two images in the brain form only one image on the gland, which acts directly upon the soul and makes it see the shape of the animal.

36. *Example of the way in which the passions are aroused in the soul*
If, in addition, this shape is very strange and terrifying – that is, if it has a close relation to things which have previously been harmful to the body – this arouses the passion of anxiety in the soul, and then that of courage or perhaps fear and terror, depending upon the particular temperament of the body or the strength of the soul, and upon whether we have protected ourselves previously by defence or by flight against the harmful things to which the present impression is related. Thus in certain persons these factors dispose their brain in such a way that some of the spirits reflected from the image formed on the gland proceed from there to the nerves which serve to turn the back and move the legs in order to flee. The rest of the spirits go to nerves which expand or constrict the orifices of the heart, or else to nerves which agitate other parts of the body from which blood is sent to the heart, so that the blood is rarefied in a different

357   manner from usual and spirits are sent to the brain which are adapted for maintaining and strengthening the passion of fear – that is, for holding open or re-opening the pores of the brain which direct the spirits into these same nerves. For merely by entering into these pores they produce in the gland a particular movement which is ordained by nature to make the soul feel this passion. And since these pores are related mainly to the little nerves which serve to contract or expand the orifices of the heart, this makes the soul feel the passion chiefly as if it were in the heart.

37. *How all the passions appear to be caused by some movement of the spirits*
Something similar happens with all the other passions. That is, they are caused chiefly by the spirits contained in the cavities of the brain making their way to nerves which serve to expand or constrict the orifices of the heart, or to drive blood towards the heart in a distinctive way from other parts of the body, or to maintain the passion in some other way. This makes it clear why I included in my definition of the passions that they are caused by some particular movement of the spirits.

358   38. *Example of movements of the body which accompany the passions and do not depend on the soul*
Moreover, just as the course which the spirits take to the nerves of the heart suffices to induce a movement in the gland through which fear

enters the soul, so too the mere fact that some spirits at the same time proceed to the nerves which serve to move the legs in flight causes another movement in the gland through which the soul feels and perceives this action. In this way, then, the body may be moved to take flight by the mere disposition of the organs, without any contribution from the soul.

39. *How one and the same cause may excite different passions in different people*
The same impression which the presence of a terrifying object forms on the gland, and which causes fear in some people, may excite courage and boldness in others. The reason for this is that brains are not all constituted in the same way. Thus the very same movement of the gland which in some excites fear, in others causes the spirits to enter the pores of the brain which direct them partly into nerves which serve to move the hands in self-defence and partly into those which agitate the blood and 359 drive it towards the heart in the manner required to produce spirits appropriate for continuing this defence and for maintaining the will to do so.

40. *The principal effect of the passions*
For it must be observed that the principal effect of all the human passions is that they move and dispose the soul to want the things for which they prepare the body. Thus the feeling of fear moves the soul to want to flee, that of courage to want to fight, and similarly with the others.

41. *The power of the soul with respect to the body*
But the will is by its nature so free that it can never be constrained. Of the two kinds of thought I have distinguished in the soul – the first its actions, i.e. its volitions, and the second its passions, taking this word in its most general sense to include every kind of perception – the former are absolutely within its power and can be changed only indirectly by the body, whereas the latter are absolutely dependent on the actions which produce them, and can be changed by the soul only indirectly, except 360 when it is itself their cause. And the activity of the soul consists entirely in the fact that simply by willing something it brings it about that the little gland to which it is closely joined moves in the manner required to produce the effect corresponding to this volition.

42. *How we find in our memory the things we want to remember*
Thus, when the soul wants to remember something, this volition makes the gland lean first to one side and then to another, thus driving the

spirits towards different regions of the brain until they come upon the one containing traces left by the object we want to remember. These traces consist simply in the fact that the pores of the brain through which the spirits previously made their way owing to the presence of this object have thereby become more apt than the others to be opened in the same way when the spirits again flow towards them. And so the spirits enter into these pores more easily when they come upon them, thereby producing in the gland that special movement which represents the same object to the soul, and makes it recognize the object as the one it wanted to remember.

361 43. *How the soul can imagine, be attentive, and move the body*
When we want to imagine something we have never seen, this volition has the power to make the gland move in the way required for driving the spirits towards the pores of the brain whose opening enables the thing to be represented. Again, when we want to fix our attention for some time on some particular object, this volition keeps the gland leaning in one particular direction during that time. And finally, when we want to walk or move our body in some other way, this volition makes the gland drive the spirits to the muscles which serve to bring about this effect.

44. *Each volition is naturally joined to some movement of the gland, but
through effort or habit we may join it to others*
Yet our volition to produce some particular movement or other effect does not always result in our producing it; for that depends on the various ways in which nature or habit has joined certain movements of the gland to certain thoughts. For example, if we want to adjust our eyes
362 to look at a far-distant object, this volition causes the pupils to grow larger; and if we want to adjust them to look at a very near object, this volition makes the pupils contract. But if we think only of enlarging the pupils, we may indeed have such a volition, but we do not thereby enlarge them. For the movement of the gland, whereby the spirits are driven to the optic nerve in the way required for enlarging or contracting the pupils, has been joined by nature with the volition to look at distant or nearby objects, rather than with the volition to enlarge or contract the pupils. Again, when we speak, we think only of the meaning of what we want to say, and this makes us move our tongue and lips much more readily and effectively than if we thought of moving them in all the ways required for uttering the same words. For the habits acquired in learning to speak have made us join the action of the soul (which, by means of the gland, can move the tongue and lips) with the meaning of

the words which follow upon these movements, rather than with the movements themselves.

45. *The power of the soul with respect to its passions*

Our passions, too, cannot be directly aroused or suppressed by the action of our will, but only indirectly through the representation of things which are usually joined with the passions we wish to have and opposed to the passions we wish to reject. For example, in order to arouse boldness and suppress fear in ourselves, it is not sufficient to have the volition to do so. We must apply ourselves to consider the reasons, objects, or precedents which persuade us that the danger is not great; that there is always more security in defence than in flight; that we shall gain glory and joy if we conquer, whereas we can expect nothing but regret and shame if we flee; and so on.

363

46. *What prevents the soul from having full control over its passions*

There is one special reason why the soul cannot readily change or suspend its passions, which is what led me to say in my definition that the passions are not only caused but also maintained and strengthened by some particular movement of the spirits. The reason is that they are nearly all accompanied by some disturbance which takes place in the heart and consequently also throughout the blood and the animal spirits. Until this disturbance ceases they remain present to our mind in the same way as the objects of the senses are present to it while they are acting upon our sense organs. The soul can prevent itself from hearing a slight noise or feeling a slight pain by attending very closely to some other thing, but it cannot in the same way prevent itself from hearing thunder or feeling a fire that burns the hand. Likewise it can easily overcome the lesser passions, but not the stronger and more violent ones, except after the disturbance of the blood and spirits has died down. The most the will can do while this disturbance is at its full strength is not to yield to its effects and to inhibit many of the movements to which it disposes the body. For example, if anger causes the hand to rise to strike a blow, the will can usually restrain it; if fear moves the legs in flight, the will can stop them; and similarly in other cases.

364

47. *The conflicts that are usually supposed to occur between the lower part and the higher part of the soul*

All the conflicts usually supposed to occur between the lower part of the soul, which we call 'sensitive', and the higher or 'rational' part of the soul – or between the natural appetites and the will – consist simply in the opposition between the movements which the body (by means of its spirits) and the soul (by means of its will) tend to produce at the same time in the gland. For there is within us but one soul, and this soul has within it no diversity of parts: it is at once sensitive and rational too, and all its appetites are volitions. It is an error to identify the different functions of the soul with persons who play different, usually mutually 365 opposed roles – an error which arises simply from our failure to distinguish properly the functions of the soul from those of the body. It is to the body alone that we should attribute everything that can be observed in us to oppose our reason. So there is no conflict here except in so far as the little gland in the middle of the brain can be pushed to one side by the soul and to the other side by the animal spirits (which, as I said above, are nothing but bodies), and these two impulses often happen to be opposed, the stronger cancelling the effect of the weaker. Now we may distinguish two kinds of movement produced in the gland by the spirits. Movements of the first kind represent to the soul the objects which stimulate the senses, or the impressions occurring in the brain; and these have no influence on the will. Movements of the second kind, which do have an influence on the will, cause the passions or the bodily movements which accompany the passions. As to the first, although they often hinder the actions of the soul, or are hindered by them, yet since they are not directly opposed to these actions, we observe no conflict between them. We observe conflict only between movements of the second kind and the volitions which oppose them – for example, between the force with which the spirits push the gland so as to cause the soul to desire something, and the force with which the soul, by its volition to avoid this thing, pushes the gland in a contrary direction. Such a conflict is revealed chiefly through the fact that the will, lacking the power to 366 produce the passions directly (as I have already said), is compelled to make an effort to consider a series of different things, and if one of them happens to have the power to change for a moment the course of the spirits, the next one may happen to lack this power, whereupon the spirits will immediately revert to the same course because no change has occurred in the state of the nerves, heart and blood. This makes the soul feel itself impelled, almost at one and the same time, to desire and not to desire one and the same thing; and that is why it has been thought that the soul has within it two conflicting powers. We may, however, acknowledge a kind of conflict, in so far as the same cause that produces a certain passion in the soul often also produces certain movements in the body, to which the soul makes no contribution and which the soul stops or tries to stop as soon as it perceives them. We experience this when an object that excites fear also causes the spirits to enter the muscles which serve to move our legs in flight, while the will to be bold stops them from moving.

48. *How we recognize the strength or weakness of souls, and what is wrong with the weakest souls*

It is by success in these conflicts that each person can recognize the strength or weakness of his soul. For undoubtedly the strongest souls 367 belong to those in whom the will by nature can most easily conquer the passions and stop the bodily movements which accompany them. But there are some who can never test the strength of their will because they never equip it to fight with its proper weapons, giving it instead only the weapons which some passions provide for resisting other passions. What I call its 'proper' weapons are firm and determinate judgements bearing upon the knowledge of good and evil, which the soul has resolved to follow in guiding its conduct. The weakest souls of all are those whose will is not determined in this way to follow such judgements, but constantly allows itself to be carried away by present passions. The latter, being often opposed to one another, pull the will first to one side and then to the other, thus making it battle against itself and so putting the soul in the most deplorable state possible. Thus, when fear represents death as an extreme evil which can be avoided only by flight, while ambition on the other hand depicts the dishonour of flight as an evil worse than death, these two passions jostle the will in opposite ways; and since the will obeys first the one and then the other, it is continually opposed to itself, and so it renders the soul enslaved and miserable.

49. *The strength of the soul is inadequate without knowledge of the truth*

It is true that very few people are so weak and irresolute that they choose only what their passion dictates. Most have some determinate judge- 368 ments which they follow in regulating some of their actions. Often these judgements are false and based on passions by which the will has previously allowed itself to be conquered or led astray; but because the will continues to follow them when the passion which caused them is absent, they may be considered its proper weapons, and we may judge souls to be stronger or weaker according to their ability to follow these judgements more or less closely and resist the present passions which are opposed to them. There is, however, a great difference between the resolutions which proceed from some false opinion and those which are based solely on knowledge of the truth. For, anyone who follows the latter is assured of never regretting or repenting, whereas we always regret having followed the former when we discover our error.

50. *There is no soul so weak that it cannot, if well-directed, acquire an absolute power over its passions*

It is useful to note here, as already mentioned above,[1] that although nature seems to have joined every movement of the gland to certain of our thoughts from the beginning of our life, yet we may join them to
369   others through habit. Experience shows this in the case of language. Words produce in the gland movements which are ordained by nature to represent to the soul only the sounds of their syllables when they are spoken or the shape of their letters when they are written, because we have acquired the habit of thinking of this meaning when we hear them spoken or see them written. It is also useful to note that although the movements (both of the gland and of the spirits and the brain) which represent certain objects to the soul are naturally joined to the movements which produce certain passions in it, yet through habit the former can be separated from the latter and joined to others which are very different. Indeed this habit can be acquired by a single action and does not require long practice. Thus, when we unexpectedly come upon something very foul in a dish we are eating with relish, our surprise may so change the disposition of our brain that we cannot afterwards look upon any such food without repulsion, whereas previously we ate it with pleasure. And the same may be observed in animals. For although they lack reason, and perhaps even thought, all the movements of the spirits and of the gland which produce passions in us are nevertheless present in them too, though in them they serve to maintain and strengthen only the
370   movements of the nerves and the muscles which usually accompany the passions and not, as in us, the passions themselves. So when a dog sees a partridge, it is naturally disposed to run towards it; and when it hears a gun fired, the noise naturally impels it to run away. Nevertheless, setters are commonly trained so that the sight of a partridge makes them stop, and the noise they hear afterwards, when someone fires at the bird, makes them run towards it. These things are worth noting in order to encourage each of us to make a point of controlling our passions. For since we are able, with a little effort, to change the movements of the brain in animals devoid of reason, it is evident that we can do so still more effectively in the case of men. Even those who have the weakest souls could acquire absolute mastery over all their passions if we employed sufficient ingenuity in training and guiding them.

1 Art. 44, p. 344 above.

PART TWO

The Number and Order of the Passions

and explanation of the six primitive passions

51. The primary causes of the passions

From what has been said above we know that the ultimate and most proximate cause of the passions of the soul is simply the agitation by which the spirits move the little gland in the middle of the brain. But this does not enable us to distinguish between the various passions: for that, we must investigate their origins and examine their first causes. They may sometimes be caused by an action of the soul when it sets itself to conceive some object or other, or by the mere temperament of the body or by the impressions which happen to be present in the brain, as when 372 we feel sad or joyful without being able to say why. From what has been said, however, it appears that all such passions may also be excited by objects which stimulate the senses, and that these objects are their principal and most common causes. From this it follows that, in order to discover all the passions, it suffices to consider all the effects of these objects.

52. The function of the passions, and how they may be enumerated

I observe, moreover, that the objects which stimulate the senses do not excite different passions in us because of differences in the objects, but only because of the various ways in which they may harm or benefit us, or in general have importance for us. The function of all the passions consists solely in this, that they dispose our soul to want the things which nature deems useful for us, and to persist in this volition; and the same agitation of the spirits which normally causes the passions also disposes the body to make movements which help us to attain these things. That is why an enumeration of the passions requires only an orderly examination of all the various ways having importance for us in which our senses can be stimulated by their objects. And I shall now enumerate all the principal passions according to the order in which they may thus be found.

53. Wonder

When our first encounter with some object surprises us and we find it novel, or very different from what we formerly knew or from what we supposed it ought to be, this causes us to wonder and to be astonished at it. Since all this may happen before we know whether or not the object is beneficial to us, I regard wonder as the first of all the passions. It has no opposite, for, if the object before us has no characteristics that surprise us, we are not moved by it at all and we consider it without passion.

54. Esteem and contempt, generosity or pride, and humility or abjectness

Wonder is joined to either esteem or contempt, depending on whether we wonder at the value of an object or at its insignificance. Thus we may
374 have esteem or contempt for ourselves; this gives rise to the passions of magnanimity or vanity and humility or abjectness, and then to the corresponding habits.

55. Veneration and scorn

But when our esteem or contempt is directed upon some other object that we regard as a free cause capable of doing good and evil, esteem becomes veneration and simple contempt becomes scorn.

56. Love and hatred

All the preceding passions may be produced in us without our perceiving in any way whether the object causing them is good or evil. But when we think of something as good with regard to us, i.e. as beneficial to us, this makes us have love for it; and when we think of it as evil or harmful, this arouses hatred in us.

57. Desire

This same consideration of good and evil is the origin of all the other passions. But in order to put them in order I shall take time into account;
375 and seeing that they lead us to look much more to the future than to the present or the past, I begin with desire. For it is obvious that this passion always concerns the future. This holds in every case involving desire – not only when we desire to acquire a good which we do not yet possess or to avoid an evil which we judge may occur, but also when we merely wish for the preservation of a good or the absence of an evil.

58. Hope, anxiety, jealousy, confidence and despair

We are prompted to desire the acquisition of a good or the avoidance of an evil simply if we think it possible to acquire the good or avoid the evil.

But when we go beyond this and consider whether there is much or little prospect of our getting what we desire, then whatever points to the former excites hope in us, and whatever points to the latter excites anxiety (of which jealousy is one variety). When hope is extreme, it changes its nature and is called 'confidence' or 'assurance' just as, on the other hand, extreme anxiety becomes despair.

59. *Irresolution, courage, boldness, emulation, timidity and terror*
Thus we may hope and fear, even though the expected outcome does not depend on us at all. But when we think of it as dependent on us we may 376
have some difficulty in deciding upon the means or in putting them into effect. The first difficulty gives rise to irresolution, which makes us disposed to deliberate and take advice; the second is opposed by courage or boldness, of which emulation is one variety. And timidity is contrary to courage, as fear or terror is to boldness.

60. *Remorse*
If we decide upon some course of action before the irresolution has ceased, this causes remorse of conscience to arise. Unlike the preceding passions, remorse does not concern the time to come, but rather the present or the past.

61. *Joy and sadness*
Consideration of a present good arouses joy in us, and consideration of a present evil arouses sadness, when the good or evil is one that we regard as belonging to us.

62. *Derision, envy, pity*
But when we think of the good or evil as belonging to other people, we may judge them worthy or unworthy of it. When we judge them worthy 377
of it, that arouses in us solely the passion of joy, in so far as we get some benefit from seeing things happen as they ought; and the joy aroused in the case of a good differs from that aroused in the case of an evil only in that the former is serious whereas the latter is accompanied by laughter and derision. But if we judge the others unworthy of the good or evil, in the former case envy is aroused and in the latter case pity – envy and pity being species of sadness. And it should be observed that the same passions which relate to present goods or evils may often also be related to those which are yet to come, in so far as we think of a good or evil as if it were present when we judge that it will come about.

63. *Self-satisfaction and repentance*
We may also consider the cause of a good or evil, present as well as past. A good done by ourselves gives us an internal satisfaction, which is the

sweetest of all the passions, whereas an evil produces repentance, which is the most bitter.

64. *Favour and gratitude*

378 But a good done by others causes us to regard them with favour, even if it was not done to us; and if it was done to us then we join gratitude to the favour.

65. *Indignation and anger*

In the same way, an evil done by others and having no relation to us merely causes us to feel indignation towards them; and when it is related to us, it stirs up anger as well.

66. *Pride and shame*

Further, a good or evil which is in us, or which has been in us, produces pride or shame respectively, when it is related to the opinion which others may have of it.

67. *Disgust, regret and cheerfulness*

Sometimes the persistence of the good causes boredom or disgust, whereas that of the evil diminishes sadness. Finally, a past good gives rise to regret, which is a kind of sadness; and a past evil gives rise to cheerfulness, which is a kind of joy.

379 ### 68. *Why this enumeration of the passions differs from the one commonly accepted*

This order seems to me the best for an enumeration of the passions. I am well aware that here I part company with the opinion of all who have written previously about the passions. But I do so for good reason. For they derive their enumeration from a distinction they draw, within the sensitive part of the soul, between the two appetites they call 'concupiscible' and 'irascible'.[1] As I have said already, I recognize no distinction of parts within the soul; so I think their distinction amounts merely to saying that the soul has two powers, one of desire and the other of anger. But since the soul has in the same way the powers of wonder, love, hope and anxiety, and hence the power to receive in itself every other passion, or to perform the actions to which the passions impel it, I do not see why they have chosen to refer them all to desire or to anger. And besides, their enumeration does not include all the principal passions, as I believe mine does. I speak only of the principal passions, because we might still

---

1 A distinction based on that made by Plato, in Book IV of the *Republic*, between the 'irascible' and 'concupiscent' parts of the soul.

distinguish many other more specific ones – indeed an unlimited number of them.

69. *There are only six primitive passions* 380
But the number of those which are simple and primitive is not very large. Indeed, in reviewing all those I have enumerated, we can easily see that there are only six of this kind – namely, wonder, love, hatred, desire, joy and sadness. All the others are either composed from some of these six or they are species of them. That is why, to ensure that readers are not confused by the multiplicity of the passions, I shall treat the six primitive passions separately, and then I shall show how all the others originate in them.

70. *Wonder: its definition and cause*
Wonder is a sudden surprise of the soul which brings it to consider with attention the objects that seem to it unusual and extraordinary. It has two causes: first, an impression in the brain, which represents the object as something unusual and consequently worthy of special consideration; and secondly, a movement of the spirits, which the impression disposes both to flow with great force to the place in the brain where it is located so as to strengthen and preserve it there, and also to 381 pass into the muscles which serve to keep the sense organs fixed in the same orientation so that they will continue to maintain the impression in the way in which they formed it.

71. *In this passion there occurs no change in the heart or in the blood*
It is a peculiarity of this passion that we do not find it accompanied by any change in the heart or in the blood, such as occurs in the case of the other passions. The reason for this is that it has as its object not good or evil, but only knowledge of the thing that we wonder at. Hence it has no relation with the heart and blood, on which depends the whole well-being of our body, but only with the brain, in which are located the organs of the senses used in gaining this knowledge.

72. *What the strength of wonder consists in*
This does not prevent it from having considerable strength because of the element of surprise, i.e. the sudden and unexpected arrival of the impression which changes the movement of the spirits. Such surprise is proper and peculiar to this passion, so that when it is found in the other 382 passions – and it normally occurs in and augments almost all of them – this is because wonder is joined with them. Its strength depends on two things: the novelty and the fact that the movement it causes is at full

strength right from the start. For it is certain that such a movement has more effect than one which, being weak initially and increasing only gradually, may easily be diverted. It is also certain that objects of the senses that are novel affect the brain in certain parts where it is not normally affected; and that since these parts are more tender or less firm than those hardened through frequent agitation, the effects of the movements produced in them are thereby increased. You will find this all the more plausible if you consider that something similar accounts for the fact that in walking we have very little feeling of any contact in our feet, since the weight of our body has accustomed the soles of our feet to a contact that is quite hard; whereas when someone tickles our feet, although the contact is much lighter and gentler, we find this almost unbearable simply because it is not part of our ordinary experience.

73. *What astonishment is*

This element of surprise causes the spirits in the cavities of the brain to
383 make their way to the place where the impression of the object of wonder is located. It has so much power to do this that sometimes it drives all the spirits there, and makes them so wholly occupied with the preservation of this impression that none of them pass thence into the muscles or even depart from the tracks they originally followed in the brain. As a result the whole body remains as immobile as a statue, making it possible for only the side of the object originally presented to be perceived, and hence impossible for a more detailed knowledge of the object to be acquired. This is what we commonly call 'being astonished'. Astonishment is an excess of wonder, and it can never be other than bad.

74. *How the passions are useful, and how they are harmful*

From what has been said it is easy to recognize that the utility of all the passions consists simply in the fact that they strengthen and prolong thoughts in the soul which it is good for the soul to preserve and which otherwise might easily be erased from it. Likewise the harm they may cause consists entirely in their strengthening and preserving these thoughts beyond what is required, or in their strengthening and preserving others on which it is not good to dwell.

384 ### 75. *How wonder, in particular, is useful*

Of wonder, in particular, we may say that it is useful in that it makes us learn and retain in our memory things of which we were previously ignorant. For we wonder only at what appears to us unusual and extraordinary; and something can appear so only because we have been ignorant of it, or perhaps because it differs from things we have known (this difference being what makes us call it 'extraordinary'). But when something previously unknown to us comes before our intellect or our senses for the first time, this does not make us retain it in our memory unless our idea of it is strengthened in our brain by some passion, or perhaps also by an application of our intellect as fixed by our will in a special state of attention and reflection. The other passions may serve to make us take note of things which appear good or evil, but we feel only wonder at things which merely appear unusual. So we see that people who are not naturally inclined to wonder are usually very ignorant.

76. *In what ways it can be harmful, and how we can make good its* 385
deficiency and correct its excess

But more often we wonder too much rather than too little, as when we are astonished in looking at things which merit little or no consideration. This may entirely prevent or pervert the use of reason. Therefore, although it is good to be born with some inclination to wonder, since it makes us disposed to acquire scientific knowledge, yet after acquiring such knowledge we must attempt to free ourselves from this inclination as much as possible. For we may easily make good its absence through that special state of reflection and attention which our will can always impose upon our understanding when we judge the matter before us to be worth serious consideration. But there is no remedy for excessive wonder except to acquire the knowledge of many things and to practise examining all those which may seem most unusual and strange.

77. *It is not the most stupid or clever people who are most carried away*
by wonder

Moreover, although it is only the dull and stupid who are not naturally disposed to wonder, this does not mean that those with the best minds 386 are always the most inclined to it. In fact those most inclined to it are chiefly people who, though equipped with excellent common sense, have no high opinion of their abilities.

78. *Excessive wonder may become a habit when we fail to correct it*

This passion seems to diminish with use, for the more we encounter unusual things which we wonder at, the more we find ourselves accustomed to stop wondering at them and to regard any we subsequently come upon as common. Nevertheless, when it is excessive and makes us fix our attention solely on the first image of the objects before us without acquiring any further knowledge about them, it leaves behind a habit which makes the soul disposed to dwell in the same way on every other object coming before it which appears at all novel. This is what prolongs the troubles of those afflicted with blind curiosity, i.e. those who seek out rarities simply in order to wonder at them and not in order to know them. For gradually they become so full of wonder that things of no importance are no less apt to arrest their attention than those whose investigation is more useful.

387 79. *The definitions of love and hatred*
Love is an emotion of the soul caused by a movement of the spirits, which impels the soul to join itself willingly to objects that appear to be agreeable to it. And hatred is an emotion caused by the spirits, which impels the soul to want to be separated from objects which are presented to it as harmful. I say that these emotions are caused by the spirits not only in order to distinguish love and hatred (which are passions and depend on the body) from judgements which also bring the soul to join itself willingly to things it deems bad, but also to distinguish them from the emotions which these judgements produce in the soul.

80. *What it is to join or separate oneself willingly*
Moreover, in using the word 'willingly' I am not speaking of desire, which is a completely separate passion relating to the future. I mean rather the assent by which we consider ourselves henceforth as joined with what we love in such a manner that we imagine a whole, of which we take ourselves to be only one part, and the thing loved to be the other. In the case of hatred, on the other hand, we consider ourselves alone as a whole entirely separated from the thing for which we have an aversion.

388 81. *The distinction usually made between concupiscent love and*
         benevolent love
A distinction is commonly made between two sorts of love, one called 'benevolent love', which prompts us to wish for the well-being of what we love, and the other called 'concupiscent love', which makes us desire the things we love. But it seems to me that this distinction concerns only the effects of love and not its essence. For as soon as we have joined ourselves willingly to some object, whatever its nature may be, we feel benevolent towards it – that is, we also join to it willingly the things we believe to be agreeable to it: this is one of the principal effects of love. And if we judge that it would be beneficial to possess an object or to be associated with it in some manner other than willingly, then we desire it: and this, too, is one of the most common effects of love.

82. *How very different passions agree in that they partake of love*
Nor do we need to distinguish as many kinds of love as there are different

possible objects of love. Consider, for example, the passions which an ambitious man has for glory, a miser for money, a drunkard for wine, a 389 brutish man for a woman he wants to violate, an honourable man for his friend or mistress, and a good father for his children. Although very different from one another, these passions are similar in so far as they all partake of love. But the men in the first four examples have love only for the possession of the objects to which their passion is related, and not for the objects themselves: for these objects they have merely desire mingled with other particular passions. Whereas the love of a good father for his children is so pure that he desires to have nothing from them, and he wants neither to possess them otherwise than he does, nor to be joined to them more closely than he already is. He regards them, rather, as other parts of himself, and seeks their good as he does his own, or even more assiduously. For he imagines that he and they together form a whole of which he is not the better part, and so he often puts their interests before his own and is not afraid of sacrificing himself in order to save them. The affection which an honourable man has for his friends is of the same nature, though it is rarely so perfect; and the affection he has for his mistress partakes largely of love, but also a little of desire.

83. *The difference between simple affection, friendship and devotion*
We may, I think, more reasonably distinguish kinds of love according to 390 the esteem which we have for the object we love, as compared with ourselves. For when we have less esteem for it than for ourselves, we have only a simple affection for it; when we esteem it equally with ourselves, that is called 'friendship'; and when we have more esteem for it, our passion may be called 'devotion'. Thus, we may have affection for a flower, a bird, or a horse; but unless our mind is very disordered, we can have friendship only for persons. They are so truly the objects of this passion that there is no person so imperfect that we could not have for him a very perfect friendship, given that we believe ourselves loved by him and that we have a truly noble and generous soul (in accordance with the explanation given below in articles 154 and 156). As for devotion, its principal object is undoubtedly the supreme Deity, for whom we cannot fail to have devotion when we know him as we ought. But we may also have devotion for our sovereign, our country, our town, and even for a particular person when we have much more esteem for him than for ourselves. The difference between these three kinds of love is revealed chiefly by their effects. For in all of them we consider ourselves as joined and united to the thing loved, and so we are always ready to abandon the lesser part of the whole that we compose with it so as to preserve the other part. In the case of simple affection this results in our

always preferring ourselves to the object of our love. In the case of devotion, on the other hand, we prefer the thing loved so strongly that we are not afraid to die in order to preserve it. We have often seen examples of such devotion in those who have exposed themselves to certain death in defence of their sovereign or their city, or sometimes even for particular persons to whom they were devoted.

84. *There are not so many kinds of hatred as of love*
Moreover, although hatred is directly opposed to love, we do not distinguish it into as many kinds because the evils from which we are separated willingly do not differ so noticeably from one another as do the goods to which we are joined willingly.

85. *Attraction and repulsion*
I find only one important distinction which is similar in both love and hatred. It consists in the fact that the objects both of love and of hatred may be represented to the soul either by the external senses, or by the internal senses and its own reason. For we commonly call something 'good' or 'evil' if our internal senses or our reason make us judge it agreeable or contrary to our nature. But we call something 'beautiful' or 'ugly' if it is represented as such by our external senses (chiefly by the sense of sight, of which we take more notice than of all the others). Two kinds of love arise from this, namely the love we have for good things and the love we have for beautiful things. To the latter we may give the name 'attraction', so as not to confuse it with the former or with desire (to which we often give the name 'love'). Two kinds of hatred arise in the same way, one relating to evil things and the other to things that are ugly; and the latter may be called 'repulsion' or 'aversion', so as to set it apart. But what is most noteworthy here is that the passions of attraction and repulsion are usually more violent than the other kinds of love and hatred, because what enters the soul through the senses affects it more strongly than what is represented to it by its reason. At the same time, these passions usually contain less truth than the others. Consequently they are the most deceptive of all the passions, and the ones against which we must guard ourselves most carefully.

86. *The definition of desire*
The passion of desire is an agitation of the soul caused by the spirits, which disposes the soul to wish, in the future, for the things it represents to itself as agreeable. Thus we desire not only the presence of goods which are absent but also the preservation of those which are present. In

addition we desire the absence of evils, both those that already affect us and those we believe we may suffer on some future occasion.

87. *Desire is a passion which has no opposite* 393
I am well aware that in the Schools they commonly contrast the passion which leads to the search for good with that which leads to the avoidance of evil, calling the former alone 'desire' and the latter 'aversion'. But there is no good whose privation is not an evil, and no evil (considered as a positive thing) whose privation is not a good. In pursuing riches, for example, we necessarily avoid poverty, while in avoiding illness we pursue health, and likewise in other cases. Thus I think it is always one and the same movement which gives rise to the pursuit of a good and at the same time the avoidance of the opposite evil. I note only this difference, that the desire we have when we are led towards some good is accompanied by love, and then by hope and joy, whereas when we are led to get away from the evil opposed to this good, the same desire is accompanied by hatred, anxiety and sadness (which causes us to judge the evil inimical to ourselves). But if we wish to consider the desire when it relates at the same time both to the pursuit of some good and equally to the avoidance of the opposed evil, we can see very clearly that a single passion brings about both the one and the other.

88. *The various kinds of desire* 394
It would be more reasonable to distinguish desire into as many different species as there are different objects that we pursue. Curiosity, for example, is nothing but a desire for knowledge, and it differs greatly from a desire for glory, as the latter differs from a desire for vengeance, and likewise for other desires. But it is sufficient to note here that there are as many species of desire as of love or hatred, and that the most important and strongest desires are those which arise from attraction and repulsion.

89. *The desire which arises from repulsion*
Now although, as already mentioned, it is one and the same desire which leads to the pursuit of a good and to the avoidance of the opposite evil, yet the desire which arises from attraction is very different from that which arises from repulsion. For attraction and repulsion, which are indeed opposites, are not the good and the evil which serve as objects of these desires. Rather, they are simply two emotions of the soul which dispose it to pursue two very different things. On the one hand, repulsion is ordained by nature to represent to the soul a sudden and unexpected death. Thus, although it is sometimes merely the touch of an earthworm,

395   the sound of a rustling leaf, or our shadow that gives rise to repulsion, we
feel at once as much emotion as if we had experienced a threat of certain
death. This produces a sudden agitation which leads the soul to do its
utmost to avoid so manifest an evil. It is this kind of desire that we
commonly call 'avoidance' or 'aversion'.

90. *The desire which arises from attraction*

Attraction, on the other hand, is specially ordained by nature to represent
the enjoyment of that which attracts us as the greatest of all the goods
belonging to mankind, and so to make us have a burning desire for this
enjoyment. It is true that there are different sorts of attraction, and that
the desires arising from them are not all equally powerful. Thus, for
example, the beauty of flowers moves us only to look at them, and that of
fruits to eat them. But the principal attraction comes from the perfections
we imagine in a person who we think capable of becoming a second self.
For nature has established a difference of sex in human beings, as in
animals lacking reason, and with this she has also implanted certain
impressions in the brain which bring it about that at a certain age and
time we regard ourselves as deficient – as forming only one half of a
whole, whose other half must be a person of the opposite sex. In this way

396   nature represents, in a confused manner, the acquisition of this other half
as the greatest of all goods imaginable. Although we see many persons of
the opposite sex, yet we do not desire many at any one time, since nature
does not make us imagine that we need more than one other half. But
when we observe something in one of them which is more attractive than
anything we observe at that moment in the others, this determines our
soul to feel towards that one alone all the inclination which nature gives
it to pursue the good which it represents as the greatest we could possibly
possess. The name 'love' is applied more often to the inclination or desire
which arises in this way from attraction than to the passion of love
described previously. Having stranger effects than the passion, this
inclination or desire provides writers of romances and poets with their
principal subject-matter.

91. *The definition of joy*

Joy is a pleasant emotion which the soul has when it enjoys a good which
impressions in the brain represent to it as its own. I say that the soul has
this emotion when it enjoys a good, for in fact the soul receives no other
benefit from all the goods it possesses; and as long as it derives no joy
from them, we may say that it does not enjoy them any more than it

397   would if it did not possess them at all. I add that the good is one which
impressions in the brain represent as the soul's own, so as not to confuse

this joy, which is a passion, with the purely intellectual joy that arises in the soul through an action of the soul alone. The latter may be said to be a pleasant emotion which the soul arouses in itself whenever it enjoys a good which its understanding represents to it as its own. Of course, while the soul is joined to the body, this intellectual joy can scarcely fail to be accompanied by the joy which is a passion. For as soon as our intellect perceives that we possess some good, even one so different from anything belonging to the body as to be wholly unimaginable, the imagination cannot fail immediately to form some impression in the brain, from which there ensues the movement of the spirits which produces the passion of joy.

92. *The definition of sadness*
Sadness is an unpleasant listlessness which affects the soul when it suffers discomfort from an evil or deficiency which impressions in the brain represent to it as its own. There is also an intellectual sadness which, though not the passion, rarely fails to be accompanied by it.

93. *The causes of these two passions* 398
When intellectual joy or sadness arouses the corresponding passion, its cause is quite obvious. For we see from the definitions that joy results from the belief that we possess some good, and sadness from the belief that we have some evil or deficiency. But it often happens that we feel sad or joyful without being able to observe so distinctly the good or evil which causes this feeling. This happens when the good or evil forms its impression in the brain without the intervention of the soul, sometimes because it affects only the body and sometimes because, even though it affects the soul, the soul does not consider it as good or evil but views it under some other form whose impression is joined in the brain with that of the good or evil.

94. *How these passions are aroused by goods and evils which concern solely the body; and what titillation and pain consist in*
Thus, when we are in good health and things are calmer than usual, we feel in ourselves a cheerfulness which results not from any operation of the understanding but solely from impressions formed in the brain by the movement of the spirits. And we feel sad in the same way when our body 399 is indisposed even though we do not know that it is. Indeed, titillation of the senses is followed so closely by joy, and pain by sadness, that most people make no distinction between the two. Nevertheless they differ so markedly that we may sometimes suffer pains with joy, and receive titillating sensations which displease us. But what makes joy ordinarily

follow titillation is the fact that what we call 'titillation' or 'pleasurable sensation' occurs when the objects of the senses produce some movement in the nerves which would be capable of harming them if they did not have enough strength to resist it or if the body was not in a healthy condition. This forms an impression in the brain which, being ordained by nature to bear witness to the body's healthy condition and strength, represents this to the soul as a good which belongs to it in so far as it is united with the body; and so this impression produces joy in the soul. For almost the same reason we naturally take pleasure in feeling ourselves aroused to all sorts of passions – even to sadness and hatred – when these passions are caused merely by the strange happenings we see presented on the stage, or by other such things which, being incapable of harming us in any way, seem to affect our soul by titillating it. And pain usually produces sadness because the sensation we call 'pain' always results from an action so violent that it injures the nerves. This sensation, ordained by nature to indicate to the soul the bodily damage suffered from such an action, and the body's feeble inability to withstand it, represents both as evils which are always unpleasant to the soul except when they cause some goods which the soul values more highly.

400

95. *How they may also be aroused by goods and evils which the soul*
     does not notice even though they belong to it, such as the pleasure
     derived from taking risks or from recollecting past evils

Young people often take pleasure in attempting difficult tasks and exposing themselves to great dangers even though they do not hope thereby to gain any profit or glory. This pleasure arises in the following way. The thought that the undertaking is difficult forms an impression in their brain which, when joined with the impression they could form if they were to think that it is a good thing to feel sufficiently courageous, happy, skilful, or strong to dare to take such risks, causes them to take pleasure in doing so. And the satisfaction which old people feel in recollecting the evils they have suffered results from their thinking that it is a good thing to have been able to survive in spite of them.

401 96. *The movements of the blood and the spirits which cause the five*
          preceding passions

The five passions I have begun to explain here are joined or opposed to one another to such an extent that it is easier to consider them all together than to treat each of them separately, as we treated wonder. Unlike the cause of wonder, which is located in the brain alone, their cause is located also in the heart, the spleen, the liver and all the other parts of the body, in so far as they help to produce the blood and hence the spirits. For, although all the veins conduct the blood to the heart, it sometimes happens that the blood in some veins is driven there with greater force than the blood in other veins; and it also happens that the openings through which the blood enters or leaves the heart are enlarged or contracted to a greater extent at one time than at another.

97. *The chief experiences which enable us to know these movements in the case of love*

In considering the various alterations which experience reveals in our body during the time our soul is agitated by different passions, I observe   402
in the case of love that when it occurs on its own – that is, unaccompanied by any strong joy, desire, or sadness – the pulse has a regular beat, but is much fuller and stronger than normal; we feel a gentle heat in the chest; and the digestion of food takes place very quickly in the stomach. In this way this passion is conducive to good health.

98. *In hatred*

I observe in the case of hatred, on the other hand, that the pulse is irregular, weaker and often quicker; we feel chills mingled with a sort of sharp, piercing heat in the chest; and the stomach ceases to perform its function, being inclined to regurgitate and reject the food we have eaten, or at any rate to spoil it and turn it into bad humours.

99. *In joy*

In joy, the pulse is regular and faster than normal, but not so strong or full as in the case of love; we feel a pleasant heat not only in the chest but also spreading into all the external parts of the body along with the blood   403
which is seen to flow copiously to these parts; and yet we sometimes lose our appetite because our digestion is less active than usual.

100. *In sadness*

In sadness the pulse is weak and slow, and we feel as if our heart had tight bonds around it, and were frozen by icicles which transmit their cold to the rest of the body. But sometimes we still have a good appetite and feel our stomach continuing to do its duty, provided there is no hatred mixed with the sadness.

101. *In desire*

Lastly, I note this special feature of desire, that it agitates the heart more violently than any other passion, and supplies more spirits to the brain. Passing from there into the muscles, these spirits render all the senses more acute, and all the parts of the body more mobile.

102. *The movement of the blood and the spirits in the case of love*

These observations, and many others that would take too long to report, have led me to conclude that when the understanding thinks of some object of love, this thought forms an impression in the brain which directs the animal spirits through the nerves of the sixth pair to the muscles surrounding the intestines and stomach, where they act in such a way that the alimentary juices (which are changing into new blood) flow rapidly to the heart without stopping in the liver.[1] Driven there with greater force than the blood from other parts of the body, these juices enter the heart in greater abundance and produce a stronger heat there because they are coarser than the blood which has already been rarefied many times as it passes again and again through the heart. As a result the spirits sent by the heart to the brain have parts which are coarser and more agitated than usual; and as they strengthen the impression formed by the first thought of the loved object, these spirits compel the soul to dwell upon this thought. This is what the passion of love consists in.

103. *In hatred*

In the case of hatred, on the other hand, at the first thought of the object that gives rise to aversion, the spirits in the brain are so directed to the muscles of the stomach and intestines that they constrict all the openings through which the alimentary juices normally flow, thus preventing these juices from mixing with the blood. This thought also directs the spirits to the little nerves of the spleen and the lower part of the liver (where the bile is collected) in such manner that the parts of blood which are normally returned to these organs issue from them and flow to the heart together with the blood which is in the branches of the *vena cava*. This causes the heat of the heart to be very uneven, in so far as the blood coming from the spleen is hardly heated and rarefied at all, whereas the blood coming from the lower part of the liver, where the gall is always located, boils up and expands very rapidly. In consequence the spirits going to the brain also have very unequal parts, and move very strangely. As a result they strengthen the ideas of hatred which are already imprinted there, and they dispose the soul to have thoughts which are full of acrimony and bitterness.

104. *In joy*

In joy, it is not the nerves of the spleen, liver, stomach, or intestines that are active, so much as those throughout the rest of the body. The nerve

---

1 Seven pairs of cranial nerves are recognized in Galenian physiology; the 'sixth pair' corresponds in modern physiology to the glossopharyngeal, vagus and spinal accessory nerves.

located around the orifices of the heart is especially active: by opening and enlarging these orifices it enables the blood which other nerves drive through the veins to enter and leave the heart in larger quantities than usual. And because the blood then entering the heart has come into the veins from the arteries, and so has passed through the heart many times already, it expands very readily and produces spirits whose parts, being 406 very equal and fine, are suited for the formation and strengthening of the impressions in the brain which give to the soul thoughts that are cheerful and peaceful.

105. *In sadness*
In sadness, by contrast, the openings in the heart are severely restricted by the small nerve which surrounds them, and the blood in the veins is not agitated at all, so that very little of it goes to the heart. At the same time, the passages through which the alimentary juices flow from the stomach and intestines to the liver remain open, so that the appetite does not diminish, except when hatred, which is often joined to sadness, closes these passages.

106. *In desire*
Finally, the passion of desire has this special characteristic: the volition to acquire some good or avoid some evil sends the spirits rapidly from the brain to all the parts of the body which may help to bring about this effect, and especially to the heart and the parts which supply most of its blood. Receiving a greater amount of blood than usual, the heart sends a greater quantity of spirits to the brain, both in order to maintain and 407 strengthen the idea of the volition and to pass from there into all the sense organs and all the muscles that can be used for obtaining what is desired.

107. *The cause of these movements in the case of love*
I derive an explanation for all this from what I said previously, namely that our soul and our body are so linked that once we have joined some bodily action with a certain thought, the one does not occur afterwards without the other occurring too. We see this, for example, in those who have taken some medicine with great aversion when they are ill, and cannot afterwards eat or drink anything approaching it in taste without immediately feeling the same aversion; and similarly they cannot think of the aversion they have for medicines without the same taste returning in their thought. For it seems to me that when our soul began to be joined to our body, its first passions must have arisen on some occasion when the blood, or some other juice entering the heart, was a more suitable fuel

than usual for maintaining the heat which is the principle of life. This caused the soul to join itself willingly to that fuel, i.e. to love it; and at the same time the spirits flowed from the brain to the muscles capable of pressing or agitating the parts of the body from which the fuel had come to the heart, so as to make them send more of it. These parts were the stomach and the intestines, whose agitation increases the appetite, or else the liver and the lungs, which the muscles of the diaphragm can press. That is why this same movement of the spirits has ever since accompanied the passion of love.

108. *In hatred*

Sometimes, on the other hand, there came to the heart a juice of an alien nature, which was unsuitable for maintaining the heat, or even was capable of extinguishing it. This caused the spirits rising from the heart to the brain to produce the passion of hatred in the soul. At the same time these spirits went from the brain to nerves capable of driving blood from the spleen and the minute veins of the liver to the heart so as to prevent this harmful juice from entering it; and they also went to nerves capable of driving this juice back to the intestines and stomach, or capable sometimes of making the stomach regurgitate it. As a result, these same movements usually accompany the passion of hatred. You can see with the naked eye that the liver contains a number of rather wide veins or ducts through which the alimentary juices can pass from the portal vein into the vena cava, and then to the heart, without ever stopping in the liver. But you can also see countless other, smaller veins where the juice might stop. These always contain blood in reserve, as does the spleen, and since this blood is coarser than that in the other parts of the body, it is better able to serve as a fuel for the fire in the heart when the stomach and intestines fail to supply any.

109. *In joy*

It has also sometimes happened at the beginning of our life that the blood contained in the veins was quite suitable for nourishing and maintaining the heat of the heart, and was so plentiful that the heart had no need for any other source of nourishment. This produced the passion of joy in the soul. At the same time it caused the orifices of the heart to be opened wider than usual; and it made the spirits flow abundantly from the brain not only into the nerves which serve to open these orifices but also generally into all the other nerves which drive the blood from the veins to the heart, thus preventing any fresh blood from coming into the heart from the liver, spleen, intestines and stomach. That is why these same movements accompany joy.

110. *In sadness* 410

Sometimes, on the other hand, it has happened that the body has lacked nourishment, and this lack must have made the soul feel its first sadness (at any rate the first which was not joined to hatred). It also caused the orifices of the heart to contract because they received only a little blood; and it caused a rather significant proportion of this blood to come from the spleen, since this is, so to speak, the ultimate reservoir of blood for the heart when it does not get enough from elsewhere. That explains why sadness is always accompanied by movements of the spirits and nerves which serve in this way to restrict the orifices of the heart and to direct blood to it from the spleen.

111. *In desire*

Lastly, when the soul was newly joined to the body, all its first desires must have been to accept things beneficial to it and to reject those harmful to it. It was to these same ends that the spirits began at that time to move all the muscles and sense organs in all the ways they can move 411 them. That is the reason why now, when the soul desires anything, the whole body becomes more agile and ready to move than it normally is without any such desire. Moreover, when the body is in this condition, the desires of the soul are rendered stronger and keener.

112. *The external signs of these passions*

There is no need for me to pause to explain any further the differences in the pulse and all the other properties I have attributed to these passions, for I have said enough already to enable their causes to be understood. For each passion, however, I have noted solely what can be observed when it is the only one present, and what enables us to recognize the movements of the blood and spirits which produce it. I have yet to deal with the many external signs which usually accompany the passions – signs which are much better observed when several are mingled together, as they normally are, than when they are separated. The most important such signs are the expressions of the eyes and the face, changes in colour, trembling, listlessness, fainting, laughter, tears, groans and sighs.

113. *The expressions of the eyes and the face* 412

There is no passion which some particular expression of the eyes does not reveal. For some passions this is quite obvious: even the most stupid servants can tell from their master's eye whether he is angry with them. But although it is easy to perceive such expressions of the eyes and to know what they signify, it is not easy to describe them. For each consists of many changes in the movement and shape of the eye, and these are so special and slight that we cannot perceive each of them separately, though we can easily observe the result of their conjunction. Almost the same can be said of the facial expressions which also accompany passions. For although more extensive than those of the eyes, they are still hard to discern. They differ so little that some people make almost the same face when they weep as others do when they laugh. Of course, some facial expressions are quite noticeable, such as wrinkles in the forehead in anger and certain movements of the nose and lips in indignation and derision; but these seem not so much natural as voluntary. And in general the soul is able to change facial expressions, as well as expressions of the eyes, by vividly feigning a passion which is 413 contrary to one it wishes to conceal. Thus we may use such expressions to hide our passions as well as to reveal them.

114. *Changes in colour*

We cannot so easily prevent ourselves from blushing or growing pale when some passion disposes us to do so. For these changes do not depend on the nerves and muscles as do the preceding ones: they proceed more immediately from the heart, which may be called the source of the passions in so far as it prepares the blood and the spirits to produce them. It is certain that the colour of the face comes solely from the blood which, flowing continually from the heart through the arteries into the veins and then back into the heart, colours the face more or less, depending on whether it fills the small veins located near its surface to a greater or lesser extent.

115. *How joy causes blushing*

Thus joy renders the colour brighter and rosier because it opens the valves of the heart and so causes the blood to flow more quickly in all the veins. As the blood becomes warmer and thinner it fills out all the parts of the face somewhat, thus making it look more cheerful and happier.

414 116. *How sadness causes pallor*

Sadness, on the other hand, constricts the orifices of the heart, causing the blood to flow more slowly in the veins and to become colder and thicker. Needing to occupy less space, the blood then withdraws into the largest veins, which are the nearest to the heart, leaving the more remote veins, such as those in the face; and since these are particularly conspicuous, the face is caused to appear pale and sunken. This happens chiefly when the sadness is great, or when it comes on suddenly, as in terror, when surprise amplifies the action which grips the heart.

117. *Why we often blush when we are sad*

But it often happens that we do not become pale when we are sad, and on the contrary we become flushed. This must be attributed to the other passions which are joined to sadness, namely love or desire, and sometimes also hatred. For when these passions heat or agitate the blood coming from the liver, intestines and other internal parts of the body, they drive it to the heart, and then through the great artery to the veins in the face. And the sadness which more or less closes the orifices of the heart cannot stop this blood except when it is quite profound. But even if it is only moderate, this sadness easily prevents the blood which has entered the veins of the face from descending to the heart, so long as love, desire, or hatred is driving other blood there from the internal parts. That is why the blood trapped in the face makes it red – indeed, redder than when we are joyful, since the colour of blood is all the more conspicuous when it flows less rapidly, and also because more blood can collect in the veins of the face when the orifices of the heart are opened less widely. We see this chiefly in shame, which is made up of self-love and an urgent desire to avoid present disgrace (which makes the blood come from the internal parts to the heart and then through the arteries to the face), together with a moderate sadness (which prevents this blood from returning to the heart). The same thing usually seems to happen also when we weep; for, as I shall explain shortly, tears are caused for the most part by a combination of love and sadness. And it is seen in anger, when a sudden desire for vengeance is often mingled with love, hatred and sadness. 415

118. *Trembling*

There are two distinct causes of trembling. One is that sometimes too few of the spirits in the brain enter into the nerves to be able to close the little passages of the muscles in just the way that, according to the account given in article 11, they must be closed in order to cause the movements of the limbs; and the other is that sometimes too many of the spirits enter into the nerves to be able to do this. The first cause is seen in sadness and fear, and also when we tremble with cold. For these passions, like the coldness of the air, may cause the blood to thicken so much that it does not supply enough spirits to the brain to permit any to be sent to the nerves. The other cause is often seen in those who keenly desire something, or are strongly moved by anger, and also in those who are drunk. For these two passions, as well as wine, sometimes make so many spirits go to the brain that they cannot be directed from there in an orderly way into the muscles. 416

119. *Listlessness*

Listlessness is an inclination felt in all the limbs to relax and remain motionless. As in the case of trembling, but in a different way, it results from too few spirits entering into the nerves. For the cause of trembling is that there are not enough spirits in the brain to carry out the directions of the gland when it drives them to some muscle; whereas listlessness results from the gland's not directing the spirits to some muscles rather than others.

417   ### 120. *How it is caused by love and by desire*

The passion that most commonly brings about this effect is love, combined with desire, for a thing whose acquisition is not imagined to be possible at the present time. For love makes the soul so engrossed in thinking about the loved object that it uses all the spirits in the brain in representing the image of this object, and it stops all the movements of the gland which do not serve this purpose. And regarding desire, it must be observed that the property of making the body more mobile, which I ascribed to it earlier,[1] applies to it only when we imagine the desired object to be something which we are able at that time to take steps towards acquiring. For if we imagine, on the contrary, that it is impossible to do anything that might serve this end, all the agitation due to the desire remains in the brain without passing into the nerves; and, serving only to strengthen the idea of the desired object, this agitation leaves the rest of the body in a listless state.

121. *It may also be caused by other passions*

It is true that hatred, sadness and even joy may also cause some listlessness when it is very violent, because it makes the soul wholly

418   engrossed in thinking about its object; this happens chiefly when these passions are combined with the desire for something which we cannot do anything to acquire at the present time. But listlessness is encountered much more in love than in all the other passions. For we pause much more to think about objects to which we join ourselves willingly than to think about objects from which we separate ourselves, or about any other objects; and listlessness does not depend on surprise but requires some time for its formation.

122. *Fainting*

Fainting is not far removed from dying, for we die when the fire in our heart is completely extinguished, and we merely fall into a faint when it is

---

1 Art. 101, p. 363. above.

smothered in such a way that there remain some traces of heat which may afterwards rekindle it. There are many bodily indispositions which may cause us to fall into a faint; but among the passions it is only extreme joy that we observe to have the power to do this. Here is the way in which I believe it causes this effect. It opens the orifices of the heart unusually wide, so that the blood from the veins enters the heart so suddenly and so copiously that it cannot be rarefied by the heat in the heart quickly enough to raise all the little membranes which close the entrances to these veins. In this way the blood smothers the fire which it usually maintains when it enters the heart in moderate amounts.

123. *Why sadness does not cause us to faint*   419
It seems that a great sadness which comes upon us unexpectedly ought to grip the orifices of the heart so tightly as to extinguish the fire; yet we do not observe this to happen, or if it happens it does so very rarely. The reason for this, I believe, is that there can hardly ever be insufficient blood in the heart to maintain the heat there when its orifices are almost closed.

124. *Laughter*
Laughter results when the blood coming from the right-hand cavity of the heart through the arterial vein causes the lungs to swell up suddenly and repeatedly, forcing the air they contain to rush out through the windpipe, where it forms an inarticulate, explosive sound. As the air is expelled, the lungs are swollen so much that they push against all the muscles of the diaphragm, chest and throat, thus causing movement in the facial muscles with which these organs are connected. And it is just this facial expression, together with the inarticulate and explosive sound, that we call 'laughter'.

125. *Why laughter does not accompany the greatest joys*   420
Now although laughter seems to be one of the chief signs of joy, yet joy cannot cause laughter except when it is moderate and mixed with an element of wonder or hatred. For we find by experience that when we are unusually joyful, the subject of this joy never makes us burst into laughter; and indeed, we are never so ready to laugh as when we are sad. The reason for this is that in great joy the lungs are always so full that they cannot be swollen any more by further surges of blood.

126. *The principal causes of laughter*
I can see only two things that might cause the lungs to swell up suddenly in this way. The first is the surprise of wonder, which may be combined with joy so as to open the orifices of the heart so rapidly that a great

quantity of blood suddenly enters its right-hand side from the vena cava, becomes rarefied there, and passes through the arterial vein to swell up the lungs. The other is the admixture of some liquid which increases the rarefaction of the blood. I cannot discover any such liquid other than the most fluid part of that which comes from the spleen. Driven to the heart by some slight emotion of hatred (helped by the surprise of wonder), this part of the blood mingles there with the blood coming from other regions of the body (which joy drives into the heart in abundance) and may cause this blood to expand much more than usual. We see the same thing in a number of other liquids, which suddenly swell up when we throw a little vinegar into a vessel containing them over a fire. For the most fluid part of the blood coming from the spleen has a nature similar to that of vinegar. Experience also reveals that in every situation which may cause such laughter to burst forth from the lungs, there is always some slight occasion for hatred, or at least for wonder. And those with an unhealthy spleen are apt not only to be sadder than others, but also at times to be more cheerful and more disposed to laughter, inasmuch as the spleen sends two kinds of blood to the heart, one very thick and coarse, which causes sadness, and the other fluid and thin, which causes joy. And we often feel ourselves naturally inclined to be sad after we have laughed a lot, because the more fluid part of the blood in the spleen has been exhausted and the other, coarser part follows it to the heart.

127. *What causes laughter in the case of indignation*

As for the laughter which sometimes accompanies indignation, it is usually artificial and feigned. But when it is natural, it seems to result from the joy we feel in seeing that we cannot be harmed by the evil at which we are indignant, together with our surprise at the novelty of the evil or at our unexpected encounter with it. So it is that joy, hatred and wonder contribute to indignation. Yet I am willing to believe that it may also be produced without any joy, by the movement of aversion alone, which sends blood from the spleen to the heart, where the blood is rarefied and then driven to the lungs, which it readily causes to swell when it finds them almost empty. In general, whatever may suddenly make the lungs swell up in this manner causes the external action of laughter, except when sadness changes it into the groans and cries which accompany tears. Regarding this matter, Vives writes that when he had gone without eating for a long time, the first pieces of food that he put in his mouth caused him to laugh.[1] This could result from the fact that his lungs, emptied of blood by lack of nourishment, were rapidly swollen by

---

1 J. L. Vives, *De Anima et Vita* (1538), ch. 3. Juan Luis Vives (1493–1540) was a humanist scholar celebrated as an educational theorist and a critic of scholastic logic.

the first juice which passed from his stomach to his heart, and which the mere imagination of eating could direct there even before the arrival of the juice of the food he was eating.

128. *The origin of tears*

As laughter is never caused by the greatest joys, so tears do not result 423 from an extreme sadness, but only from a sadness that is moderate and accompanied or followed by some feeling of love or joy. To understand their origin properly, we must observe that although lots of vapours continually issue from all parts of our body, there are none from which so many issue as from the eyes. This is caused by the size of the optic nerves and the multitude of little arteries by which the vapours get there. Just as sweat is composed merely of vapours which are converted into water on the surface of the parts from which they issue, so tears are formed from the vapours that issue from our eyes.

129. *How the vapours are changed into water*

In the *Meteorology*, to explain how the vapours of the air are transformed into rain, I wrote that this results from their being less agitated or more abundant than usual.[1] Likewise I believe that when the vapours issuing from the body are much less agitated than usual, even if they are not so abundant, they are still transformed into water; this causes the cold sweats which sometimes result from weakness when we are ill. And I believe that the bodily vapours are also transformed into water when they are much more abundant, provided they are not at the same time more agitated. This causes the sweat which occurs when we take 424 exercise. But the eyes do not weep then, because during bodily exercise the greatest part of the spirits go to the muscles used in moving the body, and less of them go through the optic nerve to the eyes. It is one and the same matter that forms blood (when in the veins or the arteries), the spirits (when in the brain, nerves, or muscles), vapours (when it issues forth in the form of air), and finally sweat or tears (when it thickens into water on the surfaces of the body or the eyes).

130. *How something that causes pain in the eye makes it weep*

I can observe only two causes that make the vapours issuing from the eyes change into tears. The first is a change in the shape of the pores through which they pass. By whatever accident this may happen, it retards the movement of these vapours and changes their order, and so may cause them to be transformed into water. Thus a speck in our eye is

---

1 *Meteorology*, Disc. 2 (AT VI 239ff).

enough to draw forth tears. For in producing pain there it changes the arrangement of the eye's pores so that some of them become narrower, and the tiny parts of the vapours pass through them less quickly. Hence, whereas previously they issued forth equidistant from each other, and so remained separated, they now come together because the order of the pores is disturbed. In this way the parts of the vapours are joined together, and so transformed into tears.

131. *How we weep from sadness*
The other cause of tears is sadness followed by love or joy, or in general by some cause which makes the heart drive a lot of blood through the arteries. Sadness is required for this, because in chilling all the blood again it constricts the pores of the eyes. But to the extent that it constricts them, it also decreases the quantity of the vapours which can pass through them, and for this reason sadness is not sufficient to produce tears unless the quantity of these vapours is increased at the same time by some other cause. And there is nothing which increases it more than the blood which is sent to the heart in the passion of love. We see, too, that those who are sad do not shed tears continually, but only intermittently, when they reflect anew upon the objects of their affection.

132. *The groans which accompany tears*
The lungs are also sometimes suddenly swollen by the abundance of the blood which enters them and expels the air they contained. As this air goes out through the windpipe it produces the groans and cries which customarily accompany tears. These cries are usually shriller than those accompanying laughter, although they are produced in almost the same way. The reason for this is that the nerves that enlarge or constrict the vocal organs, making the voice louder or shriller, are joined with those that open the orifices of the heart when we are joyful and constrict them when we are sad, and so they make the vocal organs become wider or narrower at the same time.

133. *Why children and old people weep readily*
Children and old people are more inclined to weep than the middle-aged, but for different reasons. Old people often weep from affection and joy. For when these two passions are combined together they send a lot of blood to the heart, and many vapours from there to the eyes. And the agitation of these vapours is reduced to such an extent by the coldness of their nature that the vapours are easily transformed into tears even without any preceding sadness. And if some old people also weep very readily from vexation, it is not so much the temperament of their body as

of their mind which so disposes them. This happens only to those who are so weak that they let themselves be utterly overcome by trivial matters involving pain, fear, or pity. The same thing happens with **427** children, who hardly ever weep from joy, but much more often from sadness, even when it is not accompanied by love. For children always have enough blood to produce a lot of vapours; and these turn into tears when their movement is retarded by the sadness.

134. *Why some children grow pale instead of weeping*
Yet there are some children who, instead of weeping, grow pale when they are angry. This may indicate unusual discernment and courage on their part, namely when it results from their considering the extent of some evil and preparing themselves to resist it strongly, in the same fashion as those who are older. But more commonly it indicates a bad nature, namely when it results from their being inclined to hatred or fear. For these are passions which decrease the matter of which tears are formed. We observe, on the other hand, that children who weep very readily are inclined to love and to pity.

135. *Sighs*
The cause of sighs is very different from that of tears, even though they are similar in presupposing sadness. For whereas we are moved to weep **428** when our lungs are full of blood, we are moved to sigh when they are almost empty and some imagined hope or joy opens the orifice of the venous artery which sadness had constricted. Then the little blood remaining in the lungs flows down suddenly into the left-hand side of the heart through this artery, where it is driven by the desire to attain this joy. At the same time this desire agitates all the muscles of the diaphragm and chest, so that air comes rapidly through the mouth into the lungs to fill the place vacated by the blood. And that is what we call 'sighing'.

136. *How the passions which are peculiar to certain persons produce their effects*
For the rest, so as to put in a few words all the points that might be added regarding the different effects or different causes of the passions, I shall content myself with repeating the principle which underlies everything I have written about them – namely, that our soul and body are so linked that once we have joined some bodily action with a certain thought, the one does not occur thereafter without the other occurring too; but we do not always join the same actions to the same thoughts. This principle alone can account for any particular phenomenon involving the passions, **429** whether in oneself or in others, which has not been explained here. For

example, the strange aversions of certain people that make them unable to bear the smell of roses, the presence of a cat, or the like, can readily be recognized as resulting simply from their having been greatly upset by some such object in the early years of their life. Or it may even result from their having been affected by the feelings their mother had when she was upset by such an object while pregnant; for there certainly is a connection between all the movements of a mother and those of a child in her womb, so that anything adverse to the one is harmful to the other. And the smell of roses may have caused severe headache in a child when he was still in the cradle, or a cat may have terrified him without anyone noticing and without any memory of it remaining afterwards; and yet the idea of the aversion he then felt for the roses or for the cat will remain imprinted on his brain till the end of his life.

137. *The function of the five passions explained here, in so far as they relate to the body*

Having given definitions of love, hatred, desire, joy and sadness, and dealt with all the bodily movements which cause or accompany them, we

430 have only to consider their function. Regarding this, it must be observed that they are all ordained by nature to relate to the body, and to belong to the soul only in so far as it is joined with the body. Hence, their natural function is to move the soul to consent and contribute to actions which may serve to preserve the body or render it in some way more perfect. From this point of view, sadness and joy are the two passions that have primary application. For it is only through a feeling of pain that the soul is immediately advised about things that harm the body: this feeling produces in the soul first the passion of sadness, then hatred of what causes the pain, and finally the desire to get rid of it. Similarly the soul is immediately advised about things useful to the body only through some sort of titillation, which first produces joy within it, then gives rise to love of what we believe to be its cause, and finally brings about the desire to acquire something that can enable us to continue in this joy, or else to have a similar joy again later on. This shows that these five passions are all very useful with respect to the body. It shows too that sadness is in some way primary and more necessary than joy, and hatred more necessary than love; for it is more important to reject things which are harmful and potentially destructive than to acquire those which add some perfection which we can subsist without.

431 138. *Their faults and the means of correcting them*

This function of the passions is the most natural that they can have. For all the animals devoid of reason conduct their lives simply through bodily movements similar to those which, in our case, usually follow upon the passions which move our soul to consent to such movements. Nevertheless it is not always good for the passions to function in this way, in so far as there are many things harmful to the body which cause no sadness initially (or which even produce joy), and in so far as other things are useful to the body, although at first they are disagreeable. Furthermore, the passions almost always cause the goods they represent, as well as the evils, to appear much greater and more important than they are, thus moving us to pursue the former and flee from the latter with more ardour and zeal than is appropriate. Likewise, we see that animals are often deceived by lures, and in seeking to avoid small evils they throw themselves into greater evils. That is why we must use experience and reason in order to distinguish good from evil and know their true value, so as not to take the one for the other or rush into anything immoderately.

139. *The function of these passions in so far as they belong to the soul;*   432
   firstly, of love
This would be sufficient if we had in us only a body, or if the body were our better part. But as it is only the lesser part, we should consider the passions chiefly in so far as they belong to the soul. In this regard, love and hatred result from knowledge and precede joy and sadness, except when the latter stands in place of the knowledge of which they are species.[1] And when this knowledge is true – that is, when the things it brings us to love are truly good and those it brings us to hate are truly bad – love is incomparably better than hatred: it can never be too great, and it never fails to produce joy. I say that this love is extremely good because by joining real goods to us it makes us to that extent more perfect. I say also that it cannot be too great, for all that the most excessive love can do is to join us so perfectly to these goods that the love we have especially for ourselves must apply to them as well as to us; and this, I believe, can never be bad. And it is necessarily followed by joy, because it represents to us what we love as a good belonging to us.

140. *Hatred*
Hatred, on the other hand, cannot be so mild as to be harmless, and it is   433
never devoid of sadness. I say it cannot be too mild because, however much the hatred of an evil moves us to an action, we could always be moved to it even more effectively by love of the contrary good – at least when the good and evil are adequately known. For I acknowledge that

---

1 Cf. art. 79, p. 356 above. Love and hatred result from judgements concerning good and evil, and when these judgements constitute knowledge of good or evil, they are accompanied by joy or sadness.

hatred of the evil which is manifested solely by pain is necessary where the body is concerned; but I am speaking here only about the hatred which results from a clearer knowledge, which I refer to the soul alone. I say also that this hatred is never without sadness because evil, being merely a privation, cannot be conceived without some real subject in which it exists; and there is nothing real which does not have some goodness in it. Hence the hatred which takes us away from some evil likewise takes us away from the good to which it is joined, and the privation of this good, being represented to our soul as a fault belonging to it, arouses sadness in it. For example, the hatred which takes us away from someone's evil habits likewise takes us away from his company; and we might otherwise find in the latter some good which we should be sorry to be deprived of. So too, in all other cases of hatred we can see some reason for sadness.

434 **141. *Desire, joy and sadness***
As for desire, it is obvious that when it proceeds from true knowledge it cannot be bad, provided it is not excessive and that it is governed by this knowledge. It is obvious too that joy cannot fail to be good, nor sadness bad, with respect to the soul. For the discomfort which the soul receives from evil consists wholly in the latter, and the enjoyment of the good belonging to the soul consists wholly in the former. Thus, if we had no body, I venture to say we could not go too far in abandoning ourselves to love and joy, or in avoiding hatred and sadness. But the bodily movements accompanying these passions may all be injurious to health when they are very violent; on the other hand, they may be beneficial to it when they are only moderate.

142. *Joy and love, compared with sadness and hatred*
Moreover, since hatred and sadness should be rejected by the soul, even when they proceed from true knowledge, there is all the more reason to reject them when they result from some false opinion. But it may be
435 questioned whether love and joy are good when they rest in this way on a bad foundation. It seems to me that if we consider them just as they are in themselves with respect to the soul, we may say that although joy is less secure, and love less beneficial, than when they have a better foundation, they are still preferable to any sadness or hatred resting on an equally bad foundation. Thus, in the affairs of everyday life, where we cannot avoid the risk of being mistaken, it is always much better for us to incline towards the passions which tend to the good than for us to incline towards those which relate to evil (even if we do so only in order to avoid it); and even a false joy is often more valuable than a sadness whose cause is true. But I dare not say the same about love in relation to hatred. For

when hatred is justified it simply takes us away from a subject containing an evil from which it is good to be separated; whereas a love which is unjustified joins us to things which may be harmful, or at least which deserve less consideration than we give them, and this demeans and debases us.

143. *The same passions in so far as they relate to desire*

We must take care to observe that what I have just said about these four passions holds only when they are considered exactly in themselves, and they do not lead us to perform any action. For in so far as they govern 436 our behaviour by producing desire in us, it is certain that all those having a false cause may be harmful, while by contrast all having a just cause may be useful. And even when they rest on equally bad foundations, joy is usually more harmful than sadness, because the latter engenders restraint and anxiety, and so disposes us in a certain way to prudence, whereas the former make those who abandon themselves to it rash and imprudent.

144. *Desires whose attainment depends only on us*

But because these passions cannot lead us to perform any action except by means of the desire they produce, it is this desire which we should take particular care to control; and here lies the chief utility of morality. As I have just said, desire is always good when it conforms to true knowledge; likewise it cannot fail to be bad when based on some error. And it seems to me that the error we commit most commonly in respect of desires is failure to distinguish adequately the things which depend wholly on us from those which do not depend on us at all. Regarding those which depend only on us – that is, on our free will – our knowledge of their goodness ensures that we cannot desire them with too much ardour, 437 since the pursuit of virtue consists in doing the good things that depend on us, and it is certain that we cannot have too ardent a desire for virtue. Moreover, what we desire in this way cannot fail to have a happy outcome for us, since it depends on us alone, and so we always receive from it all the satisfaction we expected from it. But the mistake we ordinarily make in this regard is never that we desire too much; it is rather that we desire too little. The supreme remedy against this mistake is to free our mind as much as possible from all kinds of other less useful desires, and then to try to know very clearly, and to consider with attention, the goodness of that which is to be desired.

145. *Those desires which depend solely on other causes; and what Fortune is*

Regarding the things which do not depend on us in any way, we must never desire them with passion, however good they may be. This holds not only because they may not happen, thus making us the more irritated the more strongly we wished for them, but chiefly because in occupying our thoughts they prevent our forming a liking for other things whose acquisition depends on us. There are two general remedies for such vain desires. The first is generosity, about which I shall speak later. The second is frequent reflection upon divine Providence: we should reflect upon the fact that nothing can possibly happen other than as Providence has determined from all eternity. Providence is, so to speak, a fate or immutable necessity, which we must set against Fortune in order to expose the latter as a chimera which arises solely from an error of our intellect. For we can desire only what we consider in some way to be possible; and things which do not depend on us can be considered possible only in so far as they are thought to depend on Fortune – that is to say, in so far as we judge that they may happen and that similar things have happened at other times. But this opinion is based solely on our not knowing all the causes which contribute to each effect. For when a thing we considered to depend on Fortune does not happen, this indicates that one of the causes necessary for its production was absent, and consequently that it was absolutely impossible and that no similar thing has ever happened, i.e. nothing for the production of which a similar cause was also absent. Had we not been ignorant of this beforehand, we should never have considered it possible and consequently we should never have desired it.

439 146. *Those desires which depend on us and on others*
We must, then, utterly reject the common opinion that there is a Fortune outside us which causes things to happen or not to happen, just as it pleases. And we must recognize that everything is guided by divine Providence, whose eternal decree is infallible and immutable to such an extent that, except for matters it has determined to be dependent on our free will, we must consider everything that affects us to occur of necessity and as it were by fate, so that it would be wrong for us to desire things to happen in any other way. But most of our desires extend to matters which do not depend wholly on us or wholly on others, and we must therefore take care to pick out just what depends only on us, so as to limit our desire to that alone. As for the rest, although we must consider their outcome to be wholly fated and immutable, so as to prevent our desire from occupying itself with them, yet we must not fail to consider the reasons which make them more or less predictable, so as to use these reasons in governing our actions. Thus, for example, suppose we have business in some place to which we might travel by two different routes, one usually much safer than the other. And suppose Providence decrees

that if we go by the route we regard as safer we shall not avoid being robbed, whereas we may travel by the other route without any danger. 440 Nevertheless, we should not be indifferent as to which one we choose, or rely upon the immutable fatality of this decree. Reason insists that we choose the route which is usually the safer, and our desire in this case must be fulfilled when we have followed this route, whatever evil may befall us; for, since any such evil was inevitable from our point of view, we had no reason to wish to be exempt from it: we had reason only to do the best that our intellect was able to recognize, as I am supposing that we did. And it is certain that when we apply ourselves to distinguish Fatality from Fortune in this way, we easily acquire the habit of governing our desires so that their fulfillment depends only on us, making it possible for them always to give us complete satisfaction.

147. *The internal emotions of the soul*
Here I shall merely add one further consideration which, it seems to me, serves very well to prevent us from suffering any discomfort from the passions. It is that our well-being depends principally on internal emotions which are produced in the soul only by the soul itself. In this respect they differ from its passions, which always depend on some movement of the spirits. Although these emotions of the soul are often 441 joined with the passions which are similar to them, they frequently occur with others, and they may even originate in those to which they are opposed. For example, when a husband mourns his dead wife, it sometimes happens that he would be sorry to see her brought to life again. It may be that his heart is torn by the sadness aroused in him by the funeral display and by the absence of a person to whose company he was accustomed. And it may be that some remnants of love or of pity occur in his imagination and draw genuine tears from his eyes. Nevertheless he feels at the same time a secret joy in his innermost soul, and the emotion of this joy has such power that the concomitant sadness and tears can do nothing to diminish its force. Again, when we read of strange adventures in a book, or see them acted out on the stage, this sometimes arouses sadness in us, sometimes joy, or love, or hatred, and generally any of the passions, depending on the diversity of the objects which are presented to our imagination. But we also have pleasure in feeling them aroused in us, and this pleasure is an intellectual joy which may as readily originate in sadness as in any of the other passions.

148. *The exercise of virtue is a supreme remedy against the passions*
Now these internal emotions affect us more intimately, and consequently have much more power over us than the passions which occur with them 442

but are distinct from them. To this extent it is certain that, provided our soul always has the means of happiness within itself, all the troubles coming from elsewhere are powerless to harm it. Such troubles will serve rather to increase its joy; for on seeing that it cannot be harmed by them, it becomes aware of its perfection. And in order that our soul should have the means of happiness, it needs only to pursue virtue diligently. For if anyone lives in such a way that his conscience cannot reproach him for ever failing to do something he judges to be the best (which is what I here call 'pursuing virtue'), he will receive from this a satisfaction which has such power to make him happy that the most violent assaults of the passions will never have sufficient power to disturb the tranquillity of his soul.

PART THREE

Specific Passions

149. *Esteem and contempt*

After having explained the six primitive passions – which are, as it were, the genera of which all the others are species – I shall make brief observations about the special features of each of the others, keeping the same order as in the foregoing enumeration. The first two are esteem and contempt. Usually the terms 'esteem' and 'contempt' signify only our dispassionate opinions concerning a thing's value. But such opinions often give rise to passions having no particular name, and it seems to me that the terms may be applied to these passions. Esteem, regarded as a passion, is the soul's inclination to represent to itself the value of the object of its esteem, this inclination being caused by a special movement of the spirits which are so directed in the brain that they strengthen the impressions having this effect. The passion of contempt, on the other hand, is the soul's inclination to consider the baseness or insignificance of the object of its contempt, and is caused by a movement of the spirits which strengthens the idea of this insignificance.

150. *These two passions are merely species of wonder*

So these two passions are merely species of wonder. For when we do not wonder at the greatness or the insignificance of an object, making no more of it and no less of it than reason deems we ought, then our esteem or contempt for it is dispassionate. And although esteem is often aroused in us by love, and contempt by hatred, this does not hold generally: it results simply from our being more or less inclined to consider the greatness or the insignificance of an object because we have more or less affection for it.

151. *We may have esteem or contempt for ourselves*

In general, these two passions may relate to all sorts of objects. But they are chiefly noteworthy when we refer them to ourselves, i.e. when it is our own merit for which we have esteem or contempt. The movement of the spirits which causes them in this case is so manifest that it changes even the appearance, gestures, gait and, generally, all the actions of those who conceive an unusually better or worse opinion of themselves.

152. *For what reasons we may have esteem for ourselves*

Since one of the principal parts of wisdom is to know in what manner and for what reason anyone ought to have esteem or contempt for himself, I shall try to give my views on this question. I see only one thing in us which could give us good reason for esteeming ourselves, namely, the exercise of our free will and the control we have over our volitions. For we can reasonably be praised or blamed only for actions that depend upon this free will. It renders us in a certain way like God by making us masters of ourselves, provided we do not lose the rights it gives us through timidity.

153. *What generosity consists in*

Thus I believe that true generosity, which causes a person's self-esteem to
446 be as great as it may legitimately be, has only two components. The first consists in his knowing that nothing truly belongs to him but this freedom to dispose his volitions, and that he ought to be praised or blamed for no other reason than his using this freedom well or badly. The second consists in his feeling within himself a firm and constant resolution to use it well – that is, never to lack the will to undertake and carry out whatever he judges to be best. To do that is to pursue virtue in a perfect manner.

154. *Generosity prevents us from having contempt for others*

Those who possess this knowledge and this feeling about themselves readily come to believe that any other person can have the same knowledge and feeling about himself, because this involves nothing which depends on someone else. That is why such people never have contempt for anyone. Although they often see that others do wrong in ways that show up their weakness, they are nevertheless more inclined to excuse than to blame them and to regard such wrong-doing as due rather to lack of knowledge than to lack of a virtuous will. Just as they do not consider themselves much inferior to those who have greater wealth or honour, or even to those who have more intelligence, knowledge or beauty, or generally to those who surpass them in some other perfections, equally they do not have much more esteem for themselves than for those
447 whom they surpass. For all these things seem to them to be very unimportant, by contrast with the virtuous will for which alone they esteem themselves, and which they suppose also to be present, or at least capable of being present, in every other person.

155. *What humility as a virtue consists in*

Thus the most generous people are usually also the most humble. We have humility as a virtue when, as a result of reflecting on the infirmity of our nature and on the wrongs we may previously have done, or are capable of doing (wrongs which are no less serious than those which others may do), we do not prefer ourselves to anyone else and we think that since others have free will just as much as we do, they may use it just as well as we use ours.

156. *The properties of generosity; and how generosity serves as a remedy against all the disorders of the passions*

Those who are generous in this way are naturally led to do great deeds, and at the same time not to undertake anything of which they do not feel themselves capable. And because they esteem nothing more highly than 448 doing good to others and disregarding their own self-interest, they are always perfectly courteous, gracious and obliging to everyone. Moreover they have complete command over their passions. In particular, they have mastery over their desires, and over jealousy and envy, because everything they think sufficiently valuable to be worth pursuing is such that its acquisition depends solely on themselves; over hatred of other people, because they have esteem for everyone; over fear, because of the self-assurance which confidence in their own virtue gives them; and finally over anger, because they have very little esteem for everything that depends on others, and so they never give their enemies any advantage by acknowledging that they are injured by them.

157. *Vanity*

All who conceive a good opinion of themselves for any other reason, whatever it might be, do not possess true generosity, but only a vanity which is always a vice, and is all the more so the less justification such people have for esteeming themselves highly. They have the least justification when they are vain for no reason at all – that is, not because they think they have any merit for which they ought to be valued, but simply because they do not regard merit as important: imagining pride to be nothing but self-glorification, they believe that those who attribute the 449 most merit to themselves actually have the most merit. This vice is so unreasonable and absurd that I would find it difficult to believe there are men who allow themselves to fall into it, if no one was ever praised unjustly. But flattery is so common everywhere that there is no man whose faults are so great that he never finds himself esteemed for things which are not praiseworthy or even for things which are blameworthy.

This causes the most ignorant and most stupid people to fall into this sort of vanity.

158. *The effects of vanity are contrary to those of generosity*
The volition we feel within ourselves always to make good use of our free will results, as I have said, in generosity. But any other cause of self-esteem, whatever it might be, produces a highly blameworthy vanity, which is so different from true generosity that it has quite the opposite effects. For all other goods, like intelligence, beauty, riches, honours, etc., are commonly esteemed so highly because so few people have them, and for the most part their nature is such that they cannot be shared by many people. The result is that vain people attempt to humble everyone else: being slaves to their desires, they have souls which are constantly agitated by hatred, envy, jealousy, or anger.

450   **159.** *Humility as a vice*
Abjectness, or humility as a vice, consists chiefly in a feeling of weakness or irresolution, together with an incapacity to refrain from actions which we know we shall regret later on, as if we lacked the full use of our free will. It involves also the belief that we cannot subsist by ourselves or get along without many things whose acquisition depends on others. Thus it is directly opposed to generosity, and it often happens that the most mean-spirited people are the most arrogant and haughty, just as the most generous are the most modest and humble. But whereas those who have a strong and generous spirit do not change their mood to suit the prosperity or adversity which comes their way, those with a weak and abject spirit are guided by chance alone, and are no more elated by prosperity than humbled by adversity. Indeed, we often see them shamefully abase themselves before those from whom they expect some advantage or fear some evil, while at the same time they insolently lord it over those from whom they do not expect or fear anything.

451   **160.** *The movement of the spirits in these passions*
It is easy to see that vanity and abjectness are not only vices but also passions. For their emotion is quite apparent in the demeanour of those who are suddenly elated or depressed by some new happening. But it may be questioned whether generosity and humility, which are virtues, can also be passions. For their movements are less apparent, and it seems that virtue is not so closely associated with passion as vice is. Yet I see no reason why the same movement of the spirits which serves to strengthen a thought which has bad foundations might not also strengthen one that is well-founded. And because vanity and generosity consist simply in the good opinion we have of ourselves – the only difference being that this

opinion is unjustified in the one case and justified in the other – I think we can relate them to one and the same passion. This passion is produced by a movement made up of those of wonder, of joy, and of love (self-love as much as the love we have for the cause of our self-esteem). On the other hand, the movement which produces humility, whether of the virtuous or the vicious kind, is made up of those of wonder, of sadness, and of self-love mingled with hatred for the faults that give rise to self-contempt. 452 And the difference I observe between these movements arises wholly from two properties of the movement of wonder: first, that surprise makes the movement vigorous from the start; and second, that the movement continues uniformly in this way, i.e. the spirits continue to move in the brain with the same degree of vigour. Of these properties the first is found much more in vanity and abjectness than in generosity and humility of the virtuous kind; the second, on the other hand, is more prominent in the latter pair than in the former. The reason for this is that vice usually proceeds from ignorance, and those with the least knowledge of themselves are the most liable to become prouder or humbler than they ought. For they are surprised by anything new that comes their way, and so they attribute it to themselves and wonder at themselves, and have either esteem or contempt for themselves depending on whether they judge the novelty to be to their advantage or not. But often one thing that makes them proud is followed by another that makes them humble; and for this reason their passion involves a variable movement of the spirits. On the other hand, there is no incompatibility between generosity and humility of the virtuous kind, nor is there anything else which might change them; this results in their movements being firm, constant and always very similar to each other. But these movements are not due so much to surprise, because those who esteem themselves in this way are well acquainted with the causes of their self-esteem. It may be said, however, that these causes are so marvellous (namely, the power to make use of our free will, which causes us to value ourselves, and the infirmities 453 of the subject who has this power, which cause us not to esteem ourselves too highly) that each time we consider them afresh they are a source of new wonder.

161. *How generosity may be acquired*
It should be noted that what we commonly call 'virtues' are habits in the soul which dispose it to have certain thoughts: though different from the thoughts, these habits can produce them and in turn can be produced by them. It should also be noted that the thoughts may be produced by the soul alone; but it often happens that some movement of the spirits strengthens them, and in this case they are both actions of virtue and at

the same time passions of the soul. There is, it seems, no virtue so dependent on good birth as the virtue which causes us to esteem ourselves in accordance with our true value, and it is easy to believe that the souls which God puts into our bodies are not all equally noble and strong (which is why, following the vernacular, I have called this virtue 'generosity' rather than 'magnanimity', a term used in the Schools, where this virtue is not well known). It is certain, however, that a good upbringing is a great help in correcting defects of birth. Moreover, if we 454 occupy ourselves frequently in considering the nature of free will and the many advantages which proceed from a firm resolution to make good use of it – while also considering, on the other hand, the many vain and useless cares which trouble ambitious people – we may arouse the passion of generosity in ourselves and then acquire the virtue. Since this virtue is, as it were, the key to all the other virtues and a general remedy for every disorder of the passions, it seems to me that this consideration deserves serious attention.

162. *Veneration*

Veneration or respect is an inclination of the soul not only to have esteem for the object that it reveres but also to submit to it with some fear in order to try to gain its favour. Accordingly we have veneration only for free causes which we judge capable of doing us good or evil, without our knowing which they will do. For we have love and devotion rather than simple veneration for those causes from which we expect only good, and we have hatred for those from which we expect only evil. And if we do not judge the cause of this good or evil to be free, we do not submit to it in order to try to gain its favour. Thus, when the pagans had veneration 455 for woods, springs, or mountains, it was not strictly speaking these dead things that they revered, but the divinities which they believed to preside over them. The movement of the spirits which produces this passion is composed of that which produces wonder and that which produces fear (about which I shall speak later).

163. *Scorn*

At the same time, what I call 'scorn' is our soul's inclination to despise a free cause in judging it so far beneath us that, although by nature capable of doing good or evil, it is incapable of doing either to us. And the movement of the spirits which produces scorn is composed of those which produce wonder and confidence or boldness.

164. *The function of these two passions*

It is generosity and weakness of spirit or abjectness which determine whether these two passions have a good or an evil use. For the more noble and generous our soul is, the more we are inclined to render to each person that which belongs to him; thus, not only do we have a very deep humility before God, but also we are not reluctant to render to each 456 person all the honour and respect due to him according to his position and authority in the world, and we have contempt solely for vices. On the other hand, abject and weak spirits are liable to sin by excess, sometimes in revering and fearing things which deserve nothing but contempt, and sometimes in haughtily scorning things which are most deserving of reverence. They often pass very rapidly from extreme impiety to superstition, and then from superstition back to impiety, so that there is no vice or disorder of the mind of which they are not capable.

165. *Hope and anxiety*

Hope is a disposition of the soul to be convinced that what it desires will come about. It is caused by a particular movement of the spirits, consisting of the movement of joy mixed with that of desire. And anxiety is another disposition of the soul, which convinces it that its desires will not be fulfilled. It should be noted that these two passions, although opposed, may nevertheless occur together, namely when we think of reasons for regarding the fulfilment of the desire as easy, and at the same time we think of other reasons which make it seem difficult.

166. *Confidence and despair*
459

Neither of these passions ever accompanies desire without leaving some room for the other. For when hope is so strong that it entirely excludes anxiety, its nature changes and it is called 'confidence' or 'assurance'. And when we are assured that what we desire will come about, then although we still want it to come about we are no longer agitated by the passion of desire, which made us await the outcome with concern. All the same, when anxiety is so extreme that it leaves no room for hope, it changes into despair; and this despair, representing the thing desired as impossible, entirely extinguishes desire, which applies only to things that are possible.

167. *Jealousy*

Jealousy is a kind of anxiety which is related to our desire to preserve for ourselves the possession of some good. It does not result so much from the strength of the reasons which make us believe we may lose the good, as from the high esteem in which we hold it. This causes us to examine the slightest grounds for doubt, and to regard them as very considerable reasons.

458   168. *In what respect this passion may be proper*

Because we ought to take more care to preserve goods which are very great than those which are less great, this passion may be right and proper on certain occasions. Thus, for example, a captain defending a very important position has the right to be jealous of it, i.e. to examine with great care all the ways by which it might be surprised; and a virtuous woman is not blamed for being jealous of her honour, i.e. for taking care not only to behave well but also to avoid even the slightest cause for scandal.

169. *In what respect jealousy is blameworthy*

But we laugh at a miser when he is jealous of his hoard – that is, when he gazes fondly at it and wants it always near him for fear of its being stolen – for money is not worth the trouble of such safeguarding. And we have contempt for a man who is jealous of his wife, because this indicates that he does not love her in the right way and that he has a bad opinion of himself or of her. I say that he does not love her in the right way, for if he truly loved her he would not have any inclination to distrust her. But

459   what he loves is not strictly her: it is only the good he imagines to consist in his having sole possession of her. And he would have no anxiety about the loss of this good if he did not think himself to be unworthy of it, or his wife to be unfaithful. Moreover this passion is related only to suspicion and distrust, for someone is not properly speaking jealous if he tries to avoid an evil about which he rightly feels anxious.

170. *Irresolution*

Irresolution is also a kind of anxiety. Keeping the soul balanced, as it were, between several actions open to it, irresolution causes it not to perform any of them, and thus gives it time to make a choice before committing itself. In this respect, indeed, it has a beneficial function. But when it lasts longer than it ought, making us spend in deliberation the time required for action, it is extremely bad. I call it a kind of anxiety even though we might remain uncertain and irresolute, while feeling no anxiety at all, when we can choose between several things which appear equally good. But this sort of irresolution proceeds merely from the object before us and not from any movement of the spirits. That is why it is not a passion, unless it happens that our anxiety of choosing wrongly

460   increases our uncertainty. But this anxiety is so common and so strong in some people that although they have no need to make a choice and they see only one thing to be taken or left, the anxiety often holds them back and makes them pause to search in vain for something else. In this case an excess of irresolution results from too great a desire to do well and from a

weakness of the intellect, which contains only a lot of confused notions, and none that are clear and distinct. That is why the remedy against such excess is to become accustomed to form certain and determinate judgements regarding everything that comes before us, and to believe that we always do our duty when we do what we judge to be best, even though our judgement may perhaps be a very bad one.

171. *Courage and boldness*
Courage, when a passion and not a habit or natural inclination, is a certain heat or agitation which disposes the soul to apply itself energetically to accomplish the tasks it wants to perform, whatever their nature may be. And boldness is a kind of courage which disposes the soul to carry out the most dangerous tasks.

172. *Emulation*
Emulation is also a kind of courage, but in another sense. For we may regard courage as a genus which divides into as many species as it has 461 different objects, and into as many others as it has causes: boldness is a species of courage in the first sense, and emulation in the second. The latter is nothing but a heat which disposes the soul to undertake tasks in which it hopes to be able to succeed because it sees others succeed in them. Thus it is a species of courage of which the external cause is an example. I say 'external cause' because in addition there must always be an internal cause which consists in our body's being so disposed that desire and hope have more power to cause a quantity of blood to go to the heart than fear or despair have to stop it.

173. *How boldness depends on hope*
For it must be observed that the object of boldness is some difficulty which usually results in anxiety or even despair. Thus it is the most dangerous and desperate affairs in which we exercise the most boldness and courage. It is essential, however, that we should hope for success in attaining the goal, or even that we should be assured of it, in order to tackle vigorously the difficulties we encounter. But the goal is different from the object; for we could not be assured of something and also be desperate about it at the same time. Thus, when the Decii threw themselves against the enemy and ran to certain death, the object of their 462 boldness was the difficulty of preserving their lives during this action, and about this difficulty they felt only despair, since they were certain to die. But their goal was to inspire their soldiers by their example and to cause them to win the victory, and they had some hope of achieving that; or else they had a further goal of gaining glory after their death, and of this they were assured.

174. *Timidity and fear*

Timidity is directly opposed to courage. It is a listlessness or coldness which prevents the soul from bringing itself to carry out the tasks which it would perform if it were free from this passion. And fear or terror, which is opposed to boldness, is not only a coldness, but also a disturbance and astonishment of the soul which deprives it of the power to resist the evils which it thinks lie close at hand.

175. *The function of timidity*

Although I cannot believe that nature has given to mankind any passion which is always vicious and has no good or praiseworthy function, I still find it very difficult to guess what purpose these two passions might serve. It seems to me that timidity has some use only when it frees us from making efforts which plausible reasons might move us to make if this passion had not been aroused by other, more certain reasons, which made us judge the efforts to be useless. Besides freeing the soul from such efforts, it is also useful for the body in that it slows the movement of the spirits and thereby prevents us from wasting our energy. But usually it is very harmful, because it diverts the will from useful actions. And because it results simply from our having insufficient hope or desire, we need only increase these two passions within us in order to correct it.

176. *The function of fear*

In the case of fear or terror, I do not see that it can ever be praiseworthy or useful. It, too, is not a specific passion, but merely an excess of timidity, wonder and anxiety – an excess which is always bad, just as boldness is an excess of courage which is always good (provided the end proposed is good). And because the principal cause of fear is surprise, there is no better way to avoid it than to exercise forethought and prepare oneself for any eventuality, anxiety about which may cause it.

464 177. *Remorse*

Remorse of conscience is a kind of sadness which results from our doubting that something we are doing, or have done, is good. It necessarily presupposes doubt. For if we were wholly certain that what we are doing is bad, we would refrain from doing it, since the will tends only towards objects that have some semblance of goodness. And if we were certain that what we have already done was bad, we would feel repentance for it, not simply remorse. The function of this passion is to make us inquire whether the object of our doubt is good or not, and to prevent our doing it another time, as long as we are not certain that it is good. But because remorse presupposes evil, it would be better never to have occasion to feel it; and we may prevent it by the same means as those by which we can free ourselves from irresolution.

178. *Derision*
Ridicule or derision is a kind of joy mixed with hatred, which results from our perceiving some small evil in a person whom we consider to deserve it: we have hatred for the evil, but joy to see it in one who deserves it. When this comes upon us unexpectedly, the surprise of wonder causes us to burst into laughter, in accordance with what I said above about the nature of laughter.[1] But the evil must be insignificant. For if it is great, we cannot believe that the one who has it deserves it unless we have a very bad nature or we bear much hatred towards him.

465

179. *Why the most imperfect people are usually the most given to derision*
Those who have some quite obvious defect (for example, being lame, blind in one eye, or hunch-backed) or who have received some public insult, are observed to be especially inclined to derision. Desiring to see all others as unfortunate as themselves, they are very pleased by the evils that befall them, and hold them deserving of these evils.

180. *The function of mockery*
When a person shows up vices in their proper light by making them appear ridiculous without laughing at them and without showing any hatred for those who have them, he engages in that gentle mockery which is not a passion, but rather the trait of a good man. It bears witness to the cheerfulness of his temper and the tranquillity of his soul, which are signs of virtue; and it often shows the quickness of his mind, in his ability to put a pleasant gloss on the objects of his mockery.

466

181. *The function of laughter in mockery*
It is not improper to laugh when we hear someone else's mockery; we may even find it hard not to laugh. But when we ourselves engage in mockery, it is more fitting to refrain from laughing, so as not to seem to be surprised by the things we say or to wonder at our wit in thinking them up. This makes them all the more surprising to those who hear them.

---

1 Art. 124, p. 371 above.

182. *Envy*

What we usually call 'envy' is a vice consisting in a natural perversity which causes certain people to be annoyed at the good they see coming to others. But I am using this word here to signify a passion which is not always vicious. Envy, then, in so far as it is a passion, is a kind of sadness mingled with hatred, which results from our seeing good coming to those
467   we think unworthy of it. Such a thought can be justified only in the case of goods due to fortune. For as regards the advantages we possess from birth – those of the soul or even of the body – the fact that we received them from God before we were capable of doing any evil suffices to make us worthy of them.

183. *How envy can be just or unjust*

But sometimes fortune gives advantages to someone who is really unworthy of them. Then envy stirs in us only because, having a natural love of justice, we are vexed that it is not upheld in the distribution of these goods. In this case our envy indicates a zeal which may be excusable, especially when the nature of the good we envy in the other person is such that in his hands it may be converted into an evil – e.g. if it is some duty or office in the exercise of which he may behave badly. When we desire the same good for ourselves and we are prevented from having it because it belongs to others who are less worthy of it, this makes the passion more violent: but it is still excusable, provided the hatred it contains relates solely to the bad distribution of the good we envy, and not to the people who possess it or distribute it. But few people are so just and so generous that they do not bear hatred towards those who forestall them in the acquisition of a good which cannot be shared by many and which they had desired for themselves, even though
468   those who have acquired it are as much, or even more, worthy of it. And what is usually most envied is glory. For although its belonging to others does not prevent us from aspiring to it ourselves, at the same time that makes its acquisition all the more difficult and its value greater.

184. *How it comes about that envious people are apt to have a leaden complexion*

There is, moreover, no vice so detrimental to human happiness than that of envy. For, apart from the fact that those tainted with it make themselves unhappy, they also do everything in their power to spoil the pleasure of others. And they usually have a leaden complexion – that is, one that is pale, a mixture of yellow and black, like a livid bruise (hence the Latin word for envy is *livor*). This agrees very well with what was said above about the movements of the blood in sadness and hatred. For hatred causes bile – both the yellow bile that comes from the lower part of the liver, and the black that comes from the spleen – to spread out from the heart through the arteries into all the veins. And sadness causes the blood in the veins to become less hot and flow more slowly than usual – which is enough to make the colour livid. But because there may be several different factors which cause the bile (whether yellow or black) to flow in the veins, and envy does not send it there in a sufficiently large quantity to change the colour of the complexion unless it is very great and of long duration, we must not think that everyone in whom we see   469 this colour is inclined to envy.

185. Pity
Pity is a kind of sadness mingled with love or with good will towards those whom we see suffering some evil which we think they do not deserve. Thus it is opposed to envy in view of its object, and opposed to derision because the object is considered in a different way.

186. *Those who are most given to pity*
Those who think themselves very weak and prone to the adversities of fortune seem to be more inclined to this passion than others, because they think of the evil afflicting others as capable of befalling themselves. Thus they are moved to pity more by the love they bear towards themselves than by the love they have for others.

187. *How the most generous people are touched by this passion*
Nevertheless those who are the most generous and strong-minded, in that they fear no evil for themselves and hold themselves to be beyond the   470 power of fortune, are not free from compassion when they see the infirmities of other men and hear their complaints. For it is a part of generosity to have good will towards everyone. But the sadness of this pity is not bitter: like that caused by the tragic actions we see represented on the stage, it is more external, affecting the senses more than the interior of the soul, which yet has the satisfaction of thinking that it is doing its duty in feeling compassion for those afflicted. There is also this difference, that whereas the ordinary man has compassion for those who complain, because he thinks the evils they suffer are very distressing, the chief object of the pity of the greatest men is the weakness of those whom they see complaining. For they think that no misfortune could be so great an evil as the timidity of those who cannot endure it with forbearance. And although they hate vices, they do not on that account hate those whom they see prone to them: they merely pity them.

188. *Those who are not touched by pity*

But those who are insensible to pity comprise only evil-minded and envious people who naturally hate all mankind, or people who are so brutish and so thoroughly blinded by good fortune or rendered desperate by bad fortune, that they do not think any evil could possibly befall them.

189. *Why this passion moves us to tears*

Moreover, we weep very easily in this passion because love sends a lot of blood to the heart and so causes many vapours to flow from the eyes; and the coldness of the sadness makes these vapours move more slowly and so change into tears, in accordance with what has been said above.[1]

190. *Self-satisfaction*

The satisfaction of those who steadfastly pursue virtue is a habit of their soul which is called 'tranquillity' and 'peace of mind'. But the fresh satisfaction we gain when we have just performed an action we think good is a passion – a kind of joy which I consider to be the sweetest of all joys, because its cause depends only on ourselves. But when this cause is not just, i.e. when the actions from which we derive great satisfaction are not very important or are even vicious, the satisfaction is absurd and serves only to produce a kind of vanity and impertinent arrogance. This is noticeable especially in those who believe themselves devout, but are merely bigoted and superstitious. These are people who – under the pretext of frequently going to church, reciting many prayers, wearing their hair short, fasting, and giving alms – think they are absolutely perfect and imagine they are such close friends of God that they could not do anything to displease him. They suppose that anything their passion dictates is a commendable zeal, even though it sometimes dictates the greatest crimes that men can commit, such as the betrayal of cities, the killing of sovereigns, and the extermination of whole nations for the sole reason that the citizens do not accept their opinions.

191. *Repentance*

Repentance is directly opposed to self-satisfaction. It is a kind of sadness, which results from our believing that we have done some evil deed; and it is very bitter because its cause lies in ourselves alone. But this does not prevent its being very useful when the action of which we repent is truly evil and we know this for certain, because then our repentance prompts us to do better on another occasion. But it often happens that weak-

---

1 Art. 128, p. 373 above.

spirited people repent of deeds they have done without knowing for
certain that they are evil; they are convinced of this simply because they 473
fear it is so, and if they had done the opposite, they would repent in the
same way. This is an imperfection deserving of pity, and the remedies
against this fault are the same as those which serve to dispel irresolution.

192. *Favour*

Favour is properly speaking a desire to see good come to someone for
whom we have good will. But here I use 'favour' to mean this good will in
so far as it is aroused in us by some good action of the person towards
whom we bear it. For we are naturally inclined to love those who do
deeds we judge good even though we get no benefit from them. Favour in
this sense is a kind of love, not desire, though it is always accompanied by
the desire to see good come to the one whom we favour. And it is usually
joined to pity because the misfortunes we see befall unfortunate persons
cause us to reflect all the more on their merits.

193. *Gratitude*

Gratitude is also a kind of love aroused in us by some action on the part
of the person for whom we have it – an action by which, we believe, he 474
has done us some good, or at least he had the intention to do so. Thus it
has the same content as favour, and the more so in that it is based on an
action which affects us and which we desire to reciprocate. This is why it
has much more strength, especially in the souls of those who are to any
degree noble and generous.

194. *Ingratitude*

As to ingratitude, it is not a passion, for nature has not placed in us any
movement of the spirits which produces it. It is simply a vice directly
opposed to gratitude, in so far as the latter is always a virtue and one of
the principal bonds of human society. Accordingly this vice belongs only
to brutish, foolishly arrogant people who think that all things are their
due, or to stupid people who never reflect on the benefits they receive. It
is also found in weak and abject people who, aware of their infirmity and
need, basely seek the help of others and then, having got it, hate them.
They do this because, lacking the will to return the favour or despairing
of their ability to do so, and thinking that everybody is grasping like
themselves and that no good is ever done without the hope of recom-
pense, they think they have deceived their benefactors.

195. *Indignation* 475

Indignation is a kind of hatred or aversion that we naturally have
towards those who do some evil, whatever it may be. Although often

mingled with envy or pity, it has an object that is wholly different. For we are indignant only towards those who do good or evil to people who do not deserve it. But we are envious of those who receive such a good, and we pity those who receive the evil. It is true that to possess a good which we do not deserve is in some way to do evil. This may be the reason why Aristotle and his followers supposed envy always to be a vice, and thus called the envy which is not a vice by the name 'indignation'.[1]

196. *Why indignation is sometimes joined to pity, and sometimes to derision*

To do evil is also in some way to receive evil. Consequently some people join pity to their indignation, and others derision, depending on whether they bear good-will or ill-will towards those whom they see committing faults. That is why the laughter of Democritus and the tears of Heraclitus could proceed from the same cause.[2]

197. *Indignation is often accompanied by wonder and is not incompatible with joy*

Indignation is often accompanied by wonder too. For we usually suppose that everything will be done in the way that we judge it ought to be done – that is, in the way we consider good. This is why we are surprised, and made to wonder, when it happens otherwise. Indignation is also not incompatible with joy, though it is more usually joined to sadness. For when our indignation concerns an evil deed which cannot harm us, and we consider that we would not be willing to do such a thing, this gives us some pleasure – which is perhaps one of the causes of the laughter that sometimes accompanies this passion.[3]

198. *The function of indignation*

Finally, indignation is observed much more in those who wish to appear virtuous than in those who really are virtuous. For although those who love virtue cannot look upon the vices of others without some aversion, they do not become incensed except at the greatest and most extraordinary vices. To be very indignant about trivial matters is to be difficult and peevish; it is unjust to be indignant about matters for which no one can be blamed; and it is impertinent and absurd not to confine one's indignation to the actions of human beings and to extend it to the works of God and nature. This is done by those who, never being content with

---

1 Cf. Aristotle, *Rhetoric* II, 9, 1386b9; *Nicomachean Ethics* II, 7, 1108b2.
2 According to a story well known in later antiquity, Heraclitus wept, whereas Democritus laughed, at the follies of mankind. The origin of the story is unknown.
3 Art. 127, p. 372 above.

their condition or fortune, dare to find fault in the way the universe is regulated and in the secrets of Providence.

199. *Anger*

Anger is also a kind of hatred or aversion that we have towards those who have done some evil or who have tried to harm not just anyone they happen to meet but us in particular. Thus it has the same content as indignation, and the more so in that it is based on an action which affects us and for which we have a desire to avenge ourselves. For this desire nearly always accompanies it, and it is directly opposed to gratitude, as indignation is to favour. But it is incomparably more violent than these other three passions, because the desire to ward off harmful things and to avenge oneself is the most compelling of all desires. It is desire, joined to self-love, which makes anger involve as much agitation of the blood as 478 courage and boldness can bring about; and hatred causes this agitation to affect primarily the bilious blood coming from the spleen and the small veins of the liver. This blood enters into the heart and there, because of its abundance and the nature of the bile with which it is mingled, it produces a heat more extreme and more intense than any that may be produced by love or joy.

200. *Why those whom anger causes to flush are less to be feared than those whom it causes to grow pale*

The external signs of this passion differ according to different personal temperaments and the various other passions composing it or joined to it. Thus we see some grow pale or tremble when they become angry, and others become flushed or even weep. It is usually thought that the anger of those who grow pale is more to be feared than the anger of those who become flushed. The reason for this is that when we are unwilling or unable to avenge ourselves except through our looks and words, we expend all our heat and energy from the moment we are first aroused, and this causes us to grow red. Sometimes, moreover, because we cannot avenge ourselves in any other way, we have such regret and self-pity that we are caused to weep. On the other hand, those who restrain themselves and resolve to take a greater vengeance become sad at the thought that 479 the action which makes them angry obliges them to take such vengeance; and sometimes they also have anxiety about the evils which may ensue upon the resolution they have taken. This makes them first turn pale and cold, and start trembling. But when they later come to take vengeance, they become warm again to the degree that they were cold to begin with, just as we observe that fevers which begin with a chill usually become the most severe.

201. *There are two sorts of anger: the most kind-hearted persons are the most prone to the first*

This shows us that we can distinguish two kinds of anger. One flares up quickly and is quite evident in external behaviour, but it has little effect and is easy to assuage. The other is not so apparent at first, but gnaws more at one's heart and has effects that are more dangerous. Those filled with kindness and love are more prone to the first; for it does not result from a deep hatred but from an instant aversion which surprises them because they are inclined to imagine that all things ought to take place in the manner they judge to be best, and so they wonder and take offence as soon as things turn out otherwise. This often happens even though the matter does not affect them personally, because their great affection makes them concerned for those they love in the same way as for themselves. Thus, what would cause mere indignation in someone else is for them a cause of anger; and since their inclination for love fills their heart with much heat and blood, the aversion which surprises them must drive enough bile into the heart to bring about a great commotion in this blood. But this commotion does not last, because the strength of the surprise does not continue, and as soon as they perceive that the object of their anger ought not to disturb them so much, they repent of their anger.

202. *It is weak and abject souls who most allow themselves to be carried away by the second sort of anger*

The other kind of anger, in which hatred and sadness predominate, is not so apparent at first except perhaps in so far as it makes the face grow pale. But its strength is gradually increased by the agitation which a burning desire for vengeance stirs up in the blood; and the blood, being mixed with the bile driven to the heart from the lower part of the liver and spleen, produces a very keen and piercing heat there. As it is the most generous souls who have the most gratitude, so it is those with the most vanity, the most abject and weak, who let themselves most readily be carried away by this kind of anger. For the wrongs that arouse our anger appear greater in proportion as vanity increases our self-esteem and also in proportion to our esteem for the good things which they take away; and the weaker and more abject our soul, the greater our esteem for these good things, since they depend on others.

203. *Generosity serves as a remedy against the excesses of anger*

Finally, although this passion is useful in giving us the strength to ward off such wrongs, there is no passion whose excesses we should take more care to avoid. For such excesses confuse our judgement and often make us commit misdeeds of which we must afterwards repent. Sometimes they even prevent us from warding off the wrongs as well as we could if we felt less emotion. But just as vanity more than anything else makes anger excessive, so I think that generosity is the best remedy that may be found against its excesses. For generosity causes us to hold in low esteem all the good things which may be taken away, and on the other hand to hold in high esteem the liberty and absolute control over ourselves which we cease to have when someone else is able to injure us. Thus it causes us to have nothing but contempt, or at the most indignation, for the wrongs at which others usually take offence.

204. *Pride*   482
What I here call 'pride' is a kind of joy based on the love we have for ourselves and resulting from the belief or hope we have of being praised by certain other persons. Thus it is different from the internal satisfaction which comes from our belief that we have performed some good action. For we are sometimes praised for things we do not believe to be good, and blamed for those we believe to be better. But both are kinds of self-esteem, as well as kinds of joy. For seeing that we are esteemed highly by others is a reason for esteeming ourselves.

205. *Shame*
Shame, on the other hand, is a kind of sadness based also on self-love, which proceeds from the expectation or fear of being blamed. Besides that, it is a kind of modesty or humility and diffidence about oneself. For when our self-esteem is so great that we cannot imagine anyone despising us, we cannot easily be ashamed.

206. *The function of these two passions*
Pride and shame have the same function, in that they move us to virtue, 483
the one through hope and the other through anxiety. It is necessary only to instruct our judgement regarding what truly deserves blame or praise in order that we should not be ashamed of doing good and not take pride in our vices, as many people do. But it is not good to rid oneself entirely of these passions, as the Cynics used to do. For although the common people are very bad judges, yet because we cannot live without them and it is important for us to be an object of their esteem, we should often follow their opinions rather than our own regarding the outward appearance of our actions.

207. *Impudence*
Impudence or effrontery, which is a kind of contempt for shame and often for pride too, is not a passion because there is no specific movement

of the spirits which produces it. It is rather a vice opposed to shame and also to pride, inasmuch as these are both good, just as ingratitude is opposed to gratitude and cruelty to pity. Effrontery results chiefly from our frequently being the object of grave insults. When we are young we all imagine praise to be a good, and disgrace an evil, of greater practical importance than our subsequent experience shows them to be. This happens when, after receiving several grave insults, we see ourselves
484 utterly stripped of honour and despised by everyone. That is why people who assess good and evil solely in terms of bodily comfort become insolent: they find that after such insults they enjoy as much of this comfort as before, or sometimes even much more of it. For they are then free from many constraints to which honour bound them, and if their disgrace involves the loss of goods, they find there are always some charitable people who will make up their loss.

208. Disgust
Disgust is a kind of sadness which results from the same cause as that from which joy came previously. For we are so constituted that most of the things we enjoy are good for us only for a time, and afterwards become disagreeable. This is evident especially in the case of drinking and eating, which are beneficial only so long as we have an appetite, and harmful when we no longer have one. Because such things then cease to be agreeable to our taste, this passion is called 'disgust'.[1]

209. Regret
Regret is also a kind of sadness. It has a particular bitterness in that it is
485 always joined to some despair and to the memory of a pleasure that gave us joy. For we regret only the good things which we once enjoyed and which are so completely lost that we have no hope of recovering them at the time and in the form in which we regret them.

210. Cheerfulness
Finally, what I call 'cheerfulness' is a kind of joy which has this peculiarity: its sweetness is increased by the recollection of the evils we have suffered, about which we feel relieved in the same way as when we feel ourselves lightened of some heavy burden which we have carried on our shoulders for a long time. I cannot see anything very remarkable in these three passions, and I have placed them here simply in order to follow the order of the enumeration which I made above. But I think this enumeration has been useful in showing that we have omitted no passions which were worthy of special consideration.

1 A play on *goût* ('taste') and *degoût* ('disgust').

211. *A general remedy against the passions*

Now that we are acquainted with all the passions, we have much less reason for anxiety about them than we had before. For we see that they are all by nature good, and that we have nothing to avoid but their 486 misuse or their excess, against which the remedies I have explained might be sufficient if each person took enough care to apply them. I have included among these remedies the forethought and diligence through which we can correct our natural faults by striving to separate within ourselves the movements of the blood and spirits from the thoughts to which they are usually joined. But I must admit that there are few people who have sufficiently prepared themselves in this way for all the contingencies of life. Moreover, the objects of the passions produce movements in the blood which follow so rapidly from the mere impressions formed in the brain and the disposition of the organs, without any help at all from the soul, that no amount of human wisdom is capable of counteracting these movements when we are not adequately prepared to do so. Thus many people cannot keep from laughing when they are tickled, even though they get no pleasure from it. For the impression of joy and surprise, which previously made them laugh for the same reason, is awakened in their imagination and causes their lungs to be swollen suddenly and involuntarily by blood sent to them from the heart. So too, those who are strongly inclined by nature to the emotions of joy, pity, fear and anger, cannot prevent themselves from fainting, weeping, or trembling, or from having their blood all in turmoil just as if they had a fever, when their imagination is strongly affected by the object of one of these passions. But there is something we can always do on such 487 occasions, which I think I can put forward here as the most general, and most readily applicable remedy against all excesses of the passions. When we feel our blood agitated in this way, we should take heed, and recollect that everything presented to the imagination tends to mislead the soul and make the reasons for pursuing the object of its passion appear much stronger than they are, and the reasons for not pursuing this object much weaker. When the passion urges us to pursue ends whose attainment involves some delay, we must refrain from making any immediate judgement about them, and distract ourselves by other thoughts until time and repose have completely calmed the disturbance in our blood. Finally, when it impels us to actions which require an immediate decision, the will must devote itself mainly to considering and following reasons which are opposed to those presented by the passion, even if they appear less strong. For example, when we are unexpectedly attacked by an enemy, the situation allows no time for deliberation; and yet, I think, those who are accustomed to reflecting upon their actions can always do something in this situation. That is, when they feel themselves in the grip of fear they will try to turn their mind from consideration of the danger by thinking about the reasons why there is much more security and honour in resistance than in flight. On the other hand, when they feel that the desire for vengeance and anger is impelling them to run thoughtlessly towards their assailants, they will remember to think that it is unwise to lose one's life when it can be saved without dishonour, and that if a match is very unequal it is better to beat an honourable retreat or ask quarter than stupidly to expose oneself to a certain death.

212. *It is on the passions alone that all the good and evil of this life depends*

For the rest, the soul can have pleasures of its own. But the pleasures common to it and the body depend entirely on the passions, so that persons whom the passions can move most deeply are capable of enjoying the sweetest pleasures of this life. It is true that they may also experience the most bitterness when they do not know how to put these passions to good use and when fortune works against them. But the chief use of wisdom lies in its teaching us to be masters of our passions and to control them with such skill that the evils which they cause are quite bearable, and even become a source of joy.

THE END

Index

Index